Cities of the World

Cities of the World

A Compilation of Current Information on Cultural, Geographical, and Political Conditions in the Countries and Cities of Six Continents, Based on the Department of State's "Post Reports"

Volume 3:
Europe and the Mediterranean Middle East

Edited by
Margaret Walsh Young

with the assistance of
Susan L. Stetler

GALE RESEARCH COMPANY
BOOK TOWER ● DETROIT, MICHIGAN 48226

Editor: Margaret Walsh Young

Associate Editor: Susan L. Stetler

Assistant Editor: Amy F. Lucas

Production Supervisor: Carol Blanchard

Cover Design: Art Chartow

Computerized photocomposition by
Lehigh Rocappi
Pennsauken, New Jersey

Library of Congress Cataloging in Publication Data

Main entry under title:

Cities of the world.

    Includes indexes.
    Contents: V. 1. Africa -- v. 2. The Western Hemi-
sphere -- v. 3. Europe and the Mediterranean Middle
East -- [etc.]
    1. Voyages and travels--1951-   --Guide-books.
2. Cities and towns--Guide-books. I. Young, Margaret
Walsh. II. Stetler, Susan L. III. United States. Dept.
of State. Post report.
G153.4.C57   910.2'02   81-20177
ISBN 0-8103-1111-9 (set)   AACR2

Table of Contents

Introduction

Cities of the World—Europe and the Mediterranean Middle East is the third volume
in a series of four books designed to provide, in one source, comprehensive
information on the world's nations and cities. The books are compiled from
official *Post Reports* issued by the U.S. Department of State for its diplomatic
personnel.

Other volumes in the series deal with Africa; the Western Hemisphere (exclusive
of the United States); and Asia, the Pacific, and the Asian Middle East. All follow
the format of *Cities of the World—Africa,* the initial volume. Data of interest only
to members of the diplomatic community and their dependents has been deleted,
and supplementary facts have been added to make the contents more relevant to
the general public. Historical background material has been expanded in many of
the reports, and current information has been incorporated into such sections as
Government, and Commerce and Industry.

Cities of the World—Europe and the Mediterranean Middle East provides coverage
of 27 countries, 78 major cities, and 543 cities of less importance. Although the
State Department has not issued separate briefings for the Principality of
Monaco, the Republic of San Marino, nor the State of Vatican City, facts about
these sovereignties can be found in the France and Italy chapters. No reports are
included for Albania, which has been without U.S. diplomatic recognition since
1939; Andorra, which is represented through the Barcelona (Spain) consular
district; nor for Liechtenstein, which is served by the U.S. consulate in Zurich,
Switzerland.

A unique aspect of the *Cities of the World* series is that it furnishes information for
the individual with specific interests. For example, in this volume, details are
given in a special subsection on the United Kingdom's many and varied
publications; full coverage is provided on the independent consular posts in both
Geneva and Palestine; and a wide range of information is offered on the countless
opportunities for recreation in the Italian cities and countryside.

Although U.S. consulates at Salzburg, Austria; Nice, France; Bremen, West
Germany; Turin, Italy; and Goteberg, Sweden have been closed since these
reports were issued, the general text remains pertinent. Information is current to
the extent possible in a constantly changing political and economic climate.

The book is arranged alphabetically by country name. The information is divided
into several sections, among which are Government, Commerce and Industry,
Major City, and Health.

A Table of Contents and an Index provide easy access to these reports. Listed
under each country in the Table of Contents are the cities which appear in the
Major City section, along with the beginning page numbers for both country and

city sections. The Index is arranged alphabetically by city name, listing page numbers for the 78 major cities as well as the 543 minor cities. Boldface numbers indicate the page on which the Major City section begins.

The editor invites comments and suggestions from the user concerning *Cities of the World*. Such letters should be addressed to:

> Editor
> *Cities of the World*
> Gale Research Company
> Book Tower
> Detroit, Michigan 48226

Austria

Present-day **AUSTRIA** is but a small remnant of the Austro-Hungarian Empire which played such a decisive role in European history. Situated between Germany and the Balkans, it served for centuries as a bridge between East and West. Austria was broken up by revolution after War War I, was incorporated into the Third Reich in 1938, and subsequently became Germany's unwilling ally until its liberation at the end of the second World War.

Vienna, Austria's capital, has a physical beauty and cultural richness which make it one of the foremost cities in Europe. Its unique geographical position and its role as a focal point in an East-West European framework give Vienna a flavor unmatched anywhere else on the continent.

Area, Geography, Climate

Austria, located in the heart of Europe, is about the size of Virginia. It shares a common border with two members of NATO, Germany and Italy; two members of the Warsaw Pact, Hungary and Czechoslovakia; neutral Switzerland; Communist but nonaligned Yugoslavia; and the Principality of Liechtenstein. Austria is primarily mountainous, with the Alps and their approaches dominating the western and southern provinces. The eastern provinces and Vienna are located in the Danube Basin.

Daytime temperatures in Vienna vary between summer highs of 85°F and −4°F in winter. October may be damp and rainy, and light snowfalls occur in November and December. Heavy snows and frost occur from January until mid-March. April, May, and early June offer pleasant spring weather, and summers are usually delightful.

Vienna sometimes becomes uncomfortably hot in July and August, especially in the city's center, but the suburbs, particularly those which are elevated, are pleasant. The city is subject to rapid and definite changes in atmospheric pressures with accompanying winds. One such wind, the Foehn, carries warm air from the south. It has a special meaning for the Viennese since many people blame it for peculiar human behavior. Average annual precipitation in Vienna is 26.89 inches.

The mountainous regions of Austria have long, cold winters with heavy snowfall and bright crisp days. The Danube Basin usually has less snow, is damper, and therefore has more gray

1

and overcast days than the higher altitudes.

Population

Austria's population is 7.5 million; about 1.6 million live in Vienna. As opposed to the ethnic diversity of the old empire, present-day society is fairly homogeneous. The only unassimilated minorities recognized as such are the Slovenes in Carinthia and the Croats in Burgenland. Many Austrians, particularly in the Vienna area, have relatives in neighboring Czechoslovakia and Hungary. German is the native language of about 95 percent of the population.

The Austrians are approximately 85 percent Roman Catholic. In contrast to the clericalism which strongly influenced Austrian affairs as late as the 1930s, the present church hierarchy is not politically active.

Government

The Republic of Austria is a federal state with nine provinces, one of which is Vienna. The government is parliamentary in form, with a Council of Ministers headed by a Chancellor, all of whom are responsible to the legislature. The directly elected President has largely ceremonial responsibilities.

Although the legislature is bicameral, only the Nationalrat (lower house) has real legistative authority. The Bundesrat (upper house) reviews legislation passed by the Nationalrat and has delaying, not absolute, veto powers.

Austria has been politically stable since World War II. From 1945 to 1966, a coalition of the two major parties governed; together they were supported by over 90 percent of the electorate. In the March 1966 elections, however, the People's Party registered an absolute majority in the Nationalrat, and formed a one-party government with the Socialist Party in the opposition. In the March 1970 national elections, the Socialist Party gained a relative majority in the Nationalrat and established a minority government, thanks to the passive support of the small Freedom Party. The Socialists called early elections in October 1971 and won an absolute majority. This feat was repeated in the seat distribution in the Nationalrat.

Extremist parties have no influence and draw a miniscule percentage of the vote. The Communist Party has not been represented in Parliament since 1959.

The Austrian State Treaty of 1955 ended the four-power occupation of the country and reestablished Austrian sovereignty. The Parliament passed a constitutional amendment proclaiming Austria's "perpetual neutrality," prohibiting membership in military alliances and the establishment of foreign military bases on Austrian soil. The Austrian Government maintains that it alone is competent to define Austria's neutrality. Despite the limitations imposed by the State Treaty, Austria is clearly sympathetic to the West.

The Austrian concept of neutrality is more active than that of Switzerland; Austria is a member of the U.N. and other international and regional organizations and has contributed troops to U.N. peacekeeping activities. Several agencies of the U.N., including the International Atomic Engergy

Agency and the Industrial Development Organization, have their headquarters in Vienna. The United States has separate missions to both organizations, supported administratively by the U.S. Embassy. In addition, the conference for mutual and balanced force reduction (MBFR), the International Institute for Applied Systems Analysis (IIASA), and the Organization of Petroleum Exporting Countries (OPEC) have established headquarters in Vienna.

Arts, Science, Education

Austria is a paradise for the arts. The Vienna State Opera (Staatsoper), the Burgtheater, and the Volksoper rank among the world's leading cultural organizations.

The great Vienna orchestras include the Vienna Philharmonic and the Vienna Symphony. The Musikverein and the Konzerthaus present special concerts and recitals by internationally famous artists.

The annual Vienna Festival in May and June, the Salzburg Festivals at Easter and in summer, the Salzburg Mozart Week in January, the Carinthian Summer Festival, the Bregenz Festival, and the avant-garde Styrian Fall Festival at Graz attract visitors from all parts of the world. Vienna is the home of the Vienna Boys' Choir and the celebrated Spanish Riding School which features the beautiful white Lipizzaner horses.

Interest in science and research is promoted by the universities, the Austrian Institute of Historical Research, and the Vienna Institute of Radium Research, one of the oldest atomic research centers. The Institute of Advanced Studies and Scientific Research is also here.

Austria has 18 institutions of higher learning, attended by some 90,000 students. About 10,000 are foreigners, many from West Germany. Austria's institutions of higher learning are open to qualified Americans in most departments. However, some fields—varying from university to university—are closed to foreigners due to limited study and laboratory facilities. American citizens should check with the pertinent department deans prior to planning their studies abroad.

While a few courses are offered in English, most of them are given in German, which is one of the prerequisites for studying at an Austrian institution of higher learning. The other requirement is at least two years of previous study at an American college or university. Excellent private teachers for instruction in the arts, particularly music and voice, are available at reasonable prices.

Also, a considerable number of American colleges and universities have branches in Austria, with programs varying from three weeks to one academic year. The Institute of European Studies has an undergraduate program for Americans in the center of Vienna, offering courses in art, history, European literature, Austrian history, political science (current events), drawing and painting, music appreciation, theater in Vienna, beginning German, and psychology. The internationally renowned Salzburg Seminar in American Studies attracts graduate students from all over Europe and the East.

Austrian education follows the traditional European system. School attendance is mandatory until age 15, when students either continue their education or enter an apprenticeship program. Literacy in Austria is 98 percent.

Commerce and Industry

Austria is a Western "free enterprise" industrialized nation. Despite the loss of its empire after World War I, extensive damage during World War II, and 10 years of occupation before 1956, the country has recovered and is enjoying the fruits of over 20 years of nearly uninterrupted prosperity. This impressive performance contrasts sharply with the sluggish and spotty economic growth of neighboring Communist countries—a significant political, as well as economic, contrast.

Manufacturing and construction contribute about 40 percent of Austria's annual wealth as measured by gross national product (GNP). Steel, textiles, paper, and pulp are highly developed industries; agriculture accounts for about five percent of GNP. Foreign trade plays an important role in the country's economy, as does tourism. Thus, Austria is quite exposed to outside influences, and much of its foreign economic policy is concerned with adjusting to events in foreign countries over which Austria has little control. This is one reason Austria is an active member of most international economic organizations.

Transportation

Rail transportation to most parts of Europe is frequent, fast, and reliable. Many major international airlines have regular direct or connection service to and from Vienna. Pam Am flies from Vienna to New York nonstop. Almost all of Europe's principal cities are easily accessible.

Salzburg is served by Austrian Airlines or Swissair from Zurich, British Airways from London, and Lufthansa from Frankfurt. More frequent and varied connections are available from Munich, a drive of one-and-a-half hours from Salzburg.

Public transportation in Vienna is excellent. A network of streetcars and buses, which maintain dependable service at reasonable fares, covers the city. A subway, currently under construction, adds a temporary burden to the traffic flow. The Stadtbahn (municipal train system) provides speedy transportation between points along the Guertel (a broad thoroughfare which more or less surrounds the heart of the city) and the Danube Canal. Public transportation operates from 5:30 a.m. until 11:30 p.m. A public bus system serves most parts of Salzburg.

Many taxis are available 24 hours a day at stands in Vienna, and by radio in Salzburg. Prices are relatively high, and drivers expect a 10 percent tip.

A private vehicle is a convenience in Austria, but maintaining an American car sometimes poses problems; service is not always satisfactory and the limited quantities of spare parts are often expensive. Stock and service are naturally directed toward automobiles made in Europe. Salzburg streets are mainly narrow, winding, and occasionally quite steep, making small cars more practical. Snow tires are necessary for the winter season, and it should be noted that Alpine passes are hazardous in midwinter.

Communications

Telephone and telegraph service to all countries is available in Austria at standard rates. International mail deliveries to and from the U.S. are reliable and frequent; transit time varies from five to seven days (airmail), and three to five weeks (surface).

Radio and TV reception is good. Austrian AM and FM stations broadcast good music with little advertising. The three FM stations also provide several hours of stereo music daily. There are two TV channels; one broadcasts in the morning and midday for about three hours and every night for about five hours, and the other is on the air evenings. Both black-and-white and color sets can be rented. Most black-and-white American TV sets can be adapted to meet local telecasting standards, although American color TV sets cannot be adapted to receive a color picture.

Radio reception in Salzburg, including broadcasts from the AF Radio Service in Munich, is good. The TV reception has four channels available, two Austrian and two German.

The International Herald Tribune is sold at newsstands and hotels throughout Vienna's First District, usually the same afternoon it is published. European newspapers and some popular American magazines are available on local newsstands, but they are expensive. A fairly good supply of books in English may be purchased at leading bookstores. Children's English-language books, however, are in short supply.

Health

Viennese hospitals, although not as modern as their American counterparts, are generally satisfactory, and many of the medical and dental practitioners throughout the city are English-speaking. Laboratories and pharmacies give good service. Adequate hospital and clinic care also is available in Salzburg.

Community health and sanitation standards in Austrian cities are similar to those in the U.S. The incidence of disease, for instance, is about the same in Vienna as in any large American city, and no serious epidemics have occurred for years. Milk in Vienna is pasteurized; so-called "baby milk" is double-pasteurized. Water is safe and pure.

Major Cities

VIENNA, Austria's capital and largest city, is located in the Danube Basin at the eastern end of the European Alpine range, near the Hungarian and Czechoslovakian borders. Initially established as a Roman outpost and trading center on the banks of the Danube, Vienna evolved, under centuries of Hapsburg rule, into one of the world's most important capitals.

In the 19th century, the city was the leading capital in Central Europe. After the Hapsburg Empire was dissolved in late 1918, however, the imperial city became the capital of a state unsure of its own identity. The political and economic crises of the 1920s and 1930s, World War II, and the postwar occupation stifled progress and reduced the city to an impoverished symbol of its once great past. It was called "a head without a body."

Since 1966, however, the city has undergone a rejuvenation. The newcomer's first impressions are those of activity—new construction, renovation, street repairs, and traffic. The city's center lies within the First District, surrounded by the Ring (site of the old city walls, but now a broad thoroughfare). The main shopping area, fine hotels and restaurants, as well as historic palaces and churches, are located in or very near to this district.

Knowledge of German is important and helpful for business or professional effectiveness and full enjoyment of Austrian culture, although English is widely spoken.

SALZBURG, "die schoene Stadt," is one of the world's most beautiful cities, both in its surroundings and in its architecture. It is at an altitude of 1,400 feet, and is divided by the river Salzach, separating the city into the "new" and "old" parts. While the city itself has a population of only 149,000, it is visited yearly by more than a million-and-a-half tourists.

The dominating architectural feature of Salzburg is the Hohensalzburg, an 11th century fortress some 400 feet above the city. Below the fortress are many examples of the baroque, featuring the ancient palaces of medieval archbishops, domed churches, and spacious squares with some of the most remarkable fountains in Europe. The tall, narrow, and well-kept houses lining the streets of the Old City testify to the pride Salzburgers have in their city's tradition. Archaeological finds date the founding of the city back to the Stone Age. During the Roman period to about A.D. 500, it was important as the center of administrative government.

Recreation

Tourism is Austria's largest industry, and the quality and number of the country's sports facilities is undoubtedly one of the main reasons.

The ski slopes at Kitzbuehel and Zell am See, only six to eight hours

from Vienna, are among the best in the world. Good skiing can also be found less than two hours from Vienna at Semmering. Skiing opportunities near Salzburg are practically limitless, with slopes ranging from beginners to competition rank, and only a short distance away. Innsbruck can be reached in two-and-a-half to three hours.

Hunting in Austria is varied and excellent. It is, however, quite expensive. The overall season for all game is long. The abundant game includes roebuck, stag, snipe, and pheasant. Both a hunting license (*jagdkarte*) and hunting permission card (*jagderlaubnis*) are necessary before taking part in a hunt. Hunting premiums are charged for the type of game taken. These charges vary, but are generally very high by U.S. standards. Hunting is by invitation only, and always done on game preserves. Contacts can be arranged to secure invitations through local tourist agencies.

To secure a hunting license the applicant must present proof of his hunting ability—usually a valid certificate from a hunting organization in another country. Lacking a valid license, a proficiency examination is administered by local authorities.

Fishing in Austria is also excellent. One can obtain permits to fish by invitation, or by joining the Austrian Fishing Association (Oesterreichische Fischerei Gesellschaft), which assigns specific sections of a stream.

Vienna has several riding stables and many tennis courts. Three 18-hole golf courses are within 20 miles of the city. One is located at the Prater Park. By joining the Austrian Golf Association, one may also gain entrance to play on some of the finest golf courses in Europe. Sailboating and swimming on the Old Danube (now a beautiful lake) and hiking in the Vienna Woods are other favorite pastimes.

Salzburg also offers good tennis (indoor and outdoor) and golf. A small but picturesque golf course is located at Klessheim on the outskirts of the city, and a rugged nine-hole course is operated by the Berchtesgaden center. Sailing is a popular summer sport on the lakes within a short distance from Salzburg.

The beauty of its rustic landscape, the network of good highways, and the comfortable accommodations of its *gasthaeuser* (inns) make Austria a paradise for those who love the outdoors.

The Wachau, an area between Melk and Krems along the Danube, is famous for its vineyards, fruit trees, castles, and churches. The monastery at Melk contains one of the world's finest old libraries and a wealth of paintings, tapestries, and art objects.

The Province of Burgenland (an hour's drive from Vienna) is an area of gently rolling hills dotted with vineyards, spas, and castles. Lake Neusiedl, a favorite Viennese resort area on the Austro-Hungarian border, has gained worldwide fame as a bird sanctuary; it also provides good sailing.

The central part of Austria, the Salzkammergut, a beautiful recreation area with high mountains, lakes, hunting, fishing, ski resorts, old castles, and churches, is about three hours from Vienna.

Eastern European points accessible by car include Budapest (four hours) and Prague (five hours). Visits to these cities require some planning,

however, due to visa requirements and other formalities connected with entering an Eastern European country.

A drive from Salzburg to Bregenz on Lake Constance provides one of the most spectacular drives in Europe, passing the length of Salzburg, Tirol, and Vorarlberg. Quiet mountain valleys, particularly in the Lungau area, afford a glimpse of native customs and dress unchanged by modern fashions. The area is rarely visited by tourists.

Visitors generally travel to vacation areas by private car, but the daily trains and buses throughout the country are excellent and inexpensive. The Salzburg-Vienna autobahn affords rapid, easy access to southern Germany and Munich.

Entertainment

Vienna is the music capital of Europe. The Vienna State Opera, the Vienna Philharmonic, the Vienna Symphony, and the Volksoper are outstanding. The talents of world-famous conductors and virtuosos are on display throughout the year, although the opera houses close for July and August of each year. Tickets are very expensive. The Vienna Festival, held annually from mid-May to mid-June, is one of the high points of Viennese cultural life.

The Vienna theater also enjoys a worldwide reputation. Paced by the famed Burgtheater, the many theaters present the classical works of Goethe and Schiller (in German) as well as the most recent Broadway hits.

Except for July and August and a short period during the winter, Sunday morning dawns with a special treat for the Viennese—the famous Lipizzaner white horses of the Spanish Riding

School perform in the Riding Hall of the Hofburg, and the Vienna Boys' Choir sings in the Hofburg Chapel.

One of the many movie theaters often has British and American films with the original English dialogue.

Vienna abounds in good restaurants with varying prices. Restaurants in the hills overlooking the city are popular, especially in summer. The wine cellars in Grinzing are famous for their *heurigen* (new wine) and folksong atmosphere.

Salzburg, the birthplace and home of Wolfgang Amadeus Mozart, is certainly one of the most music-oriented cities of the world. The Festpiele, celebrated annually from mid-July through August, draws thousands of music-loving tourists from all over the world and features widely known conductors and performers. The Berlin Philharmonic Orchestra and its conductor Herbert von Karajan are special favorites, and the highlight of the season is the open-air performance of the medieval play *Jedermann.*

Music festivals are not confined to summer, however. Throughout the year various programs are given. The Mozart festival is held in the last week of January, and during Easter week, when it again features the conductor von Karajan and the Berlin Philharmonic Orchestra in opera and concert performances. At the time of Whitsunday, concerts are also featured as separate festivals. The Salzburg Marionettes are a special attraction during the entire year.

Restaurants are good but rather expensive, and many offer sweeping panoramic views of the surrounding area.

Notes for Travelers

Vienna can be reached by direct flight from New York via Pan Am, and many other international carriers serve that city from major European centers. Salzburg is served by Austrian Airlines, Swissair, and British Airways.

Under the Austrian Passport Control Law, any person entering the country for a stay of more than three months must have a visa. No medical certificates are necessary.

Two sporting guns (unloaded) may be imported. Ammunition is available locally.

The Vienna Community Church is a Protestant English-speaking interdenominational church with an American pastor. A small chapel across from the U.S. Embassy, Zur Heiligen Maria d'Mercede, conducts services for English-speaking Roman Catholics. An Anglican-Espiscopal Church, Christ Church (affiliated with the British Embassy), a Church of Christ Scientist, and a Baptist chapel also have services in English.

The Austrian monetary unit is the *schilling* (Austrian abbreviation, S or OS; American abbreviation, AS), which is divided into 100 *groschen.* Since January 1977, the rate of exchange has fluctuated between AS14.52 and 17.26 to U.S. $1.

Austria uses the metric system of weights and measures.

The U.S. Embassy in Austria is located at 16 Boltzmanngasse, in Vienna's Ninth District. The Consulate in Salzburg is at Franz-Josefs-Kai 1, on the banks of the Salzach River.

Belgium

Taking its name from a Celtic tribe, the Belgae, which was described by Caesar as the most courageous tribe of Gaul, **BELGIUM** once flourished as a province of ancient Rome. It was successively ruled by the Franks, the Dukes of Burgundy, the Hapsburgs, the Spanish, and the Austrians; it was annexed by France; it became part of the Netherlands through the Congress of Vienna; and finally, it achieved its independence in 1830. In spite of proclaimed neutrality, Belgium was occupied twice by the Germans — in 1914 and 1940. Through the centuries it has witnessed a constant ebb and flow of cultures, whose diverse elements have created the Belgium of today.

Area, Geography, Climate

Belgium is small, about the size of Maryland, with a total area of 11,799 square miles. Thirty-nine miles of Belgian seacoast line the North Sea, and 896 miles of frontier border the Netherlands, The Federal Republic of Germany, Luxembourg, and France. The Meuse River and its tributary, the Sambre, divide the country into two distinct geographic regions: a level, fertile area to the north and west; and the hilly, wooded region, the Ardennes, to the south and east.

The capital, Brussels, is in the center of the kingdom. With Ghent and Antwerp, it forms a triangle enclosing the most heavily built-up and densely populated area of Belgium. More than half (four million acres) of Belgium is still farmland; forest covers another 18 percent.

Most places and streets in Brussels have both French and Dutch names, but in practice, the French name is more common. Belgian towns may have three names; e.g., English: Brussels, Ghent, Antwerp; French: Bruxelles, Gand, Anvers; Dutch: Brussel, Gent, Antwerpen. In Brussels, both French and Dutch names are used, but in the French- and Dutch-speaking areas of Belgium only the name in that language will be used.

Belgium's climate is characterized by moderate temperatures, prevailing westerly winds, cloudy skies, regular but not abundant rainfall, and little snow. The weather is variable. Summer temperatures average 60°F. Rare annual extremes are 10°F and 90°F.

Population

In 1981, Belgium's population was estimated at 9.8 million. The principal cities are Brussels (population about one million), Antwerp (206,000), Liege (230,000), Ghent (248,000), Brugge, and Charleroi. Density averages 831 per square mile, the second highest in Europe after the Netherlands.

Geographically and culturally, Belgium is at the crossroads of Europe. During the past 2,000 years, it has witnessed a broad diversity of peoples and cultures. As a result, Belgium is one of Europe's true melting pots with people of Celtic, Roman, German, French, Dutch, Spanish, and Austrian origins.

Today the Belgians are divided linguistically into the Dutch-speaking Flemings (56 percent) and French-speaking Walloons (32 percent), with a mixed population in Brussels, and a small region of German-speaking people in the east. Literacy rate is about 98 percent. Roman Catholicism is the predominant religion.

Government

Belgium is a parliamentary democracy with a consititutional monarch. Although the King (chief of state) is technically the executive authority, the Council of Ministers (Cabinet) makes governmental decisions. The Council of Ministers, led by the Prime Minister (head of government), holds office as long as it retains parliamentary confidence. Elections are held at least every four years by universal suffrage, with obligatory voting and a form of proportional representation.

The bicameral Parliament consists of a Senate and a Chamber of Representatives. Of 181 senators, 50 are elected by provincial councils, 25 by fellow senators, and the remainder by direct election. The 212-member Chamber of Representatives is elected directly, and traditionally is the dominant body.

A 1970 amendment to the Belgian Constitution created, within Parliament, cultural councils comprised of Dutch- and French-speaking members. The amendment granted the councils jurisdiction over certain cultural and linguistic matters. Brussels was established as a separate, bilingual area. Its Metropolitan Council is chosen by proportional representation, but parity between Dutch- and French-speaking members is required in its executive committee.

The present government, which consists of a coalition of Social Christians, (CVP/PSC), Socialists (BSP/PSB), Flemish regionalists (VU), and Brussels Francophones (FDF), easily commands the necessary majority, and is determined to move ahead with its plan for definitive regionalization described above.

The judiciary is modeled after the French system. The King appoints the Chief Justice of the highest court, the Court of Cassation. Courts do not pass on the constitutionality of legislation, but a special legal group, the Council of State, gives advisory opinions on the constitutionality of major legislation.

Belgium is divided into nine provinces, with executive power in each exercised by a governor appointed by the King.

Arts, Science, Education

Belgium is justly proud of its centuries-old artistic tradition. The nation's past is studded with the names of masters—Rubens, Breughel, Jerome, Bosch, Van Eyck—whose works are displayed in museums and churches throughout the country. Equally famous are such Belgian art cities as Antwerp, Bruges, Ghent, and Louvain. Belgium's art tradition does not end with the masters. James Ensor, Constant Permeke, and surrealists Rene Magritte and Paul Delvaux, are among the many artists considered to be outstanding representatives of 20th-century art.

Brussels is becoming a major center for the performing arts. Its Palais des Beaux Arts offers a wide range of dance and music programs each season. The Theatre Royal de la Monnaie is the home of the internationally famous "20th Century Ballet" troupe of Maurice Bejart and the Festival of Flanders. Brussels also hosts one of the world's most respected musicial competitions, the Queen Elisabeth International Music Contest. Begun in 1951, it offers material and moral support to talented young artists, pianists, violinists, and composers.

Belgian educational institutions have been famous from the Middle Ages as centers of learning. The Belgian Constitution guarantees absolute freedom of education. Most schooling is state-financed from primary school to the university level. For several years, Belgian universities have attracted large numbers of foreign students, including many Americans, but the Belgian Government recently established a quota for foreign students.

Also well known are Belgium's scientific institutions, such as the Royal Observatory and the Royal Library. Their valuable collections range from precious medieval manuscripts to specialized scientific collections.

Commerce and Industry

Belgium has a free-enterprise, industrial economy that relies heavily on foreign trade. Major industries include iron, steel, and nonferrous metals; transportation equipment; electrical equipment and machinery; chemicals, including petrochemicals; and glass, textiles, and diamond cutting. Belgian agriculture is based on small farms and intensive cultivation.

Because Belgium exports about half of its gross national product, its economy is sensitive to international economic conditions. So, Belgium has traditionally supported liberal trade policies. It firmly advocates and supports international economic cooperation, as its participation in the European Communities, Benelux, OECD, and other international economic organizations testifies.

Belgium's principal trading partners are West Germany, France, the Netherlands, the United Kingdom, and the United States. Major imports are mineral fuels, lubricants, and related products; machinery and electrical equipment; textiles; iron, steel, nonferrous metals, and related products; aircraft; and vegetable products and foodstuffs. Major exports are iron and steel products, nonferrous metals and byproducts; textiles; machinery and electrical equipment; assembled rolling stock, cars, trucks; diamonds; chemicals; stoneware, ceramics, glass, and glassware.

The U.S. is Belgium's principal trade partner outside the Common Market. Trade relations between the two countries are excellent.

Transportation

Brussels National Airport is a major international air terminal. American carriers and Sabena fly between Brussels, New York, and Boston. London and Paris, both less than an hour's flight from Brussels, offer additional air connections anywhere in the world. Excellent rail and highway systems link Belgium to neighboring countries and provide direct routes to major European cities. "Autoroutes," limited-access divided highways, run from Belgium to Paris, Frankfurt, and Amsterdam.

Trains run frequently and on schedule. Commuter service is available into and between Brussels and Antwerp. Both cities have excellent bus and streetcar systems. Taxis are expensive, but the service charge or tip is included in the metered fare.

For those planning residence in Belgium, a private car is desirable. A Belgian drivers license can be secured upon presentation of a valid U.S. license, with a photograph and a registration fee. An international drivers license will be needed for travel to other European countries which do not recognize either a Belgian or U.S. permit—principally countries in Eastern Europe. Since Belgium has one of the highest vehicle accident rates in Europe, insurance is expensive, and all vehicles registered in the country must be covered by unlimited third-party liability insurance issued by a Belgian-licensed company.

Parking is difficult in the large cities, and although most buildings have garages, those garages can accommodate only compact or subcompact cars. Good auto maintenance is hard to find for U.S. models, as many service stations are unfamiliar with cars not sold locally.

Communications

Telephone and telegraph services to and from Belgium compare to those in the U.S. Direct-dial service is available to America and most European countries. The Belgian postal system provides rapid and safe service.

Belgian radio and TV systems are government owned. French- and Dutch-language stations are separate. Flemish TV often carries American and British programs in English with Dutch subtitles. Most American and British programs on French TV are dubbed.

Although some American TV sets can be altered for reception in Belgium, it is costly and difficult. Most people rent or buy sets made for use in Europe. With a good antenna one can receive two Belgian, one Luxembourg, and one French station.

The American Forces Network (AFN) broadcasts 24 hours daily from Frankfurt and SHAPE (Supreme Headquarters, Allied Powers Europe) Belgium, offering a variety of programing, including American sports, music, and news.

La Libre Belgique, Le Soir, and La Derniere Heure are the most widely read French-language dailies published in Brussels. Het Laatste Nieuws and De Standaard are the most popular Dutch-language newspapers published there. London and Paris papers, including The Times, Daily Telegraph, Le Monde, and Le Figaro, are sold in Brussels on the day of publication. Two weekly English-language publications catering to the substantial English-speaking community appear on Fridays.

The International Herald Tribune is sold the day of publication at Brussels newsstands or through subscription. Several American periodicals, many of them European editions, are available on Brussels newsstands.

Health

A number of Belgian hospitals compare favorably with good U.S. hospitals, and many English-speaking doctors and dentists are in practice in the larger cities. Some of these have had American training.

Public health standards equal those in the U.S. Brussels and Antwerp have modern sewage- and refuse-disposal systems and water purification facilities. Tapwater is safe to drink. Dairy, meat, and other food products are safe. Living in Belgium neither involves health risks nor requires special precautions, but the climate is sometimes uncomfortable for sufferers of sinus conditions and respiratory ailments. Colds are common in winter. Epidemic diseases are rare, and are treated efficiently by Belgian public health authorities.

Major Cities

The origins of **BRUSSELS** date back to the first centuries of the Christian era. On the banks of the Senne, a small stream long since covered and lost from view, Brussels grew as a crossroads and trading center. By the 10th century, Brussels was a principal stop en route from Cologne through France to Channel ports. In 1402, the cornerstone of the Hotel de Ville, the central building of Brussels' magnificent Grand Place, was laid. During the next five centuries Brussels experienced Burgundian, Spanish, Austrian, French, and Dutch foreign rule. In 1830, Belgium won its independence from the Dutch, the Belgian monarchy was founded, and Brussels became the capital of the new kingdom.

Although retaining vivid architectural and cultural traces of its deep involvement in European history, Brussels today has all the excitement, activity, and comfort of a modern European capital. It is headquarters for the European Communities and the North Atlantic Treaty Organization, as well as the European home for many leading multinational businesses. Brussels is legally bilingual in French and Dutch. English is also widely known and used, particularly in business circles.

ANTWERP, Antwerpen in Dutch, is one of the world's greatest ports, and has held this distinction for over three centuries. It is situated on the river Schelde, about 55 miles southeast of the North Sea, 30 miles north of Brussels, and 27 miles south of the Netherlands border. Built on the flat, sandy soil typical of Flanders, it is just above, and in some areas below, sea level. The countryside is densely populated and highly cultivated. The population of greater Antwerp is about 700,000. Culturally and ethnically it is Flemish and uses the Dutch language, but many people also speak French and English.

Economic activity centers around its port, which is the third largest in the world in terms of cargo handled. It is an important transshipment point for trade with Switzerland, Germany, the Netherlands, France, and Eastern Europe. Zeebrugge and Ghent are also significant ports. Antwerp is one of Europe's petroleum and chemical centers. It is also a center for diamond cutting, shipbuilding and ship repairs, photographic film and paper, telephone equipment, forwarding agents, brokers, and ships agents. American firms in Antwerp include: ESSO and Coastal States Gas, which have refineries in Antwerp; General Motors and Ford with automobile and tractor assembly plants; eight American bank branches; ITT, Monsanto, and 3M.

Amoco Chemicals, Dupont de Nemours, Janssen Pharmaceuticals, Johns Manville, and Sperry Rand Holland. Many other American firms have businesses elsewhere in the area.

Antwerp is one of America's oldest foreign service posts. Opened in 1803 as a consular agency, it has been continually open, except for periods of Germany occupation during the two World Wars.

Recreation

In addition to the many museums and attractions found in Brussels, its central location offers unlimited sightseeing and travel opportunities, not only in Belgium but throughout Europe.

Many fine parks in the city offer a variety of outdoor activities. The Bois de la Cambre, a large green haven, features pleasant vistas for strolling, rowing, bicycling, roller skating, and miniature golf. The Parc de Tervuren has beautiful walks around lovely lakes, picnic tables, boating, and play areas for children.

A pleasant spring and summer pastime in Belgium is *petanque*, an outdoor game played with weighted balls in a marked-off court. It originated in the south of France, and reminds Americans of a mixture of bowling and horseshoes.

Swimming in indoor pools is a year-round activity in Brussels. The cool summers encourage only the hardy to venture into outdoor swimming areas. But beachcombers find the North Sea coast with its wide, sandy beaches well worth the two-hour drive from Brussels. Among the many resort areas, Ostend and Le Zoute are probably the best known. The season at the seashore is usually short, and water temperatures compare to those along the New England Coast.

Soccer, field hockey, basketball, and horse racing are popular Belgian sports. However, game shooting remains the traditional sport with boar, deer, pheasant, partridge, duck, and other small game hunted. Hunting areas are strictly controlled, either by individuals or by clubs, and shooting is by invitation or by membership. Opportunities exist for camping, boating, sailing, fishing, and skiing in the Ardennes.

Brussels has many indoor and outdoor tennis clubs, as well as good golf courses. Skating enthusiasts enjoy roller skating in the Bois de la Cambre and ice skating at Foret National and the Poseidon.

Popular attractions in Antwerp include the Antwerp Cathedral, Ruben's house, the renowned Antwerp Zoo, and several outstanding museums: the Royal Museum of Fine Arts, the Plantin Moretus Museum, the Maritime and Diamond museums, Mayer van den Bergh, Museum Smidt Van Gelder, open-air museum of modern sculpture Middelheim, and the Sterckxhof museum and park.

Various outdoor activities may also be enjoyed. Fishing is possible, but hunting is by invitation only on private preserves. Numerous bike paths exist in and around the city. Several North Sea beach resorts are one-and-a-half hours' drive from Antwerp. Paris, Amsterdam, and Cologne can be reached in about three hours. Ghent, Bruges, Courtrai, Ostend, and the Ardennes are closer.

Antwerp offers excellent participant sports opportunities. An 18-hole golf course and club in Kappellenbos is about 15 miles north of central Antwerp. Memberships in tennis clubs with indoor and outdoor courts are available. One can also join a yachting club, skeet range, squash club, and saddle clubs with horses for hire. Indoor swimming is available all year.

Entertainment

Brussels offers a full spectrum of entertainment. Operas, concerts, ballets, stage presentations (in French or Dutch), and visiting international performers provide an interesting range of cultural activities. Recently organized British and American Theater Clubs present several yearly productions. Numerous movie theaters show films in French, English, Italian, and other languages. Usually six or more American films are playing in Brussels at any one time. Inexpensive discotheques with dancing and recorded music abound in the city. The few nightclubs offering floor shows are expensive.

Brussels' many good restaurants offer Belgian cooking (based on French cuisine), as well as Italian, Chinese, Serbian, Spanish, and other specialties. Prices range from very expensive at some outstanding restaurants to reasonable at smaller establishments. Dining out is a Belgian national pastime. Numerous small cafes do a brisk beer business day and night, and sidewalk cafes flourish in good weather.

Belgian folk festival traditions, with celebrations of every kind, are some of Europe's richest. Especially colorful and exciting are those of the pre-Lenten season. The Carnival of the Gilles in Binche, a Shrove Tuesday event, dates from the 16th century, when Spain ruled Belgium. It features the Gilles, those men and boys of the town entitled to wear the brilliant costumes topped with towering Inca-inspired feathered hats. With carnival enthusiasm, the Gilles dance through the town in Indian rhythm, beating drums, shaking bells, and tossing fresh oranges to (or at) the spectators. The Ommengang in Brussels, and the Procession of the Holy Blood in Bruges, are other internationally famous Belgian festivals.

Antwerp offers operas, ballet concerts, recitals, lectures, and other entertainments. Movies from the U.S. and other countries arrive rather late, but usually are shown in the original language with Dutch and French subtitles. There are good restaurants, as well as the nightlife associated with a port city, but prices are high by American standards.

Notes for Travelers

Most travelers from the U.S. arrive at Brussels National Airport at Zaventem. The airport also serves Antwerp.

No visas are required for Americans transiting or visiting Belgium, as long as they stay less than three months in the country. Driving into Belgium, the traveler must have a valid drivers license and proof of vehicle insurance.

Belgian law prohibits importing all weapons of war, and requires registration of other firearms, with accident insurance covering their use and possession. Maximum quantities allowed are five each of pistols and revolvers, rifles, and shotguns, and 1,000 rounds of ammunition.

Among the many houses of worship in Brussels are the following which provide English-language services: Our Lady of Mercy (Roman Catholic), American Protestant Church, Holy Trinity (Church of England and American Protestant Episcopal), St. Andrew's Presbyterian (Church of Scotland), Church of Christ, Church of Jesus Christ of Latter-Day Saints, Word of God (Interdenominational Charismatic), Liberal Jewish Synagogue, and Jewish Synagogue of Brussels. Antwerp has an American Protestant Church with an American pastor, and English services also are offered at the Anglican Church of St. Boniface and at a Christian Science church. English-speaking Catholics attend services at St. Joseph's Mission, or at Holy Name Church in Brasschaet. Several Orthodox synagogues exist in the city.

The currency, the Belgian franc, is divided into 100 *centimes*.

Belgium uses the metric system of weights and measures.

The U.S. Embassy in Belgium is located at 27 Boulevard du Regent, Brussels. The Consulate General in Antwerp is at 64–68 Frankrijklei.

Bulgaria

The name **BULGARIA** is derived from the Bulgars, a Turkic people who invaded Europe in the seventh century and intermingled with the Slavic inhabitants who had earlier entered the Balkan Peninsula. Two centuries later, Bulgaria reached its zenith, and controlled all of the Balkans except Greece. The Ottoman Turks ruled Bulgaria for 500 years, until their defeat in 1878 with the help of Russia and Romania, and the country finally became fully independent 30 years later.

Bulgaria, which was allied with Germany during both World Wars, was seized without resistance by the Soviets in 1944, and after the war its monarchy was abolished and a Communist government established.

Area, Geography, Climate

Bulgaria occupies 110,000 square kilometers (43,000 square miles), and is about the size of Tennessee. Much of the country is rugged and mountainous. The Danube River, Black Sea, and Pirin-Rhodope Mountains provide natural borders on the north, east, and south. Flowing south into Greece are the nonnavigable Struma, Maritsa, Mesta, and Arda Rivers, which are important historically as invasion routes, and economically for irrigation. The Balkan range extends across the north-central part of the country, separating the wheat-growing Dobrudzha region from the Thracian plain where vegetables, fruits, grapes, and tobacco are cultivated. An international highway that crosses Bulgaria links Western Europe and the Middle East via Belgrade, Nish, Sofia, Plovdiv, and Istanbul.

From mid-May to mid-October, the climate usually is pleasantly warm and sunny. The climate is cold from November to April, with snow. Temperatures hover near 32°F (0°C), but often fall lower, sometimes to 5°F (−15°C) at Sofia, the capital. Summer temperatures rarely exceed 90°F, and the humidity is not excessive.

The only climatic problem affecting Sofia is winter smog, which is caused by industrial air pollution, soft-coal smoke, fog, and surrounding mountains that keep winds from blowing the smog away. Grey-brown dirt or coal dust, not sand, is scattered on Sofia's snow-covered streets in winter. Winters may be drab in Sofia but are quite beautiful in the nearby mountains, and abundant trees and flowers make Sofia a garden city the rest of the year. Rainfall is moderate, averaging about 25 inches per year.

Population

Bulgaria's present population is 8,885,000 (1981). About one million, or slightly more than 11 percent, live in and around Sofia. Two other cities, Plovdiv and Varna, have populations exceeding 250,000, and only four other cities (Ruse, Burgas, Stara Zagora, and Pleven) exceed 100,000.

The birth rate is low, although the government encourages larger families. About 86 percent of the population is ethnic Bulgarian, and nine percent consists of a Turkish minority. The country also has small gypsy, Armenian, and Greek minorities. The principal religious denomination is Bulgarian Orthodox, which belongs to the family of Eastern Orthodox churches that also includes Greek, Syrian, and Russian Orthodox churches. The government encourages atheism.

Like Russian and Serbian, the Bulgarian language is written in Cyrillic. Bulgarians are proud that the Cyrillic alphabet spread from Bulgaria to Russia. Knowledge of other Slavic languages (particularly Russian) is helpful in learning Bulgarian, despite significant differences in vocabulary, grammar, and pronunciation. Russian and Serbian are intelligible to most Bulgarians. The Cyrillic alphabet is not difficult to learn and can be mastered in about three hours of steady work. Among Western languages, English, French, German, and Spanish (in that order) are useful.

Government

According to the Constitution promulgated May 18, 1971, the Bulgarian Communist Party is the directing force in society and in the state. Fewer than 10 percent of Bulgarians are party members, but the party effectively controls all sectors of Bulgarian life by placing party members in all key positions. Party First Secretary Todor Zhivkov is also the Chief of State, and key ministers, including the Prime Minister, are members of the Politburo of the Communist Party.

The principal organs of the central government, in addition to the Council of State and the Council of Ministers, are the National Assembly and the judiciary. About 70 percent of the National Assembly membership is Communist. The proportion of Communists in the judiciary is probably equally high.

The Communist Party controls mass organizations, such as the Fatherland Front, Dimitrov Communist Youth Council, trade unions, and professional societies. The Bulgarian National Agrarian Union, once a potent political force, remains a nominally independent political party, but in practice fully follows Communist Party direction.

The country is divided into 27 districts (called *okrugs*), which in turn are subdivided into towns, villages, and communes administered by peoples' councils. The city of Sofia enjoys a status similar to that of an *okrug*, but in population and general importance it stands above any of the *okrugs*.

In international affairs, Bulgarian policy reflects the country's close alliance with the Soviet Union in the multilateral political, military, and economic framework of the Warsaw Pact and the Council for Economic Mutual Assistance (CEMA or COMECON). Bulgaria became a member of the United Nations in 1955 and now belongs to most of the U.N.-related agencies. It has received assistance under the U.N. Development Program and through affiliated organizations, such as the International Labor Organization (ILO), World Health Organization (WHO), and U.N. Industrial Development Organization (UNIDO).

Arts, Science, Education

Bulgarians tend to be a disciplined and conservative people who have made a conscious effort to preserve their traditions and customs. A number of villages have been restored, displaying crafts and living conditions of the last century. Festivals of folk dancing and singing are often held, with each region sending representatives.

Sofia is surprisingly Western in some ways. Clothing fads catch on a little late but they are accepted readily. Cultural events are many and varied, and cafes, restaurants, and bars are always crowded—and can be fairly expensive.

Remnants of Turkish occupation include many everyday words and gestures. For instance, Bulgarians indicate "no" by an upward and downward movement of the head (that might seem to signify "yes") and "yes" by the opposite motion.

In the performing arts, Bulgarian excellence is shown in both operatic and choral singing. Distinguished names in opera include Boris Khristov, Nikolay Gyaurov, Nikola Gyuselev, and Raina Kabaivanska.

Two symphony orchestras, several good chamber groups, and many soloists present concerts throughout the fall, winter, and spring at very low prices. Good ballet is also presented, and folk music and dance ensembles are numerous. Theater offerings include plays with 19th-century and modern Bulgarian themes, as well as Russian plays and some works by American playwrights such as Arthur Miller, Tennessee Williams, Eugene O'Neill, Edward Albee, Neil Simon, and Thornton Wilder (in Bulgarian).

"Socialist realism" remains the approved style of painting. Yet, folk themes, landscapes, and still lifes also abound, and contemporary Bulgarian art also includes modern schools. Icons are on display in museums; contemporary copies are skillfully done, but are expensive.

The Bulgarian Academy of Science, founded in 1869, today embraces numerous research and teaching institutions. Pure research is usually subordinated to applied science. The general emphasis is on matters that directly apply to industrial and agricultural development. The Bulgarian Academy of Science and the U.S. National Academy of Sciences have an agreement for cooperative research that results in several joint projects each year.

The origins of Bulgarian literature date back to A.D. 855, when the Greek priests Cyril and Methodius devised the Cyrillic alphabet to enable them to write the Slavic languages. Early Bulgarian literature was religious, but it was not until the 18th century that secular, nationalistic writings appeared. Ivan Vazov's *Under the Yoke*, which describes the 1876 revolt against the Ottoman oppression in Bulgaria, is perhaps the most widely translated Bulgarian novel. In general, the emphasis on Socialist realism in recent decades has not helped Bulgarian writers to achieve international fame.

As in most Socialist states, the educational system is charged with the dual goals of producing model citizens and meeting the economic needs for trained workers in each sector. Educational policy tends to favor the study of science and technology over the humanities.

Education is compulsory until age 15, and classes are held six days a week. Students must study the Russian language from the fifth grade on, and usually begin a second foreign language in eighth grade. English is the most popular choice.

University-level education is open to those who pass an admission test. Some special attention is given to admitting those who have worked for two years, or who come from "worker or peasant" origins. Most higher educational institutions are located in the major cities and tend to be over-crowded.

Few Bulgarians study abroad, especially outside of the Warsaw Pact countries. Most who do, study in the Soviet Union. A number of foreign students, including several hundred from Arab and African countries, study at Bulgarian universities under bilateral agreements with those countries. A handful of Americans at the predoctoral level conduct research under the International Research and Exchanges Board (IREX) program. One or two American professors conduct courses in American literature and English under the Fulbright program.

Commerce and Industry

With nearly 90 percent of its tilled land in the form of "agro-industrial complexes," Bulgaria has one of the most collectivized agricultures in Eastern Europe. However, the private sector, composed of small plots owned by collective farmers, is still important in the production of meat, eggs, milk, potatoes, fruits, and some vegetables.

Prewar agriculture featured widespread ownership of land in small holdings by farmers who lacked capital for machinery or fertilizers, but were helped by a strongly developed cooperative movement. Since World War II, Bulgaria has made rapid strides in agricultural production, and it now can feed one-and-a-half times its population. This achievement is due to good soil and a fertile climate, emphasis on high-value products in strong demand by foreign countries, more rational use of land, increased supply of mineral fertilizers, improved plant varieties, machinery, and extensive development of irrigation.

Agriculture employs a quarter of the labor force. It accounts for about 18 percent of the national income and 25 percent of total exports. Principal commodities include oriental tobacco, fruits and preserves, grapes and wines, vegetables (especially tomatoes, wheat, corn, and barley), sunflower seeds, and sugar beets. Agricultural exports include all of these, as well as meat, rose oil, dried pepper, and wool. The great emphasis on exports, especially to the U.S.S.R., often produces domestic shortages of basic agricultural commodities.

In 1970, Bulgaria began a program to organize very large agro-industrial complexes averaging 27,000 hectares in size, and including certain processing plants. Bulgaria is now experimenting with still larger, vertically integrated agricultural units. An American firm has drawn up the master plan for the huge Silistra project, involving 300,000 acres devoted to forage crops, livestock raising, meat packing, and utilization of animal by-products.

Substantial industrial growth over recent decades has converted the economy into a largely industrial one. Government plans call for industrial output to continue to increase at double the agricultural rate. Machine building, chemicals and petrochemicals, electronics, electric lift vehicles, electricity, and nonferrous metals are heavily favored. Machine tools are becoming an increasingly important part of Bulgaria's exports. So-called "industrial crops," such as flax, jute, hemp, and essential oils, remain another important segment. Principal imports are fuels and basic raw materials, as well as complete plants and heavy equipment and machinery.

Since the late 1950s, the Bulgarian Government has been developing its tourist industry. The government has paid particular attention to resorts along the Black Sea. Group tourism is favored, and these new beach and skiing facilities attract large numbers of visitors. The Federal Republic of Germany (F.R.G.) provides the largest number of visitors from Western Europe, and Poland and Czechoslovakia provide the most Eastern European tourists. The number of Soviet tourists is increasing. Turkish workers passing to and from the F.R.G., and Middle Eastern travelers en route to and from Western Europe help swell official tourism statistics. Vacations in Bulgaria are still relatively inexpensive. Current plans emphasize improved quality of services and higher prices, in an attempt to increase hard-currency earnings from tourism.

Bulgaria maintains government ownership of all but the smallest means of production and distribution. Only a few artisans continue their crafts in a private capacity. Even production from private agricultural plots is largely processed and marketed through the official system.

Foreign trade is a government monopoly. About 57 percent of total foreign trade is with the Soviet Union alone, and 23 percent is with other Socialist countries. Western trade with Bulgaria is growing, however, as the country looks for advanced Western equipment and technology.

U.S. trade with Bulgaria totaled about $42 million in 1977, including $24 million in U.S. exports (mostly feed grains) and $18 million in imports from Bulgaria (mostly oriental tobacco). During the first six months of 1978, U.S. exports were $22 million, and imports from Bulgaria were $14 million.

A decree in December 1978 opened the way for the establishment of Western commercial offices in Bulgaria, but their scope and activities are closely defined. No American firms are based in Bulgaria. A few Western firms, such as Royal Shell and Fiat, maintain Bulgarian offices, and representatives of several Western airlines that offer flights to Bulgaria reside in Sofia. Some business families live here temporarily in connection with hotel or plant construction or installation of complex equipment. A number of Japanese and other non-Communist business representatives have worked for long periods out of hotel rooms.

Transportation

No American air carrier serves Sofia. The nearest cities with daily service by American carriers are Vienna, Frankfurt, and Rome, but connections to and from Sofia vary in convenience according to the day of the week. Bulgarian airlines and other foreign carriers provide regular service between Sofia and Western European cities.

In winter, fog and heavy snow may occasionally close Sofia Airport for several days at a time.

Rail travel can be booked to Sofia from Vienna or from Frankfurt via Munich and Belgrade. First-class sleeping compartments are advisable. Dining-car service is sometimes unavailable beyond Austria, but one can usually buy snacks at stations. Current running time from Frankfurt is about 32 hours.

Bulgaria has a growing merchant marine whose freighters, sailing from the Black Sea ports of Burgas and Varna, sometimes visit U.S. ports.

A fairly good international highway (E-5) links Sofia with Western Europe via Belgrade and Zagreb (E-94). Frequent air and railway service link Sofia and the Black Sea resorts of Varna and Burgas.

Sofia is served by many streetcar, trolleybus, and autobus lines. They are sometimes crowded, but are always usable and cheap. Taxis are available at stands in various parts of the city. They do not cruise, but sometimes can be summoned by telephone (in Sofia only). Fares are reasonable.

Main roads in Bulgaria are fairly good, but most have only two lanes. Some secondary roads are poor and not well maintained. Many city streets and some intercity roads have cobblestone paving. The mountainous parts of Bulgaria have snow between October and May, which makes snow tires and/or chains advisable. Studded snow tires are useful for driving on icy roads, but they are hazardous on the wet cobblestone and brick streets common in Sofia and elsewhere in Eastern Europe. One should undercoat automobiles brought to Sofia.

Rental cars are available from the state-owned tourism agency, Balkantourist, at rates similar to those in the U.S. An international driving permit is needed. Traffice moves on the right.

Communications

Telephone and telegraph facilities from Sofia to the outside world are adequate. From the central telephone exchange in Sofia, there is direct-dial service to several Eastern and Western European countries, as well as to the U.S. International airmail is subject to inspection, and sometimes is delayed.

Bulgaria has at least 1.5 million registered radio receivers, and the number grows constantly. This total does not include portable transistors, which require no registration.

Local broadcasts are, of course, in Bulgarian. In the Sofia area, Radio Belgrade, the state-run radio, offers three schedules—the first, second, and third programs. The first program airs from about 5:30 a.m. until late in the evening. It features a varied fare, leaning heavily to folk music and dances, Turkish-language programs, children's programs, historical and ideological programs, ideologically oriented news, and classical music concerts. Some Western "pop" music is included. The second program is similar, broadcasting from 9 a.m. until about 10:30 p.m. The third program ordinarily begins at

7 p.m., and features concerts of classical music, opera, and propaganda themes.

Ordinary receivers will not pick up some Bulgarian FM broadcasts, which are at 67-100 megacycles and partly extend below the 88-100 megacycle range of Western receivers. However, the American FM band can easily pick up the third program of Radio Belgrade, with somewhat more Western music. One also can pick up Yugoslav, Greek, and West European stations on regular wavelengths in the evening. Foreigners have found it worthwhile to have shortwave radios for listening to VOA, BBC, and other foreign broadcasts.

Bulgaria's 1.5 million TV sets are served by only one TV station, which is located in Sofia and offers two channels, plus 24 relay stations. With special equipment and high antennas, one can also receive transmissions from Yugoslav TV, which feature some American and West European shows.

Television fare is of greater interest to the politically oriented than to the entertainment seeker. Each Friday evening is designated "Moscow night" on one channel, and Soviet programs are featured almost exclusively. Programs from other Eastern European capitals are often transmitted through the "intervision" network.

Almost no Western newspapers and magazines are on sale in Bulgaria. Hotels sometimes carry Western periodicals such as the International Herald Tribune and Le Monde in limited quantities.

Health

Apart from winter smog, which affects some people with respiratory or sinus problems, no special health hazards are found in Sofia. Local medical facilities are used by foreigners for minor ailments and for emergencies. Pirogov Hospital specializes in emergency care of accident and heart attack victims.

There is no need to boil drinking water in Sofia, and although dairy products are of uneven quality, they are safe for consumption. All restaurants are subject to control by food and health authorities.

Municipal services collect garbage and trash regularly, and streets are swept and washed nightly. Litter boxes are posted at street corners and in parks. The main streets of Sofia are noticeably cleaner than streets of many American cities.

Major City

SOFIA once was the ancient city of Sardica, which was destroyed by the Huns in 447, and rebuilt a century later by the Emperor Justinian I. It has been known as Sredets (under the first Bulgarian kingdom) and Triadista (under the Byzantines), and was given its present name in 1376. In 1879, it became Bulgaria's capital.

Sofia is the political, economic, cultural, and administrative center of the country. Only about an hour's drive from the Yugoslav border, it is on a plain 1,830 feet high. Some 10 miles to the north lie the Balkan Mountains (Stara Planina). Looming to the south is Mount Vitosha (7,000 feet), a national park and popular hiking and skiing area. Behind Mt. Vitosha lies Mount Musala, the highest peak in Bulgaria (9,650 feet).

Well-kept wooded parks and tree-lined boulevards make a favorable impression. Construction since 1960, along modern lines, has added apartment and office buildings and festival-congress halls to the city skyline. However, many old and impressive buildings have been preserved.

Recreation

A major point of interest accessible from Sofia is Vitosha. This 7,000-foot mountain that dominates the skyline to the south of Sofia is within a half-hour drive from the heart of town. It is a national park offering facilities for hiking and picnicking, as well as skiing in winter. Ski lifts and cable cars are available, and several above-average restaurants on the mountain offer panoramic views.

Boyana Church, just outside Sofia, contains frescoes that date from the 12th and 13th centuries and are of unusual interest to art historians.

The historic Rila Monastery in the Rila Mountains is one of the principal tourist attractions of Bulgaria. It is well worth a visit or two, particularly for camera enthusiasts. It is about a two-hour drive south of Sofia.

The city of Plovdiv also is only two hours from Sofia, along the international highway to Istanbul. This ancient capital of Philip of Macedon, father of Alexander the Great, is Bulgaria's second largest city. Plovdiv has several attractions, including a well-preserved old quarter, Roman ruins, and several museums. The city has several comfortable Balkantourist hotels. Many places of historical interest are a short drive from Plovdiv. Every September, the city is the site of a major international trade fair in which the U.S. participates.

The city of Veliko Turnovo, the ancient capital of Bulgaria, is of unusual interest. It is built in a dramatic setting on the steep slopes of the Yantra River Gorge. Veliko Turnovo is about a four-hour drive east of Sofia. In addition to the "old town," there are ruins of an ancient citadel dating back to the 12th century.

In recent years, Bulgaria has built a number of resort hotels on the Black Sea coast near the major cities of Varna and Burgas. These hotels are quite acceptable but rather expensive, and they may be overcrowded during summer. Daily inexpensive airplane flights connect Sofia and the Black Sea ports in summer. Flying time is about one hour. Inexpensive railway travel to Varna or Burgas takes eight to 10 hours.

One can enjoy automobile trips to the Aegean coast in northern Greece (seven hours) or to Istanbul (10 hours) for a change of atmosphere. Yugoslavia is also easily accessible, and Bucharest is an eight-hour drive from Sofia, via the Bulgarian city of Ruse on the Danube.

A fairly good international highway (E-5) links Sofia with Western Europe via Belgrade and Zegreb (E-94). From Salzburg, one may choose among the following alpine routes:

(1) Salzburg or Kufstein to Kitzbuehel; Mittersill; Felbertauern Tunnel; Matrei Lienz; Spittal; Villach; Wurzen Pass; Ljubljana.

(2) Bad Gastein; Boeckstein; Tauern Rail Tunnel; Mallnitz; Villach; Wurzen Pass; Ljubljana.

(3) Salzburg; Graz; Maribor.

(4) Salzburg (or Kustein); Bruck; Grossglockner; Alpine Toll Road; Spittal; Villach.

The first and third routes are preferable during winter. The Boeckstein-Mallnitz route involves a 10-minute ride aboard a railroad car-ferry. Trains leave every half hour during summer and about every hour the rest of the year. The Felbertauern Tunnel is one of the newer alpine tunnels. An alternate route from Salzburg, longer yet less mountainous and with good roads, is via Vienna and Budapest to Belgrade.

From October to April, snow tires or chains are advisable, both for the alpine passage and for the section between Nish and Sofia. Extreme alertness and prudence are required in all seasons along the E-5 highway from Zagreb to Belgrade and Sofia. This route is hazardous due to a combination of very fast- and slow-moving vehicles, inexperienced drivers of many nationalities, and unlighted farm vehicles. Travelers should avoid driving after dark.

The road trip from Trieste to Zagreb takes three hours in good weather, and from Zagreb to Belgrade, five hours. The route from Trieste to Zagreb is subject to winter snowstorms. The drive from Belgrade to the Bulgarian border usually takes about five hours, and one hour from the Bulgarian border to Sofia.

The most popular active sports among foreigners include tennis from May to October, skiing (mostly downhill, some cross-country) from December to April, and hiking and mountain climbing. Popular spectator sports in Sofia include soccer, hockey, tennis, and basketball.

Licenses are required for hunting and fishing, and may be obtained through the Foreign Ministry at high prices.

Several movie theaters in Sofia show Bulgarian and European films. American films are sometimes shown.

The opera season runs from September through June. The repertory includes well-known Western operas, as well as operas by less familiar composers from Eastern Europe. Most operas are sung in Bulgarian.

National ballet companies perform periodically at the Opera House during the season. The interesting Kutev National Folk Song and Dance Ensemble performs six to eight times a season. The Sofia Symphony Orchestra gives many concerts, often with guest soloists and conductors.

Special Note

Discretion should govern the use of cameras in view of Bulgarian sensitivity on this matter. Serious amateur photography is recognized less as a personal hobby in Bulgaria than in the U.S. Bulgarian citizens are likely to react strongly to the photographing of scenes which they may feel are unflattering, or which highlight primitive aspects of Bulgarian life. What an American may consider quaint and picturesque, the Bulgarians may consider backward. In addition, a sense of secrecy surrounds objects which might be deemed to have military significance (no matter how open they are to view from the ground or air).

Generally speaking, one should avoid photographing in the vicinity of military or police installations, airports, train stations, seaports, bridges, or border zones. Never photograph any object in the vicinity of the international "no photos" sign (a camera with a slash through it). It is also prohibited to take photos in or from an aircraft over Bulgarian territory.

Notes for Travelers

Travel from the U.S. to Bulgaria usually is via Frankfurt, Vienna, Rome, or Athens, where foreign airlines provide reasonably good connections to Sofia.

A valid visa is required, but normally does not specify an entry point. The points used by most Americans and other Western travelers include Sofia Airport, the Dimitrovgard/Kalotina-Dragoman road and rail entry from Belgrade and Nish, the Kulata road and rail entry from Thessaloniki, and the Edirne/Kapitan entry from Istanbul. A transit visa is now required for travel through Yugoslavia.

Travelers arriving from non-European points of origin must have certificates of inoculation against smallpox.

Firearms regulations permit only one hunting shotgun and a maximum of 150 shotgun shells, and these must be declared upon entry.

The only English-language church services, held every Sunday at the residence of the British Head of Chancery in Sofia, follow the order of the Anglican Church, but are considered nondenominational. The Roman Catholic Church in Sofia holds services in Bulgarian. Sofia has a synagogue and several Protestant churches (Baptist, Methodist, Evangelical, and Seventh-Day Adventist). Most churches in Bulgaria are Bulgarian Orthodox.

Bulgaria's unit of currency is the *lev* (plural, *leva*), consisting of 100 *stotinki*. The conversion rate (November 1978) is 0.8575 lev = U.S. $1.

Bulgaria uses the metric system of weights and measures.

The U.S. Embassy in Bulgaria is located at 1 Boulevard Aleksandur Stamboliyski, Sofia.

Cyprus

Cyprus, the island whose strategic position has been of value to every power that has dominated the eastern Mediterranean, has been ruled by outsiders during most of its long and unique history. It was not until August 1960 that it became a constitutional republic. Cyprian culture has been influenced by the Orient, Greece, ancient Phoenicia and Assyria, Egypt, Persia, Turkey and Great Britain, and archaeological excavations there show the existence of Neolithic civilization from 4,000 to 3,000 B.C.

Area, Geography, Climate

Cyprus is the third largest island in the Mediterranean, after Sicily and Sardinia, with an area of 3,572 square miles. It is in the eastern Mediterranean basin, 44 miles south of Turkey, 64 miles west of Syria, and 150 miles north of the Nile Delta. The island has a maximum length of 150 miles from east to west, and a maximum width of 60 miles from north to south.

Two mountain ranges dominate the landscape. The narrow and largely barren Kyrenia Range in the north (elevation 3,360 feet) lies a few miles inland from the northern coastline, and follows it from east to west for some 80 miles. The forest-covered Troodos Range rises in the southwest-

ern sector of the island, culminating in Mount Olympus at an altitude of 6,400 feet. Between the two ranges, extending from Morphou Bay in the west to Famagusta Bay in the east, lies the Mesaoria (between the mountains)—a broad, fertile, coastal plain which produces most of the island's cereal grains and other crops. Nicosia, the capital of Cyprus, is in the Mesaoria. Throughout the long summer, the plain is arid and parched, but in the winter and spring it is carpeted with a lush growth of young wheat and barley.

The climate of Cyprus may be compared to that of the Southern Atlantic States. Cyprus has hot, dry, dusty summers and fairly cold, damp winters. Nicosia's maximum mean temperature is approximately 80°F, while the minimum mean temperature is 50°. From mid-June to mid-September, temperatures sometimes exceed 100°, but after sundown usually fall 30° or more. The summer heat is endurable because humidity is usually low and high temperatures are often tempered by westerly winds. Nicosia's summer weather is generally more comfortable than in the seaside towns, where humidity is higher and temperatures are lower. Because rain falls almost exclusively from December through March, water is rationed in

Nicosia almost every summer. Winters are usually cold and damp with considerable rainfall and, on rare occasions, meager short-lived snowfalls. On the whole, the climate is Mediterranean, healthy, and enjoyable.

Population

Cyprus has had no official census since 1960. In January 1981, its population was recorded at 629,000 persons, of whom almost 80 percent are ethnic Greek and 18 percent ethnic Turk. The remainder are mainly Armenian and Maronites. The foreign population includes more than 2,000 U.N. troops, a resident British presence of over 13,000 (including retired persons and troops in the Sovereign Base areas), and some 550 American citizens, of whom 50 are official U.S. government personnel.

Although the island's heritage has created a degree of Cypriot spirit, it has not created a sense of Cypriot nationality. The population remains divided into two quite different societies—Greek and Turkish. Each maintains its distinct identity, based on custom, food, art, religion, language, and external allegiance. Historically, this population was scattered among six towns and over 600 small villages. The aftermath of the intercommunal violence of the 1960s was the enclavement of most Turkish Cypriots and, after the 1974 war, the physical separation of the two communities by a ceasefire line. Approximately 1,800 Greek Cypriots continue to reside in Northern Cyprus, and about 200 Turkish Cypriots remain in the government-controlled area. The question of displaced persons is a major element in the Cyprus problem.

Government

On August 16, 1960, Cyprus became an independent republic patterned on the democratic models of Western Europe and the U.S. But a significant factor makes the Government of Cyprus unique. The republic was created for a five-fold purpose: to end the EOKA (Greek Cypriot) uprising against the British colonial administration; to end the intercommunal strife between Greek and Turkish Cypriots; to provide means of Greek and Turkish Cypriots to govern themselves; to protect the national interests of Greece, Turkey, and the United Kingdom; and to restore and maintain peace and stability in the eastern Mediterranean.

The constitution created a central presidential system, with a Greek Cypriot president and Turk Cypriot vice president elected separately by their respective communities. A unicameral legislature, the House of Representatives, was to consist of 50 members— 35 Greek and 15 Turk. The president and vice-president were to appoint a council of ministers of 10 members— seven Greek and three Turk.

This system enjoyed a short life. Many of its provisions were suspended or modified after the outbreak of communal fighting in 1963; the system itself was basically altered by the events of 1974. The Government of Cyprus is now composed exclusively of Greek Cypriots, while the Turkish Cypriots have created an entity called "The Turkish Federated State of Cyprus," which is not recognized by the Government of Cyprus.

With major gaps, negotiations have gone on since 1968 to determine whether basic and growing differences between the two communities can be reconciled. Negotiations conducted since the spring of 1978 have taken place with the personal attendance of the U.N. Secretary General. In 1977, the late President, Archbishop Makarios, and the Turkish Cypiot leader, Rauf Denktash, agreed on a four-point set of principles for a solution to the Cyprus problem. Unfortunately, the two parties have had no formal, direct contacts since then.

Political activity in both communities has traditionally centered on personalities. The oldest established party is the Communist Party (AKEL). The governing Democratic Party of President Spyros Kyprianou controls an absolute majority in the House of Representatives, and also generally receives support from AKEL and the Socialist EDEK party of Dr. Vasos Lyssarides. The conservative, nationalist Democratic Rally Party, led by Glafcos Klerides, at the present time has no representation in the House of Representatives. Elections for the House are scheduled for 1981, and for the presidency in 1983. On the Turkish Cypriot side there are four political parties, the largest of which supports Turkish Cypriot leader, Rauf Denktash. Elections are scheduled in 1981 for the Turkish Cypriot's "Legislative Assembly."

Arts, Science, Education

Prehistoric pottery and sculpture have been excavated throughout Cyprus. Pottery-making and other folk arts are still practiced on the island, with embroidery one of the most developed of these arts.

The revival of Cypriot painting began toward the end of the British rule. Many artists still show the effects of classical European training, although others reflect the Byzantine tradition. Younger artists show a definite leaning to American "hard edge" and other modern schools.

Because Cyprus has no institutions of higher learning, Cypriots generally attend universities in Greece, the U.K., or Turkey. The lack of a university, which could act as a cultural center, restricts educational and scientific activities.

Commerce and Industry

The island's division into two economic areas has disrupted the country's economic unity and overall productive capacity. The economy in the Turkish Cypriot-controlled north is showing signs of steady recovery, but lack of managerial skills, technical expertise, foreign exchange reserves, and foreign credit financing have impeded the raising of economic activity to prewar levels.

In the south, despite the reduced economic base and the added call on resources needed to care and rehabilitate refugees, the Government of Cyprus (GOC) has successfully revitalized the economy. Care of the refugee population took first priority. Satisfactory housing facilities were provided to displaced persons under the GOC low-cost housing and self-help schemes, partially financed by the U.S. Government through the United Nations High Commissioner for Refugees (UNHCR). Under the GOC Emergency Economic Action Plans, the economy was fully reactivated. The 1977 per capita GNP of current prices in the south overtook the 1973 level. Unemployment in 1978 was reduced to less than three percent of the economically active population. A political settlement of the Cyprus problem, permitting the return to economic unity, will greatly enhance the viability of the state, and bridge the disparity of economic opportunity between the two major ethnic groups.

Commercially, vine products, citrus fruit, vegetables, clothing, footwear, and minerals provide the bulk of exports. Main imports include food and feed grains, transport and industrial machinery, equipment, and petroleum products. Invisible foreign exchange earnings remain strong, and the Cyprus pound has been relatively stable. Large inputs of foreign aid grants and loans were instrumental in keeping the government's foreign exchange reserves at satisfactory levels, covering five months' imports.

The construction boom in the Arab Gulf States has provided highly paid employment for Cypriot professionals and technicians, resulting in much needed hard currency remittances. Although the GOC economic problems are by no means solved, economic recovery is evident in all sectors of the economy. The prudent policy of the GOC and the existence of a pool of experienced and sophisticated business and managerial resources, coupled with foreign aid and favorable conditions in neighboring countries, produced the "Cyprus Economic Miracle."

Transportation

Cyprus Airways and Olympic Airways operate about 25 flights weekly in and out of the Larnaca International Airport to Athens, Beirut, and Tel Aviv. Ships carrying cargo and passengers to Cyprus call at Larnaca and Limassol. Auto ferries are available between Piraeus (Athens Port) and Limassol.

Bus and taxi service are the only forms of local public transportation, but bus service is not developed in many localities and is, at best, inconvenient and uncomfortable. In Nicosia, good taxi service is always available at moderate prices. Scheduled taxi transportation between cities, on a shared-occupancy basis, is offered at a reasonable fixed charge per passenger. Automobiles, with or without chauffeurs, can be rented reasonably by the day.

Most visitors in Cyprus consider cars a necessity for transportation. Sightseeing and recreation would be difficult without one. Traffic on the island keeps to the left side of the road, and all cars commercially imported must be right-hand-drive models equipped with turn indicators. Small British, European, or Japanese cars are preferable to large American vehicles because of narrow roads and availability of servicing. Ford and General Motors have agencies in Cyprus, but few American cars are operated on the island, mainly because of lack of service and spare parts, as well as the unavailability of right-hand-drive models. An international drivers license may be used by visitors for a three-month period, after which a local license is necessary.

Communications

Telephone service throughout the south of Cyprus is good, and dial calls can be made to all the cities and principal villages of that region. Cyprus has telephone, telegraph, and telex communications with all parts of the world, and a telephone and telegraph service with ships at sea. Calls to Europe and the U.S. usually are clear and uninterrupted. An earth satellite station in the south is scheduled for operation soon.

Postal services on the Greek Cypriot-controlled portion of the island, and international postal facilities between the U.S. and Cyprus are reliable. Letters usually arrive from New York in four to six days, and airmail service is provided daily from Cyprus.

Radio and TV reception is good. A shortwave radio is recommended for picking up foreign and Voice of America broadcasts. The British Forces Broadcasting Service offers news and some other programs. Cyprus Radio broadcasts in Greek, Turkish, and English. It offers news in English, some British Broadcasting Corporation programs from London, and also broadcasts in the languages of the national contingents of the U.N. Peace Force in Cyprus.

Television service (black and white only) covers the entire island. News and current events programs are in Greek (news in English is telecast once every evening). Many TV features are U.S. or British kinescopes with Greek subtitles. Local TV is also used for educational programs in the schools.

Nicosia's one English-language daily (except Monday) is the four-to six-page Cyprus Mail. The International Herald Tribune reaches Nicosia readers a day after publication. Several local bookshops carry foreign periodicals, technical journals, and novels in English. Local newspapers include six Greek- and three Turkish-language dailies, and 14 Greek weekly papers.

Health

Nicosia has specialists in obstetrics; surgery; ear, nose, and throat; urology; orthopedics; and internal medicine. The city has a number of small, private clinics in which Americans have been hospitalized, but cases requiring unusual diagnostic facilities may be moved to Germany or Athens, or to a hospital in Beirut or Tel Aviv. Medicine and laboratory services can usually be obtained locally. Optical care is generally satisfactory. An excellent ophthalmologist practices in Nicosia, and most lens prescriptions can be filled. Both hard and soft contact lenses are available at much lower than U.S. prices. Several good dentists, trained in Europe and America, practice in Nicosia. They use modern equipment and are highly recommended by Americans who have been treated by them.

Community and public sanitation, although lower than in the U.S., is much higher than in other Middle Eastern countries, and is perhaps comparable to that in most countries of southern Europe. Sanitary inspection laws are not always stringently enforced. Except at the top restaurants and markets, standards of sanitation are wanting. Window screening is virtually unknown. Flies are a common pest and can sometimes interfere with outdoor activities. Garbage is collected twice weekly.

Local health authorities consider the island one of the more healthful areas of the world because of the infrequency of serious diseases. Although the ordinary diseases usually found in most countries bordering the Mediterranean do occur, Cyprus is a relatively healthful area with no unusual health problems. Some cases of typhoid or diphtheria, and infrequently smallpox, are reported, principally because widescale immunization of the population has not yet been effected in rural areas. The Cyprus Government, however, conducts energetic campaigns to encourage immunization of young persons. Pollen and dust during the hot, dry summers can be a source of discomfort to those suffering from hay fever, asthma, allergy to dust or pollen, or from any chronic condition of the upper respiratory system. Rabies is nonexistent on the island. However, hydatid disease or echinococcus, attributed to a tapeworm harbored by dogs, occurs among local inhabitants. There are no known cases of Americans having been infected while in Cyprus. The island was completely free of malaria from 1951 to 1968, when two cases were reported.

Major City

NICOSIA has been the capital of Cyprus since the seventh century, and is the political and administrative center of the island. It is located inland on a wide plain, on the site of one of the greatest "city-kingdoms" of antiquity, Ledra, which today lends its name to the town's main shopping center. The estimated population is 180,000, and Nicosia has spread far outside the walled city, with modern flats and offices and attractive villas characterizing the newer sections of the town.

Nicosia, which was the scene of bitter conflict in the years prior to Cyprian independence, is an interesting city for tourists. There are distinguished collections of antiquities in its museums, and the government sponsors a permanent theater, where plays in modern Greek are presented occasionally by theatrical companies from Athens.

Good basic services are available in the city, including shoe repair, dry cleaning, and auto repair. There also is a good choice of barber and beauty shops.

Other Cities

Kyrenia, a small city of 4,900 inhabitants, is 15 miles north of Nicosia. A seventh-century Byzantine castle, which also served the Venetians in the 15th century, overlooks the picturesque harbor. The city is dominated by the Kyrenia Range and the Castle of St. Hilarion, built in 1228 on a mountain peak 2,200 feet above sea level. The castle is said to be the source of inspiration for Walt Disney's _Snow White._

Famagusta, one of the main port cities of Cyprus, with a population of about 50,000, is about 40 miles east of Nicosia on Famagusta Bay. Its center is in a well-preserved Venetian walled city. Legend has it that the citadel which overlooks the Bay of Famagusta was the setting of Shakespeare's _Othello._ The beautiful sand beaches and good hotels all along the shore give Famagusta (the Greek name Ammochostos) its name, which means "sand-hidden."

Just north of Famagusta, also on the bay, is the biblical port of Salamis, where St. Paul entered Cyprus on his evangelical tour. Most of this ancient port is now submerged, and the site, a fine swimming location, also offers a challenge to the snorkeler who might be rewarded with the discovery of antiquarian items. The Greco-Roman ruins here include excellently preserved Corinthian pillars and some fine, although headless, caryatids and statues.

Larnaca is an active seaport with a population of 20,000, located on Larnaca Bay about 25 miles southeast of Nicosia. Its salt lake is a winter haven for large flocks of flamingos. A popular belief here is that Lazarus lived in

Larnaca for many years. The nearby Tekke of Umm Haram, a beautiful mosque built on the spot where the Prophet Mohammed's aunt is said to have died, is a holy place to all Moslems.

Limassol, with a population of 55,000, is about 50 miles southwest of Nicosia on Akrotiri Bay. In this important seaport city, the marriage of Richard the Lion-Hearted and his hard-won Berengaria of Navarre was celebrated with popular dancing in the streets. Seven miles west of Limassol is the tower of Kolossi, built in the 15th century by the Knights of St. John. The ruins of Curium, an Achaean religious and political center of the second century B.C., are a few miles west of Kolossi. The site includes remains of the Temple of Apollo and a stadium. Curium is thought to have been founded by the Greeks and, in the early centuries of our era, it housed some Roman administrative and bathing facilities, found in recent excavations. Some fine mosaics and other ruins, including a fairly well-preserved Roman theater, sometimes put to contemporary use, have been unearthed.

Paphos, off whose shores Aphrodite arose from the sea foam, lies on the west littoral. It has about 9,000 inhabitants. The scenic route to Paphos from Nicosia, along the south shore, comprises the grand tour of most of the archaeological high spots in Cyprus. The Fontana Amorosa (Love's Spring), also known as the Baths of Aphrodite, in the north part of Paphos, is about half a mile from the sea. The spring was a source of poetic inspiration during the classical age, and it was said that whoever drank from it would fall in love. At Paphos, Christianity was introduced to Cyprus with the conversion of the Roman Governor Sergius Paulus. The pillar on which it is said Paul was tied to receive the 39 strokes still stands in Paphos. On the Troodos Mountains in the Paphos district, Kykko Monastery contains the cherished icon of the Virgin Mary painted by St. Luke. Warm hospitality is always extended to visitors. Not far from the monastery is a beautiful valley of 30,000 cedars.

Recreation

Cyprus offers a variety of opportunity for participant and spectator sports, and for touring. Beaches can be reached from Nicosia by private car or by shared taxi, since there is no public transportation to the beaches. Taxi service to some other cities on the island is regularly available. The proximity of the sea and the very hot summers drive most people in Cyprus to the water. The sea is about one hour away from Nicosia, with good beaches on the southern and eastern shores. A few hotels have fresh water swimming pools, which may be used for a small charge.

There also is basketball, soccer, and tennis. Picnics, sight-seeing, and camping are popular pastimes, too, because of the scenery, old castles, monasteries, and ancient ruins. Since the coup and Turkish invasion in 1974, the sites at Famagusta and Salamis have been closed to tourists.

Skin diving is available at Larnaca, and waterskiing also is becoming popular, although the sea sometimes can be very choppy. There is some spearfishing, and at a distance from the coast, there is good deep-sea fishing, for which boats can be rented. Shoreline fishing does not interest the serious angler. Some snow skiing in Cyprus has developed in recent years, and is done from December to February in the Troodos Mountains, about an hour-and-a-half by car from Nicosia. The runs are not especially challenging. Better skiing is available in nearby Lebanon. Two golf courses, previously at Pendayia and near Nicosia, have been in Turkish-controlled areas since July 1974, and are not available. Nicosia has a horse racing season extending through most of the year.

The numerous nearby archaeological sites on Cyprus are nearly all open to the public. All digs are under the jurisdiction and supervision of the Department of Antiquities, Cyprus Government, and expeditions from other nations are often at work there. Some sites charge an entrance fee of one shilling (15 cents); at others, the visitor may wander at will, picnic on or near the site, and enjoy a freedom unknown at archaeological sites in other countries. Guidebooks available in Cyprus, and brochures published by the Cyprus Museum, give details of all the antiquities.

No opera or professional symphony orchestra exists, but Cyprus does have an amateur CBC symphony orchestra. Occasionally, foreign concert artists, symphony orchestras, or popular music ensembles visit the island.

Some cinemas in Nicosia are air-conditioned; others are auditoriums without roofs for the summer. They show mostly U.S. or British films. Nightclub entertainment exists in limited scope, with a number of popular discotheques.

In addition to the restaurants offering standard European cooking and atmosphere, less expensive and simpler inns serve Greek and Turkish Cypriot dishes as well as those typical of the Near East. Most Americans like Cypriot food.

Notes for Travelers

Cyprus Airways and Olympic Airways provide 25 weekly flights in and out of Larnaca International Airport on Cyprus, through Athens, Beirut, and Tel Aviv. Ships also call at Larnaca and Limassol. Flights are available to Ercan in the north.

No U.S. citizen needs a visa to enter Cyprus. Vaccination against smallpox is required, and updating of typhoid, cholera, polio, and tetanus shots is advised.

The Cyprus Government allows importation of shotguns for hunting, but no other firearms.

The principal Christian religion of Cyprus is Greek Orthodox. Services in English are conducted in Nicosia by Nicosia Community Church (interdenominational Protestant), and at Paphos Gate by St. Paul's Episcopal Church and Holy Cross Roman Catholic Church. Most of the Cyprian holidays are ecclesiastical. For the Jewish community of about 400, services celebrating the high Jewish holidays are conducted at the Israeli Embassy.

Rotary and Lions Clubs maintain chapters in Cyprus.

The unit of currency on the island is the Cypriot pound, which is divided into 1,000 mils. Notes are issued in denominations up to five pounds, and coins are minted in values up to one pound. There are adequate British and

Cypriot-controlled banks, two with large American interests.

The *oke* is a measure of weight, and is equal to 2.8 pounds. It also is a measure of capacity, equal to 1.125 imperial quarts. Measurements of distances are in miles, yards, and feet.

The U.S. Embassy on Cyprus is located at Therissos and Dositheon Streets, Nicosia.

Czechoslovakia

CZECHOSLOVAKIA has a rich treasure in its history, with much of it still visible in the stones, palaces, and streets of Prague. The legacy of Charles IV, king of Bohemia; of Jan Jus, the religious reformer; of the educator Comenius; of such writers as Kafka and Capek; of the composers Dvorak and Smetana; and of Tomas Masaryk, the statesman, still flourishes. Few world capitals have preserved their past in such focus, and few are so picturesque.

Politically, the Czechs and Slovaks have endured centuries of storms and trials. Czechoslovakia's people, property, and institutions were nearly destroyed by the Thirty Years' War. The country was dominated by the Hapsburg Austrian Empire for 300 years; experienced a brief but brilliant period of independence from 1918 to 1938; was occupied by Hitler after Munich; had an even briefer period of independence after World War II; was subverted by the Communists in 1948; and, after the brief freedom of the "Prague Spring," was occupied by the U.S.S.R. in 1968, and remains so to this day.

Area, Geography, Climate

Czechoslovakia lies in the heartland of central Europe. It has cool summers, lush springs, and pleasant autumns. Winters are wet and cold, but not extremely so.

The main geographic subdivisions are the Czech lands—Bohemia and Moravia—and Slovakia. Moravia and Slovakia are bordered on the south by the Danube Valley, at an altitude of about 500 feet. The remainder of Moravia and Slovakia consists of valleys and forested mountains, rising to 8,700 feet in the High Tatras on the Polish-Slovak border. Prague lies on the Vltava River (Moldau in English and German), which flows northward and joins the Labe (Elbe) north of Prague. Bratislava is on the Dunaj (Danube).

Prague (altitude 800 feet) lies at the center of the Bohemian gently-rolling plain, which is almost completely surrounded by 5,000-foot mountains on the German and Polish frontiers. The surrounding mountains protect the country from the extremes of western and northern European winters. Nevertheless, high humidity makes the winter cold penetrating.

Prague's climate is temperate, with pleasant weather between May and August. Temperatures range from January's average daily high of 32°F (0°C) and low of 22°F (-4.5°C) to July's average daily high of 76°F (24.5°C) and low of 56°F (14°C).

36

From November through March, the few hours of daylight combined with smog and raw weather create a gloomy atmosphere. Average annual rainfall is about 30 inches, distributed throughout the year. Humidity averages about 80 percent. Light to moderately heavy snow can be expected during January and February.

Population

Czechoslovakia's population of over 15 million includes nine-and-a-half million Czechs, four-and-a-half million Slovaks, 600,000 Hungarians, and a quarter of a million Poles, Germans, Ukrainians, and Russians. Before World War II, about three-and-a-half million Germans lived in Czechoslovakia, but most were expelled in 1945. Of the prewar population of 360,000 Jews, only about 15,000 remain.

Although closely related, Czechs and Slovaks definitely consider themselves two separate peoples. Czech, spoken in Bohemia and Moravia, and Slovak are so closely connected that native speakers can understand each other without translation. Both Czechs and Slovaks are predominantly Roman Catholic, with a large Protestant minority in the Czech lands. Czech customs and cuisine continue to reflect 300 years of Austrian domination, while Slovak customs and cooking reflect longer Hungarian domination.

A generation of Socialist rule has largely eliminated the former social classes while creating new classes of its own. It has however, had little effect on traditional cultural ties of Czechs to Western Europe, particularly France, Italy, Germany, and Austria. Slovaks have many ties to the United States

because of extensive Slovak emigration three generations ago. From 1918 to 1938, America was intimately involved with Czechoslovak affairs. Former President Woodrow Wilson played a vital role in the creation of modern Czechoslovakia, and Tomas Masaryk, married to an American, was a great friend of the U.S.

At the time of Czechoslovak independence in 1918, the Czech educational levels were substantially higher than the Slovak levels, but the contrast is slowly disappearing. Czechs are proud of their role in European cultural and political history.

Government

Czechoslovakia is a Communist state organized as a Federated Republic of the Czech Lands and Slovakia. The highest legislative body is the bicameral Federal Assembly, comprising a Chamber of the People, elected by districts based on population, and a Chamber of Nations, elected by the Czech and Slovak National Councils. The President of the Republic is granted considerable power by the Constitution. Real authority is exercised by the Communist Party, headed by its General Secretary. Sometimes both offices are held by the same person. From the President's office and from the Presidium and Central Committee apparatus, power radiates downward through interlocking party organizations and local National Committees, the organs of local government.

Several powerless political parties and the Communist Party form the National Front. Diverse social and religious organizations continue to exist by subordinating their purposes to those of the Community Party.

Arts, Science, Education

A long tradition of devotion to the theatrical arts and the musical heritage of Mozart, Smetana, Dvorak, and Janacek are reflected in the Czechoslovak cultural scene. The leading theatrical institution, the National Theater, produces opera, ballet, and drama. Numerous theaters in Prague and the provincial cities are well attended. The Czech Philharmonic Orchestra has a worldwide reputation, and there are many other excellent musical organizations. The annual Prague Spring Music Festival is the cultural highlight of the year. Several innovative theatrical groups, such as the Laterna Magica, have gained international recognition. Czech movies of the 1960s are world renowed.

Prague's Charles University, founded in 1348, is the oldest university of central Europe. Czech science, education, and technology have compared well with the best in the world, but have suffered from the political upheavals of the last generation.

Commerce and Industry

Czechoslovakia is among Europe's most industrialized countries. Before World War II, it had a balanced industrial and agricultural economy noted for the Beta Shoe Company (which continues to exist outside Czechoslovakia); the Skoda works, producers of heavy arms for the German and Austrian armies in World War I; automobiles; and Pilsner beer. After 1945, the government placed major emphasis on heavy industry, but agriculture and consumer goods and services have recently been given renewed attention. Industry, trade, banking, and transportation were nationalized during the late 1940s under the Communist regime.

In the past, most of the country's industry was concentrated in the western half around such Bohemian and Moravian cities as Pilsen, Brno, Ostrava, and Prague. Slovakia, ruled by Hungary until 1919, was formerly an agricultural area. Since 1950, the government has been investing heavily in its industrial development. Czechoslovakia's economy is almost 100 percent nationalized. The unified labor organization is under the control of the Communist Party.

Inadequate economic growth, due to lagging labor productivity in carrying out the government's economic plan, was the major reason for the reform movement of the 1960s, which culminated in the "Prague Spring" of 1968. Adequate productivity continues to be a problem. Private-property ownership is permitted only for private dwellings. However, allocation of both parties and state-owned residential space is made by the local government. Housing shortages are chronic in major cities.

Czechoslovakia has always depended on foreign trade for its livelihood, but its traditional patterns, which used to depend heavily on trade with the U.S. and Western Europe, were changed after the 1948 Communist takeover. Primary emphasis was then placed on trade with the Soviet Union and Eastern Europe, which now accounts for two-thirds of the total foreign trade. Recent years have seen renewed emphasis on trade with the West.

The volume of trade between the U.S. and Czechoslovakia, which totaled nearly $53 million in 1939, dropped to a low of about $1 million in 1952. It has since risen, at first gradually, but faster in recent years. American imports of Czechoslovak products include canned hams, glass, jewelry, steel products, bicycles, shoes, beer, and motorcycles. Recent Czechoslovak imports of American goods consist primarily of grains, soybeans, hides, chemicals, and machinery.

Transportation

Czechoslovakia is served by a wide network of bus, rail, and air transport. However, schedules are generally slow and unreliable, and reservations are difficult to get during holidays, music festivals, and trade fairs. Except for travel between major cities, most Americans prefer travel by car within Czechoslovakia.

The only modern express train service is between East Berlin and Vienna via Prague. Train service to Bavaria is slow. Rail transport within Czechoslovakia and to other Eastern European countries is inexpensive. Daily air flights run between Prague and major European capitals.

The subway, streetcars, and buses are used in Prague and its suburbs. Frequent service is available until 11 p.m., after which all operate on a reduced schedule. Public transportation is inexpensive. Taxis are usually found at stands in the central part of town and at the airport. In outlying sections, taxis must be ordered by phone. Fares are comparable to those charged in the U.S.

Czechoslovakia's main roads are adequate, and in winter are salted and sanded heavily, although not plowed thoroughly. Compared to the U.S. or Western Europe, traffic is light on country roads, but is increasing. Gas station facilities are limited and waiting lines are common. Most gas stations are closed weekends and at night, except in major cities and along international highways. Traffic moves on the right, and road signs and traffic conventions are similar to those used throughout Europe.

A U.S. drivers license is valid in Czechoslovakia, but an international license is required for some neighboring countries and is recommended for all drivers.

Repair facilities are available for some European cars, particularly those produced or assembled in Eastern Europe. However, waiting lists for repair work are usual, spare parts are often out of stock, and the quality of repairs varies. Most foreign residents take their cars to Western Europe for service.

Communications

Local and long-distance telephone, telegraph, and telex services are available within Czechoslovakia and to other Eastern European countries. However, services to countries outside Eastern Europe are costly. International mail takes about 10 days to the U.S. for letters, and three to six weeks for parcels.

Czech, German, and Austrian AM stations can be received, as can other European stations, including VOA Munich, BBC, and on some evenings AFRN (Armed Forces Radio Network). In addition, shortwave can pick up BBC day and night, VOA morning and evening, and other European stations in English and other languages.

FM stations in Czechoslovakia broadcast regularly, but their frequency band is different from American FM receivers. However, a converter can be obtained in Prague at a reasonable cost.

Two TV stations transmit a good part of the day and evening, including several hours a day in color. They carry a few children's programs, drama, opera, sports, and foreign and Czechoslovak films and cultural programs. American sets can be converted to the Czechoslovak 625-line system, but with difficulty; Western European sets are easier to convert and can be purchased locally at reasonable prices. Television is valuable for studying the Czech or Slovak languages.

Prague has no public libraries of general interest to Americans. Non-Communist reading material is not available in local stores and newsstands, but subscriptions to European magazines and newspapers, including the International Herald Tribune, can be ordered via international mail.

Health

Medical services are provided to resident foreigners in Prague by the Foreigners' Section of the Charles University Faculty Polyclinic, staffed by an English-speaking general practitioner, a pediatrician, and a dentist. A doctor is on call at all times. The Foreigners' Section refers patients to specialists for lab tests and hospitalization as necessary. A maternity hospital with an English-speaking obstetrician is sometimes used by Americans. Local pharmacies stock locally prescribed medicines; most medicines can be obtained in West Germany. Similar services are available at regular clinics in Bratislava, although English-speaking doctors and specialists are fewer than

in Prague. Costs are lower than in the U.S.

Routine and emergency care in Prague are adequate. However, the bureaucratic organization of medical care, the lack of choice of a physician, the shortage of hospital beds, and the language barrier create problems.

Community sanitation in Czechoslovakia is high. Health controls help to prevent outbreaks of serious diseases. In Prague, except in isolated instances, the water is fluoridated and safe to drink.

The most prevalent local diseases are hepatitis, measles, whooping cough, and respiratory ailments such as bronchitis and pneumonia. Prague's damp and sooty winter often brings on or aggravates respiratory difficulties.

No special precautions are needed. Milk is pasteurized, but spoils rapidly because it is not refrigerated during distribution. Ordinary sanitary precautions, such as washing raw fruits and vegetables, are similar to those in the U.S.

Major City

PRAGUE is an old city, situated between hill and valley on the banks of the Moldau. A medley of Gothic, Renaissance, Baroque, and art nouveau architecture gives the city its basic charm. The green of its numerous parks and hills sets off its many historical monuments, making its particularly attractive in the late spring, summer, and early autumn. It is a city of fine churches and magnificent palaces (one of them, the Castle of Prague, dates from the ninth century), and its university is one of the most famous in Europe. In the old Jewish section of the city is a synagogue built in the 13th century.

Prague has a population of about 1,250,000. German is the most widely understood foreign language. In the large cities of Czechoslovakia, English also is widely understood. Within the Western foreign and diplomatic community English, French, and German are spoken.

Other important cities in Czechoslovakia are Bratislava, Pilsen, Ostrava, Brno, Kosice, and Olomouc.

Recreation

Prague is a historical and architectural gem; walking is a pleasure. Several parks, public gardens, and a zoo are located in the city. Many sightseeing and picnic areas are in the immediate vicinity of Prague, and weekend excursions to castles and historic cities and sites are popular.

Vienna, Berlin, Munich, and Nuremberg are each within five or six hours by car, and other European centers can be easily reached by air.

Skiing and ice skating are popular winter sports. The nearest ski slopes can be reached in a day's outing. Small hotels can accommodate overnight trips, but reservations must be made in advance. Indoor ice skating rinks are open to the public in Prague. Weather permitting, skaters also use outdoor rinks and ponds.

Individual hunting excursions, although expensive, can be arranged. More commonly, Czech acquaintances invite foreigners. Well-marked hiking trails cover the countryside. Fishing (with a permit), boating on both rivers and lakes, camping with tents or trailers, and outdoor bathing and photography also are popular. (Restrictions prohibit photography in frontier areas; around airports, rail lines, terminals, and military installations; and of military personnel.)

Three golf courses are available in the Prague area. The 18-hole course at Marianske Lazne is good. A diplomatic sports club has a rudimentary nine-hole course at Lisnice, 20 minutes by car from downtown Prague. A third facility, at Karlovy Vary, has an 18-hole course, but is two hours away.

Prague provides a varied and entertaining musical diet. The Czech Philharmonic, one of Europe's outstanding musical organizations, performs twice a week except in summer. During summer, the philharmonic has outdoor concerts, and light classical music is performed in Prague's public gardens. Both Western and Czech operas are performed, but most foreign ones are translated into Czech. In addition, numerous recitals and performances by the Prague Symphony, the country's second most famous orchestra, are given. The famous Prague Spring Musical Festival in May is highlighted by performers from around the world.

Numerous theatrical presentations, classical and modern, are performed, but mostly in Czech. Excellent puppet shows and pleasant operettas are presented, as are some world-renowned theatrical performances unique to Prague, including the Black Theater, Laterna Magica, and pantomime. Prague also has several movie theaters showing U.S., British, French, and Italian films in the original language with Czech subtitles.

Prague boasts several good museums and a fine national gallery of art.

Spectator events include horse racing, a famous steeplechase at Pardubice, tennis, basketball, softball, soccer, and ice hockey. Occasionally, American athletes participate in international competitions, and some exhibition teams visit Prague.

Prague has good restaurants, as do other large cities such as Brno and Bratislava. Prices are generally lower than in the U.S. and Western Europe, although variety is limited. Several restaurants have picturesque interiors, and some provide dinner music. Western jazz is popular, and good dance music can be found in the few nightclubs. Czech beer is excellent and inexpensive, and native wine is good and reasonably priced.

Notes for Travelers

Travel from the U.S. to Czechoslovakia usually is by an American carrier to Frankfurt, and then by foreign carrier to Prague. Daily flights to Prague are also scheduled from several other European cities.

A passport and a Czechoslovak visa are required for entry. Most tourist visas for American citizens, regardless of type of passport held, are valid for one trip in and out of Czechoslovakia. For each day's stay, 10 dollars worth of Czechoslovak crowns must be purchased on entry.

No immunizations are required unless the traveler arrives from areas where smallpox, yellow fever, or cholera are endemic.

No import restrictions are levied on sporting firearms or ammunition. Registration of imported arms is not required, but locally procured arms must be registered.

English-language religious services (Protestant) are conducted periodically for the foreign community by visiting Anglican ministers and U.S. military chaplains, particularly at Christmas and Easter. Regular Czech-language Protestant services are held in local churches. Roman Catholic mass is said regularly in Czech in local churches, and traditional Czech masses are sung for religious holidays. Jewish services are held despite the lack of a rabbi.

The official currency unit of Czechoslovakia is the crown (*koruna*), abbreviated Kcs, which is divided into 100 *hellers*. In addition, the TUZEX foreign trade enterprise issues coupons in crowns and *hellers*, called TUZEX crowns (abbreviated TK), which, although not legally a currency, circulate as such. The Czechoslovak State Bank maintains several different exchange rates with U.S. and other foreign currencies for different types of exchange, which are adjusted monthly.

The metric system of weights and measures is used.

The U.S. Embassy is located at Trziste 15, Prague.

Denmark

DENMARK is the oldest kingdom in Europe, tracing its written history as far back as the Viking period of the eighth and ninth centuries. A country of gentle beauty, friendly people, and cosmopolitan lifestyle, modern Denmark is an industrialized nation with a high standard of living and one of the world's most advanced social welfare societies. The homogeneity of culture, breadth of economic activity, and variety of political opinion make it a stimulating place to visit.

Area, Geography, Climate

Denmark lies directly north of Germany and south of Norway, between the Baltic and North Seas. Sweden is minutes away by hydrofoil across the narrow Baltic Straits. The country, about half the size of Maine, is comprised of the Jutland peninsula (Jylland), an extension of continental Europe, and 483 islands, about 100 of which are populated. The capital city of Copenhagen and about 40 percent of the entire population are located on the island of Zealand (Sjaelland). More than 12,000 square miles of gently rolling countryside (the highest point in Denmark is 568 feet above sea level) are devoted to agriculture. The coastline is irregular and dotted with inlets and fjords.

The Danish climate is moderated by the Gulf Stream; winters are warmer and summers cooler than in New England. The average temperatures range from 32°F in February to 61°F in July. Temperatures rarely vary from day to night, but shifting sea winds cause day-to-day temperature changes. It is seldom very hot or very cold, but humidity and wind exaggerate the temperature, especially in winter. Average annual rainfall is 24 inches; August and October are the wettest months. Nights are long in winter, with about six hours of daylight in December and January; daylight in summer lasts 18 to 20 hours.

Population

More than one-fourth of Denmark's 5.1 million people live in Copenhagen and its suburbs. Danes are friendly, especially to foreigners. The Danish language comes from the East Scandinavian group of Germanic languages, and is one of the more difficult European languages to learn. English and German are widely known and taught in Denmark, and French is spoken by a few officials and the more highly educated. The national church is the Lutheran Evangelical. The only significant non-Danish minority is a German group of about 30,000 in South Jutland.

Government

Denmark became a constitutional monarchy with the adoption of the Constitution of 1849, which removed the King's absolute power and provided for separate administrative, legislative, and judicial agencies. This system was retained in the Constitution of 1953, which is now in force.

The Danish Royal Family, the Oldenborgs, is the oldest dynasty in Europe. The present Queen, Margrethe II, ascended the throne in 1972. Her successor is her eldest son, Crown Prince Frederik. The Queen, as head of the administration, holds formal executive power, but her authority is mostly symbolic. She governs through the Prime Minister, who is chosen by the government party (or parties, in cases of coalitions) in the Parliament. The Prime Minister in turn appoints the ministers who implement government policy.

The Parliament, or Folketing, is unicameral. Its 179 members are popularly elected by universal suffrage. The normal term for the Folketing is four years, but the Prime Minister may call for national elections at any time. Eleven parties are represented in Parliament, but none has enough seats to form a majority government alone.

Arts, Science, Education

Copenhagen, the capital, offers a wide range of intellectual and artistic activities. In addition to the ballet, opera, and concerts, international artists and groups perform throughout the year. The city abounds with art galleries and fine museums.

Danish education follows the traditional European system, in which school attendance is mandatory until age 15, when most students either continue their education or enter an apprenticeship program. Danes place great emphasis on adult education. Many evening courses are offered at Copenhagen University and in high schools.

Higher education is offered at commercial and technical colleges and universities. Denmark's universities are at Copenhagen, Aarhus, Odense, Roskilde, and Aalborg. The University of Copenhagen, the oldest and largest, has five faculties: theology, law and economics, medicine, arts, and science. Other seats of higher learning include the Technical University of Denmark, Academy of Engineers, Dental Colleges, and School of Pharmacy. In addition to academic requirements, foreign students must be fluent in the Danish language.

Interest in science and the arts is promoted by universities and special foundations such as the Carlsberg/Tuborg Foundation. Research is financed by the state, and to a much lesser extent by foreign funds such as the Rockefeller Foundation. One of Denmark's best known institutes is the Niels Bohr Institute of Theoretical Physics in Copenhagen.

Commerce and Industry

Denmark's natural resources are limited to its fertile farmland and the surrounding sea. Two-thirds of the land is devoted to farming, and the production of animal products is highly developed. Only seven percent of the labor force is employed in agriculture, which accounts for eight percent of the gross national product and 30 percent of Denmark's exports.

Industrial exports are increasing in this major shipping nation. Danish labor is highly organized, and Denmark has one of the highest wage and living standards in Europe. The country relies heavily on foreign trade, importing most raw materials and semiprocessed goods and fuel. Two-thirds of its agricultural produce and one-third of its manufactured goods are exported. The country generally has an adverse trade balance and recurring balance-of-payments deficits.

Denmark joined the European Economic Community in 1973. The United States' share of Denmark's trade is about seven percent of both imports and exports.

Transportation

Copenhagen is connected to all major European centers by rail and air. Daily rail service is available to most European capitals and other large cities. Scandinavian Airlines has direct flights between Copenhagen and major U.S. cities, and Northwest Orient Airlines provides direct service between U.S. points and Copenhagen. Many other international airlines also provide worldwide flights from Copenhagen's Kastrup International Airport.

Ferries travel to Norway, Sweden, Finland, Germany, Poland, and points in England. Well-organized charter flights provide opportunities for inexpensive vacations. Copenhagen's public transportation is excellent, and includes bus and suburban train services. Fares are reasonable and monthly passes are available at reduced rates. Buses provide good service to all parts of the city. Trains provide quick service to the suburbs, but there are virtually none between midnight and 5 a.m. Taxis are readily available and not unduly expensive.

Automobile driving and registration are rigidly controlled in Denmark, and no licenses are given to those under 18. Rentals are easily obtained, but for anyone planning a long stay and wishing to buy or import a car into the country, there are strict preregistration safety inspections and modifications, which may seem unreasonable by American standards.

Some of the basic requirements include cutting the motor number into the chassis, installing three-point safety belts, and constructing a frame for Danish license plates. Brakes, steering, and window glass must meet rigorous standards; the body and underbody must be rust and corrosion free; tires must have the tread pattern intact over the entire traction area; and headlights, parking lights, and directional signals must be modified to meet Danish standards. Total inspection and modification costs vary from car to car, but labor runs a minimum of 15 to 20 dollars per hour.

Communications

Local and long-distance telephone service is good. International telephone and telegraph service is available from Copenhagen to all parts of the world, and telephone calls to the U.S. are put through immediately. Airmail and air-express service between Denmark and the U.S. is reliable and fast. Letters take three to five days from the east coast and five to seven days from the west coast.

Denmark has one TV and three radio channels operated by the Danish Government. Two Swedish TV channels can be received in Copenhagen with a good antenna, and all three transmit excellent color. Radio reception from Swedish, German, and British stations, as well as the German-based U.S. Armed Forces network, is possible with a good receiver and antenna. American and British programs and movies are often shown on all three TV channels in the original English, with Danish, or Swedish subtitles. No commercials are included on radio or TV.

Danish public libraries are good, but few volumes are in English except at the main library. Copenhagen bookstores sell the latest American and British books at about double the U.S. prices. Current English newspapers and periodicals are available at hotels, bookstores, and major train stations. Paris editions of the International Herald Tribune are usually available on the day of publication.

Health

Diagnostic laboratories and competent specialists in all fields of medicine are available in Denmark, and professional standards are equal to those in the U.S. Sometimes the doctors' fees are higher, but hospitals are reasonable in charges, and well-equipped. Most doctors and dentists speak English.

Sanitary conditions are above average. Danish law is strict about commercial processing, cooking, handling, and serving of foods. All city dairies supply pasteurized and nonpasteurized milk from tuberculin-tested cows, and all milk is safe to drink. Copenhagen is cleaner than most U.S. cities of comparable size.

Denmark has had no serious epidemics in years. Colds, influenza, and throat infections may be aggravated in winter by the dampness and lack of sunshine, and those with arthritis and sinus trouble may find the winter uncomfortable. No special health risks occur in Denmark, and no special inoculations are required. Any needed immunization is available in Copenhagen.

Major City

With nearly one-and-a-half million people, **COPENHAGEN** is Denmark's capital and its largest city. Starting as a small fishing village more than 1,000 years ago, the city has grown into a major European commercial and cultural center. Its name (Kobenhavn or Merchants' Harbor) reflects its historical association with shipping and international trade. Copenhagen's busy harbor and shipyards confirm the significant role these activities continue to play in the city's economic life.

Despite the modern pace of its commercial activity, Copenhagen maintains its Old World charm. The skyline is dominated by stately towers, their copper roofs green with age; thus its popular name, "city of beautiful towers." Many buildings in the city's center date back hundreds of years, some as far back as the 16th and 17th centuries. The old houses, which line the canals and cobblestone streets, provide a sharp contrast to modern high-rise apartment complexes that dominate the fast-growing suburbs and newer parts of the city.

The high standard of living of its citizens is reflected in the clean, well-maintained appearance of the city. Despite its size, many wooded parks and small lakes give Copenhagen an almost provincial quality. Copenhagen is a favorite of tourists, and thousands of Americans visit the city each year.

Copenhagen lies on the eastern coast of the island of Zealand, on the straits connecting the Baltic Sea to the North Sea. Between Zealand and mainland Denmark lie the island of Fyn and two channels, the Great Belt and the Little Belt. Copenhagen's strategic location on a main trade route between the Baltic and northern countries has made it one of the great transit ports of Northern Europe.

It is a truly modern city, and almost all basic services are readily available in Copenhagen, but are more costly, sometimes dramatically so, than in the U.S. There are good laundries, laundromats, dry cleaners, shoe repair shops, and barber and beauty services. Auto and electronic repairs also are adequate, and personal items are in good supply, as they are in most Danish cities and towns.

Other large cities in Denmark are Odense, Aarhus, and Aalborg.

Recreation

Facilities for sports and recreation are plentiful in Denmark. Many neighborhood gymnasiums in Copenhagen have indoor swimming pools. Tennis and badminton are popular, and several clubs have both indoor and outdoor courts. A number of 18-hole private golf courses are located near Copenhagen. Bowling, flying, gliding, and hang gliding are also available.

Summer sports are popular during the short warm season. Yacht clubs are located along the coast, and sailing is enjoyed from May to October. Many people swim in the sea during the summer, despite the chilly water temperature. Fishing on small private lakes is available. Bicycling and hiking are popular, and several reputable riding schools have indoor rings for winter riding. Excellent pheasant and duck shooting and some deer hunting are possible, but a game license is required. To obtain a license, the visitor must

pass a test, unless he holds a U.S. game license or can produce evidence of adequate experience in the use of sporting guns.

Winter sports are limited to ice skating and occasionally some cross-country skiing north of Copenhagen. Serious skiers must travel north to Norway, or south to France, Germany, Austria, Italy, or Switzerland. Oslo is 12 hours by train, or overnight by the excellent sleeper ferry from Copenhagen. The Bavarian and Swiss Alps are 18 to 24 hours away by train, and Copenhagen travel agencies offer excellent, modestly priced, eight-day package ski trips to these areas.

Many guided tours of Copenhagen are available. One popular tour goes by boat through the canals of Copenhagen, into the harbor and past the famous statue of the Little Mermaid. The airline charter industry is highly developed and competitive, providing inexpensive tour packages to all parts of Europe and many other points abroad.

Copenhagen's movie theaters show the latest American and European films. Most feature films are shown in their original language with Danish subtitles. Copenhagen has three symphony orchestras, a ballet (one of the world's finest), and a national opera company. The most famous of the orchestras is the Radio Denmark Symphony which gives weekly concerts in winter, and often features leading American and European artists. The ballet and opera each offer several performances a week from September through May.

Many fine museums are located in or near the city, including the National Museum of Art, the Carlsberg Glyptotek (with an excellent Rodin collection), and the Louisiana Museum which features modern art. The world-famous Tivoli amusement park in the heart of the city is synonymous with the spirit of Copenhagen. Open only from May to early September, Tivoli features arcades, restaurants, and concert halls in a well-maintained park.

Copenhagen has many good restaurants. Danish cuisine, lacking the refinements of the French, is good but bland. A bottle of wine is expensive, and all hard liquor is high-priced, so most Danes stick to beer and schnapps (a Danish drink made from potatoes flavored with caraway) with their meals. Danish beer is deservedly world renowned.

Notes for Travelers

Copenhagen is easy to reach by air, with direct flights from most major American and European cities.

A valid American passport is the only document needed for entry. Neither a visa nor a vaccination certificate is required.

Winter clothing is needed most of the year.

The Lutheran Church is the state church of Denmark, but complete religious freedom is practiced. Roman Catholic, Jewish, Reformist, Unitarian, Methodist, Baptist, Swedish Lutheran, and the Church of Jesus Christ of Latter-Day Saints have congregations in Copenhagen, and some churches have services in English.

The Danish monetary units are the *kroner* and *ore*. Coins are issued in 5, 10, and 25 *ore* pieces, and 1 and 5 *kroner* pieces. Notes are issued in 10, 50, 100, 500, and 1,000 *kroner* denominations. Exchange rates fluctuate.

The metric system of weights and measures is used in Denmark.

The U.S. Embassy in Denmark is located at Dag Hammarskjolds Alle, 24, DK 2100, Copenhagen.

Finland

FINLAND offers the joys that are yielded by communion with nature. The character of the nation and its people has been forged by the severity of life in this northern corner of Europe, by the challenge of existing between contending powers, and by the influence of the lakes and forests which separate the country into small communities, even as they serve to inspire a national culture.

Finnish pride focuses on Finnish independence and the modern, industrialized, democratic state, which accommodates both a generous social welfare system and a vigorous individualism. To Finns, being close to nature is an everyday occurrence: the freedom of the forests is guaranteed by law, and there they pick berries, gather mushrooms, fish, hunt, ski, and swim.

Helsinki, the capital, is the second most northerly capital in the world, after Iceland's Reykjavik. Seasonal changes in Finland are dramatic, and the country is noted for its thousands of lakes, great forests, and rocky islands. Short winter days contrast with the summer's "white nights." In addition to its wealth of unspoiled scenery, Finland offers medieval churches, ancient culture, and modern progressive cities. Finland also offers the intellectual challenge of learning its language.

Area, Geography, Climate

Finland, the sixth largest country in Europe, occupies an area of 130,120 square miles, about twice the size of the United Kingdom, and slightly smaller than the combined size of New York, Pennsylvania, and Ohio. Its coastline, excluding indentations, is 688 miles long. Finland is bounded on the east and southeast by the U.S.S.R., on the west by Sweden and the Gulf of Bothnia, on the north by Norway, and on the south by the Gulf of Finland.

Most of the country is low; hilly elevations are less than 650 feet except along the northeastern frontier with Norway, and in the extreme north (Lapland). Nearly all of Finland's 60,000 lakes, which comprise about 10 percent of the total area, are in the country's southern half, and provide important waterways and log-floating routes. An extensive and imposing archipelago—extending from the Russian border on the south coast, westward to the Aland Islands, and then northward on a diminishing scale—is an important fishing and vacation area comparable in magnitude and grandeur to the famous 60,000 lakes.

Apart from the lakes and archipelagoes, the outstanding physical feature and natural resource of Finland are its forests. These cover about 70 percent of the land area, the highest percentage in Europe. The soil, mainly moraine deposits left by the ice age glaciers, is usually so thin that the topography follows the contours of the archaean bedrock. Most of the country is low lying, but the landscape is not of the flat lowland type; on the contrary, it is extremely broken with ridges, valleys, and hollows, which usually contain lakes.

Finland is almost entirely in the northern zone of coniferous forests. A limited zone in the south and southwest, where some hardwood deciduous trees grow, resembles Central Europe in topography. In Lapland, spruce is the first tree species to disappear, followed by pine; the timber line generally is formed by dwarf birch.

Virtually all of Finland lies between latitudes 60° and 70°N, but the prevalence of warm westerly winds makes the climate several degrees warmer than elsewhere at the same latitude. Summers are short and mild (in southern Finland from June 1 to September 1) with daylight extending well into the night hours. In June and July, a two- or three-hour period of twilight separates sunset and sunrise. In the extreme north, the sun does not set for 60 days during midsummer. Winters are long and cold.

Precipitation, averaging 23 to 25 inches annually, is distributed over all seasons of the year. Generally, the wettest and least pleasant period is between late September and the first lasting snow, which usually comes before Christmas. Central and Northern Finland have snow for most of the five or six coldest months. A considerable difference often exists in temperatures from north to south, and snow coverage in southern Finland varies

from one winter to the next. However, many clear, cold days from January to the end of March are ideal for winter sports.

Helsinki's average temperature is 40°F. January and July mean temperatures are 23°F and 64°F. The nearness of the sea also affects the city's weather. The mean temperature of 21°F during February, the coldest month, is considerably higher than the average for the country as a whole, and in July, the warmest month, constant sea breezes keep it cooler. During the coldest days of winter, the mercury might dip as low as -20°F, and on the hottest days of summer rise to 85°F, but the weather tends to be more temperate than that of the United States' northern Midwest. Helsinki's maritime location also means frequent rain and high humidity. Average temperatures in Lapland are 10°F in January and 59°F in July.

Population

Finland's population of about 4,784,000, includes 2,500 Lapps. Until after World War II, most people lived in rural areas. Rapid postwar industrialization, the growth of service industries, and expanded higher-level educational opportunities, have brought about a continuous movement to urban areas. Nearly one-fifth of Finland's population now lives within 40 kilometers of Helsinki.

Finland has two official languages, Finnish and Swedish. Under the constitution, the government must meet the cultural and economic requirements of both language groups on a basis of parity. Finnish is spoken by 92 percent of the population, and Swedish by most of the rest. There are small

Lapp- and Russian-speaking minorities.

Finns are generally of light complexion with fair hair and blue or grey eyes. Racially the Finns are mixed, as are most European peoples. The main racial characteristics are derived from the East-Baltic and Nordic races. At the beginning of the Christian Era, Finland was occupied by a seminomadic people, the Lapps. Gradually the ancestors of the present-day Finns moved the Lapps northward to the Arctic.

The early Finns are believed to have come from Central Asia. Their language, unlike that of their neighbors, is not Indo-European. Like Estonian, Hungarian, and the languages of certain minorities in Central and North Russia, Finnish forms part of the Finno-Ugric family. Characteristics of the Finnish language include the use of case-endings, post-positions instead of prepositions, a great wealth of verbal forms, and a highly phonetic orthography. Finns never have trouble spelling.

After Finnish and Swedish, English is the language most commonly used, followed by German. Foreign-language study is an important part of the secondary school curriculum, and more than 90 percent of all students choose to study English. Most business firms are able to correspond in English, and English-speaking tourists have little difficulty in Helsinki.

History

King Eric of Sweden introduced Christianity to Finland in 1155. Swedish authority over Finland became effective through armed "missionary" campaigns at the end of the 13th cen-

tury. Finland became Protestant during the Reformation (92 percent of the population is Lutheran). Thereafter, Finland gradually played a greater role in the political life of the Swedish-Finnish realm. In 1809, during the Napoleonic wars, Finland was annexed by Russia and became a Grand Duchy. Assurance given by Alexander I that Finnish laws and constitutional rights would be respected became obsolete under increasingly reactionary Czars.

The cultural and political awakening of Finland in literature and in resistance to "Russification," quickened the pace towards creation of an independent Finland. On December 6, 1917, during the chaos of the Russian revolution, Finland declared its independence and was immediately plunged into a civil war between the "Whites" and the "Reds." The violence of the three-month struggle, culminating in victory for the "Whites," left wounds that are still not entirely healed. Both the left and right in Finnish politics have their own version of the events. Political affiliation could still reflect a family choice of sides in 1918. A new constitution was proclaimed in 1919.

During World War II, Finland twice fought the Soviet Union: in the Winter War of 1939-40, and again in the Continuation War of 1941-44. Finland suffered heavy casualties, lost 11 percent of its territory to the Soviet Union, and over 400,000 Finns had to be resettled. The Treaty of Peace between Finland and the U.S.S.R., signed at Paris on February 10, 1947, provided for the cession to the Soviet Union of the Petsamo area on the Arctic coast and the Karelian Isthmus in southeast Finland, for the lease of the Porkkala area near Helsinki to the U.S.S.R. for use as a naval base, and for free access to this area across Finnish territory. In late 1955, the Soviets returned the Porkkala area to Finland. The treaty also provided that Finland pay the U.S.S.R. reparations in goods valued at an estimated $570 million (completed in 1952). Finland's defense forces are limited by the Peace Treaty to 41,900 men (Army 34,400; Navy 4,500; Air Force 3,000).

In April 1948, Finland and the U.S.S.R. signed an Agreement of Friendship, Cooperation, and Mutual Assistance, by which Finland is obligated to resist armed attacks by "Germany" or its allies against Finland, or against the U.S.S.R. through Finland, with if necessary, the aid of the Soviet Union. At the same time, the agreement recognizes in its preamble, the Finnish desire to remain outside great power conflicts. This agreement was extended for 20 years in 1955, and again in 1970.

In the United Nations, which it joined in 1955, Finland favors membership for all nations, usually takes no stand on major East-West issues, stresses neutrality as policy of active participation in international life, and channels the bulk of its foreign assistance to developing countries through various U.N. agencies. Finland supports and actively participates in the U.N.'s peacekeeping activities. The Finnish military donned the blue beret of the U.N. during the Suez Crisis (1956–57), and served as observers in Lebanon in 1958, Cyprus in 1967, and in the Sinai following the 1973 war. Finland has standby military units available for the purpose of participating in U.N. peacekeeping activities as requested.

Finland's official policy of neutrality and nonalignment has led to the establishment of relations with other countries regardless of their political systems. Finland worked for the convening of the Conference on European Security and Cooperation in July 1973, involving the U.S.S.R., countries of Eastern and Western Europe, Canada, and the U.S. This conference culminated in a summit meeting of 35 heads of state and the signing of the Final Act—often called the Helsinki Act—on August 1, 1975. Finland has also supported the Strategic Arms Limitation Talks, which began in Helsinki in 1969. In the Nordic Council, an interparliamentarian organ of cooperation among Nordic nations, Finland works closely with its neighbors on matters of intra-Nordic concern.

Government

Today Finland is a Western-oriented republic. Under the constitution of 1919, the President has powers stronger than those of his counterparts in most European countries, although not as great as those of the President of the U.S. The President has full powers over foreign affairs, is the Commander-in-Chief of the Armed Forces, and can dissolve Parliament.

The Cabinet includes the Prime Minister and usually about 16 Ministers and Associate Ministers in charge of the 11 government departments. The Parliament (Eduskunta) is unicameral, and consists of 200 members directly elected every four years through proportional representation. Suffrage is equal and universal; all citizens over age 18 have the right to vote. Finland was the first country in Europe to grant full political rights to women (1906), well before the U.S.

Finnish policies on most basic domestic and foreign issues have been consistent, notwithstanding a relatively rapid turnover of cabinets since World War II, and periods when no government commanded a parliamentary majority.

The nearly equal strength of the four major parties—Social Democratic, Conservative, Center, and People's Democratic League (Communist-front party)—and the fact that they represent different economic or ideological interests, have made the formation of longlasting governments difficult. Most Finnish governments are coalitions of several parties, although at times it has been neccessary to form cabinets composed of nonparty technical experts. The average life of Finnish cabinets has been 12 months. By contrast, Finland has had only two presidents since 1946.

Justice is administered by independent courts. The public courts of justice try both civil and criminal cases. In rural areas, courts of the first instance are known as circuit courts, the judicial authority resting in a legally trained judge and a jury of lay members. Cities have municipal courts, each presided over by a legally trained magistrate and two counselors. Other courts are the Courts of Appeal and the highest judicial authority, the Supreme Court, to which appeals may be made against the judgments of the Courts of Appeal.

Judicial procedure differs from that in Anglo-Saxon countries: Finnish law is codified. There is no writ of habeas corpus or bail. Formal charges must be brought within three days of detention on suspicion, and courts of first instance must hear a case within eight days of arrest. Civil rights are deeply entrenched and strictly observed by the police and courts.

Finland has enjoyed complete freedom of worship since 1923. Some 92.7 percent of the population nominally belong to the Finnish Evangelical Lutheran Church, the state church. The Finnish Orthodox Church is the second largest congregation (about 60,000 adherents) and also enjoys the status of a state church. Several smaller church organizations have congregations totaling less than 10,000. Bishops of the six Finnish dioceses of the Evangelical Lutheran Church are appointed by the President of the Republic, on the basis of elections held in each diocese. The bishop of the Diocese of Turku is the Archbishop of the Church of Finland.

Arts, Science, Education

Helsinki and other Finnish cities have a rich theatrical life. Some 40 professional theaters in the nation offer about 20,000 performances a year. The Finnish National Theater (a government-sponsored institution) in Helsinki is among the foremost; several theaters present performances in Swedish, and occasionally English translations can be obtained.

A rich musical life in Finland is offered by 11 professional and eight semiprofessional symphony orchestras all over the country. Besides the Finnish National Opera, eight other opera associations are outside Helsinki. Two permanent symphony orchestras, the Helsinki Philharmonic and the Radio Symphony Orchestra, perform at least once a week. The National Opera, with its orchestra and ballet, and many soloist and chamber music concerts all over the city (Sibelius Academy, Church in the Rock, City Hall, House of Nobility) afford ample opportunity for concert-going.

During summer, a chain of famous festivals takes place, all featuring world-famous Finnish and international artists and orchestras. It starts with Kuopio Dance and Music Festival in June, and is followed by the Jyväskylä Arts Festival, the Savonlinna Opera Festival, the Pori Jazz Festival (one of the best jazz festivals in the world), the Folk Music Festival Kaustinen, the Kuhmo Chamber Music Festival, the Turku Music Festival, the Lahti International Organ Festival, the Tampere Theatre Summer, and finally the Helsinki Festival in late August and early September. Many Helsinki residents leave for the country during summer and much of Helsinki's cultural life closes down; however, restaurants and cinemas remain open.

Finnish architecture is justly famous. Finlandia Hall, the National Pensions Institute, the Enso-Gutzeit Building of Alvar Aalto, and the Helsinki Railway Station of Eliel Saarinen are only four of many buildings that attract students of architecture from all over the world.

Glass, porcelain, and stainless steel are some of the materials that bear the unique stamp of Finnish craftsmanship and design. The Arabia workshop is a design leader for many items from coffee cups and saucers to bathroom sinks. Nuutjärvi, Iittala, Riihimäki, and Kumela glassware are equally famous. In ladies' fashion, Finland has such famous designers as Marimekko, Vuokko and Anu Pentik.

Finland, with virtually no illiteracy, has an advanced educational system. Education is free, including all textbooks and a broad medical care program. Pupils receive a hot meal each day at school. Special schools have been established in the larger cities for children who are handicapped or have learning disabilities, and Finland has six schools for the deaf, and two state-run schools for the blind.

Like its Scandinavian neighbors, Finland has a strong adult education program. Young adults who wish to extend their education, but cannot go to a university, may attend folk high schools and folk academies. Workers' institutes offer a variety of subjects. Like folk high schools and folk academies, the workers' institutes are run privately, or by local authorities, but receive state subsidies.

The largest university in Finland is the state-supported University of Helsinki, which has spearheaded the country's intellectual life since the 17th century. Founded in 1640 as the State University in Turku, it was moved to Helsinki in 1828. Another important state school of advanced education is the Institute of Technology, established in 1908. It is now located at Otaniemi near Tapiola, on the western outskirts of Helsinki. The entire campus was designed by architect Alvar Aalto.

A major expansion of state-supported higher education facilities occurred in 1958. The Jyväskylä Teachers College, founded in 1934, was enlarged to university status. In 1959, a new university was established at Oulu in the north. It was followed by universities in Joensuu and Kuopio. The latest in Rovaniemi, established in 1979, is the world's most northerly university.

Finland has 20 university-level institutions—nine universities, three technical universities, five schools of economics, The College of Veterinary Medicine, The Swedish School for

Social Work and Local Administration, The Institute of Industrial Arts—and four language institutes. The Sibelius Academy is the most important music school, but there are also six other conservatories.

In addition to the compulsory teaching of Finnish and Swedish, most academic institutions offer English as a third language. English is widely understood in Finland and has replaced German, which was regarded as the third language among older age groups. State subsidies are provided to several private institutions. Schools receiving subsidies are subject to a degree of state supervision, but remain free from ministerial control.

Commerce and Industry

Although Finland is traditionally known for its huge forest industries, the share of forestry and agriculture in gross national product (GNP) declined in the 1960s and 1970s to about 10 percent in 1978. Manufacturing has risen to 30 percent and services to 29 percent. The forest-products industry, still the base of Finland's manufacturing, accounts directly for one-fourth of industrial output.

Finland is the world's seventh largest per capita consumer of energy, a measure of the sophistication of the economy and the severity of the climate. Income figures give further evidence of prosperity. While 1978 GNP (latest figures) was only $32 billion, the $6,690 GNP per capita is about 15th highest in the world. The growth rate for 1978 was close to two percent.

Finland's farmers operate near the northern limits of agriculture, and much of Finland's soil is poor and rolling. Finland must trade to obtain a fully nutritional and appetizing diet,

and is a net importer of foodstuffs. Finns have historically been farmers and foresters, but maintenance of Finland's agricultural sector in today's world of high-volume international trade and low-cost bulk transport requires extensive government protection and support. Major exports are dairy products, eggs, and pork. Major imports are fruits and vegetables, sugar, oil seeds, raw cotton, grains, and fertilizer.

Agricultural workers usually work in the forestry industry in winter. The annual output of forestry products is 50 to 55 million cubic meters. A limit of 58 million cubic meters cut per year has been established for maintenance of the forest resources. Finland's pine, spruce, and birch make it a leading producer of pulp, lumber, paper, blockboard, and plywood.

Mining resources are limited, but Finland does have one of Europe's largest copper deposits. Zinc, nickel, iron ore, titanium, and vanadium are also produced. Mining output accounts for less than one percent of the GNP.

A serious hindrance in the development of manufacturing industries is the total absence of coal and petroleum. Sites for generating hydroelectric power have been fully developed, and Finland is already dependent on imported petroleum, largely from the U.S.S.R. For future growth it must look increasingly to nuclear power. Three nuclear power plants have recently come into operation.

Manufacturing and service industries have become increasingly important to the life and future growth of Finland's economy. Despite wartime destruction and heavy reparations to the U.S.S.R., manufacturing has expanded rapidly and now accounts for more than one-third of exports, excluding forest-based products. Forest-based manufactured products accounted for about 45 percent of all exports in 1978. Key industries include pulp and paper, food processsing, tobacco, metal products and machinery, electrical equipment, textiles and apparel, and chemicals.

The shipbuilding industry in Finland is highly developed, using modern design and construction technology to produce a variety of special purpose ships for foreign and domestic consumers. In 1977, for example, Finnish shipyards produced a total of 51 vessels while employing a work force of some 18,000 people. This production included modern RO/RO ships, offshore drilling rigs, and icebreakers.

The metal and engineering industry, which was reorganized and expanded in order to make the large war reparations to the U.S.S.R., has since grown rapidly and diversified. Finland also has its own oil refining industry. The output of the Nordic countries' two largest refineries covers Finland's entire gasoline consumption and a major proportion of other liquid fuel consumption, as well as furnishing the basis of a new petrochemicals industry.

Foreign trade plays a vital role in the economy; exports of goods and services account for over 30 percent of GNP. Finland's high dependence on trade makes it sensitive, and indeed vulnerable, to changes in world market conditions. About 60 percent of both exports and imports are traded with the Western European countries of the European Economic Community (EEC) and the European Free Trade

Area (EFTA). Trade with the CEMA countries is mainly with the U.S.S.R. and Poland, on which Finland depends for coal. The U.S. accounts for about five percent of Finnish trade. In 1977, imports from the U.S. were valued at $356 million, and exports at $340 million.

Finland's major exports are newsprint and other paper, pulp, plywood, lumber, machinery, ships, chemicals, and copper and copper products. It also exports food specialties, design products in textiles and apparel, ceramics, glassware, furs, and furniture. Principal imports consist of machinery, crude oil, fuels and lubricants, motor vehicles, construction and agricultural equipment, tropical food products, plastics and synthetic resins, fruits, and wheat.

Finland joined the European Free Trade Association in 1961 as an associate member. It is also a member of the General Agreement on Tariffs and Trade, the International Monetary Fund, the International Bank for Reconstruction and Development, the International Finance Corporation, the Asian Development Bank, the Inter-American Development Bank, and the Organization for European Cooperation and Development. After some internal debate and conclusion of a balancing agreement with CEMA, the Soviet/Eastern European economic organization, Finland signed an industrial free trade agreement with the EEC, effective January 1, 1974.

Transportation

Finnish railways, entirely state-owned, have an operating track of 6,063 kilometers, with links to Sweden and the U.S.S.R. The northernmost point accessible by train is Kemijärvi, north of Rovaniemi. Some 674 kilometers of track have an electric power line, and electrification continues.

The Finnish highway system is constantly being expanded. As of January 1978, public roads covered 74,149 kilometers, of which 32,005 kilometers are paved. Trucking and bus services are steadily gaining in importance as carriers of passengers and goods.

Finnair, the state-owned airline, maintains regular air service to 20 Finnish cities; 29 European cities in winter and 31 in summer; and to New York, Montreal, and Bangkok. The international route network covers 49,120 miles; the domestic, 10,600 miles.

Helsinki offers excellent streetcar and bus service. Taxis are readily available at the many taxistands throughout the city, and may by reached by telephone. Fares are not excessive and drivers are not tipped. Public transportation is used by many people for getting to work, and to recreational and social activities. However, a car is still extremely useful.

In winter, main roads are kept open, but winter driving, even in Helsinki and its outskirts, can be hazardous because of frequent icy conditions. Service is available for a broad range of cars, all of which must pass rigid inspection. A U.S. drivers license is valid in Finland for three months.

Communications

The government operates the domestic telegraph and most of the country's telephone facilities. Communication services in Finland are generally excellent. A privately owned telegraph cable extends between Sweden and Finland, and nearly all cable communications to overseas destinations are transmitted by this route. International airmail normally arrives in New York about five days after being mailed in Helsinki. Postal rates are expensive.

A fair selection of musical programs is available throughout the day on Finnish AM and FM radio. Many radio channels can be received from other European countries. Good VOA and BBC reception is possible on a shortwave radio.

Television broadcasting in Finland began in 1957. Each of the two Finnish stations operates seven hours a day during the afternoon and evening hours. American, British, and Canadian movies and TV serials are regularly featured in English with Finnish subtitles. A variety of programs from other Western and Eastern European countries have Finnish subtitles. Finnish TV, which broadcasts mostly color programs, has the same technical standards as West Germany.

Time, Newsweek, and the International Herald Tribune are sold locally, although the Herald Tribune usually arrives one or two days after publication. English-language books and magazines are sold in the two main bookstores, and in lobbies of the larger hotels. A large number of American books printed in Britain are available here, as well as a good choice of standard works in Swedish, French, Italian, German, and Spanish. Type and quantity vary according to import restrictions, but in general, a good selection is available in both fiction and nonfiction.

Health

The standard of the Finnish medical profession is high. Most physicians have been educated at the University of Helsinki, and many have studied abroad as well. Most doctors speak English and German, in addition to Finnish and Swedish. In recent years, many physicians have visited the U.S. for research and study.

Numerous children's specialists practice in Helsinki. Public and private hospitals are excellent, and maternity hospitals maintain high standards. Those who have used the hospital facilities report favorably on the conditions and treatment. Charges are reasonable. The standard of Finnish nursing is good, and Finnish hospitals are usually well equipped.

Eye doctors are available, and opticians are able to fill most prescriptions promptly. Dentists are very competent, and charges are reasonable. Orthodontic treatment is available. Most medicines are available locally at a reasonable state-controlled price.

The general level of community sanitation in Helsinki is very high. Public cleanliness and controls are adequate to prevent serious outbreaks of disease, and there are no pest or vermin problems. Helsinki water is dependable but is not fluoridated; fluoride tablets for children are available locally. Pasteurized milk is available and the processing of fresh milk is closely controlled and safe. The general sanitation and safety of local goods are comparable to those in the U.S.

Some 31.5 percent of the mortality rate in Finland is attributable to heart disease, with an additional six percent caused by circulatory ailments. Helsinki's winter climate is cold and damp, and may aggravate conditions such as neuralgia, rheumatism, and sinus disorders.

Major City

HELSINKI, capital and principal city, is a Baltic port on Finland's southern coast. It lies north of such cities as Juneau, Alaska, and Churchill, Canada. In January it is somewhat warmer than such comparatively "southern" cities as Butte, Montana and Lewiston, Maine, and considerably warmer than Minneapolis, Minnesota and Lake Placid, New York. Helsinki follows East European Standard Time, which is two hours in advance of Greenwich Mean Time and one hour in advance of European Standard Time (Stockholm, Paris, etc.).

Helsinki is a modern city. Yet it has areas which give a genuine and comprehensive picture of the atmosphere and architecture of the past. The city was founded in 1550 by the Swedish King Gustav Vasa. Great fires destroyed the old wooden Helsinki many times, but it was always rebuilt. The massive walls of the Suomenlinna Island fortress date from the 18th century. Helsinki became Finland's capital in 1812. Many of the city's historically interesting sights date from the beginning of the 19th century, when the administrative center was built around the Senate Square. The Cathedral, the university, and the Government Palace, for example, are among the finest architectural achievements in Helsinki. It has been said of the Helsinki of the Empire period that it was the last European city designed as an entity and created as a work of art. The historic Senate Square is one of the most remarkable achievements of neo-classicism at its height.

Helsinki today has a modern look, with some buildings designed by internationally-known contemporary Finnish architects Eliel Saarinen and Alvar

Aalto. In planning new areas and developing old ones, the aim has been to make the city a balanced whole with several regional centers, each with its own schools, sport fields, libraries, and shopping centers. The ideal is to combine the advantages of urban living with those of rural life. Half a million people reside in the city, which is the administrative, cultural, commercial, and industrial center of Finland. Including suburbs, the population of Greater Helsinki is over 800,000.

Helsinki has many points of interest. One of the most popular is the harbor area and the Market Square, where the Havis Amanda fountain symbolizes Helsinki rising out of the waves. Other attractions include the Olympic Stadium (site of the 1952 summer games), the Sibelius monument, the "Church in the Rock," Finlandia Hall, the City Museum and the National Museum, and Seurasaari Island.

Helsinki offers a wide and interesting variety of sporting events, services, cultural activities, shopping, and entertainment, and it enjoys an unusually high standard of living.

Recreation

The sauna, a national institution in Finland, has existed for a thousand years. Finns normally take a sauna once a week and it is a custom that most Americans quickly learn to enjoy. Saunas are particularly enjoyable after physical exercise, especially cross-country skiing, and as a means of socializing, although mixed saunas are not customary. The purpose of taking a sauna is to completely cleanse the body and soul by subjecting both to great changes of temperatures. After the heat of the sauna, there is either a

shower or a swim in a pool, a lake, or the sea. The bravest roll in winter snow or plunge through a hole in the ice. After the sauna, a cold beer or soda before a warm fireplace is a necessary thirst quencher. Most Finnish apartment buildings include saunas, and their residents have regular sauna evenings. Almost all houses have saunas, some with pools; and summer houses, although quite modest, all have a sauna, usually on a lake or the sea.

Finland first rose to prominence in sports at the 1912 Olympics, where it took first place in wrestling and second place in track and field. In succeeding years Finland has become famous for long distance runners, ski jumpers, speed skaters, and marksmen. Sports unique to Finland are bandy, a form of ice hockey, and *pesupällo*, a game vaguely resembling American baseball. Soccer, hockey, and basketball are popular spectator sports.

From the first of June until late August, daylight hours are long and outdoor activities such as boating, sailing, bathing, swimming, hiking, picnicking, and motor trips may be enjoyed in the immediate vicinity of Helsinki. The time for golf and outdoor tennis is relatively short. Helsinki has an 18-hole golf course and a few excellent outdoor clay tennis courts, as well as several indoor year-round tennis courts.

Squash is becoming popular, but few courts are available. Cycling possibilities are good in the Helsinki suburbs during the warmer months, and jogging trails abound. Boating begins in May or June and extends into September. Swimming at the several municipal beaches and outside pools is popular for about two months in the summer, but swimming is possible year round at several indoor pools.

Winter sports include skiing and skating. Excellent trails for cross-country skiing are available in and around the city, many of which are lighted for evening use. Several smaller towns within a few hours' ride offer good weekend skiing; spring skiing trips to Lapland are popular. Downhill skiing is popular but facilities are limited. Several small hills are located near Helsinki, but the better locations are farther north. The city has many good outdoor skating rinks and some indoor rinks.

Salmon fishing is found in northern Lapland; moose hunting can be done in the fall. Duck and other game birds are also available, although not plentiful. Ice fishing is quite popular.

Marvelous outdoor recreation and touring opportunities are plentiful throughout Finland, particularly Lapland and the lake district. Lapland— the land of the midnight sun, northern lights, and reindeer—is the northernmost province in Finland. The principal towns are Kemi and Rovaniemi, both accessible by air (two hours) and rail (nine hours), and about 800 kilometers from Helsinki. The overnight train with space for cars is a popular way to get to Rovaniemi, a transit point to the tourist and resort areas of Pallastunturi, Kilpisjärvi, and Inari further north. The traveler can also drive north into Norway and view the fjords. Lapland is especially popular in early April, when the days are longer and skiing excellent; for midsummer's night to view the fires and festivities; and in September when the leaves change colors.

The lake district, comprising most of southwest central Finland, provides excellent opportunities for scenic travel by car and steamer ship. A wood-burning steamer offers an unusually scenic 12-hour trip from Savonlinna to Kuopio. The Olavinlinna Castle, dating back to 1475, a compact towering fortress built on an island near Savonlinna, is the site of an open air opera festival in July.

Day trips to Turku, Hanko, and Porvoo are popular. Turku, Finland's oldest city, has a population of 165,000 and was the capital of Finland until 1812. The cathedral and castle both date from the 13th century, and the open-air handicrafts museum is a popular attraction in the summer. Turku is located two-and-a-half hours west of Helsinki by car. Hanko, a coastal city two hours west of Helsinki by car, is one of the best Finnish saltwater bathing resorts during July and August. At this time, yachting regattas and tennis matches are held. En route to Hanko, many stop at Tammisaari, a charming seaside town with narrow lanes bordered by Empire-style wooden houses. Porvoo is an idyllic old coastal town one hour east of Helsinki by car. It was the home of Johan Ludvig Runeberg, the national poet of Finland, and is the site of an ancient granite cathedral.

A visit in Helsinki provides excellent opportunities to travel to Sweden and the U.S.S.R. Two shipping lines have overnight service between Stockholm and Helsinki. During summer, ships leave five times a week for Tallinn, Estonia, and twice a week for Leningrad. Daily flights are available on Finnair or Aeroflot, and daily trains to Leningrad and Moscow. Except for trips to Leningrad by ship in summer, all other excursions require a Soviet visa. Since accommodations must be booked before a visa is issued, it is best to have a travel agent in Helsinki handle this matter. Visa processing takes from 10 days to two weeks.

Entertainment

Helskinki's 13 theaters offer regular performances in Finnish and Swedish. Finnish plays and classical and contemporary American and European productions are given. Occasionally an English company presents plays. Many good movie theaters in the city and suburbs offer the latest American, British, Italian, French and other films in their original versions, as well as locally produced films in Finnish. Movies are at scheduled hours. Strict regulations exist against children attending movies featuring violence, whether accompanied by parents or not.

The Finnish Opera produces a number of operas and ballets each season. Each year Helsinki is visited by foreign ballet companies of excellent caliber, and on occasion, visiting artists of note, particularly from the U.S.S.R., appear with the local company. Two separate series of symphony concerts are given. The Radio Symphony Orchestra performs on Wednesdays. The Helsinki Philharmonic Orchestra performs every second week on Wednesdays and Thursdays (same program both nights). Some of the programs are broadcast over the state-owned radio network.

Besides the regular concert season, every summer Helsinki becomes a mecca for top performing artists who come to the Helsinki Festival. Some of the greatest groups have performed in the festival, which takes place during the latter part of August. The city offers many other entertainment opportunities for all age groups. Con-

certs, dance recitals, and marionette shows are offered. Helsinki has some nightclubs, many restaurants where it is possible to dance, and a good selection of discotheques.

Finns tend to wear suits when going to concerts, the opera, and ballet. Even when recommended dress is casual, some Finns will dress in suits.

Independence Day, December 6, and May Day are two national holidays that are occasions for parades and other forms of entertainment. Midsummer Eve in Helsinki is celebrated with bonfires and programs at the Seurasaari Open-Air Museum.

At least 21 museums are in the Helsinki area. The largest is the National Museum, with its extensive prehistoric, historic, and ethnographic collections. The largest art museum is the Art Museum of the Atheneum, located across the street from the railroad station. It contains Finnish art from the 18th century to the present, and foreign works of art. Occasionally large foreign exhibitions are shown there. The Art Collections of the City of Helsinki and the Amos Anderson Museum of Art are also noted museums which often have exhibitions, in addition to their regular collections.

Notes for Travelers

Helsinki is served by daily flights from many European cities, and Finnair flies the New York-Helsinki route. Northwest Airlines serves Stockholm, Sweden, and from there the traveler has the option of taking the ferry boat to Helsinki.

A visa is not necessary for entry into Finland, but Americans planning to stay for more than 90 days must obtain a residence permit after arrival.

No inoculation certificates are required.

Only nonautomatic and semiautomatic firearms may be imported, and local requirements for hunting licenses are handled by the police. Fishing licenses also are required.

Religious services in English are conducted in Helsinki by the International Evangelical Church at the Inner Mission and at the Church of the Rock; at Salem Full Gospel Church; St. Henrik's Roman Catholic Church; and in the small chapel (Anglican rites) of the Main Lutheran Cathedral on Senate Square.

The unit of Finnish currency, the *markka* or Finnmark (Fmk.), has a floating exchange rate. Coins are in denominations of pennies and marks.

Finland uses the metric system.

The U.S. Embassy in Finland is located at Itäinen Puistotie 1400140A, Helsinki.

France

The French share a national heritage that is both a source of pride and a burden. **FRANCE,** once an empire, and its capital city of Paris, for centuries the hub of cultural, scientific, and intellectual activity, are in the midst of a radical self-examination to determine their role in a constantly changing 20th-century society. As elsewhere in the modern world, France is confronting the economic, industrial, and scientific challenges on which the future depends.

Area, Geography, Climate

Metropolitan France covers an area of 213,000 square miles, about four-fifths the size of Texas. The landscape is varied—about two-thirds flat or gently rolling, and one-third mountainous. Broad plains cover most of northern and western France from the German border in the northeast to the city of Bayonne in the southwest. There are low hills in Normandy and Brittany and along the eastern margin of the plain. The principal rivers—the Seine, Loire, and Garonne—flow west or northwest in broad valleys across almost the entire width of the plain. Most land is used for cultivation and pasture, but numerous small areas of deciduous woods exist. The lowlands plain is bounded on the south by the Pyrenees' steep ridges; on the southeast by the low mountains and hills of Massif Central; and on the east by the massive Alps, the long, low, forested ridges in the Jura, and the broad, rounded summits of the densely forested Vosges.

France's climate varies. Western France has mild winters (early December through February) and cool summers (early June through August). Precipitation is frequent all year; most areas record 20 to 40 inches average rainfall in late autumn or early winter. Mountainous western France has greater variations in both temperature and precipitation. The Mediterranean coast and the island of Corsica have hot summers and mild winters, with less seasonal precipitation.

Paris lies in the Seine River Valley of north-central France, in the Department of the Seine. Climatic conditions in Paris are moderate. Annual rainfall averages only 26 inches, divided among all seasons. Winters are damp and not usually severe. Snowfall is light; sunshine is rare in winter, and gray, raw, foggy days are frequent. Summers are quite pleasant, but rain is heavy at times. Summer temperatures are rarely oppressive. Hot weather may occur as early as May or as late as October; conversely, June and July can be cold or rainy. Spring and autumn are long and pleasant. Winds are not excessive. Prevailing westerly winds bring moisture from the Atlantic.

Population

France's population is almost 54 million, and includes these ethnic divisions: Nordic, one percent; sub-Nordic, 40 percent; almost pure Alpine, 30 percent; Alpine with Slav admixture, 15 percent; Mediterranean, 10 percent; Basque, one percent; North African (principally Arab), one percent; and others, two percent.

By the 20th century, religion was no longer a major force in the society, but the legacy of Christian ethics has tempered national values in France as in other Western countries. Almost 85 percent of the population has been baptized Roman Catholic. About 800,000 Protestants (less than two percent of the population) and 300,000 Jews (less than one percent of the population) worship in France today.

The Region Parisienne has a population of 9.9 million, and Paris itself has about 2.3 million. Approximately 470 Americans, including civilian and military, work directly or indirectly with the U.S. Embassy. The American colony around Paris numbers 15,000. Five to six thousand American students are enrolled in university-level education in Paris and the provinces. Paris receives about 1.2 million American tourists each year.

Government

The Constitution for the Fifth Republic was approved by public referendum on September 28, 1958. Under the Constitution, the President of the Republic is elected directly for a seven-year term. The President names the Prime Minister, presides over the Cabinet, commands the Armed Forces, and concludes treaties. The President may submit questions to a national referendum, can dissolve the National Assembly, and, in certain defined emergency situations, may assume full power.

The Constitution provides for a bicameral Parliament consisting of a National Assembly and a Senate. The Assembly's 490 deputies are elected directly for five-year terms. All seats are voted on in each election. The Senate, chosen by an electoral college, has 283 members elected for nine-year terms. One-third of the Senate is renewed every three years.

The French political spectrum is expected to continue with at least four major political groups: Gaullists, Giscardian-Centrists, Socialists (headed by President François Mitterand, who was elected in May 1981), and Communists. The Gaullists and the Communists have strong political organizations. The Socialist and Giscardian-Centrist parties are more diverse in their membership and philosophies. Numerous smaller parties have limited national political impact.

Arts, Science, Education

By tradition, France has encouraged intellectual activity and has been a haven for artists; by necessity, the technician is favored today. Prestige lies with the young technicians on whom the nation's future depends, as well as with the advanced schools and institutes that prepare them.

The arts, though still lively in France, are less pertinent to the average person. Historically, arts and artists have played an outstanding role in French life. Paris is a vast monument, and museum collections speak for themselves. Contemporary painters, musicians, actors, and their critics still enjoy prestige, and any important exhibition, concert, or premiere receives much acclaim and discussion in the press and in cafes.

The intellectual, per se, is still the paragon in an educational system which encourages intelligence as an end in itself. Younger intellectuals often reject academic life and passive theorizing for active involvement in politics, social questions, journalism, and the arts (especially the innovative, productive French cinema). The Academy, founded in 1680, still tries to rule the language and the structure of French intellectual life, but it speaks to an older generation, not to the more practical, active, and iconoclastic younger generation.

The blend of the aesthetic and sensual delights of its artistic side with the active rationality and discipline of its intellectuality continues to give Paris its special excitement. The technological society is imposing change, and the resulting quarrel between traditional values and modern exigencies makes France a marketplace for ideas, a society trying to adapt to new challenges, and an interesting place to live or visit.

Commerce and Industry

Since World War II, France has been transformed from a largely agrarian economy with modest mineral resources and small, fragmented industrial sectors into a diversified, integrated, and sophisticated industrial power. Although still a large exporter of agricultural produce, France has also become a major producer and exporter of steel, chemicals, motor vehicles, nuclear power stations, aircraft, elec-

tronics, and telecommunications equipment. This rapid industrialization was fostered by France's charter membership in the European Economic Communities, and by heavy U.S. direct investment, particularly between 1955 and 1974, reaching $6 billion at the end of 1976. French investment in the U.S. also grew in the mid-70s and was $1.6 billion at the end of 1976.

In the early postwar period, several major enterprises were nationalized, including the four largest banks and certain aerospace, automotive, and other manufacturers. Railroads and public utilities were nationalized before World War II. Government intervention in the productive sectors is greater than in the U.S., but France is mainly a free market economy, and foreign investors enjoy full national treatment. In 1979, the GDP was $535 billion, about $10,010 per capita. Half of France's foreign trade is with EEC partners, headed by the Federal Republic of Germany. Imports from the U.S. in 1977 totaled almost $6 billion, or just under seven percent of all French imports. Major categories were machinery, mechanical appliances, and precision instruments.

As in most other developed countries, France's main economic problems in the late 1970s were inflation (over nine-and-a-half percent annually) and unemployment (five to five-and-a-half percent).

Transportation

Paris is the transportation center of Europe. Air and rail service connects Paris to all major European cities, and frequent, direct air service is available to the U.S. and other countries. Air service between Paris and the

U.S. is provided by TWA, National, and several foreign airlines. Extensive air and rail service also connects Paris to all other parts of France.

The two airports serving Paris are Orly, south of the city, and Charles de Gaulle to the north. TWA lands at Charles de Gaulle Airport; National flights land at Orly. Both airports are about 45 minutes by bus from the two official air terminals within the city. Frequent and convenient bus service is available between the airports and Paris. Invalides Station (Aerogare) has trains to Orly Airport; Porte Maillot Terminal has service to Charles de Gaulle Airport.

Public transportation in Paris (and in other major French cities) is excellent. The metro (subway), although crowded during rush hour, is fast, and trains are frequent. Trains and stations are well maintained and routes are clearly marked. Buses also provide excellent service; several lines run near the U.S. Embassy. Many prefer the convenient, economical public transportation to the frustrations of rush-hour driving. Taxis are plentiful and reasonable, but difficult to get during rush hour. Taxis have meters, but since rate increases are frequent, new authorized rates are posted on the windows until meters are adjusted. Rates also increase at night. A radio-taxi service operates at all hours at any location; its telephone numbers are: 205-7777, 203-9999, 200-6789, 587-6789 or 739-3333.

Because of parking problems and heavy traffic in Paris, most people use public transportation weekdays, and drive only on weekends and vacations. Garage space (or street parking) close to residences is limited, and is usually too small for large cars. Repairs are

costly and service is slow. Parts, tires, tubes, and accessories for American cars are scarce and, when available, expensive. A newer small car is preferable to an older large one.

Third-party liability insurance is compulsory and must be obtained from a company accredited in France. Rates are determined by model year and horsepower and are much higher than in the U.S.

Small garages, narrow streets, parking difficulties, and high insurance rates make it more economical, practical, and convenient to own a European car such as Audi, Austin, Citroen, Mercedes, Peugeot, Renault, Rover, Simca, Triumph, or Volkswagen.

Yellow headlights are compulsory for night driving on French highways, and cars registered in France must be equipped with yellow bulbs or plastic yellow shields. Directional signals are compulsory.

Unleaded gasoline is not available in France. Driving is on the right. The modern autoroute system is good, but tolls on these roads are high. Other roads, although narrow, are usually in good condition.

By the French Government decree of December 1959, all cars must be equipped with TV-interference resistors. These resistors (cables connecting spark plugs to the distributor) are manufactured especially to eliminate or considerably reduce radio and TV interference originating from cars. This wiring can be installed in France.

The visitor may drive in France with a valid license or with an international drivers permit. A French driving permit may be obtained on presentation of a valid license from another country.

Communications

Telephone and telegraph services to and from Paris compare to those in any large American city. Mail and parcel post service from the U.S. is good. Airmail from New York to Paris takes two or three days, and surface mail from 10 days to a month. Parcels are subject to French customs inspection in order to assess applicable duties.

Radio reception in France is usually excellent; shortwave sets are a pleasure but not a necessity. Reception from BBC-2 is clear on longwave. Radios with longwave may be purchased at reasonable prices. It is illegal to ship or hand-carry a two-way CB radio transceiver to France.

TV programs are aired on three channels from 9:30 a.m. to midnight on Sundays; on weekdays they begin at 12:30 p.m., are discontinued for several hours during the afternoon, and resume during the evening until about midnight. Reception with U.S. sets is impossible, since broadcast standard and frame frequency differ. Black-and-white and color TV sets may be rented locally.

Although newspapers and periodicals are expensive (triple American prices), almost as many copies are sold in France as in the U.S. French papers contain as much news as U.S. papers, and leading French publications generally contain more foreign news and commentary.

English-language newspapers, including the International Herald Tribune and British daily papers, are available on many newsstands each morning. European editions of Time and Newsweek are available at French newsstands (kiosks) at reasonable prices, but most magazines (Vogue, Harper's Bazaar, Holiday, Good Housekeeping) are about double U.S. prices.

Subscriptions to the International Herald Tribune, Time, and Newsweek are reasonable. Subscriptions sent via open mail cost the international postal rate. Brentano's, Galignani, and Smith's bookstores specialize in American and English books; however importing newly published books from the U.S. is cheaper and faster.

A well-stocked "American Library in Paris" at 10 rue du General Camou in the Seventh Arrondissement has good American and English literature. Library facilities are open to everyone, and the attached lending library is available to subscribing members. America's Benjamin Franklin Library, which serves as a documentation reference center on the U.S., is on the Left Bank near the major universities. The U.S. Embassy also maintains a small but excellent reference library.

Health

France (Paris in particular) has many skilled doctors, surgeons, dentists, oculists, opticians, and other specialists; but those who speak English charge high fees.

The American Hospital of Paris, in a suburb, is well equipped and has a staff of U.S. physicians, including one surgeon. The consulting staff includes outstanding French doctors. The general standard of medicine at the American Hospital is high.

Dental care is average. Many U.S.-trained French dentists are available, but fees are high. Americans coming to Paris to live should first have dental work done at home.

French hospitals are of two types: state hospitals (considered below American standards), and private clinics, mostly for surgery, many of which are comparable to small U.S. hospitals.

Some American drugs have French equivalents available locally, produced and marketed under French names. Many of the latest U.S. drugs, however, are unavailable locally.

France's general level of community sanitation is adequate, but handling of meats and other foods in the open markets appears to be below U.S. standards.

Upper respiratory infections occur frequently, mainly due to the damp climate. Many persons have chronic colds and sinusitis; children are particularly susceptible. More serious diseases are not prevalent. Occasional outbreaks of various contagious diseases occur, but no more so than in any other country.

Few precautionary measures need be taken with respect to health conditions in Paris. Warm clothing is advised for those arriving from tropical areas or from the U.S., where offices and homes are kept warmer than is customary in Paris. Influenza immunizations should be taken in the fall.

Fatty foods, French wines, and rich sauces are responsible for some gastrointestinal disorders. Paris water is safe to drink, but is hard due to high amounts of calcium carbonate. Some mothers perfer to give their children bottled water. Rural sanitation is not as advanced as in Paris, so one should use caution in the use of drinking water in towns or villages. Pasteurized milk is available.

Major Cities

PARIS, one of the world's loveliest cities, has grown from a tiny settlement on an island in the Seine to a great metropolis with an atmosphere completely its own—and incomparable to any other. It is renowned as a center of intellectual, cultural, and artistic life, and for centuries has attracted writers and painters from every part of the earth. Paris is a city of wide, tree-lined streets; beautiful historical monuments, squares, and parks; distinguished educational institutions; a broad range of industries and commercial facilities; and a well-deserved reputation for both haute couture and haute cuisine.

Some of Paris' most notable tourist attractions are the Louvre, the magnificent Cathedral of Notre Dame, the Arc de Triomphe, the Avenue des Champs-Elysees (the famous street whose name means "Fields of Paradise"), the Eiffel Tower, La Madeleine (Church of St. Mary Magdalene), and the beautiful Place de la Concorde. There is an almost endless list of historical and interesting places to visit.

Benjamin Franklin, the first American diplomatic agent to France, established his office in 1771. The first consul chosen for this post was selected by Congress in 1776, and the archives of the Paris consular office date back to October 1, 1801.

Many places of special historical and architectural interest near Paris can be visited within one day; the Palace of Versailles (royal residence of Louis XIV), Malmaison (residence of Napoleon and Josephine), Palace of

Fontainebleau (2,000 rooms showing the luxury in which French kings and emperors lived), and Chartres (grandest Gothic cathedral in France).

Greater **BORDEAUX** , with a population of 598,800, is the fourth largest city in France (Bordeaux proper has 267,000 people). The capital of the Department of the Gironde and of the Region of Aquitaine, it lies on the Garrone River, some 35 miles inland from the Atlantic Ocean.

American representation in Bordeaux dates from March 1778, when a commerical agent, John Bondfield, was appointed after France formally recognized the independence of the Thirteen Colonies. Since President George Washington commissioned Joseph Fenwick of Maryland as consul to Bordeaux in 1790, Bordeaux has had a U.S. Consulate continuously, except during the Franco-American dispute of 1798–1800 and the Nazi occupation of 1941–1944.

The city hosts 40 other diplomatic establishments; 10 are career posts.

Bordeaux has beautiful 18th-century architecture and several new modern areas. The river flows through the city's center, and ocean-going vessels usually are docked within a few yards of the U.S. Consulate General. Beyond Bordeaux lies some of the world's foremost wine producing country (divided into five major districts—Medoc, St. Emillion, Graves, Entre-deux-Mers, and Cotes de Bordeaux). Resident and visitor alike can visit beautiful vineyards and their chateaux, drink great wines, and learn something of the intriguing, colorful, and complicated winemaking process.

The Bordeaux consular district includes 19 Departments in southwestern France, covering an area of 47,810 square miles, or almost one-fourth of the country. About eight million people live in this area. Other important cities in the district include Toulouse (383,176 inhabitants); Limoges (147,406); Pau (85,860); and Poitiers (79,725).

About 2,200 American citizens reside in the district. Of these, 150 live in the Bordeaux area. In addition, about 300 American students attend universities in Bordeaux, Poitiers, Pau, Biarritz, and Toulouse.

LYON, which forms the core of the second largest metropolitan area in France with a population of about two million, is the country's third largest city. It is at the confluence of the Rhone and Saone Rivers, some 300 miles southeast of Paris. Old Lyon lies between the rivers and up the hill on the west bank of the Saone. More recently, the city has grown on the east bank of the Rhone and west into the foothills bordering the Saone. The climate is similar to that of Washington, D.C.; it is humid, but snow or long hot spells are rare.

Lyon takes pride in its history, which goes back to Gallo-Roman times when it was Lugdunum, the Roman capital of Gaul. Many remaining buildings and artifacts remind residents and visitors alike of Lyon's origins in antiquity, its importance in the growth of French Catholicism, and its role at one time as the leading silk and cloth manufacturing city in the Western world.

However, the city is not all history. It has a new metro system, a shopping center (the largest in Europe), and a modern international airport, Satolas. Lyon is a well-maintained and clean city where the old and the new are integrated into an attractive whole. Houses virtually unchanged since the 17th century, multistoried office complexes reaching for the sky, wide tree-lined boulevards, and beautiful parks blend to make this a lovely, livable city, whose residents still consider the traditional art of French cooking important enough to take a two-hour lunch.

Lyon, a world-famous medical center, particularly in cancer research, has excellent medical facilities readily available. Lyon has many fine hospitals, but Americans have used the French Clinque or private hospitals for their needs.

The first U.S. Foreign Service post in Lyon opened in 1826, when James Fenimore Cooper was appointed as its consul.

MARSEILLE, with a population of one million, is France's second largest city and a cosmopolitan Mediterranean crossroads. As well as residents of French stock, thousands of Italians, Armenians, North Africans, Greeks, and other Mediterranean peoples live in Marseille.

About 1,500 Americans, many of them students, reside in the U.S. consular district, which comprises the 10 Departments of Aude, Aveyron, Bouches du Rhone, Gard, Herault, Lozere, Pyrenees Orientales, Tarn, Var, and Vaucluse. About 75 Americans live in the city proper. Thousands of American tourists transit Marseille each year, but few stop over because the city is not an important tourist attraction. English-speaking residents of all nationalities other than French

number about 1,000, and a few of the French speak English.

Marseille, the ancient city of Massilia (2,500 years ago), is a contrast of old and new. Along with modern buildings and conveniences are narrow winding streets and centuries-old structures. The city is colorful with its picturesque harbor, cliff drive along the sea, and tree-lined boulevards—a typical Mediterranean port city, full of life and vitality, dependent largely on maritime traffic. France's largest port, Marseille handles more cargo than any other Mediterranean port, and ranks third in Europe. The new deep-water port in nearby Fos handles tankers up to 250,000 tons, and is linked with pipelines to the north and Germany. In a few years, Fos will produce about eight million tons of steel a year.

Marseille is 20 miles east of the mouth of the Rhone River. The old city surrounds a small natural harbor, which for centuries gave Marseille importance as a port, but today is little more than a picturesque setting for fishing boats and yachts at the foot of the Canebiere, the city's main street.

The modern port, a man-made harbor, with its docks, other ship-handling facilities, and annexes extends north from the old port. The hills around Marseille rise to over 1,000 feet, and the nearby coast is rocky, with only a few beaches. The vast modern city is varied in character.

The climate resembles that of Los Angeles, but with little or no smog. The wind, the mistral, sometimes blows at gale strength, making winters seem much colder, but also alleviating summer heat.

NICE, in the Department of Alpes Maritimes, is in the renowned

Riviera resort area, 30 miles from Italy and 135 miles from Marseille. The city's international airport is two-and-a-half miles from the center of town. It handles more passenger traffic than any airport in France outside Paris. Daily flights link Nice with all parts of the world. Work is now in progress south of the airport to extend the airport to meet the demands of the area.

Besides an advantageous location, Nice has an excellent climate and a stimulating variety of official, social, and cultural contacts. The population of Greater Nice, which stretches from the Var River to the independent corporation of L'Abadie, is now 350,000, making it the fifth largest city in France. Most of its labor force is in tourist-related occupations. Next to tourism in economic importance is the cut flower trade. The Nice wholesale flower market ships its products to distant points and to the large perfume essence industry in nearby Grasse. Light industry, electronics, and construction are also important employers in the Nice area.

As a resort town, Nice has a pleasing, well-rounded character. It has miles of lovely promenades on the sea, an opera house, theaters, casinos, and many good restaurants. Nearby mountains serve as a scenic backdrop and as a protection from cold winds. Most of all, Nice has sunshine; the sun shines about 325 days a year.

The U.S. consular district of Nice comprises five French Departments: Alpes Maritimes, Ales de Haute Provence, Hautes Alpes, Corse du Sud, and Haute Corse. The Consulate, opened in 1818, is one of the oldest consular offices. Except during a 10-year gap in the 1870s and during the German occupation in World War II, it has been operating continuously. Nice was a part of the Kingdom of Piemont when the Consulate was opened—well before the region became a part of France in 1860.

Principal diplomatic officers assigned to Nice are accredited also to Monaco. That Principality covers an area of 447 acres, roughly the size of New York City's Central Park, and has 25,000 inhabitants. France conducts Monaco's foreign relations in most areas abroad, and provides a French citizen to act as Minister of State. These relations are based on an 1861 treaty signed by Napoleon III and the Prince of Monaco. This treaty was last renegotiated on July 17, 1918. The present sovereign is Prince Rainier III of the Grimaldi family, the oldest reigning dynasty in Europe. He has been married for 25 years to American actress Grace Kelly.

Monaco is divided into four sections: La Condamine, containing the commercial section, market, and port; Monaco-Ville, the "capital city" area where the palace and most of the government buildings are located; Monte-Carlo, containing the casino, opera-theater, luxury apartments, beaches, and beach clubs; and Fontvieille, the industrial section, containing a new commercial port. Monaco has the character of a deluxe resort city; it is built on a series of terraces with steep roads and street stairways; gardens, lovely plants, and palm trees are everywhere.

Located on the Franco-German border in Alsace, **STRASBOURG** is a charming city with much cultural activity. The surrounding country is picturesque and full of recreational opportunities. The city, like others in the Rhine Valley, enjoys a moderate climate, although temperature changes can be sudden and, for most Americans, sunny days are too few.

Strasbourg, a proud and historic city with a 2,500-year-old past, retains a pleasing provincial character without the hectic rush of a large capital. Yet, as the seat of the Council of Europe, and as the meeting place for several international organizations (such as the European Parliament), the city has a cosmopolitan air which draws upon its binational past. A good speaking knowledge of French is essential in Strasbourg. German is helpful in understanding the Alsatian dialect, which is widely spoken in the smaller towns and rural areas of Alsace.

The U.S. consular district covers a large portion of Eastern France, with nine Departments that include all of the regions of Alsace and Lorraine, most of Franche Comte, a part of Champagne, and the Territory of Belfort. The scenic Vosges Mountains run through the middle of the district, dividing areas subject to Germanic influence from those that are not. The district has about 4.7 million inhabitants and, besides Strasbourg, has several important cities: Nancy and Metz in Lorraine, Colmar and Mulhouse in Alsace, Chaumont in Champagne, Besancon in Franche Comte, and Belfort. Heavy industry and mining are in northern Lorraine and southern Alsace, but agriculture and light manufacturing predominate in the rest of the district. Alsace, in particular, has a reputation as one of the most export-oriented areas in France. Large numbers of migrant workers in the area's industries, combined with a significant number of French workers from the area working in Germany and Switzerland, add special dimensions to labor conditions in the district.

The universities of Strasbourg, Nancy, Metz, and Besancon are leading centers of higher education in France, and make an important contribution to the area's intellectual life.

Strasbourg itself (population 260,000), the district's largest city, is also the cultural and commercial center of Alsace. The city has been an important Rhine port for over 2,000 years, and its historical traditions and monuments are rich and varied. Dominating the city is the single spire of one of the most beautiful cathedrals in Europe. Cultural opportunities include the outstanding Opera du Rhin, a fine city orchestra, and the only national theater outside Paris. The University of Strasbourg, with 24,000 students from all over the world, is a recognized leader in the fields of law, economics, and medicine.

Strasbourg's role as a major commercial and manufacturing center is enhanced by its key positions near the geographical center of the European Common Market. Already the hub of an international rail and water transportation network, the city has the largest coal port in France and is becoming an important petroleum refining center. It also has several well-known breweries and a large metal-working industry.

International organizations, such as the Council of Europe, most of whose 20 members have resident ambassadors, give the city an interesting diplomatic character. Also, periodic meetings of the Council's Consultative Assembly and the European Parliament bring parliamentarians from all over Europe to Strasbourg, and provide a good sampling of the European perspective on the continent's problems.

Established in 1949, the Council of Europe represents the first formal attempt in the postwar period to draw the nations of Western Europe into closer political union. Although overshadowed today by the European Communities, it is nevertheless a broader-based organization whose pioneering actions in human rights have brought it justified renown. Also, its work in regional and local planning; harmonization of national legal systems; public health; and youth, educational, cultural, and environmental affairs has made solid progress in developing a European body of doctrine and practice in these fields.

Besides the seasonal influx of tourists, the American presence in the district is considerable. More than 50 large U.S.-owned multinational corporations have plants and subsidiaries in eastern France, and American investment in French-controlled businesses is extensive. American Chambers of Commerce are located in both Alsace and Lorraine.

About 1,000 Americans attend universities in the district each year as full-time or part-time students, and many American colleges have junior year programs at French universities— eight in Strasbourg alone. U.S. professors come to the area's universities on sabbatical or as exchange professors. Also, several hundred retired Americans, mostly of French origin, have settled in the area. Four of the largest American military cemeteries in France are in the district.

Strasbourg is considered one of the best medical centers in France. Excellent doctors and surgeons are available, as well as the best in hospital care. All the latest drugs are known and in use, and the Hospital Civil and some of the clinics are equipped with diagnostic laboratories.

Recreation

Paris

Paris has more museums, art galleries, and places of historical interest than one could normally visit, except on an extended stay. French- and English-language tours of Paris and its environs are always available.

Touring around Paris is a popular leisure activity. Many world-famous French chateaux are within a one-day drive. The Bois de Boulogne in Paris, and the Forest of Meudon, Versailles, and Fontainebleau provide hundreds of acres of parks and woods for hiking, picnicking, and horseback riding.

Weekend trips can be made to English Channel coastal resorts (Deauville, Honfleur, Trouville, Le Touquet), about 125 miles from Paris, as well as to Mont St. Michel and the chateau country of the Loire Valley. One can also make long weekend visits to Atlantic Coast resorts (La Baule is about 250 miles away); Luxembourg and Belgium, and Baden-Baden, Stuttgart, and Frankfurt in Germany. Rail transportation from Paris is excellent. Local tourist agencies arrange bus trips.

Well-equipped public playgrounds do not exist, but Paris has many neighborhood parks where children can play. Children can ride bicycles safely in the suburbs but not in the city. There are some recreational facilities in and around Paris for adults and children. Ice skating is available at indoor and outdoor rinks during winter. Private clubs provide facilities for tennis, but permission to play is difficult to obtain. White tennis clothing is required at all private courts in France. More public tennis facilities are becoming available, but still not enough to fill the demand.

Indoor and outdoor swimming pools are available, but quite crowded during summer. The closest sand beaches on the English Channel are 125 miles from Paris at Deauville-Trouville.

There is some fishing within 100 miles of Paris. To fish in public lakes or rivers one must have a "permit general." To fish in private lakes or rivers, a permit must be obtained from the district (Department) in which the waters are located. Those who wish to hunt in France either must belong to a hunting club such as St. Hubert, by buying a yearly share which provides hunting on reserved grounds, or must be invited to private hunting grounds.

Ski resorts in the French Alps, Switzerland, and Austria (overnight by train) provide slopes for all levels of skiing.

The availability of entertainment in Paris is practically unlimited. The Opera House, one of the city's most elegant buildings, provides grand opera on a lavish scale. Excellent plays are staged at many theaters, but one must speak French to enjoy them fully. Many concert halls host a variety of musicians. Younger persons may join clubs entitling them to student rates for musical and theatrical events. Cinemas show American films with French subtitles as well as European films.

Bordeaux

The only public sports facilities in Bordeaux are eight swimming pools and a gym which are ordinarily re-

served for private athletic associations or school groups. The city has several private tennis clubs and a golf club. Also, a good golf club and tennis clubs are at Arachon, 40 miles away. Membership dues and initiation fees are high; club facilities are limited. The area has several clubs for flying, sailing, riding, fencing, archery, judo, sculling, and gymnastics; for team sports like baseball, rugby, and hockey; and for organized activities such as bicycle touring and skiing.

The most interesting spectator sports events are football (soccer) and rugby association matches.

Children can enjoy a formal public garden in the center of the city and a large park on the outskirts. Only neighborhood kindergartens and the two public parks have playgrounds with swings and other equipment. Organized sports and activities for children are available at schools or clubs.

Boating, fishing, swimming, or other water sports abound at many area coastal resorts. A broad sandy beach stretches southward 150 miles from the mouth of the Gironde to the Spanish border. Principal resort colonies are Arachon (40 miles), Biarritz (113 miles), and St. Jean de Luz (120 miles). The Basque country near the Spanish border is popular for hiking, cycling, and camping. Skiing in the Pyrenees (three hours by car) begins in December and continues until April. Ski resorts are expanding rapidly and facilities are excellent. The picturesque Dordogne River Valley has good hunting, fishing, and camping facilities.

Good entertainment is available during the season (October to April). The Grand Theatre presents plays, operas, ballet, and symphony concerts, and eminent artists from Paris often take leading roles. Since 1950, a three-week music festival in May has brought instrumentalists of world rank, chamber music groups, choruses, orchestras, and theatrical companies to the city. A number of plays in French are presented each season by out-of-town groups. Several modern movie houses show French, American, British, and other films, all with French dialogue, except for a few features in English with French subtitles. Bordeaux has several excellent small museums.

Lyon

Lyon is a convenient point for travel within France or to nearby Switzerland and Italy. An inexhaustible supply of touring sites, historical monuments, and museums is available for every taste. Virtually every known recreational activity has its followers in Lyon, and the district abounds in recreational advantages. In fact, the area probably has a greater variety of recreational advantages, facilities, and resorts than any other in France.

All major sports are popular. Most of the French Alps lie within the district and provide excellent skiing, hiking, and climbing. Lyon has many sports facilities which provide facilities for swimming, golf, tennis, and other sports.

The types of entertainment found in any major U.S. city are readily available, popular, and reasonably priced in Lyon. However, Lyon is conservative compared to Paris, and the nightlife is surprisingly quiet.

Marseille

Marseille is convenient to many large cities—Paris (500 miles), Rome (600 miles), and Barcelona (325 miles).

However, the district itself also has varied scenery and points of interest.

Marseille is linked to Lyon, Paris, and the north by an excellent autoroute. To the east at Toulon is the French Navy Mediterranean Headquarters, which is visited regularly by units of the U.S. Sixth Fleet. To the west are the blooming university cities of Montpellier and Perpignan on the Spanish border.

The region around Marseille offers excellent touring, sight-seeing, hiking, and picnicking. Also available in the district are skiing and mountain climbing in the Alps, as well as fine seaside amusement and recreation on the Cote d'Azur.

One should not swim at Marseille beaches, as sewage is pumped into nearby water. It is possible to swim from the rocky coast in or near the city. The best beaches are around Cassis, a scenic resort town 13 miles away, or beyond. Good beaches are also the same distance west of Marseille.

The historic cities of Arles, Avignon, Nimes, and Orange, to the northwest, are easily reached by train, bus, or car; and the charming university town of Aix-en-Provence is less than an hour away.

Sports facilities in the area are good. Marseille has a large public sports center with two indoor swimming pools. Several private clubs also have pools. Rowing, yachting, and tennis clubs charge nominal dues. There is a golf club near Aix-en-Provence, about a 30-minute drive from the city. Hunting and fishing are good, and skin diving and spearfishing are popular. Horseback riding, rugby, soccer, volleyball, and basketball are other popular sports.

Most French sports equipment is expensive, but skin diving and fishing gear (masks, spears, etc.) is cheaper than in the U.S. Camping equipment is of excellent quality and reasonably priced, but sports clothing is more expensive.

Hunting weapons, or the use of animals in hunting, is not restricted. However, hunters must buy annual licenses, and each community maintaining a hunting preserve charges a yearly fee for use of its property.

There is a variety of entertainment in the Marseille district. Several good movie houses show European and American films with French soundtracks. On occasion, an English-language film with French subtitles is shown. Frequent plays, operas, operettas, and concerts are performed during winter. An open-air theater is used in summer. The July music festival of Aix-en-Provence is internationally famous. Plays and operas are held in the Roman theater at Orange and in many other cities.

Marseille has a zoo, and several museums and art galleries. A few Marseille bookstores carry small selections of English books, mostly classics, and there is an English bookshop in Aix-en-Provence.

Each September the city hosts an international fair, consisting mainly of industrial and commerical exhibits. A smaller Spring Fair, begun in 1963, features boats, camping, "do-it-yourself" equipment, furniture, antiques, and household appliances.

On Sundays during the summer, bullfights are held at the ancient Roman amphitheaters in Aries and Nimes. Horse races are held often at Marseille's two tracks and at one in Aix-en-Provence, except in winter.

Many restaurants can be used for dinner parties, but they are expensive. American-type nightclubs are few and expensive.

Nice

As a tourist site, the Riviera is justly famous. Nice, its most famous resort, is in Provence, a region with numerous places of scenic beauty and historical and artistic interest.

Mountain resorts are nearby for winter sports. The ski stations of Valber, Auron, and Isola 2000 can be reached by car in less than two hours, and several Italian resorts are within four hours. All sports equipment and attire are sold locally, but prices are higher than in the U.S. Styles in sports clothing are the same. Equipment may be rented at the ski resorts, and lessons are available.

Ample facilities also exist for other sports. Four golf courses are located from 30 to 45 minutes from Nice, and several tennis clubs are in Nice and nearby cities. The most popular outdoor activity is ocean swimming. The moderate climate permits swimming about five months a year on the many area beaches. Wind surfing is a new sport which has become very popular.

The Riviera handles thousands of tourists each year and has ample entertainment facilities. Carnivals, flower shows, film festivals, auto shows, and open-air theaters are operated in various municipalities and by private groups. Many movie theaters show American films with French soundtracks. Art exhibits and concerts are frequent. Large casinos at Nice,

Cannes, Monte Carlo, and Juan les Pins sponsor dances, concerts, and theatrical attractions, in addition to gambling. Many excellent restaurants offer regional French and Italian cuisine, as well as traditional French specialities. Prices for theaters, opera, and restaurants are about the same as in the U.S.

Monaco's National Day celebration on November 19, the feast of Prince Rainier's patron, St. Rainier, includes a mass and *Te Deum* at the Cathedral, luncheon at the Palace, an afternoon football match, and a gala at the Monte Carlo Opera in the evening.

In the Nice area, facilities and services for photography are ample. All varieties of film are sold, but prices for film and film processing are about 20 percent higher than in the U.S.

The International Herald Tribune and popular American magazines are sold at local newsstands. An English bookstore in Nice carries a good selection of classic and contemporary writers. An English-American library on the grounds of the English church has a varied, although somewhat dated, selection of books. The Nice-Matin is the most important local daily newspaper. Several weekly and biweekly papers are also published.

Strasbourg

The plain and the foothills of Alsace (the Strasbourg area) are dotted with small, picturesque villages. In spite of wartime destruction and intensive rebuilding, many houses remain from the 15th and 16th centuries, and the distinctive Alsatian architecture is attractive and interesting. Fine examples of Romanesque and Gothic religious architecture, as well as 18th-

century civil architecture, can be found all over Alsace. On the foothills and lower slopes of the Vosges are the vineyards of Alsace, which are the sources of some fine white wines and an unusual rosé. Higher up on rocky promontories, the ruins of medieval castles look out over the Rhine plain to the Black Forest in the distance.

The Alsatians are French citizens with a Germanic cultural background. In Alsace, both French and Alsatian, a German dialect, are spoken by nearly everyone. In the countryside, Alsatian predominates, and many older peasants do not understand more than a few words of French. German is widely understood and spoken.

Several Western European countries are easily accessible from Strasbourg. In Switzerland, Basel is about 80 miles away; Bern, 170; and Geneva, 219. Paris is 300 miles away. The distance to Heidelberg, Germany, is 85 miles; to Munich, 170; to Frankfurt, 138; to Bonn, 214; to Luxembourg, 130; and to Innsbruck, Austria, 260. Opportunities to visit interesting places are innumerable, and exceptionally good guidebooks are available in Strasbourg. Baden-Baden, 45 minutes away, has a golf course and a famous casino with a fine restaurant and dancing.

Trains are fast, relatively inexpensive, and reliable. Across the Rhine in Germany, the excellent toll-free Autobahn (expressway) system connects Strasbourg with Basel, Frankfurt, Stuttgart, and Munich. A newly completed French autoroute (expressway) makes Paris an easy four-to-five-hour drive from Strasbourg, but tolls are high. Traffic on French secondary roads is intense, particularly at certain times of the day and in the summer, and the American driver may have initial difficulty adjusting to the aggressive driving habits of some French motorists. Bicyclists, motorcyclists, and pedestrians also encumber the roads both in town and country. Gasoline prices are the highest in Europe. Although unleaded gasoline is not available in Strasbourg, it is available in nearby Germany.

Strasbourg's three tennis clubs have good clay courts, and one club has covered courts. The Strasbourg Golf Club, about four miles from the city, set in the charming countryside, has a nine-hole course generally playable all year.

Year-round swimming is possible indoors at the Schiltigheim municipal pool and at the older Strasbourg municipal bath. There are beautiful outdoor swimming pools in Strasbourg near the Rhine Bridge, in nearby Kehl across the river, and at Obernai, an attractive town in the Vosges foothills about 30 minutes away. Skiing is available in season in the Vosges and in the Black Forest within 50 miles of Strasbourg. The season generally lasts from December through March. Strasbourg has a fencing club and a bowling alley.

Some trout fishing is possible in the small streams of the Vosges and the Black Forest. For hunters, Alsace offers excellent shooting. Quail, partridge, pheasant, and hare are abundant, and deer and wild boar are in the mountains. Opportunities for horseback riding and lessons are plentiful at Strasbourg, and the surrounding areas of Alsace have numerous clubs for both ring and trail riding. The Vosges mountains offer the serious hiker and camper invigorating air and scenic vistas. L'Orangerie and the Contades, are two favorite parks for afternoon walks.

Athletic competitions of all kinds, including soccer, basketball, tennis, water polo, swimming, boxing, and wrestling can be seen in and around Strasbourg.

Two municipal theaters provide a full program of plays, concerts, ballets, operas, and operettas. The city's radio-TV station gives free tickets to various concerts throughout the year. The opera, symphony orchestra, and municipal ballet are particularly good, and many well-known chamber orchestras, quartets, and soloists come to Strasbourg on tour. A music festival is held every June, with eminent visiting artists and first-class orchestras.

Strasbourg has about 20 cinemas. Movies are in French and German, and occasionally in English. Most English and American pictures are shown with French soundtracks.

Notes for Travelers

Frequent, direct air service to Paris is available from the U.S. and most countries of the world. There is also excellent rail service into Paris from other parts of Europe.

Unless a French identity card is obtained, a visa is required for those who plan to be in France more than three months. No vaccination or health certificate is required of travelers from the U.S., Canada, or Western Europe.

The importation of hunting weapons and ammunition is strictly controlled by customs regulations. Allowable weapons are classified as "rifles and carbines with fixed barrels, rifled bore, single-shot or repetition fire, or center-fire cartridge, with the caliber of the arm less than 6.5 mm., or more than 8.2 mm. Immediate registration is required.

Practically every faith has a church in Paris. There are two prominent American churches—the American Pro-Cathedral (Episcopalian) and the American Church in Paris (an interdenominational Protestant organization)—as well as St. Joseph's Roman Catholic Church for the English-speaking community. In certain Catholic parishes, where English-speaking foreigners ordinarily reside, the French priests speak English. The two Protestant churches mentioned have American pastors, and members of the congregations are mainly U.S. citizens. Several Jewish synagogues in the Paris area hold services in French and Hebrew.

Bordeaux, Lyon, and Marseille each have an Anglican Church which offers services in English; in Strasbourg, English-language services are held in the Temple Neuf Chapel (Anglican and interdenominational); and in Monaco, an American priest is attached to St. Charles Roman Catholic Church. Throughout France, particularly in the large cities, most major denominations are represented, but their services usually are conducted in French. Strasbourg also offers German-language services.

A number of well-known international service and charitable organizations have affiliations in Paris (YMCA, Red Cross, Rotary, and others).

The French unit of currency is the franc, with an exchange rate of 4.48 francs to U.S. $1 (March 1980).

The metric system of weights and measures is used in France.

The U.S. Embassy in France is located at 2 avenue Gabriel on the historic Place de la Concorde, Paris. There are Consulates General in Bordeaux, at 4 rue Esprit-des-Louis; in Lyon, at 7 quai General Sarrail; in Marseille, at No. 9 rue Armeny; and in Strasbourg, at 15 avenue d'Alsace. The Consulate in Nice, at 3 rue du Docteur Barety, also serves the Principality of Monaco.

German Democratic Republic

The **GERMAN DEMO-CRATIC REPUBLIC** (G.D.R.), whose state and society are dominated by the role of the Social Unity Party of Germany (SED), is composed of the former German provinces of Western Prussia, Brandenburg, Mecklenburg, Thuringia, and Saxony. It was founded in 1949 as a separate entity, and formal diplomatic relations with the United States were established on December 9, 1974. Its capital, East Berlin, is part of a "divided city," but travel in this Communist country is different and exciting. Excellent opportunities exist for touring and sight-seeing in the many charming towns, villages, and castles. The people of the G.D.R. are generally hospitable to foreign visitors.

Area, Geography, Climate

The G.D.R. covers an area of 41,767 square miles and is roughly the size of Kentucky. It has a population of 16,759,000 (1981), with an average population density of 409 per square mile (compared with 628.3 in West Germany). The most heavily-populated areas run along the Dresden-Leipzig-Erfurt axis to the south; the lowlands between Berlin and the Baltic Sea are more sparsely settled.

The G.D.R. is located on the northern European plain and is com-posed of two distinct geographic areas: the northern lowlands, which stretch from the Baltic coast south to the Leipzig Basin, covering two-thirds of the country; and the southern high-lands, which make up part of the mid-dle European sub-Alpine system. The northern lowlands, having been formed by glaciation, are characterized by a sandy topography dotted with forests and lakes, as in the Mecklen-burg lake district and the Brandenburg midlands around Berlin.

A belt of loess loam separating the northern lowlands and the high-lands to the south comprises the agri-cultural heartland of the G.D.R. The southern highlands contain several distinct regions, including, from west to east, the Harz Mountains, the Thu-ringian Forest south of Erfurt and Weimar, the Erzgebirge south of Karl-Marx-Stadt, and the Elbsandstein Ge-birge (often referred to as Saxon Swit-zerland) southeast of Dresden near the Czech border.

The G.D.R. shares a 1,381-mile border with the Federal Republic of Germany to the west and southwest; a 430-mile border with Czechoslovakia to the south; and a 456-mile border with Poland to the east. To the north it borders the Baltic Sea. The G.D.R. lies in the temperate zone and has a continental climate somewhat moderated by the Baltic. The climate in Berlin is similar to that in the northeastern U.S., with cooler summers and milder winters.

The principal rivers of the G.D.R. include the Elbe, the Saale, the Spree, the Havel, and the Oder. Over one-fourth of the G.D.R.'s territory is covered by forest, most heavily concentrated in the north. The least forested region is the Leipzig-Halle-Magdeburg area, which is an important industrial district. The G.D.R. has lignite coal reserves estimated at 25 billion tons, 60 percent of which are located near Halle, Leipzig, and Cottbus. The country has suffered from chronic water shortages because the Thuringian basin, one of its principal industrial areas, has traditionally been one of the most poorly watered regions in Europe. The G.D.R.'s coefficient of water use is nearly 100 times higher than the world average, a problem that has been met by the construction of numerous water reservoirs in the area.

Population

The G.D.R. and East Berlin have a combined population of 16,759,000, subdivided into urban and rural. The country has experienced a decline in population since 1967, when its birth rate dropped to −0.2 percent. The population of the territory that now constitutes the G.D.R. was 16,745,385 in 1939 and rose to 19,102,000 in 1947. An estimated two million citizens have emigrated to West Germany since the republic was founded in 1949. This emigration resulted in a critical loss of manpower, which was reduced only by the construction of the wall along the boundary with West Germany and around West Berlin in August 1961.

The G.D.R. is divided into 14 districts, plus East Berlin. Its major cities, in addition to East Berlin, include Leipzig (pop. 547,000), known for the biannual Leipzig Trade Fair and as the home of Johann Sebastian Bach; Dresden (502,000), formerly the capital of Saxony and a city still rebuilding after its near total destruction in World War II; Karl-Marx-Stadt (302,000), formerly the industrial city of Chemnitz; and Rostock (210,000), the principal port on the Baltic Sea. The ethnic population of East Germany is 99 percent German; a small Slavic group, the Serbs, form a minority of 100,000 around Cottbus and Dresden. The entire population speaks German, which is the official language. Thirty-five years after World War II, women still outnumber men by 116 to 100 in the G.D.R. Over three-fourths of the female population is employed. The divorce rate is among the highest in the world. Fifty percent of the population are affiliated with the Protestant Church; eight percent are Roman Catholic; and 42 percent have no religious affiliation.

Government

The Socialist Unity Party of Germany (SED) dominates all facets of the G.D.R. society. The program and decisions of the SED are binding on all state organs. The heads of the principal state organizations, and Council of State, the Council of Ministers, and the National Defense Council, are all high-ranking members of the SED. Four other parties officially exist in East Germany: the Christian Democratic Union, the Liberal Democratic Party of Germany, the National Democratic Party of Germany, and the German Peasants Party. However, all four have recognized the leading role of the SED in their party programs.

The SED was founded in 1946 in the Soviet-occupied zone of Germany by the forced merger of the Communist Party of Germany (KPD) and one wing of the Socialist Democratic Party. The SED holds a party congress at five-year intervals to set down the guidelines for the next five-year plan. The SED Central Committee meets about four times a year to review and implement policy decisions. The day-to-day leadership function is performed by a 25-member Politburo. It is headed by a General Secretary, currently Erich Honecker, and is effectively the ruling political body in the country.

Mass organizations and mass media in the G.D.R. are controlled by the SED and serve to integrate and mobilize the population to support party policy. The largest organizations include: the Free German Trade Union (FDGB); the Free German Youth (FDJ); the Democratic Women's Alliance of Germany (DFD); the Society for German-Soviet Friendship (DSF); and the Society for Sport and Technik (GST).

The Volkskammer (People's Chamber) meets about five times a year to adopt new laws initiated by the SED. The votes are, with rare exceptions, unanimous. Volkskammer delegates are elected every five years from a single list presented by the National Front, an umbrella organization composed of all parties and organizations in the country and a prime vehicle for political integration. The G.D.R. adopted a new Civil Code in 1974 to replace the German Civil Code adopted by the Reichstag of the German Empire in 1896. The original code, with subsequent amendments, is still used in the Federal Republic of Germany and in West Berlin.

Arts, Science, Education

The main direction of much artistic endeavor is the building of a Socialist society and culture. However, the foreign resident and the G.D.R. citizen are also able to enjoy the classic accomplishments of the past, as well as the "probing of the outer limits of permissibility," especially in the fields of literature and drama. Thus, on the stage one can enjoy a classic drama by Goethe or a controversial contemporary reinterpretation of a Goethe theme like Plenzdorf's *The New Sorrows of Young Werther*. East Berlin has two opera houses and a variety of theaters, including the internationally known Brecht Theater. Performances are in German, except for some operas, which are performed in the original language. Excellent museums can be found, particularly in Berlin, and there is the world-famous collection of the old masters in Dresden. The woodcuts of German classic artists such as Duerer and Gruenewald can be viewed, plus exhibits of the genius of the architects, designers, and artists of the famous Bauhaus School.

Scientifically and technologically, the G.D.R. represents a nonhomogeneous mixture of the Soviet system of polytechnical training and the classic German university. This situation leads G.D.R. scientists, as well as the authorities themselves, to turn strongly toward the West in an effort to bridge the scientific-technological gap which has developed during 35 years of isolation. However, despite the gap, the G.D.R. remains one of the leading scientific-technological countries of the world, and nourishes the long-time German tradition of excellence in these fields.

Commerce and Industry

Gross national product of the G.D.R. was $89.1 billion in 1979, quoted in 1979-value dollars. The annual growth rate is 2.3 percent. Fifty-eight percent of the land is arable. Major agricultural products are feed grains, potatoes, sugar beets, meat and dairy products. Major industrial products are steel, chemicals, machinery, precision engineering, and fishing vessels.

The G.D.R. has one of the world's largest deposits of brown coal and also has substantial amounts of potash and some uranium. It is a member of the Council for Economic Mutual Assistance (CEMA), and the U.S.S.R. and other Eastern European countries are the major trading partners. The Federal Republic of Germany (F.R.G.) is the major trading partner in the West. Exports in 1979 were $17.3 billion, led by machinery and equipment and chemical products. Imports during the same period were 19.2 billion; raw materials, fuels, and agricultural products were the major items.

Transportation

Good all-weather roads connect the major cities of the G.D.R. Important towns and places of interest are served by trains, which are inexpensive and punctual. The larger cities are also served by the government airline Interflug at moderate prices. There is a country-wide network of bus lines, but since they are not very comfortable and are often crowded, they are not usually used by Americans, except for short tours or trips.

Berlin is serviced by a number of airlines, which makes it possible to fly directly to and from all Eastern European capitals as well as the Western European capitals. One can also travel by rail or car and, with a valid visa, can enter the G.D.R. at all authorized border crossing points without difficulty.

In East Berlin one may travel by streetcar, subway, bus, and taxi. During rush hours, public transportation is crowded, but traffic delays of any duration are seldom encountered. Taxis are difficult to flag down from the street, but can be obtained if requested by phone. Fares for all intercity transportation are relatively inexpensive. The streetcar and subway systems service all of East Berlin, and also cross to West Berlin under carefully controlled circumstances at limited crossing points. The major interchange point (Friedrichstrasse Station) is easily reached by intercity transport. Residents of the nearby Leipziger Strasse apartment complex often walk across Checkpoint Charlie to West Berlin and use its excellent subway and bus system.

Ambulances are cream colored with a red cross on the side; fire trucks are red; and police vehicles are normally green and white with blue lights on top.

Adequate repair facilities for personal cars are available in West Berlin, and most Americans use the European Exchange System garage. Delays are often encountered, since the garage does not carry a large inventory of spare parts and must have them shipped in. However, cost of repairs is fairly reasonable, and most of the work is guaranteed for up to 90 days. German repair facilities are also used, but repairs are somewhat more expensive, and there is also a shortage of the necessary parts for American cars. At the present time there are no repair facilities for American-made cars in East Berlin.

Communications

International phone service is available to Western Europe, the U.S., and to most countries in the world through an international operator. Direct-dial calls are available to most Eastern European countries and to some Western countries. Cables for the West normally are sent through West Berlin Bundespost. Transit time for mail from East Berlin to the U.S. is slow (one month plus), but international mail from Bundespost (Berlin West) takes only three to five working days.

Armed Forces Network operates AM and FM radio stations, and these stations can be heard throughout Berlin. In addition to the U.S. network, the British and French Forces also operate radio stations in Berlin on a 24-hour basis.

A U.S. Military TV station (AFN) in West Berlin can be received in East Berlin with an outdoor antenna. The picture ranges from snowy to adequate. Reception is excellent for two West Berlin and one East Berlin UHF stations, and one West Berlin and one East Berlin VHF stations. German stations broadcast about 10 hours a day; AFN-TV, about 12 hours a day. News coverage on AFN-TV and West Berlin stations is excellent for local and international news. The West Berlin stations broadcast at least one program a week in English.

The International Herald Tribune is sold at newsstands in West Berlin on the afternoon of publication. Also available on newsstands are major American and English newspapers, which generally arrive on the newsstands in West Berlin about one day after publication.

Health

Many German doctors and dentists practice in West Berlin, and some Americans consult them. A list of English-speaking doctors is available at the U.S. Embassy. Health insurance is available in East Berlin, and includes ambulance service and full medical and dental treatment. Emergency medical treatment is also available.

Health standards in East Berlin are generally comparable to those in the West. There are no epidemic contagious diseases, and no special health precautions are necessary. In Germany's sea climate, though, rheumatic conditions and upper respiratory diseases may be aggravated. Drinking water, dairy products, and other food products are under strict government control, and generally meet American standards of sanitation.

Rural sanitation is not as advanced as it is in East and West Berlin, so care should be taken in drinking water or eating raw fruits and vegetables in outlying towns or villages.

Major City

Berlin is located well within the German Democratic Republic. It is situated 110 miles south of the Baltic Sea on the North German Plain. The G.D.R. considers **EAST BERLIN** to be its capital, but the U.S. Government views it as one sector of the four-power city of Berlin. In 1945, the 20 districts of Berlin were divided among the four Allied Powers for administrative purposes, with the U.S. taking charge of six districts in the southwest; the British assuming responsibility for four districts in the west; and the French taking two districts in the northwest. The Soviet Union received the eight eastern districts, including the governmental and cultural center of pre-war Berlin. On October 7, 1949, the G.D.R. was founded, and it claimed the Soviet Sector of Berlin as its capital. The Soviets delegated rights and responsibilities to the G.D.R. at that time. The Western Allies do not recognize East Berlin as the capital of the G.D.R., and refer to East Berlin officially as the Soviet Sector of Berlin.

In the mid-13th century, Berlin began to develop from the smaller villages of Berlin and Coelln, located along the banks of the Spree River. It served first as the capital of the Mark Brandenburg, then of Prussia in 1701, and finally in 1871 of a united Germany. The city underwent a phenomenal population growth in the last quarter of the 19th century, from 827,000 in 1871 to 2,700,000 in 1900. Administrative changes, plus additional growth, brought the population to 3,800,000 in 1930. The present population of East Berlin stands at 1.1 million (compared with 1.9 million in the Western sectors of Berlin), with males constituting only 44.5 percent of the total population 35 years after World War II.

East Berlin was severely damaged near the end of World War II, and although the G.D.R. has restored some of the downtown area to its original 18th century style and has replaced some of the most famous examples of early 19th century "Berlin classic" architecture, there are sections of East Berlin, especially in the center along

the wall, which still bear the scars of wartime destruction. The center of modern East Berlin has been relocated away from the area close to the wall toward Alexanderplatz, a complex of modern buildings dominated by an imposing television tower, the second highest structure in Europe. There is currently much building in progress in downtown East Berlin, including modern hotels and a trade center being constructed by the Japanese.

The area of Berlin near Unter den Linden contains some of the most famous museums in Germany, such as the Pergamon, which houses the Pergamon Altar and the world-famous Ishtar Gate from Babylon. However, many of the art treasures once housed in these museums were removed during the war and are currently in West Berlin, a point of contention between East and West Germany preventing the signing of a cultural agreement between the two states. Also located in the center of East Berlin are two opera houses and 14 theaters. A smattering of movie theaters show mainly Soviet and East European films, but an increasing number of Western films is being shown.

Foreign diplomats can travel between East and West Berlin easily through one of the five checkpoints connecting the two sides of the city. Since February 1974, West Berliners have been able to take their cars into East Berlin, which has increased traffic in a city that still is free of the traffic problems found in most large cities. There are few Americans living in East Berlin, although the large American community in West Berlin has access to the East.

Americans living in East Berlin find that virtually all basic services and supplies are available from the local community, or on the market in West Berlin.

Recreation

Travel in the G.D.R. is interesting and exciting. Berlin is located east of center in the country, in the middle of a north-south axis. With the exception of Rostock on the Baltic coast, all the northern half of the G.D.R. is comprised of fairly small cities and towns with no major roads connecting them. Besides Rostock, about four hours by car from Berlin to the northwest, there are interesting cities along the Baltic coast to the east. The island of Ruegen off the northeast coast is popular for summer vacations. Ruegen is about five hours by car from Berlin. Just southeast of Ruegen, the small town of Greifswald offers a charming annual Bach festival in May. The main road from Ruegen-Greifswald to Berlin passes the villages of Ravensbruck and Oranienburg.

South of Berlin and due east and west, a network of highways (autobahns) connects all the major cities of the country. Close by, and actually contiguous to the southwestern crossing of West Berlin, is Potsdam, one of the showplaces of the G.D.R. Besides the summer and winter residences of Friedrich the Great, one can also visit the elaborate Orangerie and the Cecilienhof. It was at the Cecilienhof that the Potsdam Treaty of 1945 was signed, and the various meeting rooms have been maintained as a museum, with handout scripts in most languages explaining the G.D.R.'s view of what happened at Potsdam. About two hours due south on the autobahn from Berlin is Dresden, a city almost completely destroyed during World War II and rebuilt since, with part of the

inner city rebuilt in the original character. Close by Dresden is the "Saxon-Switzerland" and Meissen, with its factories that produce world-famous porcelain. The mountain range in this southeast area of the country, known as the Erzgebirge, borders on Czechoslovakia.

Moving west along the southern border, the next interesting area is in the southwest section centered around Erfurt, Weimar, and Jena. Known as the Thuringia from the forest south of the area, these cities and their outskirts offer a range of sight-seeing activities. Naumburg has as its center a 13th century cathedral; Jena prides itself on its university, founded in 1558, which has had Schiller, Viktor, and Hegel as professors. Eisenach is famous for the Wartburg Castle where Luther translated the Bible into German, and counts Johann Sebastian Bach as one of its former citizens. Suhl and Oberhof are climate and health resort areas, and Oberhof serves as the training center for the national teams in ski jumping and ice skating.

For in-town sight-seeing, Weimar offers a very pleasant and inexpensive hotel, said to have been the favorite of Napoleon. The city has prohibited cars in the center of town, but visitors can walk from the Goethe house to the Schiller house and through parks and museums. Proceeding north along the western border, the Harz Mountains provide a number of charming small towns very popular in both winter and summer. To the southeast is Leipzig, second largest city, and home of the spring and fall Leipzig fairs.

There are few opportunities for participating in active sports in and around East Berlin, but within the city limits are some public tennis courts.

Hunting also is available to visitors in the area. West Germany, however, provides an extravaganza of sports facilities.

Good entertainment can be found throughout the East Berlin district. Movies are limited in scope and by scarcity of theaters, and are shown in German. Live entertainment, on the other hand, is found throughout the season (September to June), is quite reasonable by Western price standards, and ranges in quality from good to outstanding. In addition to several theaters, including the famous "Bertolt Brecht Berliner Ensemble," there are, as centers of opera and ballet, the Staatsoper and the Komische Oper located in the downtown area. These two theaters feature operas ranging from Grand Italian to modern German, and, they serve occasionally for concert performances.

Notes for Travelers

Visitors can arrive at Schoenefeld, the G.D.R. international airport which services East Berlin from Copenhagen, Amsterdam, and Paris. It is also possible to arrive by train from Copenhagen, or to drive by private car from Denmark, Sweden, or the Federal Republic of Germany. In the latter case, much time can be lost at border crossings, in passing railroad crossings, or in the small towns en route. Speed limits are rigidly enforced.

Persons wishing to visit the G.D.R. are advised to obtain a visa entitlement certificate through a travel bureau, which then can be presented at any G.D.R. embassy, or at a border crossing point, for a visa. No visa is necessary for a one-day (returning before midnight) visit to East Berlin from West Berlin. A passport should be carried.

Types of weapons which may be imported (after application approval) are sporting rifles, shotguns, pistols, and revolvers. Rules are strictly enforced.

Only limited religious facilities are available in East Berlin. For the most part, Americans attend West Berlin churches and synagogues, both local and military.

The official currency unit of East Germany is the Mark, which is divided into 100 *pfennigs*. The East Mark is pegged to the West German Mark one to one. The rate of exchange with the U.S. dollar fluctuates.

Standard units of weights and measures follow the metric system.

Special note: Visitors to East Germany should not attempt to assist anyone to leave the country illegally, should not make critical comments of the regime, and should photograph only obvious tourist sights.

The U.S. Embassy in the German Democratic Republic is located at Neustaedtische Kirchstrasse 4/5, East Berlin.

Germany, Federal Republic of

The **FEDERAL REPUBLIC OF GERMANY** (F.R.G.), formed from the Länder which comprised the three Western Occupation Zones and the Saarland, has been a sovereign state since 1955. It is a country of broad variations in its geography and culture, and is today one of the world's great industrial powers, and probably the most dynamic of the major Western European countries.

Area, Geography, Climate

The F.R.G. is composed of 10 states or Länder in addition to Land Berlin (West Berlin), which has a special status and is not a constituent part of the Federal Republic. Of these, North Rhine Westphalia (where Bonn, the capital, is located) is first in population although fourth in area, Bavaria being the largest. West Germany's total area is 95,930 square miles (about the size of Wyoming).

West Germany has five distinct geographical areas and a wide variety of landscapes. From north to south the areas are: the North German lowlands; the hills and low mountains of the Mittelgebirge; the West and South German plateaus and mountains (including the Schwarzwald); the South German Alpine foothills and lake country; and the Bavarian Alps with the Zugspitze (Germany's highest mountain—9,721 feet) near Garmisch. The greatest rivers are the Rhine, the Weser, the Elbe, and the Danube. The first three flow to the north and empty into the North Sea. The Danube starts as a spring in the beautiful and historic town of Donaueschingen in southwest Germany, and flows east 1,725 miles to the Black Sea. Lake Constance (Bodensee) is the largest lake (only part is in Germany), and lies between Germany, Switzerland, and Austria.

Germany is in the temperate zone and has frequent changes of weather. The average temperature in January (the coldest month) varies at sea level from 34° F to 27° F, and in the mountains drops to under 21° F. In July, the hottest month, average temperatures range from 61° F to 68° F.

Population

The F.R.G., including West Berlin, has a population of 61,388,000 (1981). Today, more than 85 million people speak German as their mother tongue.

Many American soldiers, government employees, businessmen, and their dependents live in Germany, and their relations with the German population are generally good. Most Germans recognize and deeply appreciate the considerable help rendered after the war by the Marshall Plan, and the aid given by millions of individual Americans, churches, and charitable organizations. Many Germans have been in the United States and speak English; most are interested in sharing their views with Americans.

Government

West Germany's constitution is called the Grundgesetz (basic law) and provides strong guarantees of individual rights. Only those matters requiring centralized direction, such as foreign policy, foreign trade, defense, and monetary policy, are reserved to the federal government. Other tasks of government, such as education, social service, public order, and police, are left to the control of the Länder.

The Lower House of Parliament, the Bundestag, has 496 members popularly elected every four years. The Upper House, the Bundesrat, composed of 41 deputies appointed by the Land governments, insures the cooperation of the Länder and must consent to important legislation. The Federal President is elected every five years. The Federal Chancellor, who defines and administers policy, is replaced during any legislative period when the Bundestag votes "no confidence" and agrees upon a successor. The largest political parties are the Christian Democratic Union (CDU) and its associated group, the Christian Social Union (CSU), and the German Social Democratic Party (SPD).

The City of Berlin, both East and West, has a special status. Since 1945, it has technically been under the military occupation of the U.K., France, the U.S., and the Soviet Union. In 1948, Soviet measures forced the German administration of the city to restrict its activities to the part occupied by the Western Powers, now known as West Berlin. West Berlin has its own local government with a mayor and an elected assembly. All federal laws must be expressly adopted by this assembly if they are to apply to Berlin.

Arts, Science, Education

Cultural life in present-day Germany is rooted in the rich and abundant past. Bach, Mozart, Beethoven, Brahms, and Wagner in music, and Goethe, Schiller, Kleist, Heine, Buechner, and Hauptmann in literature have their secure place among many other composers, poets, painters, and sculptors of the classical, romantic, and modern ages.

It was only after 1945 that the German reading public, conscious of its own classical poets and writers and those of the first decades of the 20th century, came to know again or for the first time the works of the writers who had left Germany after 1933. At the same time, foreign literature found its way once more to Germany. Names like Anouilh, Faulkner, Eliot, Hemingway, Sartre, and Thornton Wilder are as familiar in Germany as they are in their own countries. Meanwhile a new generation of German authors has come into its own. Young writers like Grass, Boell, and Uwe Johnson combine the command of contemporary novel techniques with concern about social reality.

The Federal Republic occupies fourth place in the book-publishing world. The Munich State Library with two-and-a-half million volumes is the largest in Western Germany. The principal university libraries are located in Goettingen, Cologne, Frankfurt, Munich, Freiburg, Heidelburg, and Tübingen.

Contemporary painters reflect the achievements of the great German art movements of this century—the Bruecke of 1906 in Dresden (Kirchner, Heckel, Schmidt-Rottluff, Macke, Nolde); the Blue Rider of 1911 in Munich (Kandinsky, Klee, Marc, Feininger, Jawlensky); and the Bauhaus and the Dadaism and Expressionism of the twenties (Grosz, Schlemmer, Dix, Beckmann, Baumeister, Hofer, Schwitters). Abstract art was born in Germany more than 50 years ago. Architects have been faced with the task of blending that which remained of the old cities with new conceptions, thus combining requirements of the modern age with respect for ancient traditions. The artistic form is characterized mainly by the clean, functional building.

The museums have been rebuilt, and in most cases rearranged, according to modern taste. Many have been converted into exhibition halls which change shows frequently. The Deutsches Museum in Munich and the Germanisches National Museum in Nuremberg, as well as the Romano-Germanic Museum in Mainz, the Roman-Germanic Museum in Cologne, and the Alexander Koenig ornithological museum in Bonn, are unique.

Germany is a classical land of opera. Some 60 regular opera companies with orchestras are under contract to the state or to a municipality, and have soloists and choruses with permanent tenure. The Bayreuth Festival is the outstanding one of all such festivals, each year showing new productions by the grandson of Richard Wagner. Operettas are equally popular. Symphony concerts are popular in the

cities. The Berlin Philharmonic Orchestra, the Munich Philharmonic, and the Bamberg Symphony Orchestra are exclusively concert orchestras. In addition, radio orchestras have won an outstanding place in music.

Germany has many theaters, and the subsidies they receive from the Länder and the municipalities are substantial. Theater is part of the cultural life of a German community. It occupies a lively place in intellectual life, and seasonal schedules are arranged to blend opera, concerts, plays, and ballet. More than a third of all plays staged are by foreign authors. Stage festivals with programs of theatrical plays are held at regular intervals and on special occasions. The most famous of these is the Oberammergau Passion Play, which is given every 10 years. Annual events are the Shakespeare Week at Bochum, the Hersfeld Festivals, and the Ruhr-Festival at Recklinghausen.

The educational system of the Federal Republic provides for compulsory school attendance from the ages of six to 18. Adult education is encouraged by evening courses at "Peoples' Universities" (Volkshochschulen), and by a system of public libraries.

The term "science" (*wissenschaft*) as used in Germany includes the humanities, and social and natural sciences. Germany has about 3,500 scientific centers of teaching and research of all kinds, both in and out of the universities.

Including West Berlin, the Federal Republic has 47 universities, many technical institutions, and a large number of teacher-training institutions and ecclesiastical seminaries. Tuition is free. German universities are considered to be at the upper division and graduate level by American standards. Admission by an American directly from high school is therefore not possible.

Germany has no state church. The two main churches are independent of the state, but they can still claim the historically based state services and receive financial support. Their ecclesiastical property rights are guaranteed. The state also guarantees freedom of religion. About 49 percent of the population is Protestant Lutheran and 45 percent is Roman Catholic.

Commerce and Industry

The Federal Republic is the leading industrial country in Europe. Its main industries include coal, iron and steel, machinery, electrical goods, vehicles, and chemicals. Germany imports food, raw materials, and a wide range of manufactures; it exports machinery, vehicles, electrical goods, and other industrial and handicraft products. Germany has a favorable balance of trade.

Until the winter of 1973, job openings outnumbered the unemployed, despite the presence of over two million foreign workers. However, unemployment has risen during the past five years, and now over one million workers are jobless. Workers belong to large and powerful trade unions which bargain collectively for wages and working conditions and participate in industrial policy and managerial decisions.

The Federal Republic is a member of the European Economic Community (EEC) and also continues to trade on a large scale with a second block of

European countries, the European Free Trade Association (EFTA), and with the U.S. The Federal Republic accounts for almost 10 percent of total world trade.

Transportation

The transportation system of Germany's major cities consists of electric trains, streetcars, and buses. Subways are found in Berlin, Hamburg, Frankfurt, Munich, and Bonn, and are under construction in Düsseldorf. All cities have taxi service, with rates slightly higher than those in New York City. As in other heavily populated areas, transportation facilities are overtaxed.

Germany's biggest transport undertaking is the Federal Railways (Deutsche Bundesbahn) with about 25,000 miles of track. Besides the famous international express trains, a number of new international express services, called TEE trains, have been brought into service. Connections to and from the larger cities are excellent, and most capitals in Europe can be reached within 24 hours. Since it is not normal practice for conductors to call the station on German trains, and trains stop only a minute or two, one should be at the door of the train ready to leave immediately on its arrival. Rail fares in Germany are lower than in the U.S.

Due to its geographical position in the heart of Europe, Germany is a center of European air traffic. Almost all important international airlines operate services to and within the Federal Republic. Frankfurt has the principal international airport.

Because of its extensive network of roads, Germany is an ideal country for motoring. Most people find a car desirable not only for transportation to work, but also for shopping and recreational purposes. With the express highways or autobahns, which connect most major cities in Germany, and good secondary roads, all parts of the country can be reached easily by car.

Driving in Germany is on the right. The speed limit in cities, unless otherwise posted, is 50 kilometers (31 miles) per hour; on state roads, 100 kilometers (62 miles). There is no longer a general speed limit on the autobahns, but certain stretches may have posted limits. Road signs are in keeping with the international system.

Since foreign cars brought into Germany, or purchased after arrival, are imported duty-free, certain rules must be observed when selling them in Germany. German law permits the sale of private cars without payment of duty after they have been registered in Germany for two years. If a car is sold within two years, customs duties must be paid by the buyer unless he is a member of a diplomatic mission or consular establishment. Cars must be inspected by the German Technical Inspection Team before they can be licensed, and then must be reinspected every other year.

Communications

Worldwide telephone and cable service is available throughout West Germany, and postal facilities provide excellent service. Airmail to the east coast of the U.S. usually is delivered in two to three days.

Two large regional radio stations, the North German Radio in Hamburg and the West German Radio in Cologne, provide much of the programing for local stations. Music and entertainment make up 50 percent of the programs, cultural subjects are 13 percent, and the remainder is news reporting. The British and American Armed Forces in Germany have their own networks, and USICA (International Communication Agency) operates RIAS (Radio in the American Sector) in Berlin, broadcasting to German citizens in the Eastern Sector of Berlin and the Soviet-occupied zone of Germany.

Two Germany-wide government-operated television networks (called programs) and a third regional "program" broadcast daily, carrying a variety of plays, operas, documentaries, sports, movies, news broadcasts, and general entertainment. About 85 percent of all households have TVs; about two-thirds of those are color.

Radio reception is good. The British and American Forces networks provide AM and FM newscasts, entertainment, and music. German stations also broadcast FM stereo.

The operation of citizen's band communication radios is not allowed in Germany. The frequency band 26960 KHz through 27280 KHz is allocated to other uses, such as public safety, law and order, commerce, and trades and sports clubs. The prohibition is directed against every type of radio equipment capable of transmitting a radio signal in this frequency band, regardless of power, including home installations, walkie-talkie type portable sets, and toy radios if the toy is capable of emitting a radio signal.

The Federal Republic and West Berlin have some 1,200 daily newspapers with a total circulation of 17 million copies. About 6,500 periodicals have a total distribution of 152 million copies. More than 20 illustrated magazines have a total circulation of more than 20 million. The German Press Agency (Deutsche Presse Agentur-DPA) is the leading German news agency, with offices throughout the world. The two leading U.S. news agencies, Associated Press and United Press International, also service German newspapers.

The International Herald Tribune and the Stars and Stripes (daily) are available. Time and Newsweek magazines are current, and a wide selection of other American periodicals are for sale on the stands. British newspapers are available. Excellent bookstores in the larger cities have limited selection of books in English.

Health

Throughout West Germany, particularly in the large cities, medical and dental care is excellent, and a full range of services and facilities is available. The Bonn University Clinics belong to one of the most advanced medical research centers in the country, and the clinic standards are similar to those in the best U.S. hospitals; Berlin offers good medical and dental care and provides many and varied hospital facilities; Düsseldorf University has good clinics and fine doctors and dentists (a large number speak English); both Frankfurt and Hamburg offer good hospitals and competent English-speaking doctors and dentists; Munich's health facilities are very good and include Harlaching Hospital, one of the largest and most modern in Germany; and Stuttgart also is known for its excellent hospitals and competent medical care.

The F.R.G.'s community sanitation and public cleanliness are about the same as those in American cities of comparable size.

Most of Germany has a moderate sea climate with no extreme differences in temperature; rheumatic conditions and upper respiratory diseases may be aggravated, though. Children especially are bothered with respiratory problems and colds. No epidemic contagious diseases of a serious nature exist. Sporadic cases of polio, typhoid, diphtheria, and scarlet fever occur, but never in epidemic proportions. The frequency is no greater than that in the U.S. Americans are exposed to seasonal epidemics of chicken pox, measles, and mumps.

Drinking water, dairy products, and other food products are under strict German Government control, and generally meet or exceed American standards of sanitation.

Major Cities

BONN differs from other Western European capitals in several important respects. Although it has become the political nucleus of the Federal Republic, it is in no sense the cultural and economic center, and is by no means the largest city in the country. For the last 200 years Bonn has been primarily a university town, and many would like to see it stay this way. On the other hand, it must meet the rapidly expanding requirements of the federal government. With its heavy traffic, somewhat antiquated road network, and extensive new construction, Bonn gives the impression of bursting at the seams.

Until Bonn was chosen as the provisional capital of West Germany in 1949, it was known chiefly for its university and as the birthplace of

Ludwig van Beethoven. The house in which he was born is now a museum and is probably the best known of Bonn's attractions. Between Cologne and Bonn is the Palace of Bruehl which is used during state visits for large receptions and during the summer months for public concerts. Bonn has a large concert hall (the Beethovenhalle) and a new city theater. One of the museums in Bonn contains the skull of the famous Neanderthal man. The University Medical Clinics on the Venusberg are famous, and there are several good hospitals.

The city was badly damaged by the war and had not been restored by 1949, when it became the provisional capital. Facilities had to be found or built to provide housing and office space for the German ministries and the various embassies, foreign journalists, and others. Existing facilities were converted to government use and new ministries were built in simple and functional style. Most embassies were able to find or build structures for chanceries in Bonn, but residences of the diplomatic corps are located throughout the area from Cologne to Remagen—a distance of some 40 miles.

Bonn has a population of 300,000.

Although **WEST BERLIN** (actually the western sectors of the City of Berlin) is often depicted as a beleaguered isle in a "red sea," it also is an enclave of vitality, prosperity and courageous democracy within the East. Despite the threat from the East during the postwar years, West Berliners carried on with confidence and courage—a confidence and courage measured by the excellence of their theater, music, and art; the gaiety and

humor of their cabarets; and the impressive physical reconstruction of the city and investment in its economic future. To remain detached from the personality and the problems of Berlin is impossible. Living in this indomitable city is a singular experience.

Berlin lies well within East Germany, about 110 miles south of the Baltic Sea on the North German Plain. Besides having a unique geopolitical position, the city is unusual in that it remains under protective military occupation by the three Western powers—the U.S., France, and Great Britain. These three powers share with the Soviet Union rights and responsibilities for the City of Berlin as a whole. The U.S. Ambassador to the Federal Republic of Germany doubles as Chief of Mission in Berlin, and as such, maintains both an office and a residence there.

Once the fourth largest city in the world, and the largest in Europe in 1939, Berlin developed from a cluster of settlements on the banks of the Spree River in what was once a glacial drainage valley. In its growth the city sprawled beyond the valley onto the surrounding flat sandy plains. The latitude of Berlin is the same as southern Labrador, but the climate is about the same as that of the northeastern U.S., except that summers are generally cooler and rainier. Winter temperatures range from 20° to 40° F, although they occasionally drop to 0° and below. There are periodic snowfalls, and spring arrives rather late. Graceful tree-lined streets, extensive woods, parks, and lakes spare Berliners much of the harshness and aridity of big city living.

As a showplace behind the Iron Curtain for Western economic, cultural, and political ideas, West Berlin has a high standard of living. It is the largest industrial city in Germany, and is also the most populous. The American community alone, including families, numbers about 14,000. There are, of course, the usual complements of journalists, students, educators, and representatives of business and religious organizations living in Berlin, as well as some 50,000 American visitors each year. In recent years, foreign workers from southern Europe and Asia Minor have come to constitute an increasingly significant portion of the labor force.

At the end of World War II Berlin, like the rest of Germany, was divided into four occupation sectors. Unlike the Federal Republic, however, Berlin formally remains occupied territory. The Allied Kommandatura, an inter-Allied governing body established in 1945 by a Four-Power agreement, continues to exercise ultimate authority in Berlin. Since 1948, the Soviets have not participated in the work of the Allied Kommandatura. The establishment in that year of a separate administration in the Soviet sector began the unnatural division of the city, which became virtually complete in 1961 with the erection of the Berlin Wall. In the Western sectors (West Berlin) the Allies gradually reduced their direct control over municipal affairs, exercising only those specific powers which they deemed necessary for the continued maintenance of their rights and responsibilities.

The working relations between the Allied Kommandatura and the Berlin City Government have been marked by close cooperation and reflect the fact that since the Airlift, the Berliners have looked on the Western Allies as protectors rather than as occupiers. With Allied approval, Berlin has developed close political, legal, economic, and cultural ties with the Federal Republic of Germany. These ties are vital to the continued maintenance of a free and prosperous city, and the Quadripartite Agreement of 1971 provided that they are to be maintained and developed.

The Berlin Constitution, adopted in 1950 with the approval of the Allies, provides for the governing of Berlin as a city-state, comparable to Hamburg or Bremen. A unicameral legislature, the House of Representatives, is popularly elected every four years. This parliament in turn chooses the Governing Mayor and votes on his nominations for the position of the Mayor (the Governing Mayor's Deputy) and the Senators—the department heads who make up the Governing Mayor's "cabinet." Responsibility for communal affairs is shared between the Senate and the administrations of the 12 districts which make up West Berlin. Berlin has a judicial system similar to that found in the various states of the Federal Republic.

West Berlin is an integral part of the West German economy and currency area. The city lives by importing raw materials and fuel and by exporting finished products. Tourism, administration, and education are also of importance. Free access to the territory of West Berlin is thus essential to the functioning of the economy. West Berlin is prevented from acting as a regional distribution center by its isolation from the surrounding German Democratic Republic. It is a distribution center only for its own population.

BREMEN is one of the oldest

and most interesting cities in Germany. It has a population of about 600,000. Its cultural attractions include a number of museums, art galleries, theaters, an opera, libraries, fine old buildings of considerable architectural and historical interest, and a number of parks.

The oldest and largest part of Bremen—including what was the walled city of the Middle Ages, now marked by the fomer moat—lies on the east bank of the Weser River. The area is now an attractive park. A newer part of the city, Bremen-Neustadt, is on the west bank of the Weser. In addition, there are numerous suburban housing developments including Neue Vahr, the largest of its type in Germany. The port and warehouse district lies to the north along the banks of the Weser.

Bremen's position as a port has been long established, and it is today an important processing and distributing center for such products as coffee, wool, cotton, grain, and tobacco. Its industrial life has expanded greatly and the city now has several large shipyards, a growing electronics industry, a large and modern steel mill, and an important aircraft firm.

Bremerhaven, 40 miles from Bremen with a population around 150,000, was an important transocean passenger port, but with the decline of that trade has become specialized in container shipment. It is also the largest single fishing port on the European Continent.

DÜSSELDORF, with more than 700,000 people, has the commercial, industrial, and cultural vigor of one of the largest population concentrations in the world—the Ruhr district of North Rhine-Westphalia. The city itself covers 93 square miles and is the district capital.

Although it is not in the Ruhr, Düsseldorf is often called the desk of the Ruhr because it is the financial and commercial center for industries of the Ruhr area. It is also an extensive shopping center, a popular city for culture and amusement, and one of Europe's leading sites for trade fairs and exhibitions. It is the seat of a stock exchange, a Land Central Bank, and regional headquarters of major German banks and of various regional organizations. The list of trade and professional associations with central offices in Düsseldorf is long, and the city serves as headquarters for the German Federation of Trade Unions, as well as for several trade unions. It is also considered the fashion center of West Germany.

Although Düsseldorf traces its founding back before the year 1100, most of the city today is of quite recent construction. Offices and residential buildings in contemporary style, wide straight streets, and heavy traffic, especially during rush hours, characterize its modern appearance. The city has attractive parks and ponds. Its center is marked by the well-known Koenigsallee with smart shops, sidewalk cafes, and a swan-inhabited lagoon. Certain suburbs, however, are highly industrialized.

FRANKFURT AM MAIN is the largest city in the State of Hessen. Since it is located in the center of the continent, it is a transportation hub. Frankfurt, with a population of 690,000 and dense suburbs, is 328 feet above sea level on the banks of the Main River, about 25 miles east of its confluence with the Rhine River at Mainz.

Frankfurt is a commercial and financial center. Some 500 American businesses have branches in the Frankfurt area. It is really Germany's financial capital, with nearly 270 credit institutes, branches, subsidiaries, and/or representative offices of major domestic, continental, and foreign banks. Twenty American financial institutions are represented in one way or another in Frankfurt. It is the seat of the Bundesbank, the equivalent of our Federal Reserve.

Frankfurt has a long and distinguished history of which it is justifiably proud. Not only has it been a center for trade fairs, book fairs, and banking for some 700 years, but until the Prussians took over in 1866, the Free City of Frankfurt was for 400 years the site of and responsible for the election of the Holy Roman Emperor. It has long, enduring, and illustrious ties with the New World—early visitors to Frankfurt included such distinguished Americans as William Penn, Benjamin Franklin, and Thomas Jefferson. The first Frankfurt Consulate in America opened in Philadelphia in 1826, and the first U.S. Consulate in Frankfurt opened in 1829.

There is a large foreign colony in Frankfurt, mostly Americans with the U.S. military, other government agencies, and American business organizations. Currently 47 countries have consular representation in Frankfurt.

The city of **HAMBURG** has a population of about 1.7 million. To some extent cut off from its hinterland in the German Democratic Republic and Eastern Europe since World War II, it remains a commercial gateway to the East and to the Scandinavian countries, and is Germany's "Opening to the World." With 75 foreign consulates, it is surpassed only by New York City in consular representation.

About 5,565 Americans live in the U.S. consular district, with an estimated 1,900 in the city of Hamburg. Among the large American business concerns with offices or plants in Hamburg are EXXON, Texaco, Conoco, Mobile Oil, Dow Chemical, U.S. Lines, Pan American, Swift Packing Co., Libby's Foods, Citibank, Chase Manhattan, Bank of America, and American Express Company.

MUNICH (München), capital of Bavaria and a metropolis of almost 1.3 million people, is the dominant commercial, travel, and political center of southern Germany. It attracts numerous conventions, meetings, fairs, and exhibits spanning a broad range of economic activities. Munich is also one of the world's outstanding metropolitan centers of culture and entertainment. Its excellent theaters, museums, and galleries present an unending round of high-quality cultural performances and exhibits, while the traditional Bavarian love of fun sustains a wide variety of spirited festivals, atmospheric night spots, and entertainment. It is a dynamic city with a multitude of recreational and intellectual possibilities.

Munich is Germany's third largest city, after Berlin and Hamburg. The city long ago outgrew its medieval walls, leaving a well-defined inner city or downtown area of concentrated activity. Munich is also Germany's fastest growing major city. Expansion continues at a fast pace with the construction of new suburbs.

The city lies about 1,600 feet above sea level on the southern edge of a relatively flat plain stretching from the foothills of the Alps, about 25 miles away, north to the Danube River. The Isar River flows through the eastern section of town on its way to join the Danube.

The climate is like that in northern parts of the U.S. Winters are cold but not severe, although temperatures on rare occasions fall below 0°F, and two to three feet of snow may blanket the ground in January and February. In spring and fall there are times of pleasant, clear, warmish weather, or prolonged stretches of rain and cloudiness. The temperate summers are relatively short with a fair amount of rain. The Foehn, an adiabatic wind, occurs here mostly in the fall and spring. It creates an anticyclonic atmosphere and a drop in barometric pressure which can cause headaches, listlessness, insomnia, and irritability.

STUTTGART, the cultural and political capital of Baden-Württemberg, is a city of more than 600,000 people, or if adjoining suburbs are included, more than 1.5 million. It is perhaps best known as the manufacturing site of Mercedes and Porsche cars.

Stuttgart's burgeoning chemical, electronic, and precision machine tooling plants have only partially changed the city's old world charm. Although thousands of U.S. troops are stationed in the area of Stuttgart, American influence on the city itself is slight, and a knowledge of at least some German is usually required to shop in the city's well-stocked stores.

HEIDELBERG, in the Land of Baden-Württemberg, has about 125,000 people, and is famous as a tourist attraction. It escaped the bombing of World War II and is thus a combination of the old and new, considered by many the ideal German city to visit. Its most distinct disadvantage is probably its very humid and overcast climate. It is neither very cold in winter nor very hot in summer.

The Land of Baden-Württemberg is an area of rolling hills and forests with a population of nearly nine million. In an area about the size of Switzerland (13,000 square miles) are such landmarks as the Black Forest and the classical university towns of Heidelberg, Tübingen, and Freiburg. Baden-Württemberg's climate is generally mild, with an average winter temperature of slightly above freezing and summer temperatures of 60° to 70°F. Humidity is relatively high, and average annual rainfall is 20 to 30 inches.

Heidelberg is the seat of Headquarters, U.S. Army, Europe (USAREUR), and of the Seventh Army, at which post the Foreign Service is represented by a Political Adviser (POLAD).

Recreation

Bonn

The Bonn area has excellent opportunities for cycling and hiking. The beautiful countryside invites motorists to explore the many charming villages, castles, and Roman ruins. During the winter months there is some skiing in the Eifel Mountains, about an hour away.

Within easy range of Bonn, the Rhine, Mosel, and Ahr valleys—with their vineyards, castles, and restaurants—offer opportunities for intensive exploration. In more distant parts of Germany, innumerable points of cultural and historical interest are easily accessible by rail or car on weekends.

Several challenging golf courses are available in the area, as are an international riding school, German tennis clubs, swimming and rowing clubs, and athletic clubs. American children may join the Plittersdorf (local German) soccer teams.

Hunting opportunities for both big and small game are good. Fishing opportunities are somewhat less extensive but well worth exploring.

Theater, art galleries, museums, and musical performances may be found in any German city with a population of 100,000. Although Bonn provides fewer recreational and cultural facilities than most European capitals, it has excellent facilities for a city of its size. Besides a small but good art gallery and museums, it has an excellent hall for musical events, the Beethovenhalle, in which concerts are given two or three evenings a week. The theater presents plays, ballet, or opera every evening. Düsseldorf is only one-and-a-half hours away by car, and Cologne is half an hour away. Operas, plays, first-rate symphony orchestras, nightclubs and good restaurants are found in both cities.

Berlin

Within the confines of West Berlin are a wide range of recreational and entertainment possibilities. There is boating and swimming (the latter discouraged for safety reasons in the numerous lakes, except at Wannsee); some skiing on natural snow slopes and on one of the "rubble" mountains in the city; rod and gun club activity;

and other outdoor sports such as golf, tennis, baseball, and football.

Berlin art museums have outstanding permanent collections, and in addition sponsor special exhibits from time to time. The Botanical Gardens and Museum and the extensive Grunewald and Tegel Forests have excellent facilities for family outings. Sections of the Grunewald and the Wannsee area are designated nature preserves; the best known of these is Peacock Island, a bird sanctuary in the Wannsee.

For the concert- and theater-goer, West Berlin presents a host of cultural attractions. The season is long, and the selection of programs rich and varied, offering an extensive classical and modern repertory. In addition to several modern concert halls (including the exciting new Philharmonic Hall and the Radio Symphony Orchestra Hall), there are 14 legitimate theaters, plus one theater for musicals and operettas, and one opera company in West Berlin. One of the highlights of the fall season is the Berlin Cultural Festival, which features a number of internationally famous ensembles and soloists. In addition, there are many local movie theaters. During the annual Berlin Film Festival in June many foreign-language films are shown.

A large number of fair to excellent local restaurants, hotels, cabarets, and nightclubs are available. Two restaurants, catering to the French community, offer first-class food at reasonable prices. Most German restaurants with German, international, or various national cuisines charge moderate to expensive prices.

An attempt has been made since the war to build up a Fasching (Mardi Gras) tradition in Berlin, and several big formal balls are given just before Lent.

Bremen

Bremen and the surrounding area provide adequate opportunities for sports and outdoor life. A country club, The Club zur Vahr, has two golf courses, tennis courts, and a swimming pool. Several tennis clubs, including one with three indoor courts, are available. Fees are reasonable. There is a large indoor swimming pool, and a number of public outdoor swimming pools in and near Bremen. However, the weather is seldom warm enough (by American standards) to make outdoor swimming enjoyable. Riding is available, using English saddles. Skiers may go to the Harz Mountains or further south to the Alps. Excellent hunting for boar, deer, hare, and fowl is available within easy distance of the city.

Bremen's North Sea weather has a reputation worse than it is. On average, the temperature ranges from slightly above freezing in winter to the mid-60s in summer. In the fall and winter, occasional prolonged periods of gray days are to be expected. For the rest of the year, however, the weather is tolerable to pleasant, although in the cooler range. Cloudless days are few, but many days are fine except for a short shower.

Bremen has many good movie houses showing the latest American as well as German and foreign films. Foreign films normally have German soundtracks. Opera, theater, and concerts are available in Bremen throughout most of the year.

Düsseldorf

Düsseldorf has several new and modern public indoor swimming pools, three miniature golf courses, and two bowling alleys. Except for an ice rink, no winter sports facilities are in the immediate area. The mountains of the Sauerland and the Eifel have some acceptable skiing slopes when the weather is favorable. Many well-marked hiking trails and bicycle paths are along the Rhine and in the woods around Düsseldorf and neighboring cities. Hunting and fishing opportunities sometimes can be arranged with local authorities. Public tennis courts and numerous private tennis clubs with membership fees ranging from moderate to expensive are also available. Membership fees for the golf courses in Düsseldorf, Cologne, and Krefeld are high.

An extensive program of opera, concerts, and theater, running for about 10 months of the year, has found an enthusiastic audience. Subscription and box office rates are moderate to expensive. The City Symphony Orchestra gives monthly concerts, as do several chamber music groups. The Düsseldorf Opera performs nightly from September through June, with occasional performances by the Corps de Ballet. The city's repertory theater offerings are diverse, and a political cabaret—the Kommoedchen—is widely known. The Amerika Haus in Cologne and Die Bruecke, an English-German society in Düsseldorf, present varied programs. The Film Forum presents high quality films from many countries, some of which are in the original language.

Frankfurt

Nearly every type of participant and spectator sport is available in the Frankfurt area. Golf, tennis, bowling, swimming, and riding facilities are good.

Opera, ballet, concerts, recitals, theater, and cinema also are available in Frankfurt and Wiesbaden at reasonable costs. Festivals and pageants are held several times a year, while commercial exhibitions and trade fairs are periodically held in Frankfurt.

The International Women's Club and the Steuben-Schurz Society are two German organizations with membership open to non-Germans. The latter is for both men and women and also has a youth group. The membership of the Union International Club is composed of American and German business and professional people and members of the consular corps. It has a swimming pool, tennis and badminton courts, and an excellent bar and restaurant. Teenager clubs, Boy and Girl Scouts, Brownies, PTA, and church groups are also available.

Hamburg

There are many playgrounds and parks in Hamburg. Beautiful woods and lakes in the vicinity are good for walking and picnics. Also, several golf clubs and an old, established tennis club offer facilities to foreigners, as do horseback riding and bowling clubs, and some rowing, gliding, and scuba diving groups.

Kiel, one of the Baltic resorts, is about one-and-a-half hours from Hamburg (direct Autobahn connection). Boats of the British Kiel Yacht Club are available for rent to members and sometimes to nonmembers. Membership in German clubs in Hamburg as well as in Kiel is also possible.

German theaters, cinemas, nightclubs, and restaurants offer entertainment comparable to that of other cosmopolitan cities in Europe. The Hamburg State Opera ranks with the first two or three in Germany, and is noted especially for its modern productions. Theater in Hamburg is considered among the best in Germany.

Non-German films are dubbed in German, although there are performances in English at one of the local theaters each Sunday morning.

Munich

Bavaria is a paradise for those interested in sports. World renowned German, Austrian, and Swiss ski resorts are within easy reach of Munich. Many of them feature learn-to-ski weeks. Several Munich sport shops sponsor ski weeks at popular resorts, as well as special ski plans which provide transportation and instruction at a different slope every weekend. Most large sport shops offer ski equipment rentals.

The city of Munich maintains three large public ice skating rinks, four large indoor swimming pools, and several large outdoor swimming pools. A number of golf courses are also available. For those interested in horseback riding, there are a number of riding clubs.

The facilities built for the 1972 Olympics have given Munich the opportunity to play frequent host to international sports events, such as equestrian competition, soccer matches, and cycling competition. Racing is also a popular spectator sport.

Bavaria is an excellent hunting and fishing area. Game includes deer, boar, chamois, capercaille, black cock, hare, fox, pheasant, partridge, and duck. The streams are well stocked with trout and there is some river char and pike fishing.

Walking tours through Munich are popular. From the various observation towers one can see the city of Munich and as far as the Alps. Many old churches are interesting to visit. Numerous art galleries and museums are free of charge, or charge only a small entrance fee. The Deutsche Museum, for instance, is the largest technical museum in the world. Several large castles in and around Munich are well worth visiting. Many miles of pleasant and scenic trails are in the Alpine regions and in the Isar valley on the outskirts of Munich. Also in Munich are several parks, the largest being the English Garden. Trips to Munich's Botanical Garden and to its Hellabrunn Zoo, one of the largest in Europe, are also worthwhile.

The nearness of the Alps and a host of interesting cities offer unlimited opportunity for touring in Bavaria. There are interesting museums, castles, and architectural monuments, and perhaps the most impressive points of interest are the towering Alps of Upper Bavaria and the Austrian Tyrol, with world-famed spas and sports facilities. Skiing is particularly popular, but the beautiful scenery, picturesque villages, and colorful people provide year-round attraction.

Visitors to Munich have many opportunities to attend the theater and opera. The large Bavarian State opera house and about 20 theaters give nightly performances. Concert lovers will find that the musical fare is frequent, varied, and of outstanding quality.

Munich is world renowned for its Oktoberfest (a combination of carnival and beer festival which lasts about two weeks starting in mid-September) and for its Fasching (carnival) which begins on January 7 and ends on Shrove Tuesday. Munich is famous for its excellent beer, and the city features many beer halls. Europe's largest circus has its home in Munich, and performances are given from Christmas until the end of March. The Europa cinema in Munich's downtown area features English-language (usually American) films of recent vintage.

A number of interesting cities are only a few hours away. Included are Nuremberg, Ulm, Augsburg, Salzburg, Regensburg, and Bayreuth (site of the annual Wagner Music Festival). The so-called Romantic Road connects the walled towns of Dinkelsbühl, Noerdlingen, and Rothenburg ob der Tauber, which are preserved virtually as they were in the 16th century. Eastern Austria, Czechoslovakia, Northern Italy, and Switzerland are within a day's drive.

Stuttgart

Hunting and fishing opportunities abound in Baden-Württemberg, and both the city of Stuttgart and the surrounding areas offer an excellent choice of sports—horseback riding, ice skating, swimming, bowling, tennis, and golf.

Stuttgart's ballet is among the best in Europe, and performances by it and the city opera are given throughout the year except for two late summer months. Frequent concerts are given by the State Symphony Orchestras, other local groups, and a wide variety of visiting artists from all over the world. Stuttgart has several museums, and the Württemberg Art Association offers periodic exhibits of paintings, sculptures, and graphic arts. One of Stuttgart's most colorful festivities is the annual fall Volksfest.

This harvest festival is second only to Munich's renowned Oktoberfest and unfailingly attracts large crowds. Almost every village in the district has one or two similar fests during the year. Downtown cinemas show many first-run American and international films, dubbed in German.

Heidelberg

Heidelberg offers a wide variety of recreational activities. Several excellent swimming pools are in the area, and there is hiking, cycling, hunting, and fishing. The nearest good skiing area is the Black Forest, two or three hours away by car; when the weather is not cold enough there, the German, Swiss, or Austrian Alps can be reached in five to eight hours.

Heidelberg also has many cultural activities of good quality at reasonable prices. Concerts, theater, opera, ballet, etc., are available at all times, and the U.S. Army sponsors a limited number of cultural events. A small museum is in town. The nightclubs and restaurants are also good for a city of this size. Many German movie houses are available, and the Army shows American films nightly in five theaters in the Heidelberg area.

Notes for Travelers

Most travel from the U.S. to Germany is by air. There are modern airports in Berlin, Bremen, Düsseldorf, Frankfurt, Hamburg, Hannover, Cologne/Bonn, Munich, and Stuttgart. Frankfurt, the largest airport, has daily Pan Am and TWA flights to and from New York (about seven hours). Le Havre, Rotterdam, and Bremerhaven are the nearest European ports for steamship lines.

American visitors to Germany need only a valid passport for entry.

Reasonable quantities of hunting firearms and ammunition may be imported into the country. Regulations may be checked with the Office of Munitions Control, Department of State, Washington, D.C., concerning the export and eventual reimport of arms from and to the U.S.

Regular religious services (Catholic, Protestant, and Jewish) are conducted in all the major cities of West Germany, and where there are no local services conducted in English, chaplains of the U.S. Army make provisions for the English-speaking communities. Berlin has local American and British churches, and a regularly-scheduled Jewish service conducted in German. In Hamburg, there is an Orthodox Jewish service in English each Friday evening and Saturday morning.

The unit of German currency is the Deutsche Mark (DM), which is divided into 100 *pfennigs*. The current rate of exchange is about two DM to the U.S. dollar.

The metric system of weights and measures is used.

The U.S. Embassy is located at Mehlemer Avenue, Bad Godesberg, 5300 Bonn. The Mission in Berlin is in the Headquarters Compound, 170 Clayalle, Berlin-Dahlem; the Consulates General are at 1 Praesident Kennedy Platz, 28 Bremen; 5 Cecilien Alee, Düsseldorf; 27/28 Alsterufer, 2 Hamburg 36; 21 Siesmayerstrasse, Frankfurt (the largest in the world); 5 Koenigstrasse, 8000 München (Munich) 22; and 7 Urbanstrasse, 7000 Stuttgart. The office of the Political Adviser in Heidelberg is at Roemerstrasse 166, 6900 Heidelberg.

Greece

History recounts the background and the struggles of **GREECE,** publications and official reports tell of the problems and the virtues encountered there—but few narratives can adequately describe Olympia in the spring, Delphi in the October light, a taverna by the sea in August, or the islands on any clear day. Life in Greece is good, its people are warm and hospitable, and the natural beauties of the land still provide a setting fit for the gods.

Area, Geography, Climate

Greece, a mountainous country, is bounded on the north by Bulgaria, Yugoslavia, and Albania; on the east by Turkey and the Aegean Sea; and on the south and west by the Mediterranean and the Ionian Seas. The land area, including the islands, is some 50,270 square miles (about the size of Alabama). Only 25 percent of the land is arable, and much of that is dry and rocky.

Greece has mild, wet winters and hot, dry summers. There is considerable variation in climate between southern (including its islands) and northern Greece.

Athens. This southern city, the capital of the country, has a dry and generally agreeable climate, ranging from subtropical to temperate. December through March temperatures average 40°F; April and May temperatures are similar to those in Washington. From June through September, daylight temperatures average slightly less than 90°F, often reaching 100°F. Moderate humidity, from 40 to 60 percent makes summer tolerable. Fresh sea and mountain breezes temper even midsummer heat. Nights are generally comfortable.

Rainfall occurs mainly in winter. Summers are usually dry and dusty. Cold northerly winter winds occasionally bring a brief snow flurry to the city and a light blanket of snow to the surrounding mountains. The moderate climate has no adverse effects upon health, clothing, or furnishings.

Thessaloniki. In northern Greece, temperatures and humidity from the end of May till the end of September (especially from mid-July to mid-September) are high. Summer heat is sometimes tempered by late morning and early evening breezes. July and August nights are often uncomfortable for sleeping. The hot summer comes and goes abruptly, and temperature changes for all seasons are frequent and sudden.

In winter, periods of mild, sunny and springlike weather are usually interspersed with cold snaps which can be uncomfortable. Periods of chilly and damp weather with considerable rainfall and occasional snow occur, and temperatures often dip below freezing. Although snow does not usually linger, the city has been struck by blizzards.

One feature of Thessaloniki's climate is the *Vardari*, a high and northwesterly wind which appears suddenly and at irregular intervals from the area of the Axios (Vardar) River Valley. Winds sometimes continue for several days, and during winter bring cold, biting weather. In summer the *Vardari* gives relief from the heat, but also brings dust clouds.

Population

The total population of Greece is 9,556,000 (January, 1980); metropolitan Athens (including Piraeus), 2.8 million; greater Thessaloniki, 570,000. Other large cities include Patras, Volos, Iraklion, Kavalla, Larissa, Kalamata, and Tripolis. About 45 percent of the people live in rural and semi-urban areas of less than 5,000 people; over 40 percent of the population work on farms. Due to a continuing exodus from villages to urban areas and Greece's economic development, these percentages have declined since 1971.

The established religion is the Eastern Orthodox Church. Other religions (Protestants, Roman Catholics, and about 0.3 percent Moslems) follow their own worship practices, dress, dietary laws, and holy days.

The American community in Athens consists of personnel and dependents of the U.S. Embassy and other government agencies. Many private companies, including Mobil Oil, PAA, TWA, Union Carbide, and Exxon, maintain branch offices in Athens, headed by Americans. Six U.S. banks also maintain branch offices in Athens with U.S. managers. American educational, religious, and welfare organizations in Greece, the American Red Cross, and U.S. tourists complete the group.

Government

Democracy was restored in Greece in July 1974, following the collapse of the seven-year military junta. Constantine Caramanlis returned from his self-imposed exile to head a government of national unity which prepared the country for parliamentary elections in November. Caramanlis led his new Democracy Party to victory in the elections, gaining 54 percent of the popular vote, and governed the country with a majority of 215 seats in the 300-member Parliament for the next three years.

New elections were held in November 1977, in which the New Democracy Party suffered a decline in the popular vote (to 42 percent), although it retained a majority of 173 seats in the Parliament. Caramanlis continued as prime minister. The Panhellenic Socialist Movement (PASOK) led by Andreas Papandreou, which finished third in the 1974 elections, took second place and became the principal opposition party, with 92 seats. The Union of the Democratic Center, which had been the second party, fell to third place with 15 seats.

The Orthodox Greek Communist Party (KKE-Exterior) gained 11 seats, while the United Democratic Left and the Eurocommunist Greek Communist Party (KKE-Interior) each won a single seat. The rightist National Camp Party won five seats and the centrist New Liberal Party holds the remaining two seats.

Greece is a parliamentary democracy with a president as head of state. Constantine Tsatsos was reelected President of the Republic in 1977 for a five-year term. The judiciary consists of several levels of administrative, civil, and criminal court systems. The constitution provides for religious freedom, but the prevailing religion in Greece is the Eastern Orthodox Church of Christ. It is self-governing, and is administered by the Holy Synod under the leadership of the Archbishop of Athens and All of Greece.

Arts, Science, Education

In view of Greece's rich cultural roots, visitors expecting to find a flourishing intellectual and artistic life may find themselves disappointed. The heritage is there, but although modern Greek writers such as Nikos Kazantzakis and Nobel Prize poet George Seferis are as famous abroad as at home, and the Greek painters Spyropoulous and Ghikas are as familiar to gallery visitors in New York as in Athens, the arts are not cultivated today in Greece. Athenian art suffered during the centuries when Greece was under foreign rule and Athens was but a forgotten village.

Art is now beginning to flourish anew, but the main emphasis is on classical art and literature, almost neglecting anything since Byzantium. Contemporary Greek theater often jumps from Aristophanes to Arthur Miller, but the theater is not too popular with the public, playing to full houses only during the summer, and then mostly to foreign audiences.

The ancient Acropolis is the setting for the Athens Festival which presents national and international theater, and dance and music at the Herod Atticus Theater, between July and September. Ancient Greek comedies and tragedies in Demotic Greek are performed in July and August at the ancient theater in Epidaurus, two-and-a-half hours from Athens.

First-run foreign films in English, French, and Italian (with Greek subtitles) are popular in Greece. The winter's favorites are usually rerun in the summer in outdoor theaters.

Folk art survives in Greece mainly for commercial reasons. It is often difficult to distinguish between souvenirs and work of genuine cottage artisans. The Greek countryside is delightfully genuine in flavor, and Greek folk dancing is pleasurable whether spontaneous or a performance. A professional group of dancers, with an international reputation for professionalism, performs nightly in Athens. The group, the Dora Stratou dancers, consists of genteel ladies and gentlemen from fashionable social strata.

The Karagiozi shadow theater, with Byzantine and Turkish antecedents, is well worth seeing. Performances are held in the main squares nightly in summer.

One can hear *bouzouki* (a stringed instrument) music throughout Greece. However it is difficult to find unamplified music, *bouzouki* or any other kind, except in rural Greek villages. *Rebetika* (turn of the century, popular folk music) is experiencing a real revival throughout the country.

Greece abounds in priceless sights, sounds, and experiences, ranging from Minoan frescoes to Byzantine splendors.

Although conservative, science and education are revered in Greece. Because of the impressiveness on a job application, the hunger for education in both the humanities and sciences remains high. The Greek mind is among the keenest in the world. Greeks attach great value to higher education abroad, probably due to the uneven, and at times antiquated, quality of higher education in home. The result is that young Greeks obtain graduate degrees overseas and decide not to return home, despite the fact that a growing need exists for their knowledge and skills.

Commerce and Industry

During the past decade, Greece has changed from a primarily agrarian to a semi-industrial economy. This shift has resulted in rapid urbanization so that increasing numbers of people now live in towns of more than 10,000. In the late 1970s, agricultural output represented only 18.1 percent of total GNP, but secondary output accounted for 30 percent and services for 51.9 percent.

With rapid industrialization, annual budgets now emphasize, in addition to defense and social service expenditures, improvements in irrigation, roadbuilding, and tourism. Shipping is another major economic element. The Greek flag flies on more than 25 million tons of ships. Over 20 million tons are controlled by Greek interests under foreign flags.

The most valuable industry, leading in employment and productivity, is textile manufacturing (mainly cotton). Other industries are food processing,

tobacco, nonmetal minerals, and metallurgy.

Bauxite is Greece's most important mineral deposit. For domestic use of the bauxite ore, an aluminium smelter was built on the Gulf of Corinth. Large amounts of Greek magnesite and nickel ore are exported. Lignite, fuel for the country's thermal electric power plants is abundant. Iron and steel producers rely on scrap metal and imported billets as raw material. Two recently built blast furnaces use domestic and imported iron ore as well as scrap metal.

A mill, in conjunction with the $200 million Esso Pappas industrial complex, is being built in Thessaloniki for the production of finished iron and steel. Financed by U.S. private investors, the complex also includes an oil refinery and an ammonia plant. U.S. investments include a $16.5 million Ethyl chemical plant and the $13 million Goodyear tire plant established in Thessaloniki. Four petroleum refineries operate in Greece, one government-controlled. Oil deposits have been found off the island of Thassos, and exploration has begun in a nearby area.

Major new industrial development projects include shipyards; a new Athens airport; a Europort near Thessaloniki; thermal, hydroelectric and nuclear power plants; an aerospace industry; the Athens subway; nonmetallic and metallurgical industries; and petrochemical plants.

Industrialization is requiring more capital-goods imports. The growth of per capita income is being manifested in increasing imports of consumer goods. Greece's payments for imports are being financed in part by export earnings and by invisible earnings from tourism, shipping, and emigrant and worker remittances. As these sources of foreign exchange have not been enough to cover the trade deficit, Greece depends on the inflow of private foreign capital and official loans.

About eight percent of Greece's imports and 13 percent of exports are with Eastern European Communist countries. Some 60 percent of the exports are foodstuffs and tobacco. Most of Greece's trade with the Communist countries is carried out under bilateral clearing agreements requiring a balanced flow of trade. In the past these trade balances have favored Greece, further complicating the economic position, as few Eastern products are imported.

Since January 1, 1981, Greece has been a full member of the Common Market. In 1975, the country applied for early full membership in the European Community and in February 1976, the Council of Ministers accepted the application in principle. Formal negotiations opened in July 1976.

From 1964 to 1973, the Greek economy achieved GNP real growth rates of 5.2 percent to 9.3 percent per annum, averaging 7.7 percent. In 1974, following the Cyprus crisis and the world recession, GNP fell by two percent in real terms. In 1978, real GNP growth reached 5.9 percent. However, the economy is still plagued by those structural weaknesses normally associated with developing economies. Particularly troublesome is the failure to develop a progressive and competitive agricultural sector. The government, relying on private initiative for economic modernization, actively encourages the inflow of foreign capital and limits its own direct economic activities to infrastructure projects and other projects which lack private investments.

A small proportion of Greek workers belong to labor unions, as compared to membership in U.S. and Western European unions. Greek unions are playing an increasing role in determining wages, fringe benefits, and working conditions. Demand for skilled labor exceeds supply, and unemployment is low—approximately four percent. Some 200,000 Greek workers are employed in West Germany. Underemployment has been a serious rural problem, although agricultural labor is becoming scarce during peak periods. Per capita income was $4,210 at current prices in 1979.

Transportation

Athens is centrally located. Olympic, BEA, TWA, Air France, Ethiopian, SAS, Swiss Air, KLM, Sabena, and Lufthansa connect Athens with the Near and Far East, North Africa and Europe, often with daily service. Daily service within Greece is available from Athens to Thessaloniki, Alexandroupolis, Kalamata, Kavalla, and the larger islands.

The Orient Express to Istanbul, Ankara, Aleppo, Belgrade, and Western capitals also services Athens. Railroad service within Greece is good, but not extensive.

Except for an occasional cruise ship, there is no direct service between Greece and the U.S.

Main streets and highways in Greece are macadam; secondary roads are rough and ungraded. Most roads are two-lane, except for parts of the National Road. The highway network is fairly good and constantly being expanded and improved. In response to tourism, road surfaces are improving; however, in some more remote areas they are often no more than wagon roads or mule tracks. The road to Belgrade is good, and the border between Greece and Yugoslavia is open to private automobiles.

Greek buses and taxis provide adequate and inexpensive local transportation, except during rush hours. Emergency vehicles are designed as follows: firetrucks are red; ambulances are white or white striped with yellow; police vehicles are all black or all white. All emergency vehicles are equipped with sirens and flashing lights. Motorcycles are used by traffic police.

A car is necessary for trips outside the cities. Maintenance is slightly less expensive than in the U.S., and spare parts are available for almost any make of vehicle. A valid U.S. or international drivers license is recognized. Traffic moves on the right.

Communications

Facilities for telephone and telegraph are good. Direct-dial, long-distance calls to the U.S., Western European countries, and Tel Aviv can be made for moderate fees, and telegraph service is readily available. Local phone calls are quite inexpensive. Public telephones are located at some of the newspaper kiosks in the cities. Mail service is excellent.

Radio reception, AM and FM, is good. Few English-language programs are on standard broadcast, but the local stations offer a variety of good musical programs, both classical and modern. The VOA broadcasts locally in Greek and by shortwave in English.

Neighboring stations can be picked up on standard broadcast, and London BBC can be picked up on shortwave radios. The Armed Forces Network offers news, entertainment, and recorded popular and classical music.

Greek TV has two channels, but broadcasting hours are limited. American TV sets cannot be used without modification.

Athens has two English-language dailies, except Monday. The Rome Daily American, an eight-page newspaper printed in Rome, is received the day after publication. The International Herald Tribune is available in late afternoon or evening on the day of publication. The airmail edition of the London Times is on local newsstands a day after publication. Foreign magazines such as Paris Match, Oggi (Italian), Punch, etc., are available, as are the international editions of Time and Newsweek. The Athenian, a monthly magazine in English, can be obtained by subscription or on the newsstands.

Health

Emergency major surgery can be adequately handled by local specialists. A modern, medical center and laboratory opened in Athens in the fall of 1975. Competent English-speaking Greek dentists are also available. Several are American-trained and use U.S. equipment. Cost of dental care (and also eye care) is often lower than in the U.S.

Most pharmaceutical supplies and medications of American, French, and German origin are available locally.

Greece loosely enforces general food and drug regulations. Prevalence of tuberculosis and intestinal parasites constitutes a health hazard, and

Americans should use common sense in selecting places to eat. Disease-reporting and quarantine practices are not adequate. Although a few quarantine wards exist in hospitals for the more dangerous communicable diseases, no home quarantine practices are enforced.

Sanitation practices in the cities are good. In Athens, garbage is collected three times a week and sewage drainage is adequate. Athens water is potable. Insects and vermin pose no particular problem, although mosquitoes and garden insects are often annoying.

The major endemic communicable diseases are dysentery (amoebic and bacillary), infectious hepatitis, and TB. Americans should be immunized against smallpox, polio, typhoid, diphtheria, and tetanus. Official American personnel in Athens, however, enjoy high standards of health. No cases of TB among Americans have been reported, but some cases of hepatitis have been found.

No unusual health risks are involved in living in Athens as long as precautions are taken in disinfecting fresh fruits and vegetables, and in choosing foods when eating in Greek restaurants. Eating raw clams and oysters and improperly cooked pork and beef is hazardous. In rural areas, one should drink beer or bottled soda instead of water. Pasteurized milk from local sources can be used safely.

Major Cities

ATHENS, the capital of Greece, is situated 300 feet above sea level on the Attica Plain, bordered by the Aegean Sea and Mts. Parnes, Penteli, and Hymettus. Athens proper is built around the historic Acropolis and picturesque Lycabetus Hill. The Attica Plain is agriculturally rich, but surrounded by semiarid hills and mountains.

Athens is the commercial and political center of Greece. Architecture varies from the antiquity of the Acropolis to the modern suburbs. The city is burgeoning with construction, especially apartment and office buildings in central Athens. Like Boston, Athens is a "mother city," the central point of a group of suburban townships with separate entities. The northern suburbs are Psychico, Philothei, Kifissia, and Ekali, about a 15- to 35-minute drive from Athens. Old Phaliron, Ellinikon, Glyfada, and Vouliagmeni are on the seafront, about a 20- to 30-minute drive.

Basic services in Athens are generally satisfactory. Tailors and dressmakers offer a wide variety of services and prices with good results. Many moderately priced beauty and barber shops are in Athens, although sanitation is not quite up to U.S. standards. Shoe repairs, dry cleaning and laundry service are reasonably priced, and workmanship ranges from fair to good There are several local laundromats. Electrical and radio repair is good; prices are reasonable.

THESSALONIKI, in the northern province of Macedonia, is 300 miles from Athens and is Greece's second largest city. Originally called Therme, it was renamed in 315 B.C. in honor of the daughter of Philip of Macedon (Alexander the Great's father). The name Thessaloniki, meaning victory in Thessaly, was given to her in honor of Philip's great victory at Chaeronea. The city achieved its greatest prominence during the late Roman Empire and the Byzantine Empire, when it surpassed Athens, and became the first city of the Greek "province." It suffered a decline under the 482-year Turkish occupation.

Because of its location, Thessaloniki became the center of great commercial activity in the 19th century, regaining the importance it enjoyed under the Byzantine Empire. The city was a strategic prize in both Balkan Wars and in two World Wars. Turkish rule of Thessaloniki ended in 1912, an event commemorated yearly on October 26, name day of the city's patron, Saint Demetrius. A year later, additional parts of Macedonia were integrated into the Kingdom of Greece.

The city is on the northeastern shore of the Thermaic Gulf, off the Aegean Sea. Central Thessaloniki was rebuilt after a disastrous fire in 1917. The city has recently seen a building boom. The old unburnt city below the citadel remains quaint and picturesque. Other areas, reflecting the effects of war, occupation, and thousands of refugees, are now being replaced by worker-housing developments.

Before World War II, the city's chief importance derived from transshipments of goods that originated in or were destined for the Balkan hinterland. Shipping is increasing, and upon completion of port expansion, should play a vital role in the city's economic life.

Of Thessaloniki's 645,000 inhabitants, 98 percent are of Greek origin and the rest are foreign (Sephardic Jews, Armenians, White Russians, etc.).

Many persons in the Greek community speak English, and some English is spoken by shop and restaurant staffs. English is the second language of the young; older persons may speak French or German as a second language. Knowledge of a little modern Greek is indispensable for getting to know the people and for traveling with ease in the smaller cities, towns, and villages.

With construction and highway improvements and modern hotels, tourism in the area is rapidly increasing. Tourists coming from Europe by rail or car, en route to southern Greece or the Near East, pass through Thessaloniki. More international airlines are making regular stops at Thessaloniki's airport, where facilities are being expanded.

The U.S. consular district of Thessaloniki includes all of Greek Macedonia and western Trace, extending from Albania and Greek Epiros on the west to the Turkish border on the east, and from the Aegean Sea and Thessaly on the south to Yugoslavia and Bulgaria on the north.

Recreation

Athens

Sight-seeing spots abound in Greece, and the Athens area alone has various spots of historical and architectural interest. Athens also has 10 major museums. Archeological treasures and Byzantine art and icons predominate, but trophies of the War of Independence in 1821 and Greek folk art are also included.

Patras, largest city in the Peloponnesus and third largest in Greece, is west of Athens and can be reached in about four hours by car. Old fortifications and the famous Clauss winery are the principal points of interest. In addition, Patras is the center of the pre-Lenten carnival celebrations.

Delphi, famed seat of the oracle, is a three-hour drive from Athens. Both the ruins and scenery at Delphi are worth return visits. Interesting ruins may be visited in Olympia, Corinth, Mycenae, and Epidavros, all within a few hours from Athens by car.

In addition to the better known and larger Greek islands such as Corfu, Rhodes, and Crete, innumerable smaller islands offer pleasant travel and can be reached by boat or plane. Excursion boats operate daily in spring, summer, and early fall.

Island-hopping and trips on the mainland offer a change from the metropolitan life of Athens and a view of the "other" Greece. The ruins of ancient Greece provide a photographer's and painter's paradise, as well as an inspiration for delving into the early history of Western civilization.

Transportation and accommodations costs are rising.

The Greek Touring Club sponsors excursions and tours throughout Greece. The club, affiliated with the Club Mediterranee, has established huge recreational areas on Corfu island and Lambiri at Eglon, two of the most beautiful summer resorts of Greece. Open from May through the end of September, they offer waterskiing, sailing, water polo, swimming, volleyball, basketball, Ping-Pong, dancing, concerts, and lectures free of charge.

The most popular sport in Greece is soccer. Numerous stadiums dot the country; the most important are in Athens, Piraeus, and Thessaloniki, and

are owned by Greek athletic associations. The two main soccer grounds in Athens are the Panathenaikos and the A.E.K. Another soccer field is in Piraeus. Soccer matches begin in mid-September, climaxing with the national championships around the last of June.

Horse racing takes place every Wednesday and Saturday at the Phaleron Race Course, Athens. The sport is popular among the Greeks and the foreign colony, with betting at the track.

Americans interested in horseback riding patronize various riding stables—Varibobi, Greenfield, Paradisos, and Gerakas. The latter two have extremely high initiation fees but extensive facilities. English-speaking instructors are available at most stables.

Athens has several tennis clubs, including the Philothei Club, the Ekali Club, Paradisos Tennis Club, the Athens Tennis Club, and the Panhellinion. It is possible to play outdoor tennis eight to nine months of the year. The Glyfada Golf Club, located near Athens, has an 18-hole championship course. Other golf courses are located on the islands of Rhodes and Corfu.

Yacht racing is held off Phaleron Bay on Sunday afternoons, weather permitting. Yachting is a popular and delightful sport among the islands of Greece, and many residents own boats. Yachts may also be chartered with full crews.

Swimming is popular. Beaches, complete with changing cabins, restaurants, and snack bars are 20 minutes from Athens. Swimming is possible year round, but from November to

April, swimmers must be hardy. The waters around many of the islands offer ideal spearfishing. A few pools exist.

Waterskiing is growing in popularity; boats and instructors are available at several beaches. Sailing and canoeing are available through the Greek Yacht Club, and the Minos Yacht Club.

Good ski slopes can be found on several Greek mountains between December and March, while some, like Mt. Olympus, Mt. Parnassus, and the Pindus Range offer good skiing through May. Principal ski centers served by chair lifts are on Mt. Vermion, 18 kilometers from Naoussa; on Mt. Pelion 28 kilometers from Volos; and on Metsovon, Mt. Parnassus, Mt. Olympus, and Mt. Parnes. Ski rental equipment is not available.

The Greek seas abound with sole, bass, pike, mullet, tuna, perch, and other fish. Weather conditions, bright sunshine, and calm seas permit sea fishing year round. Within three to five hours from Athens are several trout streams. As most streams are narrow, deep, and fast, spinning tackle is preferred.

The hunting season lasts from September to mid-May. Aquatic birds are numerous near Athens, and passage birds are found in central Greece. The season for hunting partridge and rabbit is September through mid-January. Limited boar hunting is possible in northern Greece, but Americans seldom hunt there as the area is almost inaccessible. The country-wide annual hunting license is expensive.

The Association of Greek Mountaineers organizes hiking and camping excursions to the mountains and excursions to foreign countries. The club runs a mountaineering school near Athens with lectures, instruction, and films. The Hellenic Alpine Club, with 600 members in Athens, sponsors mountain climbs, hikes, spelunking, and snow skiing.

Entertainment in Greece is characterized by informality, spontaneity, simplicity, and individuality. Indoor and outdoor movie theaters are found in Athens and the suburbs. Recent American films are popular and widely shown in addition to Greek, French, Italian, Spanish, and German films.

The theater, a tradition firmly rooted in classical days, operates in modern Greece year round. A revival of the ancient outdoor theater, with the plays of Sophocles, Euripides, Aeschylus, and Aristophanes, is the basis of the annual Epidavros Festival in June, and an important part of the Athens Festival in August and September.

The National Theater sponsors a repertoire of ancient Greek tragedies and comedies, on three or four consecutive weekends in the old amphitheater of Epidavros, built in the fourth century B.C. This theater is noted for its acoustics and beautiful setting. Its program receives international acclaim, and is repeated at the Athens Festival in the Ancient Roman Herod Atticus Theater below the Acropolis. It is supplemented with performances of the Athens State orchestra, and by various foreign orchestras and ballet companies.

Winter theater offers a varied repertoire in Greek of classical and new plays by well-known foreign playwrights.

A variety of lectures and musical programs are offered. Greek commercial firms regularly organize recitals and theater and ballet performances with foreign artists and troupes during winter. In addition, the Athens State Orchestra and the Athens State Opera offer regular year-round programs.

Athens' better restaurants and hotels serve Greek and continental food; some serve exotic foods. Night life in Athens is diversified and interesting. "Taverna-style" restaurants throughout the city and suburbs offer music for dining and dancing. Some more sophisticated tavernas offer floor shows. In summer, many move outdoors in the suburbs or on the seafront.

At national and religious festivals foreigners are usually spectators rather than participants. Those events are interesting and worth seeing. Typical of such festivities are Epiphany (January) and the pre-Lenten carnival season.

Cameras are allowed everywhere, but the visitor should use common sense and good taste in photographing certain religious festivities.

Thessaloniki

Pella, ancient capital of Macedonia and birthplace of Alexander the Great, is 45 minutes from Thessaloniki. Several beautifully preserved mosaics and numerous artifacts are on display. Archeological excavations are still conducted. Naousa (one to one-and-a-half hours) is noted for its variety of fruit trees and its wine; Edessa (two hours), for its dam and picturesque waterfalls. Phillipi, named by Alexander in honor of his father, and the site of St. Paul's first sermon in

Europe, is about two hours to the east by car.

Within the district are several other picturesque towns, such as Kavalla, Xanthi, and Kastoria, all within five hours from Thessaloniki. Buses and trains link Thessaloniki with other provincial centers. Kastoria, noted for its Byzantine churches and scenic beauty, is important for its fur industry. Kavalla, with its old quarters, Turkish fortress, Roman aqueduct, and excellent beaches, is a scenic jewel.

The monasteries of the Mt. Athos peninsula, forming an independent ecclesiastical government dating from medieval times, are also within the district. The approach is usually made as far as Ouranoupolis by road, then by small boat and ultimately by mule or on foot. No women, or boys under 18, are allowed to enter the region of the Holy Mountain. A good hotel now exists in Ouranoupolis, but like many tourist hotels, is open only from May until mid-October.

Two islands, Thassos and Samothrace, which are accessible by sea from Kavalla and Alexandroupolis, are well worth seeing. A visit to either island can be made on a long weekend. Samothrace (a three- to four-day trip), an important archaeological site, has an excellent small museum as well as a modern tourist rest house. Thassos, while less known archaeologically, has interesting ruins, an excellent small museum, lovely landscapes, and picturesque villages. In addition, the visitor will find the crystal-clear waters of Thassos' bays and inlets excellent for swimming and snorkeling. A new hotel on Thassos has brought increased tourist trade.

Istanbul and Belgrade can be

reached from Thessaloniki either by rail or car, or by air via Athens. Sofia can be reached in six hours by car or one to two hours by plane from Athens.

There is ample opportunity for sports in the Thessaloniki area. Swimming is excellent from May through October at nearby beaches, and about 50 to 75 miles from the city, crystal-clear water and isolated beaches are available for spearfishing and snorkeling. There are three yacht clubs providing anchorage, but only limited service, for small craft.

A small but good tennis club with four courts is available through membership. There are also two tennis courts at Anatolia College which may be used with special permission. Golf is not available. Good hiking is possible in nearby mountains, and ambitious hikers can climb 10,000-foot Mt. Olympus, allowing two to three days for the round trip to and from Thessaloniki.

Partridge, quail, dove, and hare can be hunted in fall, but hunting is poor in the immediate vicinity of Thessaloniki. Waterfowl hunting can be arranged. Hunting licenses for foreigners are expensive.

Ski slopes are two hours away at Selli in the Vermion Range. Local taxis, private cars with chains, or excursion buses will take skiers to the mountains. One hotel and a ski lift are in operation. Skiers can also stay in guest quarters, without modern conveniences.

American films, old and new, predominate at local indoor cinemas; English, Italian, German, Spanish, and Greek films are also shown. The best theaters compare with U.S. neighborhood types. Movies for families are limited, as 60 percent of foreign films are classified unfit for children. From May to September, films are shown in outdoor theaters.

The Opera Company, the National Theater, and other Athens companies are in Thessaloniki annually for runs of one to two weeks. The State Theater of Northern Greece presents a variety of plays throughout the year. Athens musicians and lesser-known American and European soloists occasionally present recitals or concerts during the fall or winter. The National Symphony Orchestra of Northern Greece performs Monday nights from fall through spring.

The archeological museum has a fine collection of antiquities from various ages. The Macedonian Museum has an interesting collection of Northern Greek artifacts and costumes.

Several dancing places, restaurants, tavernas, and nightclubs are in the Thessaloniki area. The distinct types are places with food and dancing to *bouzouki* music; tavernas serving typical Greek food, the famous *mezedes*; nightclubs with orchestras and discotheques for youth; and coffee and tea rooms.

Special events are sponsored by the USIS (United States Information Service), the French Institute, and the Goethe Institute. The International Fair of Thessaloniki is held annually during September with industrial exhibits, consumer goods, entertainment features, and an amusement park. A wine festival is held during the fair. A Greek song festival, and a week-long cinema festival have recently become part of the festivities. An outdoor flower exhibit is sponsored each May; Demetria Cultural Festival is held in October.

Good Friday candlelight procession, midnight Easter services, blessing of the sea at Epiphany (January 6), and pilgrimages throughout the year on patron saint's day of churches possessing notable icons are some of the religious festivities.

Notes for Travelers

Many major international airlines, including TWA, serve Greece. Some visitors travel by sea from New York to Europe, and then on to Athens by air.

Passports are required, but visas are necessary only for a stay of more than two months. Public health regulations require certificates of inoculations against smallpox (travelers arriving from Asia or Africa), and against yellow fever and cholera (travelers arriving from infected areas).

Concealable firearms may not be imported. There are strict regulations on other arms and ammunition.

Interdenominational English-language services are conducted at St. Andrew's American Community Church in Athens. Protestant services are held at the U.S. Air Base Chapel, Kifissia Protestant Church at the American Club, St. Paul's Church (Episcopalian) in Athens, First Church of Christ Scientist, Church of Jesus Christ of Latter-Day Saints at Athenai Airport, and Trinity Baptist Church in Sourmena. St. Dennis Cathedral in Athens, St. Paul's Catholic Chapel in Kifissia, the Air Force Chapel at Athenai, and the Chapel of the Ursuline School conduct Roman Catholic masses. Jewish services are held at Athenai and at Beth Shalom Synagogue in Athens.

In Thessaloniki, English-language services are conducted at the American Community Church at Anatolia College, the Church of the Immaculate Conception, and Kalamaria Chapel. The city also has a Jewish synagogue.

The official unit of Greek currency is the *drachma* (Dr.), with an official exchange rate of approximately 37 *drachmas* to the U.S. dollar (1979).

Greece uses the metric system of weights and measures.

The U.S. Embassy in Greece is located at 91 Queen Sophia Avenue, Athens. The Consulate General is at 59 King Constantine Street, Thessaloniki.

Hungary

HUNGARY considers itself the eastern outpost of Western civilization in Europe. A monarchy for nearly one thousand years, it was a forceful nation during the Middle Ages, when it dominated parts of the territory now included in Czechoslovakia, Romania, and Yugoslavia. In the 16th century, Hungary was conquered by the Turks. Later it was ruled by the Austrians, and in 1867 became part of the dual monarchy of the Austro-Hungarian Empire, which determined an important part of the history of central Europe.

Hungary was allied with Nazi Germany in World War II, and fell to Soviet troops. Discontent over its subservience to Russia precipitated an uprising in 1956, but the revolution was suppressed, and Hungary remains today a Communist state.

Area, Geography, Climate

Hungary is an exclusively inland country, 36,000 square miles in area (roughly the size of Indiana). It is bounded by Czechoslovakia and the Soviet Union on the north, Romania on the east, Yugoslavia on the south, and Austria on the west. Some parts of Hungary are flat but other sections offer pleasant scenery, such as the Matra mountains in the north and the area around Lake Balaton, the largest lake in Central Europe.

The climate in Budapest, the capital, is temperate. Winters, although damp and cold, are less severe than in Washington, D.C. Light snow falls from late November through February, but usually disappears on the Pest side of the Danube after three or four days. (The capital was formed in 1873 by the union of the cities of Buda, Pest, and Obuda.) In the hills of Buda, small amounts of snow may remain on the ground for weeks. January, the coldest month, has an average mean temperature of 31° F. During the late November through February period, the minimum daily temperatures are below freezing. Rainy weather, with accompanying fog, is common from November through January and is often associated with smog.

The July mean temperature is 71° F. The occasional spells of hot, dry weather are easier to take than Washington's summer humidity. In Buda, the temperatures are generally a bit lower. The yearly average precipitation is 25.2 inches.

Population

Of Hungary's 10.7 million population, 2.5 million reside in Budapest. Hungary is the most densely populated

117

country in East Central Europe, and trends indicate a steady urbanization. The ethnic composition is approximately 96 percent Hungarian (Magyars, the original settlers from the Ural Mountains of Russia), three percent German, and one percent Slovak, Romanian, Serb, and Gypsy.

Roman Catholics account for 60 percent of the population. The Calvinists and Lutherans make up 20 percent. The Jewish population approaches 100,000. All churches receive limited state financial aid, and religion can be practiced in relative freedom. Religious education, although possible to an extent, is controlled.

Government

The organization and style of the Hungarian People's Republic Government is similar to other member states of the Warsaw Pact. In theory, the unicameral Parliament is the supreme organ of state authority, but it only meets four times a year, and routinely adopts all proposed laws. The Presidential Council, chaired by President Pál Losonczi, is the organ representing the function of a "chief of state." The highest executive authority is the Council of Ministers, headed by Prime Minister György Lázár. Policies are established by the Central Committee of the Hungarian Socialist Workers (Communist) Party (HSWP), and in particular by its Political Committee, both chaired by the First Secretary Janos Kadar.

A nominally non-Communist political organization, the Patriotic People's Front, organizes elections and engages in domestic political activity under supervision of the ruling Hungarian Socialist Workers Party (HSWP). A number of nonparty members are in Parliament but not as members of any non-Communist political organization. All political activity centers around the HSWP, which has about 700,000 members.

Except for members of the HSWP Secretariat (the administrative arm of the Central Committee), who traditionally hold no other jobs, many members of the Central Committee and the Politburo also hold key positions in the government. Monopoly of the HSWP in the creation of policy and its administration is not only a continuing central theme of Communist ideology (the leading role of the party), but is carefully guarded and exercised in practice as well. Nonetheless, nonparty members are officially allowed to participate in any aspect of Hungarian life, except the party, and currently hold several significant offices.

The government's collective "chief of state" is the Presidential Council or Presidium, and President Losonczi or one of the vice-presidents of this body represents the council on ceremonial occasions such as the accreditation of foreign ambassadors. The head of government, the Prime Minister (Minister President), is Chairman of the Council of Ministers (the Cabinet, which is composed of ministers of departments and deputy prime ministers). Janos Kadar has been First Secretary of the party since 1956, and exercises leadership and direction over a small group of Central Committee secretaries and members of the Political Committee (Politburo) who make the basic policies for Hungary. These policies are periodically reviewed and approved by the Central Committee, which has more than 100 members.

Various mass organizations serve

multiple purposes: to transmit the ideas and programs of the party and state authorities to the masses, to secure mass support, and to create among the masses a sense of participation in the processes of government. Among these organizations are the Patriotic People's Front (about 150,000 members), the Communist Youth League (over 800,000 members), the Pioneers (for ages 10 to 16), the National Trade Unions Council, the National Council of Hungarian Women, the National Peace Council, the National Federation of Sports Associations, and the Hungarian Red Cross. The last two organizations are less politically oriented than the others.

Arts, Science, Education

Hungary has enjoyed a long and rich cultural tradition that has produced important leaders and innovators in the fields of music and science. Among the most famous are Franz Liszt, Bela Bartok, Zoltan Kodaly, Edward Teller, and Nobel Prize winner Albert Szent-György, the latter a participant in the delegation which returned the Crown of St. Stephen to Hungary in January 1978.

Hungarian cultural life has also produced a number of outstanding writers and poets. Although translation of their works is increasing, the language barrier continues to inhibit their rise to international eminence.

Budapest is the focal point of Hungary's cultural life. It has 16 permanent theaters as well as a number of open-air stages that offer performances in the summer. The State Opera House and the Erkel Opera Theater present good, sometimes superior, opera productions, ballets, and concerts, often featuring foreign guest artists.

The city's highly rated symphonies, chamber groups, and soloists perform at the Academy of Music in the winter, and on Margit (Margaret) Island in the Danube in the summer. Budapest Music Weeks, arranged each year in the autumn, and the Liszt-Bartok Piano Competition held every third year, are internationally known. The Hungarian State Folk Ensemble and the Budapest Ballet Perform regularly during the winter season.

Hungarian film-making has achieved a high level of sophistication, and a number of Hungarian films and directors have received international recognition. Budapest has many first-run movie theaters which show both Hungarian and foreign films. Often these foreign films will be presented in their original language with Hungarian subtitles.

As a consequence of efforts to preserve Hungary's historical and cultural relics and treasures, Budapest abounds in museums of all types. Among the most interesting are the Buda Castle Museum, which recreates the atmosphere of the Middle Ages with its artful blend of authentic medieval artifacts and skillful reconstructions; the Hungarian National Gallery, which focuses on Hungarian painting, sculpture, and graphic art from the 19th and 20th centuries; the Museum of Fine Arts, that houses an extensive collection of both Hungarian and foreign artists; and the Hungarian National Museum, which is the current repository of the Crown.

A number of galleries and exhibition halls display the work of contemporary Hungarian artists. Among them are the Mucsarnok and the Ernst Museums. Hungarian artists are well versed in Western art movements and tendencies, which often find expression in their work.

For all cultural events, tickets are priced considerably lower than in the U.S. Information on cultural programs and performances is published in each of the daily papers, while such publications as Pesti Musor and Budapest Musorfuzet provide details on a weekly and monthly basis.

Budapest is the center of Hungarian education. In addition to the Eotvos Lorand University, consisting of the faculties of law, liberal arts, and the natural sciences, there are the Semmelweiss Medical University, Karl Marx University of Economics, Budapest University of Technology, and a number of institutes and academies for fine arts and technical fields. The Hungarian Academy of Sciences, the country's highest scientific body, maintains more than 80 research institutes and centers, most of which are located in Budapest.

Commerce and Industry

Most of Hungary is flat plain or rolling terrain, where agricultural products typical of a temperate zone country are produced. Hungarian industry, largely developed since World War II, is mostly in the Budapest and the Diosgyor-Miskolc areas. Hungary lacks sufficient natural resources to support large-scale heavy industry and, except for bauxite, some coal, and natural gas, it must import almost all of its basic raw materials.

After World War II the Communist Government of Hungary proceeded to reconstruct a war-torn economy according to orthodox Marxist precepts. This reconstruction involved a wide expansion of industry, with special emphasis on heavy industry, and establishment of a centrally directed, planned economy. The government also undertook partial collectivization of agriculture. Roughly two-thirds of the country's production is now industrial; one-third is agricultural.

Following the 1956 revolution, the government completed agricultural collectivization by requiring individual farmers to join cooperatives, and it placed emphasis on types of industry that were more compatible with Hungary's economic resources. It also adopted economic development policies intended to bring about a steady rise in the standard of living. However, Hungary's economic ills, caused mainly by an inflexible economic bureaucracy and doctrinaire rigidity of central planning, were not completely solved. As a result, the economic growth rate slowed down in the early 1960s, and the need for further economic reform became more evident.

The need to modify the economic system culminated in the New Economic Mechanism (NEM) introduced in January 1968. NEM's aim has been to encourage economic efficiency by substantially reducing detailed, central, decision making and increasing the role of market forces in the Hungarian economy while preserving a planned economy.

Under the NEM, detailed central directives to individual companies were abolished and replaced by more general economic and financial mechanisms, designed to steer diversified decisions into the planned directives. A considerable amount of leeway in investment decisions was permitted to economic enterprises. Profitability became a primary yardstick for measuring performance. A system of bonuses was established for management and workers. Prices, which had previously been rigidly set by central authorities, were divided into three categories. About 40 percent of prices for consumer commodities remained centrally determined; other prices were either freed or allowed to fluctuate within certain centrally determined limits.

Laws were also passed affecting the organization of agricultural cooperatives, land ownership, foreign trade, labor, and investments. The aim was to increase the responsibility of individual enterprises and decrease the direct role of central government. The state retained basic control over the economy through the planning process, economic regulations, ownership of enterprises, appointment of enterprise managers, control over labor unions, laws on cooperatives, and monopoly of foreign exchange and credit.

The NEM has been a successful innovation, and in the years since its introduction the Hungarian economy has grown at a healthy rate which most recently has exceeded five percent. Agriculture has been a particular beneficiary of the new system, and both agricultural production and the incomes for farm workers have increased dramatically. Rises in the production of corn, wheat, and meat, all of which are important hard-currency earners, have been most impressive. There have, of course, been problems.

A number of industries which ran into difficulty were brought back under more direct state supervision through stringent central controls over investment decisions. Price subsidies for essential consumer goods continue and are expensive, although the government has allowed prices to increase

somewhat to reflect the higher cost of inputs, while gradually reducing reliance on subsidies. Nevertheless, the fixed prices of many items often cause distorted economic decisions.

The relative roles of enterprise managers and trade unions have become an issue. A substantial reorientation of industry is underway to make Hungary competitive on world markets. Modifications of the economic system to meet these issues have been essentially conservative in nature, although the basic intent and effect of the policy has remained intact. Hungary is a member of the Council for Economic Mutual Assistance (CEMA), which links the economies of Central and Eastern European Communist countries with that of the Soviet Union.

As a member of CEMA, Hungary receives from other participating countries raw materials, some finished goods, and fuels, which are paid for with telecommunications and transport equipment, machinery, pharmaceuticals, meat, and grains. Hungary is in the midst of a major export expansion program. Almost 67 percent of Hungary's foreign trade is conducted with other CEMA states and 33 percent with the West, from which it imports raw materials, advanced machinery, instruments, and special materials. One-third of Hungary's trade with the West is conducted with West Germany alone. Trade with the U.S., while expanding in recent years, is still modest; in 1977, U.S. exports totaled more than $60 million, and imports from Hungary amounted to about $50 million. Exports by American companies based in or through third countries, as well as their purchases from Hungary, add considerably to these figures. To pay for imports from hard-currency countries, Hungary's chief exports are light industrial and agricultural products. Basic imports from the U.S. are soybean cake and meal, chemicals, and farm machinery; exports are canned ham, rear axles, and light bulbs.

The internal market in Hungary is one of the best organized in the Communist world, and substantial quantities of goods are available. It is still marked, however, by poor distribution, quality, and selection. Although a variety of good fruits and vegetables is available in season, the seasons for individual commodities are extremely short. Fruits are difficult to obtain out of season and, when available, are quite expensive.

Hungarian stores stock a variety of canned and frozen foods, and while their canning and freezing techniques are below Western standards, they are adequate. Products and industries in which Hungary is strong, such as pharmaceuticals, shoes, and clothing, are good by East European standards, but fall below Western norms.

Transportation

Air service between Budapest and cities in Western Europe is adequate but, as is common in Europe, expensive. Service is provided by Pan Am, KLM, Swissair, Austrian Airlines, Sabena, SAS, Air France, Alitalia, Lufthansa, BEA, and Malev. Pan Am provides service to and from New York via Frankfurt once weekly in winter, and twice weekly in summer.

Two trains run daily to Vienna, where one can get surface transportation to any place in Western Europe. The trip takes about five hours. The present train schedules prohibit long weekends in Vienna, as there are no

trains leaving for Vienna on Friday evenings and returning Sunday evenings.

During the summer, daily except for Sunday, hydrofoil boats travel on the Danube to Vienna. The ride is pleasant and takes about five hours. Reservations usually must be made in advance, because the trip is scenic, and is popular with Hungarians as well as tourists.

Public city transportation is excellent. Budapest and its environs are well serviced with a network of buses, streetcars, and a new, second metro line. Crowded conditions prevail during rush hours. Taxis are numerous and are available at taxi stands throughout the city. They may be ordered by phone, but during peak periods are slow to arrive. Taxis usually do not cruise looking for fares, but some will occasionally stop.

The main roads in Hungary are well-maintained, and many points of interest in the country are easily reached. The drive to Vienna takes from three to four hours, depending on weather conditions, traffic, and whether a delay is encountered at the border.

All private motor vehicles must be registered with the Hungarian authorities in Budapest, and third-party liability insurance is mandatory.

Communications

Telephone and telegraph service to virtually all countries is available, but past experience has shown that telegrams often do not reach their destinations. Phone calls can be monitored; that, plus old and worn equipment, makes telephoning difficult and frustrating.

International mail arriving in Hungary is susceptible to interception by Hungarian authorities.

Radio Budapest is heard on two frequencies, identified by the names Radio Kossuth and Radio Petofi—named for two patriots of the 19th century. The broadcasts are similar in format to Western European stations—lectures and radio plays—and the music is largely Western. While contemporary serious American music is rarely heard in live performances, many American popular recording artists, jazz bands, vocalists, and beat groups can be heard daily on the radio.

Hungarian TV leaves much to be desired from an American point of view. It often consists of long discussions on economic, political, and agricultural problems. However, Hungarian, French, Italian, East and West German, and even vintage American films are televised in synchronized versions. These films, as well as the newscasts, help improve a foreigner's Hungarian language skill.

Occasionally, live concerts are scheduled. Sports events are televised regularly. A member of the East European Television Network called Intervision, Hungarian TV sometimes carries West European Eurovision telecasts of events such as song and dance festivals and sports matches. Budapest has two channels, but well-placed antennas in receptive areas may pick up Bratislava in Czechoslovakia. Hungarian TV sets are of excellent quality, offering fine definition and clear pictures. Rentals are available.

English-language newspapers can be obtained. The International Herald Tribune, published in Paris, and international editions of American and European news periodicals such as Time, Newsweek, or Paris Match are available on request in first-class hotels in Budapest. They generally sell out quickly. A complete range of Hungarian publications is available locally, including an eight-page English/German-language daily newspaper published by the Hungarian news service.

Health

Budapest has no American doctors or dentists, but many qualified Hungarian practitioners are available. Many of the local hospitals have inadequate facilities, obsolete equipment, and low standards of cleanliness; however some Americans have been satisfied with hospital care in Budapest. Often, facilities in Vienna are used.

Public health services are adequate but not up to U.S. standards. Organized programs covering tuberculosis detection and mass immunization exist. Tapwater is potable. In times of drought, however, it may be necessary to boil tapwater in certain parts of the city as a precautionary health measure. Budapest is also a source of naturally carbonated water, which is customarily sold in restaurants and foodstores. It is not necessary to boil milk, but because it is not heated to a high enough degree during pasturization, it spoils easily. Therefore, some Americans boil milk only to prevent it from spoiling rapidly. Raw fruits and vegetables are safe to eat.

Sewage and garbage disposal in Budapest are adequate. The community has an effective program of pest control.

Except for the heavy smog covering most of the city during certain periods in winter, (aggravating sinus and respiratory ailments), and for high pollen levels in spring and summer, Budapest involves no undue health risks.

Major City

Despite heavy damage during World War II and the Hungarian Revolution of 1956, **BUDAPEST** is still one of the most beautiful cities of Europe. It is a combination of three originally distinct cities: Buda on the western bank of the Danube River, Pest on the eastern bank, and Obuda located north of present-day Buda. The three are now linked by a series of bridges across the Danube.

Buda, built on rolling hills rising in places to 1,700 feet, contains many attractive residential sections and wooded areas. Pest, built on level ground at an altitude of 300 feet, contains the city's airport. Obuda, located north of Buda, is the fastest growing area of the city. It has, in recent years, almost lost its separate identity, and now only a small vestige of its past remains. It is located at the western base of the Arpad Bridge.

During the 19th century, and in the early years of the 20th, Budapest was famed for its literary, musical, and theatrical life. It was a metropolis of beautiful parks and historical buildings, and one of its major attractions, still popular with tourists, was Margaret Island (Margit Sziget), where St. Margaret, the daughter of King Bela IV (13th century), lived in a convent.

Recreation

Many pleasant excursions can be made within the city of Budapest and the surrounding area. The hills of Buda provide numerous attractive areas for pleasant weekend walks and picnics. Szentendre, an art colony lo-cated on the Danube River north of Budapest, and Esztergom, which is the seat of the presiding Bishop of the Roman Catholic Church in Hungary, are worthwhile nearby visiting places. They can be reached in less than an hour by car from the center of the city.

Farther away from the city, Lake Balaton, the summer retreat of the greater part of Budapest's population, offers good possibilities for swimming and sailing. The principal Balaton resorts of Balatonfured, Siofok, and Tihany are about 90 minutes from Budapest by car, and all offer adequate hotel facilities at international prices. In addition, cottages for rent by the season are available at the Balaton.

Other interesting points in the countryside include the attractive city of Eger, which has traditionally been an important center of the Roman Catholic Church in Hungary. It also was the site of a particularly fierce battle between Hungarian defenders and Turkish invaders in the 16th century. A well-preserved minaret located in the city is one of the most visible reminders in Hungary of the century and a half of Turkish rule during the 16th and 17th centuries. In addition, Eger is a most important center of the Hungarian wine industry, and wine cellars located outside the city are open to visitors. The countryside north of Eger provides some scenic contrast to the flat plain which accounts for the greater part of the Hungarian countryside.

Eastern Hungary offers the well-known Hungarian Puszta, where one is able to look for 10 miles in any direction without seeing even the smallest hill. At Hortobagy, in the middle of the Puszta, visitors can arrange to see displays of traditional horsemanship executed by costumed *csikos* (Hungarian cowboys), and view the unique gray longhorn breed of Hungarian cattle, which have vanished from the landscape elsewhere. An overnight stay in the 250-year-old Hortobagy Inn, which offers charming if not deluxe accommodations, can be a most enjoyable experience.

Half an hour east of Hortobagy lies Debrecen, the largest city in eastern Hungary and the center of Hungarian Protestantism. Debrecen's Protestant College, which is one of Hungary's oldest learning institutions and also the seat of the provisional Hungarian Government during the revolution against Austrian rule in 1848, is exceptionally interesting. Other provincial cities worth visiting are Szeged and Cyula, both of which have annual summer festivals; Kecskemet, which is in the heart of the country's fruitgrowing region about an hour from Budapest; and Pecs, where two Turkish mosques remain, and which has a modern ballet.

In Budapest, the Margit Island, the Central City Park (Varosliget), and a number of smaller parks offer greenery and play areas for children. The Varosliget also contains the city zoo, an ice skating rink, an amusement park, and a first-rate circus.

A number of museums of old and modern art, several of oriental art, and of Hungarian folklore are located in Budapest. The Szechenyi Library contains old Hungarian publications and manuscripts.

Budapest has a variety of facilities for active sports. Many of the city's large, public, open swimming pools are filled from Budapest's natural hot springs, permitting outdoor winter swimming. Tennis, skiing, skating, sledding, and horseback riding are popular sports with Hungarians, and good possibilities exist for hunting pheasant, deer, and even wild boar.

Entertainment

Budapest's cultural life is rich: operas, concerts, chamber music, ballet, theater, and nightclub performances are presented almost daily. Budapest's two opera houses present a wide range of operas and ballets concurrently six days a week, September through June. They are often well staged and directed, with a wide repertoire of German, Italian, Russian, and Hungarian operas. All are sung in Hungarian. A number of foreign and Hungarian guest stars appear in Budapest during the opera season. There is also an Operetta Theater which specializes in light musicals.

Numerous concerts by orchestras and chamber music groups are presented. Legitimate stage plays are performed at more than a dozen theaters. Although translated into Hungarian, many Western and American musicals and plays, including works by Albee, O'Neill, Williams, Miller, and even Neil Simon, are performed.

More than 100 cinemas in Budapest feature films from all over the world—often some recent American ones. Many theaters show films in the original language with Hungarian subtitles. Folklore programs by the Hungarian State Folk Ensemble and other leading groups are presented every evening at the Folklore Center, and occasionally at other places during the year. Budapest is also well known for its restaurants, many of which feature gypsy orchestras.

During the summer, performances of operas, ballets, operettas,
concerts, and folklore programs are
staged in the outdoor theater on Margit Island, at the Buda Castle, the
Kiscelli Museum, and in some of the
other towns in Hungary. A music
festival is held each summer in the city
of Szeged. Youth concerts by various
popular music groups are given at the
Buda Youth Park.

Notes for Travelers

Many international carriers provide flights to Budapest via connections in major European cities.

Passports and visas are required
for entry. In general, immunization
certification is the same as for Western
Europe.

A permit to import shotguns may
be obtained from the Hungarian mission which issues the traveler's visa.

Budapest has many Catholic
churches, the best-known being the
Matyas Templom (the Matthew
Church) in the Var. There are also
several synagogues and Protestant
places of worship. Christ the King
Chapel (Catholic), the Church of Scotland (Presbyterian), and the British
Embassy (Anglican) provide English-
language services.

The units of Hungarian currency
are _forints_ and _fillers_. The official exchange rate as of July 1979 was 20.31
florints to one U.S. dollar. There are
severe penalties against unauthorized
currency exchanges.

Hungary uses the metric system
of weights and measures.

Special note: Pictures may be taken
in Hungary, provided they are not of a
military nature. Forbidden areas usually are marked, but in case of doubt,
cameras should not be used.

_The U.S. Embassy in Hungary is
located at Szabadsag ter 12, Budapest._

Iceland

ICELAND is a highly-developed Western European nation, and its citizens enjoy an advanced standard of living in an unpolluted and almost untouched environment. Born in the distant geological past when volcanic forces burst through a weak spot in the earth's crust, Iceland abounds in rugged lava flows, rushing rivers, massive glaciers, hot springs, and active volcanoes, giving rise to the name, "The Land of Ice and Fire."

A visit to Iceland is especially attractive to those who enjoy pure air and water, wide open spaces, and such outdoor sports as hiking, fishing, skiing, and ice skating. The small population and its full range of political and social institutions also offer opportunities to observe at first hand the many aspects of a developed nation.

Area, Geography, Climate

Iceland, the second largest island in Europe (39,706 square miles), is slightly smaller than Virginia. Three-quarters of the country is a wilderness of deserts, lava fields, glaciers, and extinct volcanoes. The landscape is lunar in many areas, so much so that American astronauts trained in Iceland in the early sixties in preparation for the first moon landings. A distinct beauty is found in the bareness of the landscape, and often the combination of crystal-clear air and brilliant sunshine creates vistas which can only be described as breathtaking. Lakes, rivers, and waterfalls are abundant, but trees are few. In summer, the inhabited coastal area is green and the pastures are filled with sheep, horses, and cows, but in the dark of winter the same area is windswept and forbidding, and often inaccessible. Large numbers of varied species of birds live on the coasts throughout the year.

Despite its location at 64°N latitude, close to the Arctic Circle, Reykjavik's (the capital) climate is similar to that of the U.S. northern marine west coast, although cooler and windier. The Gulf Stream helps keep the annual mean temperature at 41°F. Changes between summer and winter are not extreme. It is rarely very cold in winter, and never really warm in summer. Winter temperatures below 20°F are unusual, as are summer temperatures above 60°F. The wind blows year round and a wind-chill factor between −15°F and 10°F is common in winter.

Cooler weather lasts from October through April. Snow may fall in Reykjavik as early as September and as late as June, but often doesn't come until October or November and is rarely seen after April. Even in mid-winter, rain is as likely as snow, and a large accumulation of snow is rare. Average annual rainfall is 50 inches in Reykjavik. During winter and spring, winds in the capital can reach hurricane force. Overall, the climate is not as severe as that of New England or the Great Lakes winters. But, on a year-long basis, Iceland's weather has never been considered pleasant.

Iceland is so far north that the amount of daylight varies considerably throughout the year. Following the winter solstice on December 21, there is an average gain of six minutes of light each day and a loss of six minutes following the summer equinox on June 21. In December and January, there are four hours of dim light unless the weather is clear. In February, the days begin to increase rapidly, and by April are as long as in midsummer in the U.S. From late May to late August there is no darkness at all—20 hours of sun (or clouds) and four hours of twilight. Following this period of "light nights," the sun slowly retreats, and by October the days begin to decrease as rapidly as they increased.

Since the climate is cool, mildew and insect pests are rare, but on windless days flies, moths, and annoying gnat-like insects surround the lakes, and fishermen sometimes find a face net useful.

Earthquakes are common in Iceland but are rarely felt in Reykjavik. Volcanic activity is infrequent but rather spectacular when an eruption does occur. In May 1970, Mt. Hekla, thought to be the mouth of hell during the Middle Ages, began a series of minor eruptions which lasted for two months. The underwater volcano which created the new island of Surt-sey in the Westman Islands off the south coast began erupting in November 1963, and remained active through mid-1967. In January 1973, a volcanic eruption on Heimaey Island in the Westman Islands forced the evacuation of all 5,000 residents and destroyed over 300 homes and buildings. About 4,800 persons have returned to Heimaey and have restored the town to its former prosperous state. In early 1977, an eruption lasting for a few hours occurred in the Krafla area near Lake Myvatn.

Population

Iceland is the most sparsely populated country in Europe, averaging just over five persons per square mile. About 55 percent of the 229,000 Icelanders live in the Reykjavik-Kopavogur area. These two cities are respectively the first and second largest in Iceland. Akureyri, on the central northern coast, with 12,000 people, is Iceland's third largest city. Keflavik, the city nearest the NATO Base and 32 miles from Reykjavik, has a population of 6,422. The NATO Base has about 3,000 military personnel and 2,000 dependents. Most other Icelanders live in small fishing villages or farming communities around the coasts with from 200 to 2,000 inhabitants. The center of the country is completely uninhabited.

Excluding the American-manned NATO Base, only 300 U.S. citizens reside in Iceland. However, the number of tourists, business representatives, and other Americans visiting the country totaled 23,500 in 1978.

Icelanders are descended from Nordic and Celtic peoples who first arrived in the year 874. Most Icelanders are knowledgeable about their family history, very often back to the time of the settlement. The Icelandic language is of Germanic origin and was introduced from western Norway in the ninth century. The language has gone through so few changes since the Viking Age that an Icelander of today can read and understand 12th and 13th century literature, notably the famous *Sagas*. Although the Icelandic language is difficult, some foreign diplomatic personnel learn to read newspapers and carry on basic conversations. Their efforts are greatly appreciated by Icelanders.

Foreigners are often confused by Icelandic family names. Few continuing family names are used. The given name is the primary name, and the surname tells only the given name of the father. Surnames for males are formed by adding "son" to the father's given name. For females, the suffix "dottir" is added to the father's given name. The wife keeps her maiden name. The Icelandic telephone book, as a result, is arranged alphabetically by the first name.

The population of Iceland is 98 percent Lutheran, but although Lutheranism is the state religion, there is complete religious freedom. Catholics number about 1,000 and have their own church and hospital. The population also includes some 1,500 members of other Christian denominations.

Icelandic modes of dress, housing, and foods are similar to those in other Nordic countries. About 9.5 percent of the population earns its living from farming, 13.4 percent from fishing and fish processing, 16.6 percent from manufacturing, and the rest from service industries (26.3 percent), commerce (18.4 percent), construction (8.8 percent), etc. The country has virtually no unemployment.

Government

Denmark ruled Iceland until 1918, and both countries shared the same sovereign until 1944, when Iceland declared its independence. Since then it has been a constitutional republic, with a parliamentary government headed by a Prime Minister and nine Cabinet ministers elected by and responsible to Parliament. A President, elected every four years, has largely ceremonial powers. Iceland's Parliament (called the Althing) was established in the year 930, and is the oldest parliament in the world. It has 60 members, 40 in the lower house and 20 in the upper. All are elected for four year terms (barring an earlier dissolution of Parliament) by universal suffrage from citizens over 18. Elections are based on a system of mixed proportional and direct representation.

Iceland has four principal political parties. Based on the December 1979 national elections, the largest is the Independence Party (with 35.4 percent voting strength), followed by the Progressives, the Social Democrats, and the People's Alliance Party.

The Prime Minister is Gunnar Thoraddsen, and the President is Vigdís Finnbogadóttir.

Legislative power rests with the Althing and executive power is vested in the Prime Minister and his Cabinet. The constitution provides for a system of national and local courts to administer justice and specifically guarantees personal liberties.

District and town judges form the independent judiciary of Iceland. A Supreme Court sits in Reykjavik. Criminal cases are handled by the State Prosecuting Attorney. The judicial system also includes a Maritime Court and an Arbitration Court for adjudication of labor disputes.

Iceland is divided into 34 districts and 22 towns. Each district and town is administered by a magistrate and an elected council of seven to 15 members. Magistrates are directly responsible to the national government. Their principal responsibilities include police administration, tax collection, and the administration of state old-age pensions and other social benefits.

Arts, Science, Education

Icelanders have traditionally had a strong interest in education and the arts. The literacy rate is 99.9 percent. Reykjavik has a wide variety of bookstores including one devoted exclusively to English-language books. Book prices are high.

Painting, sculpture, theater, and music are enthusiastically supported. Museums and legitimate theaters feature Icelandic creative works as well as some of the better foreign productions, including American productions. The Reykjavik Music Society and the Icelandic Symphony Orchestra offer frequent concerts of classical music, and local social clubs sponsor Icelandic and visiting concert artists. The Icelandic Symphony Orchestra offers a concert series every other week during the fall, winter, and spring, often featuring internationally famous guest artists. Well-known jazz musicians perform several times a year in Iceland.

The City of Reykjavik sponsors a Spring Arts Festival every two years. It features classical, rock, jazz, and folk music concerts by well-known performers, as well as art exhibits. The nine cinemas in Reykjavik mainly feature U.S. movies, and a university film club offers classic and foreign films.

A National Research Council conducts research and administers government policy in scientific and technological matters. A variety of research is conducted by institutes of marine science, fisheries, agriculture, industry, and building. Research on Surtsey Island is conducted under the auspices of the Surtsey Society, which was created to coordinate international scientific efforts concerned with the newly formed volcanic island.

Education is compulsory for children aged seven to 15. The University of Iceland in Reykjavik has about 2,000 students. The University faculty oversees departments of law, philosophy, economics, Icelandic language and literature, theology, medicine, dentistry, and engineering. The *Saga* manuscripts, which were returned from Denmark in 1971, are housed in the University's Manuscript Institute.

Commerce and Industry

Iceland's 1979 estimated GNP was over U.S. $2.3 billion, or $10,600 per capita. The economy is based on private enterprise, cooperative societies, and government ownership. The cooperative movement plays a major role in manufacturing, fish processing, importing, retailing, and insurance.

The national and municipal governments, directly and through the banking system and investment funds, control a large share of the financial resources available to Icelandic business firms. Government involvement is widespread in shipbuilding, fish processing, cement and fertilizer production, communications, and electric power generation and distribution.

Iceland depends on imports for many of its needs. Fishery products comprise about 83 percent of the exports. The biggest overseas market for Iceland's cod and other ground fish fillets is the U.S., which bought about 36 percent of fish products in 1978. The U.S. is also Iceland's best customer in overall exports, taking over 29 percent of total Icelandic exports in 1978. Other major trading partners are the United Kingdom, the Federal Republic of Germany, and Denmark. Iceland depends largely on the U.S.S.R. for petroleum. A bilateral agreement with the Soviet Union provides for the exchange of Icelandic fish, wool products, and paint for Soviet petroleum.

Iceland's future industrial development will hinge on its abundant hydroelectric and geothermal power, and the government's attitude towards foreign investment. Apart from the fish processing industry, hydroelectric power installations, a diatomite plant, a ferrosilicon plant, and a Swiss-owned aluminum smelter, industry is rather small scale and geared mainly to meet local consumption needs.

Transportation

Iceland has no railroads or streetcars. Except for the paved road to Keflavik and the new road to the town of Hella, roads outside Reykjavik are mainly dirt or gravel and are of only fair to poor quality. However, nearly all inhabited parts of Iceland can be reached by ordinary car during summer (early June to mid-September). A four-wheel-drive vehicle with high road clearance is needed for trips to remote areas in winter. For trips to much of the country outside Reykjavik during summer, a four-wheel-vehicle is not needed. Automobile travel outside of Reykjavik often is impossible during winter.

Loftleider and Flugfelag Island (both Icelandic air carriers) are the only air transport to Europe and the U.S. A car ferry operates between Seydisfjordur, 461 miles to the east of Reykjavik, the Faeroe Islands, Scrabster, Scotland, and Bergen, Norway. This ferry leaves Iceland on the weeklong trip every Saturday from June 14 to August 23.

Local taxi and bus service is safe and efficient. Taxis are metered and zoned and are widely used and readily available, but they cost more than in New York or Washington. Tipping is not customary.

Although it is advisable to buy a new car abroad rather than in Iceland because of high prices, Reykjavik has dealers representing most major auto manufacturers, and any popular American or foreign car can be serviced locally. Repair service, however, is expensive and not guaranteed. There are only 120 miles of paved roads in the country, and the poor quality of the remaining road system, combined with the harsh climate, make it inadvisable to buy an expensive car for Iceland. A valid U.S. or other national drivers license is required, and all vehicles must be inspected. Car rentals are available.

Communications

State-owned telephone service is available to all parts of Iceland and principal points throughout the world. Connections to the U.S. are reasonably quick and clear. Reliable worldwide telegraph service is also maintained. International airmail to the U.S. takes three to six days depending on destination. Mail is not censored in Iceland.

The Keflavik Base operates a TV and radio station. The latter operates daily for 24 hours. The base TV cannot be received in Reykjavik.

Icelandic radio operates on LW and FM and offers popular and classical music and conversation programs. In the evening, the latter programming seems to prevail. Icelandic television transmits on both black and white and color about four hours a day, every day except Thursday and during the month of July, when the station is closed. Many programs are in English. Icelandic radio and television are state owned and operated.

A good shortwave radio is recommended for long-term visitors. VOA and BBC reception is good and gives an excellent supplement to world and U.S. news sources.

The New York Times is delivered to Reykjavik the day after publication, while the Paris edition of the International Herald Tribune arrives two to four days late. European editions of Time and Newsweek are sold at local newsstands. Reykjavik has six daily newspapers, all in Icelandic.

Health

Reykjavik medical facilities equal those in U.S. cities of comparable size. The University of Iceland has its own medical school, but many Icelandic doctors and dentists have been trained in the U.S. and Europe. Reykjavik has four reasonably well-equipped and -staffed hospitals, but they are usually crowded. Iceland has a state medical program, and doctors' fees are reasonable by American standards. Drugs and pharmaceuticals are expensive for foreigners.

Facilities for standard laboratory work are available, but for more sophisticated evaluation the tests must then be sent abroad. All medicines are sold only by prescription.

Official U.S. personnel may use the modern Keflavik base hospital, although illnesses or medical conditions requiring specialists are frequently referred to Icelandic physicians. Icelandic dentists are competent, but prices are high. Orthodontistry is available in Reykjavik, also.

Obstetric care is extremely satisfactory. Iceland has one of the lowest infant mortality rates in the world.

Reykjavik is a remarkably tidy city, relatively free of pollution, except when the fishmeal plants are operating. No serious endemic diseases or health hazards exist in Iceland. In fact, disease is less prevalent than in the U.S. or Western Europe. Influenza, whooping cough, measles, chicken pox, and pneumonia are the most common ailments. The long, damp winter causes at least one bad cold a year for most people.

Garbage is collected by the city about once a week. Water throughout Iceland is potable, pollution free, and so tasty it is often called "Icelandic Champagne." It is not fluoridated. One can drink water from streams without boiling it. Government standards for food inspection are high, and foods bought on the local market can be eaten without special preparation or treatment. Milk is pasteurized and government-controlled.

Major City

REYKJAVIK is the capital of Iceland and its largest city. It is on the southwest coast, situated on a peninsula extending north into the sea. It is a modern, picturesque city. New buildings of reinforced concrete are rapidly replacing older wooden frame and corrugated iron structures similar to those found in northern Norway. Small, detached, and semidetached houses and numerous apartment buildings are found in the city. The well-built homes are comfortable, small, and modern.

Most of the city has central heating supplied by natural hot springs. In 1928, the use of hot springs for space heating began and has been expanded to serve the entire city. Reykjavik is often referred to as the "smokeless city" because of this heating method.

Reykjavik is the seat of government and the focal point of Icelandic cultural activities. It is the site of the University of Iceland, founded in 1911. It has a museum of natural history; a national museum; theater and orchestra; art galleries; libraries; an outdoor stadium and indoor arena; and state radio and television. The city has thermally heated outdoor swimming pools open all year, three small lakes teeming with wild bird life year round, and several parks.

Reykjavik's terrain is essentially barren lava. However, the mountains and natural harbor form a scenic setting for the capital. The harbor, with its extensive shipping and fishing activities, has been the lifeline of the city.

Reykjavik enjoys a high standard of living, with per capital income ($10,600) similar to that in other Western European nations. The country has one of the highest inflation rates in Europe. All of the usual basic services are available, but at expensive fees. Barber shops and beauty salons do have reasonable prices, however.

Recreation

The Icelandic countryside is unusual and beautiful, and summer sightseeing can be delightful if the weather is good. Many sights are within easy driving distance of Reykjavik. The Krisuvik hot springs are 22 miles south. Thingvellir, seat of the ancient Icelandic Parliament, is about 30 miles east and has a magnificent view of the mountains. It is on the north shore of Thingvallavatn, Iceland's largest lake. Hveragerdi, a small settlement 25 miles east of the capital, has geothermal steam experiments in progress including large, steam-heated greenhouses that grow fruits and flowers. Laugarvatn, 60 miles east of Reykjavik, has a summer hotel and a lake warmed by the Earth's subterranean heat which makes swimming possible. At Geysir, a few miles farther east, is the world-famous spouter from which the word "geyser" derives. In the same area is Gullfoss, a magnificent waterfall. The well-known, semidormant volcano, Hekla, is located just east of Gullfoss.

Trips to remote areas are frequently organized by local travel agencies. Camping tours on four-wheel-drive buses are a common way to see remote places. The Akureyri area is about 280 miles north of Reykjavik. Fnjoskadalur, an eight to 12-hour drive, depending on road conditions, but only an hour's flight, is an excellent camping and picnic area. Nearby is Dettifoss, one of the world's largest waterfalls; Godafoss, another beautiful waterfall, and Lake Myvatn, an unusual area of lava, hot mud, and striking scenery are also in the Akureyri area.

Vestfirdir (the Westfjords), on

the northwest peninsula, although the least visited by tourists, has magnificent and breathtaking scenery. The chief town, Isafjordhur, is about 200 miles from Reykjavik and can be reached by car, air, or ship. The roads, like those elsewhere in the countryside, are poor, and passable only in summer.

On the east coast of Iceland lies Vatnajokull, the largest glacier in Europe. About 185 miles from Reykjavik, the area has some of the most spectacular scenery in the country. It takes two days by car to reach this glacier. Hotel accommodations are scarce in this area, so the visitor should take camping gear, unless he has booked hotel reservations well in advance.

Another site of particular interest is the island of Heimaey in the Westman Islands. It was here in 1973 that the Volcano Eldfjall was created by an eruption in a pasture near the city. The island was evacuated during the eruption, but most of the population have since returned. Quite a contrast exists between the active city and the desolation of the volcano area. Part of the city still remains under lava and ash.

The most popular family sport in Iceland is swimming, done year round in pools with natural hot water. Reykjavik has two outdoor and two indoor pools. Charges are nominal and facilities are excellent. The major spectator sports are soccer, European handball (a combination of basketball and soccer), and basketball.

Three ski tows are near Reykjavik but one cannot count on sufficient snow for skiing every year. Trips to Akureyri, where skiing conditions are more reliable, are frequently arranged. Skiing usually starts in January and

continues through April. Glacier skiing is good throughout summer.

Three golf courses are in the Reykjavik area and another course is available near the base. Although weather conditions have to be considered, Iceland has many golfing enthusiasts.

Except in winter, horseback riding is possible on trails and unpaved roads in the Reykjavik area. Icelandic horses are small, powerful, independent-minded creatures. Horse shows are held on summer weekends; these include racing—not comparable to thoroughbred racing. No betting is allowed in Iceland.

Iceland is world famous for many kinds of birds, and birdwatching is a popular activity. Lake Myvatn, located in the north, is a beautiful stretch of water high above sea level. It is noted for its waterfowl, including some which are not found anywhere else in Europe.

Some game-hunting opportunities exist. The season for geese and ptarmigan varies from one-and-a-half to three months in the fall. Reindeer hunting is permitted in the eastern part of the country when government permission, based on the size of the herd, allows it. Only the most dedicated hunters care to make this arduous trek, since the game is carried on foot or horseback to the nearest road.

Fishermen from all over the world are attracted to the outstanding salmon streams in Iceland. Most of the better streams are rented to Icelandic clubs or to individuals, and fishing time must be reserved months in advance. Unless one is lucky enough to be invited as a guest, the average charge per rod a day is a startling U.S. $150-$250. Trout fishing is also excellent and much less expensive. Sea trout and German brown trout live in streams near Reykjavik. Faxa Bay has good deep sea fishing, especially codfish, halibut, and haddock. A boat may be chartered for fishing parties.

Iceland has no tennis courts. Interest in track and field is strong, and a handful of joggers run at parks or the university's 400-meter track.

Extensive and unusual camping opportunities are available during the short summer in Iceland. It is easy to find an area affording complete privacy, and once in the countryside a tent can be pitched almost anywhere. A few organized campsites with modern facilities are also available. Campers must be hardy, since temperatures during summer range from 35°F to 60°F, and rain and wind are prevalent. Hunting and fishing licenses are not required by the Icelandic Government, but fees and permission are required by the landowners.

Hiking and mountain climbing also are interesting and rewarding. The enthusiast must come equipped with sturdy hiking boots and suitable clothes for these activities.

During summer vacation, several schools and institutions in the country are used as tourist facilities.

Entertainment

There are adequate entertainment facilities available in the Reykjavik area. Nine movie theaters show mainly English-language films with Icelandic subtitles. The films are usually one or two years old, but a few are more recent. Regular stage performances are first-rate, but sometimes difficult to understand without knowledge of the language. Occasionally the National Theater presents operas and musicals.

The Icelandic Symphony Orchestra performs every other week during winter, often with guest soloists and conductors from the U.S. and Europe.

First-class restaurants are few, but Reykjavik has six or seven nightclubs including three at local hotels. All restaurants and nightclubs are expensive. Liquor is not sold on Wednesdays in Iceland.

Notes for Travelers

Travel between the U.S. and Iceland is by air. Icelandic Airlines (Loftleidir) flies at least once daily from Kennedy Airport in New York, and several times weekly to and from Chicago and Baltimore. Many European connections are available, and all international flights use Keflavik Airport.

Visitors staying less than three months need no visa.

Icelandic law forbids importing animals into the country.

There are restrictions on the importation of firearms for hunting and target practice. Handguns are not authorized.

All local church services are in Icelandic, but many clergymen speak English. Religious services in English are conducted monthly by NATO Base chaplains at the University of Iceland chapel.

The official basic unit of currency is the Icelandic crown (*krona;* plural *kronur;* abbreviated IKr.). The exchange rate fluctuates, due to a policy of slow devaluation. Hotels and (some) restaurants accept U.S. currency.

The U.S. Embassy in Iceland is at Laufasvegur 21, Reykjavik.

Ireland

IRELAND today is being enlivened by powerful influences which are transforming it from a nostalgic land of legends into a forward-looking modern state. Notable illustrations of this progress are its increasingly influential role in the United Nations, its economic development program, and its entry into the European Economic Community. Known everywhere as the Emerald Isle, Ireland enchants travelers with its green meadows and striking scenery, but perhaps most of all with the friendliness and hospitality of its people. Some say that the Irish are the world's greatest (and most eager) storytellers. Loquacity certainly is an Irish trait.

Area, Geography, Climate

The island of Ireland is divided politically into two parts—Eire, informally, but not officially, called the "Republic of Ireland"; and Northern Ireland, a part of the United Kingdom. Of the island's 32 counties, Ireland has 26 and Northern Ireland has the rest. The partition of the island (since 1922) has been a subject of sensitive political controversy.

The area of the 26 counties is 27,136 square miles. The country is roughly 135 miles wide and 300 miles long, and is situated to the extreme northwest of the Continent. The Irish Sea separates it from Great Britain.

Annual rainfall in Ireland averages 29 inches, distributed fairly evenly during the year. Ireland is noted for its "soft" weather, and rarely do several days go by without at least a shower. Temperatures occasionally drop below freezing during five months of the year. Light snow may fall during winter. Mild winds and fog are fairly common, and winds of gale proportions sometimes occur, especially at night from November to May. Humidity is fairly even throughout the year, averaging about 78 percent. The climate is somewhat similar to that of Seattle, London, and The Hague.

Newcomers are immediately impressed with the beauty and charm of Ireland. Dotted with beautiful and historic landmarks, it offers widely varying landscapes, from mountain lake country to rolling agricultural and pastoral areas.

Population

The largest municipalities are Dublin, the capital city, with a population of 620,000; Cork, with 130,000; and Limerick, with 60,000. Shannon Airport, near Limerick, is the gateway to Ireland for many travelers. On the west coast is Galway, an ancient sea-

136

port, and the main city in that part of the country.

Business hours and attitudes in Ireland are easygoing. The average per capita income is now more than $4,500, but still much lower than in the United States or the more industrialized countries of Europe. English is the official language, but the government is making serious efforts to revive the native tongue, Gaelic. It is generally spoken in small enclaves in the south and west, particularly in the Aran Islands, off the coast of Galway.

Ireland is 95 percent Roman Catholic.

Government

Ireland is a sovereign, independent, democratic state, and functions under a constitution adopted by plebiscite in 1937. Its government is a parliamentary democracy, with a Parliament, a Prime Minister, and an elected President. The National Parliament (Oireachtas) consists of a President, a House of Representatives (Dail Eireann) and a Senate (Seanad Eireann).

The three major political parties are Fianna Fail, Fine Gael, and Labor. Garrett FitzGerald, leader of the Fine Gael Party, was narrowly elected Prime Minister June 30, 1981. He heads a minority coalition whose government business takes place in the lower house, the Dail Eireann. The Prime Minister and other Ministers, with the exception of the Attorney General, are members of the Dail.

The Dail has 148 members elected by secret ballot under a complicated system of proportional representation. An election must be held at least every five years. The Senate is composed of 60 members, 11 nominated by the Prime Minister. Of the rest, six are elected by the universities and 43 by various vocational and cultural interests. The Senate has no power to veto legislative proposals, and is allowed a maximum of 90 days to consider and amend bills sent to it by the Dail.

The President is elected by direct popular vote for a seven-year term and is eligible for only two terms. With Dail approval, the President appoints the Prime Minister who, in turn, names the other Cabinet ministers. The Cabinet exercises the executive power of the state and is responsible to the Dail. The head of government is the Prime Minister.

Modern Irish law is based on common and statute laws. All judges exercise their functions independently, and are subject only to the constitution and the law. They may be removed from office for misbehavior or incapacity, but then only by resolution of both houses of Parliament. Ireland's highest tribunal is its Supreme Court.

Arts, Science, Education

The Irish Department of Education provides free primary and secondary education and substantially aids vocational schools and universities. In addition, many private secondary schools are run by boards of governors, religious communities, or individuals.

Two universities are in the Republic of Ireland—the University of Dublin (world-famed Trinity College) and the National University of Ireland, comprised of four constituent colleges (Dublin, Cork, Galway, and Maynooth), and known as University College. Each receives an annual state grant and is a self-governing institution. Both offer courses in the humanities, social sciences, pure and applied sciences, and the professions.

St. Patrick's, at Maynooth, a recognized college of the National University of Ireland, is a pontifical university with faculties in theology, canon law, and philosophy. Law students also may enroll. The National Institute for Higher Education, Limerick, recently opened, and has programs leading to diplomas in applied science and engineering, business studies, electronics, European studies, and secretarial science.

A vital force in the life of Ireland is the Royal Dublin Society, founded in 1731 to encourage agriculture and industry and to promote science and art. The society's many activities include sponsorship of the famous Dublin Horse Show. The Royal Irish Academy devotes itself to the promotion of natural sciences, mathematics, history, and literature. The Royal Hibernian Academy encourages the fine arts.

Ireland has many other famed institutes and learned societies. Some of the better known are: National College of Art; Royal Irish Academy of Music; Abbey Theatre School of Acting; Dublin Institute of Advanced Studies, a research institution which specializes in Celtic studies, theoretical physics, and cosmic physics; Irish Academy of Letters, a society for the promotion of creative literature; The Arts Council; and Royal Society of Antiquaries of Ireland, which encourages the diffusion of knowledge of Ireland's cultural heritage.

Commerce and Industry

Until the mid-1950s, Ireland depended largely on its agricultural sector. Consecutive governments over the past two decades have favored a policy of rapid industrialization, and various inducements have attracted a significant amount of industrial investment from overseas sources, especially from the United States. Agriculture now directly contributes about 17 percent of the gross national product, and employs about 23 percent of the work force. Its importance is much greater by virtue of its indirect impact. Industrial output provides 35 percent of GNP. Important industrial categories include chemicals and chemical products, mines and quarries, textiles, metals, engineering, paper and printing, food, beverages, and tobacco products.

International commerce is crucial to Ireland's economic welfare, in terms of imports of essential goods, and in terms of national income, since exports account for over 40 percent of GNP. Industrial exports exceed more than half of the total, but meat and dairy products remain very important. Ireland has close and growing economic ties with the U.S., which is Ireland's second largest trade partner, after the United Kingdom. Irish exports to the U.S. consist mostly of manufactured goods, such as nonelectric machinery, chemical elements and compounds, glassware, cable, transistors, and photocells, as well as beef to American forces in Europe.

U.S. investors are prominent in Ireland in areas as diverse as banking, chemicals, automobile production, electronics, and hydrocarbon exploration and development. A big attraction to many of these firms, in addition to financial incentives offered by the government, is the prospect of entering their products into the Common Market—an access they might not otherwise enjoy.

The tourist sector is of great importance to Ireland as both an employer and foreign exchange earner. Earnings from tourism have climbed to over $400 million, one-fifth derived from U.S. sources.

In addition to membership in the European Communities (European Economic Community, the European Atomic Energy Community, the European Coal and Steel Community), Ireland belongs to the Organization for Economic Cooperation and Development (OECD), the Council of Europe, and the General Agreement on Tariffs and Trade (GATT).

Transportation

Public transportation in Ireland, a government monopoly, is sporadic. While the scheduling is adequate, performance leaves much to be desired. Buses and trains nearly always are crowded, and taxis are in short supply. Buses do not operate after 11:30 p.m.

London is only an hour by air from Dublin, and ferryboats operate frequently between Ireland and England. Flights are on daily schedules from both Shannon and Dublin to the Continent and to the U.S.

Automobiles are a necessity for any extensive travel in the Irish countryside. Traffic moves on the left, and right-hand-drive vehicles prevail, but there is no restriction on cars with left-hand-drive. Gasoline is very expensive.

Communications

Telephone, telegraph, and wireless communication facilities are not on a par with those in the U.S., and telephoning within Ireland can be time-consuming and often frustrating. Overseas calls, however, require relatively little delay. Air and surface mail is reliable.

Ireland operates two TV stations, and one radio station known as RTE (Radio Telefís Eireann). Radio Eireann operates 16 hours a day, and reception, especially in the evening, is good. The Irish Television Network (Telefís Eireann) broadcasts daily from 5 p.m. to 11 p.m. Coverage is greater on weekends, however, and includes sports activities. Four other TV stations—British Broadcasting Corporation (U.K.), Ulster Television (Northern Ireland) and Harlech Television (Wales)—can be viewed locally in certain areas, and all the stations broadcast in color.

Six daily papers are published in Ireland, all in English. They emphasize local and national news, so it is necessary to look to British and American newspapers for complete international news. British papers are available on local newsstands. Overseas editions of Time and Newsweek are sold in Dublin, and occasional issues of other American publications are available. Dublin has public and rental libraries and many good bookstores. Few American publications are available, mainly because of limited demand.

Health

Competent specialists in all fields of medicine and dentistry provide excellent services, but their equipment is not always as modern as in the U.S. Public hospitals are adequate, and medical charges are moderate. Private hospitals and nursing homes provide more modern facilities. Community sanitation in some areas is below U.S. standards, but there is no special health hazard.

Because of dampness and lack of

sunshine, arthritis and respiratory diseases are prevalent. There have been no serious epidemics in Ireland for several years. Immunizations of every kind are available in the large cities, and the Irish Department of Health offers free X-rays to all.

Major Cities

DUBLIN, Ireland's capital, is a vital and interesting city, long renowned for the vigor of its intellectual life. It is one of the most charming cities of Europe, and still retains much of the flavor of the 18th century, which is particularly noticeable in its Georgian architecture. Many small parks (the Irish call them "greens") separate blocks of buildings, adding personality to the conglomeration of narrow, twisting streets and series of wider thoroughfares.

Dublin, at sea level on the eastern seaboard of Ireland, extends north and south of the River Liffey along Dublin Bay for 10 miles in either direction. It is surrounded by rolling hills, called the Dublin Mountains.

There is a wealth of activity in Dublin, and legitimate theater is excellent. Abbey Theater is the most famous, but there are four other large legitimate groups, as well as a number of small theater clubs. Frequently, British organizations take productions to Dublin. French and German groups, with productions in those languages, also have appeared in Dublin. Grand opera, operetta, ballet, and other musical groups from England and the Continent perform frequently, and symphony orchestras and internationally known artists also appear.

About 26 movie theaters operate in Dublin and its suburbs, and most films shown are American or British.

Recently released films are shown on schedules comparable to American schedules, particularly in the more popular theaters in downtown Dublin. Nightclubs are limited. Most common are the pubs, which range from common beer halls to elaborate drinking lounges. Those licensed for singing are called "singing pubs," the most popular being the Abbey Tavern, The Old Shieling, and The Embankment. Dancing is a favorite pastime in Dublin, as it is everywhere else in Ireland.

The Royal Dublin Society's Spring Show and the Horse Show in August offer trade, livestock, flower displays, and some of the finest horse and pony jumping to be seen in Europe. The Horse Show, in particular, attracts many thousands of visitors from England and the Continent. Other international festivals being developed are the Wexford Music Festival, the Waterford Music Festival, the Cork Film Festival, and the Dublin Theater Festival.

Dublin has one principal museum and two major art galleries open all year.

CORK, on the River Lee, is an important port city, with a long history of rebellion against English oppression. Many of its lovely public buildings were destroyed in the fight for independence in 1920. Nearby is Ireland's greatest tourist attraction, Blarney Castle.

The many travelers who use Shannon Airport are familiar with **LIMERICK,** which is nearby. It is a busy city, and one replete with relics of Ireland's past. Salmon fishing is one of its major industries.

GALWAY, on the west coast, is an old city, and the Spanish influence of its early traders still is conspicuous in much of its architecture, and in the colorful dress of its people. It is considered the most Gaelic city in Ireland. Galway and the surrounding area are known for unsurpassed salmon fishing (in the River Corrib) and for the many and extensive oyster beds. An international oyster festival is held annually at Kilcolgan in County Galway.

Recreation

The Irish are enthusiastically athletic. A national sport, hurling, is strictly an Irish game, and is not for the less-than-hardy. Hockey sticks and head injuries symbolize this rough-and-tumble game. Irish football (a version of soccer) is probably more popular than hurling, and when the all-Ireland finals are played, excitement is in the air, and the crowds rival those of any U.S. bowl game.

"Hunting" in Ireland does not mean with a gun, but rather is on horseback or on foot with hounds. Hunting ranks with racing in popularity, with no fewer than 30 packs of foxhounds, 35 of harriers, two of stag hounds, and 17 of beagles. Visitors are always welcome at the hunting clubs and are assured of the excellent sport in the tradition of the Irish hunting fields. Hunting in Ireland is less expensive than in most countries.

What is ordinarily called hunting for game, is referred to in Ireland as "shooting." Excellent shooting grounds, especially in the west of Ireland, are under control of the Irish Land Commission, Merrion Square, Dublin, from whom information about leasing can be obtained.

There is scarcely a district of importance in Ireland without a golf course. The total is some 200—many of them splendidly laid out 18-hole courses, situated in ideal surroundings. Visitors are always welcome at any club. Fishing, too, is very popular in Ireland, and good angling is available in the many lakes and rivers, and all around the Irish coast. An abundance of salmon and trout fishing is free except for boat hire.

Horse racing is one of the most important features in the sporting life of Ireland. Irish horses have a fine record in classic events in England and other countries. Several leading courses are within easy reach of Dublin, and many others exist throughout the country. The world famous Irish Derby, the Irish St. Leger, the Guinness Oaks, and other classic events are held at the Curragh in County Kildare. The flat racing season is March to November. Steeplechase meetings are held throughout the year.

Greyhound racing is well-established with many tracks throughout the country. Clonmel in County Tipperary is the headquarters of the Irish Coursing Club, and many thousands of dogs are registered in the Irish stud book each year. Although it is not generally known, greyhounds are one of Ireland's big exports.

Camping, walking, and cycling are very popular in Ireland. Access to mountain and moorland trails is free. Strong winds and rough seas, however, limit water activities. Swimming is popular among the Irish, who are not afraid of extremely cold water. Yachting is a sport for those who can afford it, but more popular than yachting is rowing. Rowing clubs are found throughout the length of Ireland, with rowing regattas held annually. The rivers and canals afford boating and beautiful countryside. The Shannon River cruise is a splendid experience.

Ireland has many scenic and historic attractions, and any place in the country is within a few hours' driving time from Dublin. Trinity College, at College Green near the heart of Dublin, was founded in 1591. Its famous library houses the 1,200-year-old Book of Kells, one of the most beautifully illuminated manuscripts in the world.

At Kilmainham, in the western suburbs of Dublin, is Kilmainham Prison, where generations of Irish patriots were incarcerated and the leaders of the 1916 uprising against British Rule were executed. The prison is now a historical museum.

Dublin Castle, whose construction was begun between 1208 and 1220, is currently the headquarters of the police forces (Gardai) of Ireland. The castle stands on the high ground west of Dame Street, where the Danes had erected a fortress four centuries earlier, and was the nucleus around which the city slowly grew. Those parts of the original building still in existence represent the oldest surviving architecture in Dublin (except for some early cathedrals). In addition, the castle was the nerve center of British rule in Ireland from 1220 until 1922. The Bedford Tower portion of the castle houses the Heraldic Museum (the only one in the world) and Genealogical Office where family trees are traced and grants of arms are issued. Also in the castle are the medieval Record Tower and the oak carvings in the Church of the Most Holy Trinity.

Another Dublin attraction is the Chester Beatty Library, the most valuable and representative private collection of oriental manuscripts and min-

iatures in the world. It contains the oldest manuscript of the New Testament and unique Manichaean Papyri.

Phoenix Park (1,760 acres) is the largest enclosed urban park in the world. One of its attractions is Dublin Zoo (founded in 1830), which is world famous for breeding lions. The Dublin and Wicklow Mountains, with their splendid scenic beauty, offer a grand opportunity for an unforgettable weekend of camping and hiking. These mountains are only a few miles from the city center.

All major roads from Dublin to the other cities are paved and are generally good, but narrow. Excellent bus service is available from downtown Dublin to all local points of interest and to other cities. Within an hour's drive, visitors can tour the historic and picturesque monastic village of Glendalough, which is the sixth century ruins of St. Kevin's monastery and church. Twenty-three miles northwest of Dublin is the Hill of Tara, which was the ancient religious, political, and cultural capital of Ireland. Sixteen miles northwest of the Hill of Tara is the village of Kells, where the Books of Kells, the manuscript of the Four Gospels (in Latin), was written in the eighth century.

Blarney Castle and the magic Blarney Stone are just 162 miles southwest of Dublin near the city of Cork. Southwest of Cork are the beautiful Lakes of Killarney. A complete tour of the area includes a combination of motor vehicle transport, jaunting cars, ponies, or walking, and a boat trip on the lakes. Traveling by automobile from the city of Killarney, one can drive through the famous "Ring of Kerry," 110 miles of beauty and enchantment. Twenty miles northwest of

Killarney, near the western coast of Ireland, is the city of Tralee (where William Mulchinock wrote the renowned song *The Rose of Tralee* during the mid-1800s), and 58 miles northwest of Tralee is the historical city of Limerick. Seventy-five miles northwest of Limerick is the ancient and storied city of Galway.

In Galway Bay are the Aran Islands, 30 miles west of Galway City. The everyday language of the islanders is Gaelic, and their songs and stories enshrine Ireland's ancient folklore and culture. Many pre-Christian remains are found there.

Notes for Travelers

Most air travel to Ireland from the United States is directly into either Dublin or Shannon airports on U.S. airlines, but alternate routing is available on the Irish line, Aer Lingus, or on British Airways.

Passports should be carried if the traveler plans to cross the Northern Ireland border. No visa is necessary for Americans or British, and no travel restrictions exist.

Roman Catholicism is Ireland's religion, but several Protestant churches are represented, particularly in Dublin. Among them are the Church of Ireland (Episcopal), Presbyterian, Methodist, Congregational, Christian Science, Baptist, Moravian, Society of Friends, and Unitarian. In Dublin and the surrounding area are several synagogues and two Mormon churches.

The Irish pound is the basic currency; the rate of exchange is on a par with the British pound and British currency is accepted (at par value) in Ireland. However, Ireland has recently decided to participate in the European Monetary System, while Great Britain has opted for nonparticipation. Therefore, the future of this relationship is doubtful.

The avoirdupois weight system and long measure are used. Liquid measure is based on the English imperial gallon. Ireland changed to the metric system in 1976.

The U.S. Embassy in Ireland is located at 42 Elgin Road, Ballsbridge, Dublin.

Israel

The modern State of Israel was created in 1948 after more than half a century of Zionist efforts to provide a homeland for Jews dispersed throughout the world. The official design for this new nation was formed in 1917 with the Balfour Declaration, which avowed the British Government's support of a Jewish homeland in Palestine. Other countries, including the United States, upheld the declaration, and after World War I, the United Kingdom assumed the Palestine Mandate.

Nazi persecution of Jews during the 1930s and 1940s increased the incentive for immigration to Palestine, and international support grew for establishment of a Jewish state. In November 1947, the United Nations adopted a plan to divide the area into an Arab state and a Jewish state, but as the end of the British Mandate approached, disorders between the two segments of the population of Palestine degenerated into civil war. The State of Israel was proclaimed on May 14, 1948. The years since then have been marked with tension, border disputes, and open warfare—interspersed with cease-fire agreements and internationally-sponsored peace talks. Presently, hostilities have risen again in the long and bitter Arab-Israeli dispute.

Area, Geography, Climate

Israel is a narrow strip of land at the eastern end of the Mediterranean, wedged between the sea and the Jordan Valley. About the size of New Jersey, Israel is 280 miles long and 10 to 41 miles wide, with a total area of 8,000 square miles.

Since June 1967, Israel has administered the West Bank of the Jordan River, the Golan Heights, Gaza, and the Sinai Peninsula, thus more than trebling the area under its jurisdiction. The highest point within the pre-1967 boundaries is Mt. Hermon, 3,692 feet; the lowest point is also the lowest point on earth—the Dead Sea, 1,286 feet below sea level.

The climate varies considerably. The coastal plain has wet, moderately cold winters with temperatures of 38° to 55°F; a beautiful spring; a long, hot summer (79° to 90°F); and a cool, rainless fall. The inland hills are cooler than the plains and may have snow in the winter. The southern section, the Negev, is a hot, barren desert. The only rain in Israel falls during the winter and spring, usually in heavy downpours and thunderstorms. After the rainy season, drought becomes serious. As much winter rain as possible is held for irrigation; water from springs and rivers is also diverted for this purpose.

Sandstorms, the *sharav*, or *ham'seen*, are quite common during spring and summer. This hot, parching wind from the inland desert carries with it fine sand. The sun becomes brassy, and the temperature may climb as high as 100°F in Tel Aviv, and higher in the Negev. July and August are generally the most uncomfortable months. Pleasant, warm weather usually extends into early November. Insects, flies, mosquitoes, and cockroaches are abundant; scorpions are found in the Tiberias area, and there are poisonous snakes in the Negev. None present a major problem.

Population

Israel's population is about 3.8 million—3.2 million Jews and 600,000 Arabs. By ratio, 85 percent are Jews; 11 percent, Moslems; and the remainder, Christians and Druze. The Jewish population has increased nearly fivefold since Israel's establishment as a state.

Most of the Arab population live in the Galilee and in villages along the border between Israel and the occupied territories. Nazareth is the largest primarily Arab town within pre-1967 borders. An additional one million Arabs reside in the cities and villages of the territories. Bedouins still live in the Negev near Beersheba and in other southern areas.

In some Arab and Druze villages of the north and among the Bedouin in the south, many old, traditional Palestinian ways survive, little changed either by the British Mandate or by the State of Israel.

The people who live in Israel come from many different parts of the world. Although most of them learn Hebrew and are quickly absorbed into the life of the country, their diverse origins are apparent. The most striking evidence is the variety of languages spoken: English, German, French, Yiddish, Romanian, Bulgarian, Russian, Polish, Spanish, and Ladino. Hebrew and Arabic are the official languages of the country, but many Israelis speak excellent English. The government welcomes Jews from all over the world. Immigrants are taught Hebrew in *ulpanim*, intensive courses operated by the government. The *ulpanim* are only one arm of a phenomenally successful revival of the Hebrew language; it is also taught in schools and during compulsory military service. Virtually everyone speaks Hebrew, but for some 50 percent of the population it is the second or third language.

Government

Israel is a parliamentary democracy with supreme authority vested in the Knesset, a unicameral legislature of 120 members. Knesset elections are held every four years, or more frequently in the event of a Cabinet crisis, which leads to a Knesset vote for new elections. For electoral purposes, the country is treated as a single national constituency. Each party provides a slate of 120 candidates, and Knesset seats are apportioned according to each party's percentage of the total vote, starting at the top of each list. The current Knesset was elected in June 1981.

The President of Israel is chosen for a five-year term by the Knesset; his duties are largely ceremonial and nonpartisan.

The Cabinet, headed by the Prime Minister, is responsible to the Knesset.

Ministers are usually members of the Knesset, although nonmembers may be appointed. As no political party has commanded a majority in the elections, all Cabinets have been coalitions. In the June elections the Likud (right of center) block narrowly emerged as the largest single party, and Prime Minister Menachem Begin is endeavoring to form a new government.

Civil and religious courts serve the three major Jewish, Moslem, and Christian communities. Religious courts have exclusive jurisdiction concerning marriage and divorce, which they decide according to their own religious laws.

Since the Israeli Government considers Jerusalem the country's capital, most Israeli Government Ministries are located in that city. The Israeli Knesset (Parliament) is also in Jerusalem, as are the official residences of the President and Prime Minister.

Scores of social, religious, scholarly, and philanthropic institutions and organizations—Israeli, Moslem, and Christian—are located in Jerusalem. Included are the Hadassah Medical Organization; the Keren Hayessod, several enterprises supported by the Women's Zionist Organization of America; the Friends' School in Ramallah; Lutheran and Mennonite Schools in Beit Jala; and the Helen Keller School for the Blind in Beit Hanina.

Jerusalem's Role

Before the June 1967 hostilities, the eastern sector of Jerusalem and all of the West Bank of the Jordan River were governed by the Kingdom of Jordan. When Israeli Defense Forces overran this territory in 1967, the West Bank was placed under military government and is still considered "occupied territory." The Arab sector of Jerusalem was, however, incorporated into the State of Israel and is now considered by Israel to be an integral part of the State. Arab Jerusalemites (about 85,000) retain their Jordanian citizenship and passports, but are considered by Israel to be "residents" of Israel. The administration of the enlarged city is entrusted to the Jerusalem municipality headed by Mayor Teddy Kollek.

Jerusalem is one of the two independent consular posts in the American Foreign Service. The other is Geneva, Switzerland. Personnel assigned to Jerusalem are accredited to neither the Israeli Government nor to the Jordanian Government.

While the U.S. has had consular representation in Jerusalem for over 100 years, the post's present status in the city is based on the 1947 U.N. "Partition of Palestine" resolution. This resolution divided Palestine into two states, one Jewish and one Arab. Jerusalem, because of its unique religious and historical significance, was not included in either state. The city was set aside as a _corpus separatum,_ an international area under the aegis of the U.N.

The "Partition of Palestine" resolution was never implemented. Immediately after the termination of the British Mandate in Palestine, war broke out between Arabs and Israelis. At the conclusion of the hostilities, Jerusalem was a divided city with Arab forces in control of the Walled City and the suburbs to the north and east, and Israeli forces in control of West Jerusalem.

This division of Jerusalem was recognized *de facto* but never *de jure* by the U.S. Government and most of the international community, the rationale being that the resolution of the status of Jerusalem should be determined in the context of peace between Israel and Jordan.

The *de facto* division of the city continued until the Six-Day war in June 1967, when the Israeli Defense Forces conquered the entire city of Jerusalem and the West Bank of the Jordan River. Shortly after the war, the Israeli Parliament passed legislation which, by administrative decree, enlarged the Jerusalem municipal boundaries to include what was formerly Arab Jerusalem, as well as areas of the West Bank, and effectively incorporated the entire area into the State of Israel.

The U.S. has refused to accept the legitimacy of this annexation and continues to regard "Arab Jerusalem" as occupied territory. American policy on the question of Jerusalem was clearly stated by the Secretary of State on December 9, 1969: "We believe Jerusalem should be a united city within which there would no longer be restrictions on the movement of persons and goods. There should be open access to the united city for persons of all faiths and nationalities. Arrangements for the administration of the united city should take into account the interests of all its inhabitants and of the Jewish, Islamic, and Christian communities. And there should be roles for both Israel and Jordan in the civic, economic, and religious life of the city."

Arts, Science, Education

Israel's cultural, scientific, and educational institutions have played a significant role in blending a population of mixed geographic and cultural backgrounds into one nation.

Free, primary education is compulsory until age 15. Secondary education, which is not compulsory, is also free. Most schools are state-operated, but many primary and secondary schools are run by Jewish and Christian groups. In addition to Tel Aviv University, Bar Ilan University in Ramat Gan, the Hebrew University in Jerusalem, Haifa University, and Ben Gurion University in Beersheba, there are several other institutions of higher learning. They include the Technion Institute of Technology in Haifa, the Holon Technical College, the Bezalel School of Arts and Crafts in Jerusalem, and the Rubin Academies of Music in Tel Aviv and Jerusalem.

Israel, enjoying a worldwide reputation in the sciences, can boast of one of the highest levels of scientific manpower and competence in the world. Because of this competence, Israel ranks at the top of those countries receiving U.S. Government funds in absolute quantity for research, and gets the highest per capita share of the U.S. Government's international research dollar. Israel's principal private research institution is the Weizmann Institute of Science at Rehovot, which also offers graduate degrees in the basic sciences.

Tel Aviv provides Israel's liveliest cultural life with five publicly supported theaters and many small off-Broadway type theaters. Most productions are in Hebrew. Occasionally, there are simultaneous translations into English.

The Israel Philharmonic Orchestra, under the direction of Zubin

Mehta, is superb—one of the world's top 10 orchestras. Its home is the Frederic R. Mann Auditorium in Tel Aviv, but regular concerts are also given in Haifa and Jerusalem. Season tickets are practically sold out each year; there are some 24,000 subscribers in Tel Aviv alone. Occasionally tickets are available for individual concerts, as well as for special concerts not covered by season tickets.

Other symphonic orchestras are the Jerusalem Symphony, Haifa Symphony, and Galilee Symphony. Chamber orchestras include Tel Aviv's Israel Chamber Orchestra, the Beersheba Orchestra, and the Holon Chamber Orchestra. Tel Aviv has several internationally known chamber groups, including the Yuval Piano Trio, the Tel Aviv String Quartet, and the Israel String Quartet. Other excellent groups are the Israel Piano Trio, the Tel Aviv Piano Quartet, and the United Kibbutz Chamber Orchestra and Choir, sponsored by the *kibbutz* movement.

The Israel Museum in Jerusalem, the Tel Aviv Museum, the Haifa Museum of Modern Art, and Kibbutz Ein Harod's Mishkan LeOmanut are the principal public art museums in the country. Also, innumerable art works are found in other sites—from the Chagall stained-glass windows at Hadassah Hospital in Jerusalem to modernistic sculpture dotting the countryside. Private art galleries abound in main cities and smaller towns. Some excellent small art and archeological museums are in some 10 *kibbutzim*. Art galleries may also be found in the art colonies of Safed, Ein Hod, and old Yafo (Jaffa).

The Israel Museum also houses the outstanding collection of Dead Sea Scrolls, Jewish ceremonial objects, and archeological finds.

Tel Aviv's Museum Haaretz includes glass, ceramics, numismatic, ethnological, science, and technology museums, as well as the Archeology Pavilion, a pre-history museum, and a planetarium. The Archeology Museum, in a former Turkish bath in old Yafo, contains many local unearthed findings.

Commerce and Industry

Israel's economic growth has been among the world's highest, averaging almost 10 percent in the first 25 years of the state's history. However, the growth rate has declined since 1973. Between 1975 and 1977, real growth rates averaged about one percent, but by 1978, had climbed to 5.2 percent.

Israel today is a highly industrialized nation. Only about six percent of its 1.2 million labor force work in agriculture. A large part of the agricultural sector is dominated by cooperative or communal settlements—the famous *kibbutzim* and *moshavim*. Even so, many *kibbutzim* have developed industry to supplement their agricultural endeavors. The 1979 per capita GNP of about $4,640 put Israel on a par with many European countries.

Limited in natural resources and manpower, Israel has always had to rely heavily on imports to supply its large defense needs, to provide inputs for its industries, and to supply demanded consumer goods. Until 1973, Israel could finance an excess of imports over exports with gifts and loans from abroad. Following the 1973 war, the balance-of-payments deficit rose from one billion to three billion dollars. Financing this enormous deficit, much of it defense-related, is one of the central economic problems facing the Israeli Government today. Another is continuing inflation.

The Israel Labor Party and its predecessor, the Mapai Party, set economic policy from the foundation of the State, until the Likud coalition took power in mid-1977. The Labor Party had organized a mixed economy of a socialistic bent, with strong government intervention. The government sector was very large compared to the private sector, and together with industry owned by the Histadrut (the Israel Federation of Labor), provided the main thrust of economic growth. In the 1977 Likud coalition, the Liberal Party took over economic policymaking positions. The Liberal Party leans toward laissez-faire, free market principles, and favors lessening the government role in the economy. The Liberals have made wide-ranging changes in the structure of Israel's economy, including the lifting of foreign exchange controls, cutting subsidies on exports and on basic consumer items, and adopting a floating exchange rate for the Israeli pound.

The U.S. is an important trading partner with Israel. Israel's other major trading relationship is with the European Community. On July 1, 1977, Israel became an associate member of the EEC, and all exports of manufactured goods now enter the European Community duty free. Israel also benefits from the U.S. Generalized System of Preferences (GSP); over 2,700 of its products enter the U.S. duty free.

The U.S. extended to Israel $11 billion in assistance from fiscal year 1949 through fiscal year 1977. Half of it was in grants. In 1978, the approved assistance level was about $1.8 billion. The only other country giving major assistance to Israel is the Federal Republic of Germany, which provides annually about $300 million in personal restitution payments, and $50 million in long-term loans.

Transportation

Arkia (Israel Inland Airlines) operates daily flights between Tel Aviv and Rosh Pina, near the Sea of Galilee, and between Tel Aviv, Eilat, and Sharm-el-Sheikh. Arkia also flies a Tel Aviv-Jerusalem route and conducts air/land tours for those with less time than money. Arkia flights service Tel Aviv-Jerusalem and Santa Katharina in Sinai.

Steamship service is frequent, particularly in the summer, between Haifa and Cyprus, Greece, Turkey, and western Mediterranean ports. During summer, weekly auto ferries run between Haifa and Piraeus, touching at Cyprus and Rhodes en route; frequent sailings are available to Corfu and Venice.

Traveling to other countries from Israel is often inconvenient. Air links exist with many points in Europe, but fares may be considered high for the short distance involved. It is possible to travel to Arab countries only by either first going to Cyprus, or by going across the Allenby Bridge to Jordan.

Trains run from Nahariya near the Lebanese border to Beersheba and Dimona in the Negev, and between Tel Aviv and Gaza. Frequent and inexpensive service operates between Tel Aviv, Jerusalem, and Haifa.

Hitchhiking, or "tramping," is a way of life in Israel. Drivers are quite willing to stop for needy travelers. However, sudden pickups pose a traffic hazard.

Taxis are quick, easy to get, and usually metered. Group taxis, or *sherut* (Hebrew for service) operate within and between cities along predetermined routes. These run frequently, but only from central *sherut* stands for interurban runs.

Tel Aviv has an extensive bus system which is uncomfortable and crowded in rush hours. Service on interurban buses is good, although time consuming. Reasonably priced tour buses are both comfortable and enjoyable.

Municipal buses, trains, and Israeli airlines do not run between sundown Friday and sundown Saturday (*Shabbat*). Taxis, *sheruts,* and a tour bus line are available for the determined tourist on *Shabbat.*

A car is essential for most people who work in Tel Aviv—certainly for those who live outside the city proper. Almost any American car, even a compact, will be large by Israeli standards and may be difficult to maneuver through narrow, congested streets in some older parts of Tel Aviv. Parking in town increases in difficulty proportionally. Apartment parking facilities in Tel Aviv are cramped, and much maneuvering is often required to get into and out of the space provided. Families who live in the suburbs, where parking is not a problem, often consider the safety aspects of a large, heavy car versus the convenience of smaller models. Road accidents, many of them serious, are a fact of life in Israel.

Compulsory "no fault" third-party liability insurance rates are fixed by the Israeli Government; most Americans find that they pay more than they did in the U.S. for the same coverage. Many people also carry a U.S. comprehensive policy which includes collision and theft insurance. Israeli insurance companies give a discount for each year one has not made a claim against his previous policy.

According to Israeli law, headlights on all cars must be asymmetrical and this should be specified when ordering a new car. It is much cheaper to have them factory-installed than to have it done locally. If American manufacturers don't have these headlights, they can be purchased in Israel at an average cost of $30 a pair.

The damp, salty air and heavy dew at night make it difficult to start newer cars in the morning. Car covers will help protect against salt corrosion and rust. Many people find air conditioning useful during hot summers.

Auto repair in general, and even the smallest replacement parts, can be quite expensive. One should be prepared with spare parts for those that might not last. Windshield wipers, antennas, and side mirrors have disappeared from cars parked in Tel Aviv. Spare parts ordered from the U.S. may require a long delivery time. Service and parts for some foreign cars whose manufacturers cooperate with the Arab boycott are not available in Israel.

Communications

Israel has a country-wide, government-owned dial telephone network. Although it is a modern and growing system, a shortage of long-distance lines, especially to Jerusalem, can make dialing outside Tel Aviv frustrating. International calls are easily made and are usually clearer than calls placed locally. Satellite-telephone relay equipment connects with most parts of the world except the Arab countries. Reliable cable service, too, exists to all but the Arab countries. Direct-dial service is available through selected subscribers to the U.S. and most European countries. This service is continually being expanded.

Mail facilities are good.

Israel Broadcasting, the government radio network, broadcasts on several standard AM and FM frequencies. Newscasts in English and French can be heard in the early morning, early afternoon, and mid-evening. In addition, Radio Cyprus, VOA, and BBC are received on AM and FM. Shortwave reception is spotty. Local broadcasting includes American and European popular and classical music as well as Hebrew and Arabic programs. Classical music is also aired on FM stereo.

The national television network airs a number of English-language programs originating from the U.S., England, and Canada. At a moderate expense, an antenna can be rigged to receive TV broadcasts from the Amman, Jordan station which also has several English-language programs. Both Israeli and Jordanian TV operate on the European system. Except for prestige programs, Israeli TV broadcasts in black and white (CCIR), Amman in color. The color system used in both countries is PAL.

Receivers purchased in the U.S. work on the American system, and, if color, on NTSC. They will not operate in Israel without adaption. This can be done locally, but it is expensive and not always satisfactory.

The Jerusalem Post, a small independent daily, is the only English-language paper in Israel. It covers most significant events concerning Israel, but is sketchy on world news. Local dailies are also available in Arabic, Yiddish, Hungarian, Polish, Bulgarian, Romanian, German, and French. Several Hebrew-language papers are sold, including two in easy Hebrew for new immigrants. The International Herald Tribune, published in Paris, arrives a day late. Major European newspapers are also available with short delays.

Most major American periodicals are available at local newsstands; prices are double those in the U.S. Subscriptions by surface mail arrive irregularly in four to eight weeks. International editions of Time and Newsweek reach Tel Aviv within a day or two of publication, but subscription-copy delivery of air editions is slower.

Health

Israel has one of the world's highest ratios of medical doctors per patient. Doctors are highly competent and well-trained. English-speaking specialists, dentists, oculists, and opticians are available. Several hospitals have laboratories, diagnostic clinics, obstetrical services, and other facilities meeting the modern standards expected by Americans.

Most hospitals in Israel are good but crowded. Medical fees differ slightly from U.S. fees. American women who have given birth in Tel Aviv believe hospital maternity facilities rank favorably with those in the U.S.

Reliable and well-stocked city pharmacies are usually closed in mid-afternoon, but a rotating-duty pharmacy is open nights and holidays.

Community health conditions in Tel Aviv and Jerusalem are generally much better than in other Middle Eastern cities. Jerusalem, including the bazaar or *suq* area, is one of the cleanest cities in the Middle East.

Municipal health controls are satisfactory. The water is safe to drink; public cleanliness, sewage, and garbage disposal are good. As in most tropical climates, cockroaches and ants in homes are not uncommon, especially in kitchens and pantry areas. The problem is most acute during summer, but insect-repellent shelving paper and other defensive weapons are available.

Tel Aviv has the usual contagious and communicable diseases, but none presents a major problem. Some amoebic dysentery and infectious hepatitis exists, but much less so than in other countries in the area. Fungus infections are frequent. Those allergic to dust, molds, and pollens may have trouble at times, and some people find the long, humid summers debilitating.

Major Cities

TEL AVIV is Israel's largest city, with a population of 368,000 in a metropolitan area of over one million. Located about midway on Israel's Mediterranean coast, the city is bounded on the north by the small Yarkon River and on the south by the ancient city of Yafo (Jaffa). Between Tel Aviv and Haifa to the north, the numerous small communities give the appearance of a megalopolis interspersed with farms and sand dunes.

Tel Aviv was founded in 1909 as a Jewish suburb of the Arab town of Yafo. The city grew rapidly and quickly became the financial and commercial center of Israel. Banks, insurance companies, and business firms have their main offices in Tel Aviv/-Yafo. Manufacturing firms, a new uni-

versity, research activities, and the international airport give the feeling of living in a bustling metropolis. The pace of the city is Mediterranean with its hectic traffic, sidewalk cafes, and crowded noisy streets; but the newness and lack of greenery and open space set it apart from most Mediterranean locations.

Tel Aviv began as a garden suburb and, without apparent thought or planning, it expanded. As a result, streets are narrow and buildings are crowded together. Among these are some modern glass and concrete office towers, including the tallest building in the Middle East. In the newer parts of the city, improved construction and planning can be seen.

Shabbat, the Jewish Sabbath, begins late Friday afternoon and ends after sundown on Saturday. All banks and business firms are closed during that time. Some restaurants are open, and there is public transportation. Sunday is a regular working day for Israelis. The American Embassy is in Tel Aviv. Although Israel claims all of Jerusalem as its capital, the U.S. and most countries which maintain diplomatic relations with Israel accept only West Jerusalem in a *de facto* sense as the working capital. They regard the international status of Jerusalem as still undecided, pending final peace treaties between Israel and its Arab neighbors. So, most countries maintain their embassies and legations in Tel Aviv, although they transact much of their business with Israeli Government offices in Jerusalem. The U.S. Consulate General in Jerusalem is an independent post not subject to direct Embassy jurisdiction, but it receives administrative support from Tel Aviv.

JERUSALEM is situated in the

Judean Hills about 40 miles from the Mediterranean, at an altitude of 2,710 feet. The physical setting is dazzling. On a clear day one can look to the east and see the Dead Sea (1,300 feet below sea level), the Jordan Valley, and the Mountains of Moab.

Jerusalem's population is about 370,000, with some 285,000 Israelis living primarily in the western part of the city, and some 85,000 Arabs concentrated in the Old (Walled) City and East Jerusalem.

The U.S. consular district in Jerusalem also includes the West Bank of the Jordan River, which has a Palestinian Arab population exceeding 650,000. More than 90 percent of the Arab population in East Jerusalem and the West Bank is Moslem, but substantial concentrations of Christians live in Jerusalem, Bethlehem, and Ramallah and environs.

The official language is Hebrew. Many Israelis are fluent in several languages, and English is widely spoken. In East Jerusalem and on the West Bank, Arabic is the principal language, but many Arabs—particularly in Jerusalem—speak fluent English.

Jerusalem has vast emotional and symbolic significance for Judaism, Christianity, and Islam. It is a short walk from the Dome of the Rock (the third holiest site in Islam) to the Western Wall (the Western Wall of the Second Temple platform—once known as the Wailing Wall), and to the Church of the Holy Sepulchre (the site of Christ's tomb). Religion is an important element in city life, and religious holidays of the three major faiths are felt and observed as in no other city in the world.

Jerusalem contains many of the most important Jewish, Moslem, and Christian shrines in the world. The Old City is a showplace of outstanding examples of Islamic, Byzantine, Crusader, and Ottoman architecture.

Present-day Jerusalem is also an important educational and cultural center. The main campus of Hebrew University, the Bezalel School of Arts and Crafts, and the Hebrew Union College are located in the city. Two newly established four-year colleges on the West Bank are Bir Zeit University and Bethlehem University. The Ecole Biblique (famous for the New Jerusalem Bible) and the Albright School of Oriental Research are two of the many archaeological and theological research centers in Jerusalem. Tantur Ecumenical Studies Institute near Bethlehem is a new important institute.

Jerusalem's first-class concert hall features performances by internationally renowned artists and by the Israel Philharmonic Orchestra. There are also several art galleries, theaters, and dance studios in the city.

Traditional Palestinian handicraft activity (embroidery, olive wood carving, mother-of-pearl, and gold work) are centered around the Jerusalem and Bethlehem areas.

Tourism is Jerusalem's leading industry. About a million tourists visit Israel annually and most find their way to Jerusalem. Some 40 hotels are in East Jerusalem, and about 20 are in West Jerusalem. In addition, scores of shops, travel agencies, and restaurants cater primarily to the tourist trade. The climate is mild, with a long summer (May to October) of warm days and cool nights and a chilly, often rainy winter (November to March). Summer temperatures seldom go above 85°F. Humidity is low and mildew is rare. In winter, temperatures average 55°F, with occasional dips to freezing. Jerusalem gets an occasional *ham'seen* or sandstorm. These occur infrequently and are not as strong as in other parts of the Middle East.

Recreation

Tel Aviv

Swimming is possible about eight months of the year and even year round for the hardy. Tel Aviv and nearby coastal suburban areas have beaches, but these are generally crowded and full of tar. Some very attractive beaches are about an hour's drive north or south of the city. Bathing is prohibited at unguarded beaches due to a dangerous undertow, but this does not hinder popular seaside picnics from April to November.

The large, public saltwater pool in Tel Aviv and several freshwater pools in nearby Ramat Gan are usually crowded. Hotels in Tel Aviv and Herzelia, as well as the Kfar Shmaryahu Community Club, have large pools. The Tel Aviv Country Club, five minutes north of the city, has excellent sports facilities, a double, Olympic-size freshwater pool (heated in winter), 11 tennis courts, and a large gym. Skin diving, fishing, snorkling, waterskiing, and scuba diving are also popular in Israel. Diving classes with instruction in English are given in Tel Aviv and at Red Sea resorts.

Small boats can be rented for the day in Haifa and on the Sea of Galilee at Tiberias. Skin divers can explore interesting underwater ruins off the coast of Caesarea. The Gulf of Aqaba, off Eilat, has an incredible variety of tropical fish and coral reefs; an excursion by glass-bottom boat to see them is enjoyable. Eilat also offers excellent skin diving, waterskiing, and scuba diving.

Israel has one golf course, located at Caesarea, 45 minutes north of Herzelia. Near Tel Aviv, there are riding stables; a ranch north of Tiberias in the hills of Galilee offers trail riding. One ranch in the hills of Galilee runs guided horseback tours with camping and Western-style dining. Horse shows are frequent.

Hunters find a variety of game, including partridge and wild boar, but duck and geese are scarce. It is illegal to shoot gazelle. One can shoot up to 10 game birds a day during the September through February hunting season. Guns of any caliber can be licensed in Israel, but one cannot hunt with guns of "military caliber" (larger than .22). Twelve-gauge shotguns and .22-caliber rifles are recommended, since ammunition for these sizes is more available in Israel. Ammunition costs much more than in the U.S.

An advantage of a small country is that excursions can be made to almost any location in one or two days. Tour buses throughout Israel take in ruins, Crusader castles, old Roman and Phoenician cities, and Biblical sites, as well as modern towns.

Occasionally, arrangements have been made for volunteers to join archeological digs. Some search for old coins and artifacts on weekends. An archeology class in English, including excursions, is offered at Tel Aviv University.

For hiking enthusiasts, a four-day, cross-country march to Jerusalem is held each spring, yielding stories enough to last the rest of the year. Hiking in the mountains in Galilee is excellent; it is especially beautiful in spring, when the view from every mountaintop compensates for the climb. One of the most popular outings is to Mount Tabor; a monastery on top serves meals and runs a guesthouse (by reservation). One can either drive up the mountain by winding roads or climb straight up. The climb takes about an hour.

Without detracting from the splendor of Jerusalem or the lovely setting of Haifa, the beauty of Israel lies not only in its cities, but in the land. From rich northern greenery to rugged southern deserts, the land is for exploring, strolling, picnicking, and just enjoying. For added pleasure, in harmony with the natural beauty are sites with histories dating from the Crusades and Biblical times. Some spots connect with Israel's modern history and striking development. Among the interesting places are:

Caesarea. About an hour north of Tel Aviv, on a main highway, this ancient, partially excavated city was founded by King Herod, and was the Roman capital in Palestine. A long aqueduct from Roman times parallels the beach. The Roman theater hosts visiting artists during the summer music festival. Between these two remnants of ancient times is a Crusader city. The wall and moat are almost intact; inside the wall, much original pavement and several buildings have been preserved.

Megiddo. About one-and-a-half hours from Tel Aviv, archaeologists have uncovered 20 superimposed cities here. The lowest stratum dates back to the fourth millennium B.C.; the most recent one from the fourth century B.C. Megiddo was an ancient fortress and played a role in defending the

country against Thutmose III. Later, it was one of Solomon's "cities for chariots." The Hill of Megiddo in Hebrew is *Har Megeddon*— the Biblical Armageddon.

Tiberias, some two-and-a-half hours from Tel Aviv, is a winter resort on the Sea of Galilee. The drive to Tiberias through the hills of Galilee is probably one of the most beautiful in the world. The whole area around Tiberias is famous from the New Testament; Capernaum, Jesus' city, is nearby, as is the Mount of Beatitudes where Jesus preached the Sermon on the Mount.

Nazareth is roughly 45 minutes from Tiberias. Again, the natural beauty of the surrounding countryside alone would be worth a trip. Nazareth is the best known Christian shrine in Israel, as well as the largest Arab and Christian town in the country.

Acre (Akko) is about two hours from Tel Aviv. The fortress which the Crusaders built fell to the Turks, but the Turkish fortress which resisted Napoleon still stands. An impressive underground Crusader fortress was excavated in recent decades. Walls remain around most of the city; a British Mandate-era prison is now a museum. Acre is an Arab town and, like Nazareth, is a reminder that Israel is indeed part of the Middle East. On the Lebanese border, a half hour north, are the grottoes of Rosh Hanikra. The road heading east along the border is beautiful.

Haifa is about one-and-a-half hours from Tel Aviv. Israel's principal port, it spreads inland from the Bay of Haifa up the western slope of Mount Carmel. The view of the city and the bay from above is unforgettable. Most of Israel's heavy industry is concentrated in Haifa. The city's most interesting history dates from just after World War II, when it was the center of illegal Jewish immigration into Palestine. Museums in Haifa include the Museum of Antiquities, the Museum of Modern Art, and the Ethnological and Folklore Museum.

The Galilee is within three hours of Tel Aviv. The area has some of the best scenery throughout the year and has such interesting sights as the Crusader castle at Montfort, the ancient synagogue at Bar'am, the nature preserve at Tel Dan, and numerous *kibbutzim* which, until 1967, were frequently under Syrian artillery fire. Just to the east, within the Israeli-occupied Golan Heights, are the Banyas Waterfalls, the crater at Birkat Ram, and Mt. Hermon, where skiing is possible several months of the year.

The Dead Sea is the lowest spot on earth. On its southern shore is the infamous Sdom (the Biblical Sodom), which is now the site of Israel's Dead Sea Works where salt and chemicals are extracted from the sea. A few miles north of Sdom is the well-preserved and -excavated mountain fortress of Masada, where Jewish defenders held off the Roman siege in the first century. The climb to the top is a must for the hardy, but a cable car is also available. Farther north is the oasis of Ein Gedi—lush greenery amid the desert. A waterfall at Ein Gedi creates a pool which is excellent for swimming.

The Negev. Beersheba, 66 miles from Tel Aviv, is the gateway to the Negev. The city has historical interest as the home of Abraham. Currently, it is the site of the Bedouin camel market on Thursday mornings. To the south are the ruins of Shivta and Avdat. At

Avdat, a Byzantine church and Roman acropolis were superimposed on an ancient Nabatean foundation.

Eilat, 212 miles from Tel Aviv, is the southernmost point in Israel and its only port on the Red Sea. The port is bordered on both sides by mountains; the Sinai range on one side and the Jordanian Mountains of Edom on the other. It is a major tourist attraction and winter resort with swimming, boating, waterskiing, fishing, skin diving, and a world-famous aquarium and underwater observatory.

Just south of Eilat in the occupied Sinai desert is a Scandinavian-type fjord and the beautiful Coral Island. Farther along the coast of the peninsula down to Sharm-el-Sheikh are fine beaches, with tropical fish and coral reefs for swimming, and outstanding snorkeling and skin diving.

In touring and traveling, visitors should not drive through strictly religous towns or sections of cities on Friday night or Saturday, nor drive anywhere on the Day of Atonement, Yom Kippur.

Entertainment

In addition to the theaters, orchestras, and museums described, Israel has several repertory theaters as well as amateur and professional groups. Plays are performed in Hebrew, but many are familiar works translated from other languages, and some programs provide an English synopsis. Theater in English is sometimes possible to find, but not always worth the effort. Opera is not of European standard. Internationally known entertainers in all fields appear frequently.

More than two dozen movie theaters, including a drive-in, are in the suburbs of Tel Aviv. American and European films are shown in their original language with subtitles in Hebrew and English or French. Most films are at least a year old when they are shown in Israel. To avoid waiting in line to buy tickets, one can buy them in advance from a booking agency located near the U.S. Embassy.

Yafo (Jaffa), directly south of Tel Aviv, abounds in nightclubs, cafes, and other evening diversions. The renovated artists' quarter glows by night; most little shops and galleries in the Old City remain open late into the evening.

The celebrations for Purim, the Feast of Esther, include folk dancing and popular street entertainment, costume parties, and a beaux arts ball in the artists' colony of Ein Hod (near Haifa). A week-long Passover music festival is held at Kibbutz Ein Gev on the Sea of Galilee, and a festival of Christian liturgical music is given at Abu Gosh (near Jerusalem) in May. Each summer the Israel Festival of Music and Drama brings outstanding groups and individual artists from many countries, especially from the U.S.

Jerusalem

The drive to Jerusalem through the Judean hills is beautiful, with several interesting places to stop along the way. The countryside changes with every season; barren in winter, bright with green fields and blossoming wild flowers in spring, and parched in summer. Within the city is the Israel Museum with its collection of Dead Sea Scrolls, the Billy Rose Sculpture Garden, and fascinating exhibits within the main buildings. The Israeli Government buildings, Hadassah Hospital,

the Kennedy Memorial, Mt. Herzl, and the scale model of the old city are all worthwhile. Mt. Zion with King David's tomb and the room of the Last Supper are outside the walls of the Old City. Inside the walls are the Church of the Holy Sepulchre, the Wailing Wall, and the Dome of the Rock. Many interesting places in East Jerusalem outside the walls are also accessible, as are other West Bank sites such as Bethlehem, Jericho, and Hebron.

Present-day Jerusalem is divided into three areas: the Walled City (with its Christian, Moslem, Jewish and Armenian quarter), West (Israeli) and East (Arab) Jerusalem.

The Walled City, a relatively small area covering less than a square mile, is the religious, emotional, and touristic heart of Jerusalem. Contained within the walls are the Western Wall, the Church of the Holy Sepulchre, David's Tower, Via Dolorosa, Dome of the Rock, Al Aqsa Mosque, and other religious, historic and archaeological sites.

The Walled City is inhabited by about 20,000 people. Its narrow streets and bazaars are often thronged with pilgrims, tourists, and residents going about their daily business. Immediately to the east of the Old City, across the Kidron Valley, is the Mount of Olives, the lower reaches of which contain the Garden of Gethsemane.

West Jerusalem is that part of the city controlled by the Israeli Government prior to June 1967, and has a population (almost entirely Jewish Israeli) slightly exceeding 270,000. The western sector is a mixture of older stone houses, vast modern housing developments, government ministries, and educational and cultural institutions. Most shops, theaters, restaurants, and commercial institutions are located in West Jerusalem.

Jerusalem does not have an international airport, but one can fly from a small airfield north of the city to various points within Israel and to the Sinai Peninsula. Excellent plane connections from Ben Gurion (Lod) Airport (about an hour's drive from Jerusalem) are available to principal European cities, Cyprus, and America. Travel by ship is also available from Israel to Cyprus and to various other Mediterranean ports. TWA is the only regularly scheduled American airline operating in and out of Israel.

Sight-seeing, picnicking, and amateur archaeology are by far the most popular pastimes in and around Jerusalem where short, half-day trips are possible. Many organized sight-seeing tours are available for a modest fee. These tours go to almost every part of the country, and guides are usually good.

Numerous places of archaeological and religious interest are within a few hours drive from Jerusalem. Bethlehem is a 15-minute ride from the city. Nablus, home of the Samaritans and the site of the Roman city Sebastia, is an hour's drive. Jericho, one of the world's oldest inhabited cities and a winter resort for Jerusalem's Arabs, is located near the Dead Sea, less than an hour away.

The religious sites at Nazareth and the Sea of Galilee are less than three hours from Jerusalem by bus or car. The ancient port of Caesarea with extensive ruins, a bathing beach within the Old City, and an excellent golf course is two hours away; Eilat, five hours by car or bus or 40 minutes by plane, is a popular Red Sea resort, particularly in the fall or spring when it is not so hot.

Both Israel and the West Bank abound in historical sites ranging from the Biblical to the Crusader period. Jericho, Masada, Lachish, Hazor, Megiddo, Gezer, Sebastia, Caesarea, Askelon, Hebron and Acre (Akko) are a few of the many places of significance for those interested in the area's history. Most can be seen in a day; reasonable and adequate hotel facilities can be found for longer trips.

Except for soccer, which is very popular, organized team sports are not common in Jerusalem. The YMCA and YWCA do, however, offer excellent facilities for swimming, tennis, squash, volleyball, basketball, and gymnastics. Membership fees are modest. The YMCA and YWCA have summer day camps for children seven to 14 years of age with swimming, gym, outdoor games, handicrafts and outings.

Several attractive, clean swimming pools are within 20 minutes of Jerusalem, and three hotel pools are in the city proper. Ocean bathing at Mediterranean resorts (about an hour or two from the city) is popular. Pools and beaches are crowded on Saturdays in summer.

Horseback riding is available in Jerusalem. Hunting for birds and wild boar is permitted in Galilee and Golan, but there is no shooting on the West Bank.

Entertainment

Movies are a popular form of evening entertainment in Jerusalem. Jerusalem's 12 movie theaters are somewhat spartan, but feature many

American and English films. There is also a Cinematheque, and the Israel Museum and the Jerusalem Theatre run art films on a twice-weekly basis.

Israel's Philharmonic Orchestra plays regularly in the Jerusalem Concert Hall during the winter and spring. Many world famous conductors and renowned guest artists appear with the Philharmonic throughout the season. There are also a Jerusalem Symphony Orchestra and excellent chamber music groups.

There are two major archaeological museums in Jerusalem, and frequent lectures are held at the Hebrew University, many of them in English.

Although Jerusalem is not generally considered a gourmet's paradise, many hotels and restaurants in the city are more than adequate. The American Colony Hotel in East Jerusalem offers a unique atmosphere and good cuisine; the King David Hotel in West Jerusalem and the Intercontinental on the Mount of Olives both have adequate dining facilities. The latter offers dancing two or three times a week.

Photography is popular in Israel. Local processing of black-and-white film is satisfactory, but color film should be developed in the U.S. Photographers should be wary of taking pictures of Orthodox Jews or traditionally dressed Arabs, especially if they are at worship.

A number of holidays in both Israel and the West Bank offer interesting festivities. In the Arab sector of Jerusalem, the pilgrimages and ceremonies of the Eastern and Western churches during the Christmas and Easter seasons are impressive, and the Samaritan Passover at Nablus is an unusual event. In Israel, Purim (or Carnival) is celebrated by young and old in costumes. Passover is commemorated by *Seder*, or ritual family dinner.

Notes for Travelers

The normal travel routes from the U.S. to Israel are by air (direct from New York to Tel Aviv), or by ship to Naples, and then on to Haifa. Travelers arriving in Tel Aviv may proceed to Jerusalem by bus or *sherut* (group taxi).

No visas are required in tourist passports, but are issued at time of entry. Bearers of diplomatic and official passports (who enter on assignment) must have Israeli visas. All travelers are required to have smallpox vaccination certificates; if arriving from the Far East, cholera inoculation is necessary, and from Africa, yellow fever vaccination is required. In addition, typhoid/paratyphoid and tetanus shots are recommended.

Only the following nonautomatic firearms are allowed: in Jerusalem, .22, .38, or .45 pistols (1); .22 or 30/30 rifles (1); and 12 or 16 gauge shotguns (1); in Tel Aviv, .22 rifles (1); and 12 or 20 gauge shotguns (1). One hundred rounds of ammunition (600 for shotguns) are allowed.

Israeli pounds are the official currency. The pound (IL) is divided into 100 *agurot*. American dollars and hard currency of other countries are easily convertible at banks and through authorized money changers. Certain shops accept foreign currency, but in general, business transactions are made in pounds. Because of increasing inflation, the currency exchange rate fluctuates.

The metric system of weights and measures is used. An exception is the *dunam* (one-quarter acre or one-tenth hectare), a land measure which dates back to Ottoman times.

Special note:

Synagogues abound throughout Israel. Several churches are found in Yafo: St. Anthony's Church and St. Peter's Church (Roman Catholic); the Greek Orthodox Church; the Anglican (Episcopalian) Church; and the Church of Scotland (Presbyterian). Christian worship services in English (ecumenical, Anglican, Episcopalian, and Roman Catholic) are conducted every Sunday in Herzelia Pituach in private homes.

A Baptist Mission near Petach Tikva is about a 20-minute drive from Tel Aviv. A Christian Science group meets Sundays in the Hilton Hotel.

Jerusalem probably has the world's highest per capita number of churches, synagogues, and mosques. Many buildings have historical, religious, and architectural significance.

The Old City has Roman Catholic, Greek Orthodox, Armenian Orthodox, and Coptic partriarchates, and an Anglican church presided over by an archbishop. There are also bishoprics of the Syrian Orthodox and various Uniate churches and a large Lutheran church. In West Jerusalem there are Roman Catholic, Scottish Presbyterian, Greek Orthodox, Anglican, and Baptist churches, as well as congregations of smaller fundamentalist denominations.

Interdenominational and Protestant services are held weekly in the YMCAs in both East and West Jerusalem. Many visitors enjoy attending midnight mass on Christmas Eve in Bethlehem or Easter services in the Church of the Holy Sepulchre, and visiting synagogues on Jewish holidays.

The U.S. Embassy in Israel is located on the seashore at 71 Hayarkon Street, Tel Aviv. The Consulate General has two offices—one in West Jerusalem at 16-18 Agron Road, and one in East Jerusalem on Nablus Road.

Italy

ITALY, whose cultural and artistic heritage has made a major contribution to Western civilization, is today a nation in transition. Its striking political and economic challenges seriously affect the stability of the country, and constant crises have become a way of life. Yet, in spite of this turmoil, Italy continues to maintain equality and partnership in the community of democratic nations.

Area, Geography, Climate

Italy's 116,300 square miles make it about the size of New York and the New England states combined. Most of this territory lies on a mountainous 500-mile-long, boot-shaped peninsula, which thrusts southeastward into the Mediterranean Sea. North of the peninsula lies the Po Valley-Venetian Plain area, which extends some 300 miles east to west, bounded to north, east, and west by the foothills of the Alps. This region is the agricultural and industrial center of Italy.

To the west and south, Italy includes the large islands of Sardinia and Sicily, plus many small islands, the most important being Elba, Pantelleria, and the Eolian (Lipari) group. Its position on the main routes between Europe, Africa, and the Middle East has given Italy throughout history great political, economic, and strategic importance. The western tip of Sicily is only 80 miles from Africa.

Except for the Po Valley in the north, Italy is generally rugged and mountainous. The Alps and their foothills occupy a large part of the north. The Apennines cover most of the peninsula, except for the heel of the boot in the south and certain limited coastal areas.

Italy's climate is generally mild and "Mediterranean," but wide variations occur. Sicily and the south are broadly comparable, although warmer on the average, to southern California. The Alps and Dolomites in the north have a climate similar to that of our Mountain States.

Population

Italy has about 57 million people. Population density is about twice as great as in the similar-sized New York State-New England area. Population growth rates have slowed markedly in comparison with pre-World War II levels. Millions of Italians, mostly from the economically depressed south, have emigrated in the last 100 years, mainly to the United States, Brazil, Argentina, Venezuela, Canada, and Australia. About two million Italians now work in other European countries, mainly France, Germany, and Switzerland.

Outside of Rome and the main tourist centers, few Italians speak second languages. English and French are the most common, but in many areas it is often difficult to find anyone who speaks anything but Italian.

Ethnic minorities are small; largest are the German-speaking people of Bolzano Province and the Slovenes around Trieste. In addition, ancient communities of Albanian, Greek, Ladino, and French origin exist.

Over 99 percent of Italians are nominally Catholic. About 150,000 are Protestants (two-thirds of whom belong to the Waldensian sect which predates the Reformation), about 35,000 are Jewish, and a small number are Greek Orthodox.

The position of the Catholic Church in Italy is governed by a series of accords with the Italian state, the most recent being the Lateran Pacts of 1929, which were confirmed by the present constitution. The Vatican is recognized as an independent sovereign state. Although Roman Catholicism is the official religion of the state, the constitution provides for religious freedom.

Government

Italy has been a democratic republic since June 2, 1946, when the monarchy was abolished by popular referendum. The constitution, which came into effect on January 1, 1948, established a bicameral Parliament, a separate judiciary, and an executive branch composed of a Council of Ministers (Cabinet) headed by the President of the Council (or Prime Minister).

The Cabinet, which in practice is composed of members of Parliament, must retain the confidence of both houses. In addition, the President of the Republic is chief of state. He is elected for seven years by Parliament sitting jointly with a small number of regional delegates. He nominates the Prime Minister who chooses the other Ministers.

Except for seven senators appointed for life, both houses of Parliament—the Chamber of Deputies (630 members) and the Senate (322 members)—are popularly and directly elected by proportional representation. The political parties have a predominant role in the selection of legislators, since individual members of parliament are selected by each party from its electoral ballot list in proportion to the party's percentage of the vote in each district. Thus, direct communication between legislators and constituents is relatively rare, as citizens usually deal with their representatives through their party. Both houses are elected for a maximum of five years, but either may be dissolved by the President of the Republic before the expiration of its normal term. Legislative bills may be introduced in either house, but must be approved by a majority in both.

The Italian state is moving from a highly centralized system to a plan which gives greater authority to the regions. The chief executive of each of the 95 provinces (including Valle d'Aosta), the Prefect, is appointed by and answerable to the central government. In addition to the provinces, the constitution provides for 20 regions (five of which have special status) with limited governing powers.

Since 1953, no party has held an

absolute majority in either house of Parliament. For their parliamentary majorities, Italian governments have had to depend on coalitions of political groups, in each case centered around the Christian Democratic (DC) Party. Until the early 1960s, postwar governments were generally "center" coalitions (the DC plus the Liberals, Social Democrats, and Republicans). From 1962 to 1972, most governments were "center-left" (the DC plus Social Democrats, Republicans, and Socialists). Thereafter, a variety of formulas were attempted. The present coalition, formed in July 1981, is headed by Prime Minister Giovanni Spadolini, leader of the Republican Party and the first non-Christian Democrat since World War II to head the government.

The following are the major parties with representation in the national Parliament:

Christian Democrat Party (DC)— the core of postwar governments. United by Catholicism by representing a wide range of views.

Italian Communist Party (PCI)— the world's largest nonruling Communist party (1.8 million members). The PCI holds a majority in many municipal and provincial governments and is particularly influential in many areas of Italian life, including labor, media, education, and the arts.

Italian Socialist Party (PSI)—Italy's oldest party, with a long and troubled history of internal problems and schisms. Having alternately cooperated with the PCI and the DC, it now seeks to establish an identity independent of both.

Italian Social Movement-National Right (MSI-DN)—a far right party which includes new-Fascist and Monarchist elements.

Italian Social Democrat Party (PSDI)—formed when the PSI split in July 1969.

Italian Republican Party (PRI)—a small but influential left-of-center lay party which has participated in most postwar governments.

Italian Liberal Party (PLI)—a conservative, business-oriented, center party which was badly battered in the 1976 elections.

Arts, Science, Education

Despite centuries of political disunity and poverty, and surprisingly (in light of its reputation) poor agricultural land and raw materials, Italy has enjoyed several epochs during which it was at the center, or was the center, of the Western cultural tradition. The Roman Empire and the time of the Italian Renaissance are obvious examples, but artifacts from the Etruscans and the Roman Republic show astonishing imaginative fertility; the Dark Ages saw Italy as a crossroads of the relation between Europe and "higher" cultures to the east and south; preeminence in university education began during medieval times; and contributions to pre-Renaissance European culture, to Western philosphy and all the arts, to the Romantic movement in Europe, and to modern science, arts, and scholarship are formidable.

Any examples are arbitrary. Throughout much of this century, Italian playwrights were receiving regular productions throughout the world, just as their predecessors, the composers in the great tradition of Italian opera, make up the heart of every opera company's repertoire. Following the war, Italian new realism became the most important force in cinema, and Italian design shaped the look of the postwar world. The postwar film giants, such as Rossellini and DeSica, were followed by Fellini and Antonioni, and then by Pasolini, Bertolucci, and Rosi.

Italian education has suffered from politicization, especially in the overcrowded universities, so that while individual Italian scholars are renowned in their fields, the reputation of the education system of today has declined.

Transportation

Public transportation is modern, efficient, and reasonably priced, but plagued by strikes. Modern buses operate between major cities, with connections to smaller towns. Fast modern trains, diesel and electric, provide two classes of service and operate between all important points. Major international air carriers serve the large cities. Alitalia and ATI (Italian Airlines) furnish quick service to most main cities, as does a smaller airline, Itavia. Generally speaking, ground transportation is less expensive than in the U.S., and air travel more expensive.

Transportation within the cities, whether by bus or tramway, is good, although crowded at rush hours. The hill cities also have public elevators and funicular railways.

Taxis, fairly inexpensive, are usually available. They do not cruise looking for fares, but wait at taxistands throughout the cities. They are metered, and a minimum fare is imposed. A small additional charge is made for service at night and for transporting bulky articles such as trunks. It is possible to phone a stand for a taxi; the driver starts his meter when he leaves the stand. It is customary to tip about 10 percent of the fare. One should avoid unmetered taxis—they are privately owned and usually charge outrageous prices.

Traffic moves on the right in Italy. The highways are generally well-maintained but, except for the superhighways (called *autostrade*), they are narrow and winding. Standard American cars are rather large for the narrow roads, so an American compact or small foreign car is best.

Liability insurance must be placed locally; several American companies have affiliates and prices are comparable to those in the U.S. Cars driven into Italy must have an international "green card" certificate of insurance. Collision and theft insurance is also available locally, or from American insurers such as Clements in Washington, American International Underwriters, or USAA.

Present regulations allow non-Italian nationals to drive in Italy if they have valid drivers licenses. If the license is not Italian, an Italian translation must be carried with it at all times. If one does not have a valid license, he must obtain an Italian license, which requires oral and road driving tests.

Shops experienced in repairing American cars can be found in Rome and Naples, but not in other communities.

Communications

Telephone and telegraph connections within Italy and to international points are good. International mail service between Italy and the U.S., however, is rather slow. It may be some weeks before a letter arrives by airmail. Surface mail takes six to eight weeks, and packages are subject to customs inspection.

Italy has three state-controlled radio programs, broadcasting day and evening hours on both AM and FM. Program content varies from comedy and popular music to lectures, panel discussions, classical music, and opera. All three offer frequent newscasts. In addition, a growing number of private FM stations broadcast a mix of popular and classical music. A shortwave radio can receive VOA, BBC, the Armed Forces Network in Germany, and other European stations.

The two TV channels controlled by Radio-Televisione Italiana offer varied programs—news, operas, plays, documentaries, musicals, and films—all in Italian. Some programs are now offered in color. A roof antenna will bring in nearby stations from France, Switzerland, Yugoslavia, and Monaco. In Italy, the past several years have seen the growth of private TV stations which also broadcast a varied schedule of movies and talk shows.

American TV sets must be converted to receive both sound and picture, but this can be done locally at reasonable cost. Radios and TV sets are available locally at only slightly more than U.S. retail prices.

Two local English-language newspapers, the Daily News and the Daily American, appear throughout Italy, and include local and international news, syndicated columns, and classified ads. The Paris International Herald Tribune is received in Rome in the early afternoon the day of publication. It is not available in some cities until the following morning. European editions of Time and Newsweek are available one or two days after publication. Foreign newspapers and magazines are available on newsstands and current U.S. magazines also can be found. Rome has several English-language bookstores with a varied, but high-priced, stock. A more limited selection in English is found in Italian bookstores in other cities.

Health

Medical facilities including physicians, specialists in most fields, hospitals, and clinics are available in the large cities. However, because of funding limitations, public hospitals often are understaffed, and without up-to-date equipment. Private hospitals are usually on a par with those in the U.S., but are rather expensive. Medicines are available from local pharmacies.

Sanitary controls throughout Italy are generally good. The water in the large cities is usually safe, but not fluoridated. Good pasteurized milk is available. Uncooked shellfish and rare meats are unsafe. Precautions, such as washing fresh fruit and vegetables and avoiding raw seafood, are the same as those advisable in the U.S.

No unusual diseases are common in Italy. Respiratory ailments are quite prevalent during winter, particularly in cities with smog problems, such as Milan and Turin. Inoculations against hepatitis and influenza are recommended.

Major Cities

ROME, probably the most famous city in the world, has been the capital of Italy since 1870. It surrounds the small independent Vatican State, historic center of the Roman Catholic Church. It is located about halfway down the southwest side of the peninsula, in the center of a small rolling plain known as the Roman Campagna. The hills on which the city is built range from 44 feet above sea level at the Pantheon, in the oldest part of the city, to 462 feet at the top of Monte Mario, a modern residential district. Rome is 15 miles inland on the Tiber River.

A city of over three million people, Rome is primarily a government and commercial center. It is a metropolis with modern shops, stores, restaurants, hotels, and apartments. Many foreigners live in Rome, but foreign colonies are not clearly defined. Foreigners include employees of various governments, international organizations, and private firms, as well as students and retired persons. About 15,000 Americans permanently reside in the U.S. consular district.

Since the Lateran Treaty of 1929, signed by Cardinal Gasparri for Pope Pius XI and Benito Mussolini for Victor Emmanuel III, Vatican City has been an independent state. Completely surrounded by Rome, the Vatican is a triangular tract of land on 109 acres, populated by about 1,000, with the pope as its absolute ruler. Saint Peter's Church lies in its southeast corner. To the north are administrative buildings and Belvedere Park. The pontifical palaces and the Vatican Gardens are located in the western part of the state. There are several basilicas, churches, and other buildings in Rome which are granted the rights of extraterritoriality and tax exemption, but not papal sovereignty.

The Sistine Chapel, whose ceiling

was painted by Michelangelo from 1508–12, is in the Vatican. The Swiss Guards are the bodyguards of the pope. Founded in the 16th century, the corps is comprised of a small group of Roman Catholic Swiss who wear uniforms designed by Michelangelo.

The political freedom of the Vatican is guaranteed and protected by Italy. The state has its own citizenship, issues its own currency and postage stamps, and has its own flag and diplomatic corps. It has its own newspaper (Osservatore Romano), railroad station, and broadcasting facilities.

The Vatican is open to visitors all year and the pope receives callers in public and private audiences. U.S. citizens should send requests for papal audiences to The North American College in Rome. The address is Casa Santa Maria dell' Umilta, Via dell'- Umilta 30, 00187, Rome, Italy. The telephone number is 679-2256.

Described by Petrarch as the "Pearl of Cities," **FLORENCE**'s glorious past and dynamic present never cease to fascinate students and visitors from all parts of the world. The splendors of the Italian Renaissance are not only manifested in its famous churches, palaces, and museums, but are kept alive in the tradition of craftsmanship, making Florence and the region of Tuscany one of the world's major handicraft centers.

Florence is in the heart of a rich agricultural region whose principal products are cereal grains, vegetables, olives, and the famous Chianti wine. The city has a population of 450,000. About 3,000 are non-Italian residents, mainly American, British, and Swiss citizens.

Most members of the foreign colony, and the Italians who move in this circle, speak English. However, very few of the general Italian population, and virtually none of the Italian officials, speak or understand English. Shopkeepers, travel agencies, and hotels catering to tourists have English-speaking personnel; otherwise, only Italian is used.

Florence receives hundreds of thousands of American visitors each year. The U.S. consular district there comprises all of Tuscany and all of Emilia Romagna except for the provinces of Parma and Piacenza. These provinces have a population of about six-and-a-half million. Major cities include Florence, Bologna, Pisa, Ferrara, Arezzo, Siena, Livorno, Modena, and Ravenna.

The consul general is also the U.S. representative to the Republic of San Marino, the world's oldest and smallest republic. Believed to have been founded about 300 A.D., the Republic covers an area of 24 square miles and has 19,000 inhabitants. Its principal exports are wine and building stone quarried on Mount Titano. San Marino, the capital city, has a population of about 5,000 and was built around a hermitage in 441 A.D. The city's main industry is the manufacture of silk.

A number of excellent schools in the Florence area—graduate and undergraduate—specialize in the fine arts, Italian language and culture, and music. These include the Pius XII Institute, the University of Florence Center of Culture for Foreigners, the Luigi Cherubini Conservatory of Music, the Instituto Statale d'Arte, and the Accademia delle Belle Arti. Tutoring is available in art, music, or Italian.

GENOA is the capital of the Italian region of Liguria. The city, at the head of the Ligurian Sea, is about 330 miles by road from Rome.

Sunshine and mild weather predominate most of the year, although in winter, cold days made dismal by piercing gusts and chilling drizzle are a reminder that Genoa is a northern city. It is, in fact, located at the same latitude as Augusta, Maine. The usually mild climate is due to the mountains which shield the area in winter from the full effect of northerly winds coming down from the Alps.

Greater Genoa is dominated by its port. Much of the city's commercial life is directly involved or related to shipping. Major industries include a large steel plant owned by Italsider (the largest steel producer in Europe) and major shipbuilding and ship repair yards. Genoa is also the starting point of several oil pipelines which link the Mediterranean with central European countries.

The city is an important producer of heavy machinery, electric motors, generators, and allied products. Major industries in the area are mostly government-owned. Relatively few are the privately owned, medium-size concerns which played such an important part in the "Italian Economic Miracle" of the early 1960s in the other northern industrial centers.

Genoa's population is about 800,000. The city is built on different levels in, on, and about the hills which dominate the area. Splendid palaces are found in all parts of the city; the best known is the Palazzo Doria, home of the famous 16th-century Italian naval hero, Andrea Doria. The ancient, narrow streets, called *vicoli* (alleys), still exist in labyrinthine profusion near the central port basin. In other parts of the city, steep, winding footpaths lead to various levels, giving Genoa a distinctive atmosphere and appearance which persists despite all efforts at modernization.

To Americans, Genoa is first of all the city in which Christopher Columbus was born and raised. The Genoese themselves are proud of this fact. Genoa maintains a sister-city relationship with Columbus, Ohio, and official visits and gifts are sometimes exchanged.

Apart from the Columbus tradition, many events tie Genoa to the United States. For example, Genoese shipbuilders secretly sold ships to the American Republic during our Revolutionary War. Genoa was hit extremely hard during World War II, and many people still remember that important segments of local industry were rehabilitated with Marshall Plan aid.

However, this is not to say that Americans can expect to be eagerly welcomed into Genoa's social life. The Genoese are by tradition conservative, laconic, and inclined to be suspicious of outsiders, even other Italians. This is probably the result of centuries of isolation.

Until the advent of the railroad, the Apennines were an almost impenetrable barrier to communications with the hinterland, and except for several hostile incursions from the north, Genoa had little overland contact with the rest of Europe, or even with the rest of Italy. Although Genoa was among the first great maritime trading centers as well as a leading seapower, the ancient Genoese city-

state suffered several devastating invasions from the sea. The Saracens sacked the city several times. Thus, Genoa's role in maritime matters did not render its populace more cosmopolitan, but instead tended to strengthen the traditional distrust of aliens, which is still part of the Genoese character.

This attitude appears to be changing, however, judging from the way the Genoese joke about themselves. The considerable influx of people from other Italian cities, notably immigrants from the south in search of employment, has also had a moderating effect. Still, one should expect considerably more reserve in personal and social contacts with the Genoese than is encountered in official dealings with them.

Italian is, of course, the principal language, but some of the Genoese speak their own language, Genoese, among themselves. Genoese is definitely more of a language than an Italian dialect, and there is an Italian-Genoese dictionary as well as a small body of literature in Genoese. Although the "level of living" in Genoa is high by almost any standard, the city has not yet experienced the degree of modernization found in Milan, Turin, and other industrial centers of the prosperous north. Americans will find most of the goods to which they are accustomed available in Genoa, but often at higher prices than in the U.S.

Some 100 Americans families in business or engineering live in the greater Genoa area. In addition, about 3,000 Americans, largely of Italian origin, live in the district. During summer, numerous American tourists pass through the city every week. Most of them do just that, pass through, on their way to or from the French and Italian Rivieras. Thus, the city itself has remained relatively untouched by international tourism, and the Genoese, it would seem, prefer it that way.

MILAN is Italy's largest city (population about 1,700,000) and principal industrial, commercial, and financial center. In the heart of the rich Po River Valley, Milan is linked to important European highway, rail, and air networks.

Milan is a city of contrasts. Old buildings, some dating from the fourth century, line the narrow, winding streets of the central portion of the city, while modern glass and marble skyscrapers and wide boulevards characterize the newer areas.

The city has a bustling atmosphere reminiscent of New York or Chicago, and has been called the least Italian of all Italian cities. It is surrounded by an extensive and growing industrial area. A number of satellite cities are being built, many characterized by two- to six-story low cost apartment developments interspersed with park and garden areas. Milan itself is a city of apartment buildings; most range from six to eight stories. Practically all Milanese live in apartments, and the American one-family house with its yard and garden is almost unknown.

Milan is not a tourist city, although some 500,000 tourists (30 to 35 percent are Americans) travel through Milan, usually on their way to other destinations. Most stop briefly to see the principal tourist attractions: the Milan Cathedral (Duomo), an amazing structure in flamboyant Gothic, the third largest cathedral in the world; the Palazzo di Brera, one of Italy's outstanding galleries; the Santa Maria delle Grazie Church, the rectory of which contains Leonardo da Vinci's "Last Supper"; or to attend a performance at the world-famous La Scala opera house.

For the resident, one of the finest aspects of life in Milan is its nearness to such recreational, scenic, and historical attractions as the Italian lake district, the Alpine ski and summer resorts, the Italian Riviera and Adriatic beaches, and the tourist centers of Florence and Venice. By train or plane, practically all of continental Europe can be reached within a day.

Milan, at about the same latitude as Ottawa, Canada, has a temperate climate. Winter temperatures average 40° to 50°F; summer temperatures range from 65° to 85°F. Milan receives about 30 inches of rainfall a year; snow appears only a few times from December to March.

Many of the largest Italian industrial firms (Montecatini, Edison, Pirelli) are located in Milan. Here also are the headquarters of many of Italy's leading industrial and trade associations and largest banks. The city hosts many specialized trade fairs, national and international, throughout the year. The most famous is the Milan International Samples Fair, held each April at the large, well-equipped Milan Fair Grounds.

A U.S. Trade Center, financed by the Department of Commerce, is located there and holds exhibits of American products most of the year. In addition, the U.S. Department of Agriculture exhibits agricultural commodities at the Trade Center, usually during the April fair.

The permanent foreign colony in the area numbers many thousands, including at least 1,800 Americans and a slightly smaller number of British. Swiss, German, and Austrian nationals compose a large part of the foreign colony.

The general standard of living for Americans is about that of the U.S. The amenities of urban life—electricity, gas, central heating, elevator service, potable water, garbage collection, telephone service—are on a par with those in America.

The sun, sea, and scenery of **NAPLES** and its surroundings made the area the playground of ancient Rome. The centuries have endowed it with a rich, artistic patrimony that, coupled with its natural beauties, attracts hundreds of thousands of visitors annually. Naples is nestled in a semicircle of hills on a bay, dominated by the graceful rise of Mount Vesuvius, and flanked by the islands of Capri, Ischia, and Procida.

It is a major seaport, industrial complex, and distribution center of southern Italy, with a population of over 1.2 million. Most of the business quarter has been rebuilt since World War II, and the new apartment buildings have gone up in the older residential areas and in new sections of this growing city.

Many foreigners live in Naples, but Americans are most numerous. A small American business community and nearly 10,000 American military personnel and their dependents live in the Naples area.

PALERMO is the capital of the region of Sicily, an area given broad powers of self-government by the na-

tional government in 1947. The Palermo U.S. consular district has the same geographical limits as the region. The city (population 640,000) lies in a valley delineated by sharp rocky mountains which reach to the sea, with the bay of Palermo presenting a topographical outline of striking natural beauty. The city proper, although consisting of a fair number of up-to-date commercial structures and many modern apartment buildings, is also rich in the architecture of Arab, Norman, Saracen, and other cultures which figured so importantly in its history.

Winters are mild, and temperatures seldom drop below freezing. The famed Sicilian sunshine is no myth, and the weather is clear and sunny most of the year, with little rain during summer and fall.

Daily routine in Sicily is strongly influenced by the hundreds of years of Spanish rule. Meals are served late— lunch at 1:30 or 2 p.m. and dinner at 8:30 to 9:30 p.m. The noon meal is generally the larger of the two. A siesta after lunch is common, and all shops and government offices are closed from 1 to 4 p.m. or later, remaining open until 7:30 or 8 in the evening.

TRIESTE is Italy's only border post. It is also one of the oldest American consulates, having been opened in 1797. For many years, until the end of World War I, Trieste was the major port of Italy. It remained so until the end of World War II, when conflicting territorial claims between Italy and Yugoslavia led to the creation of the Free Territory of Trieste, administered by the Allied Military Government composed of American and British Forces.

In October 1954, the London Memorandum of Understanding was signed by Italy, Yugoslavia, Britain, and the U.S., ending the military occupation of the city.

In early 1964, the Province of Trieste was grouped with the Provinces of Gorizia, Udine, and later Pordenone, into the fifth special autonomous "region" of Friuli-Venezia Giulia; this region, plus the Veneto Provinces of Venezia, Padova, Belluno, Treviso, and Rovigo, constitute the present consular district.

Trieste's 300,000 inhabitants are principally Italian, but there is also a 10 percent Slovene minority, and the German and Austrian colonies are fairly large. American tourism to the district is concentrated in Venice and, during winter, to the major ski resort of Cortina d'Ampezzo.

The climate is pleasant. Summers are seldom hot and humid, and winters are usually without snow. From December to February, the famous Trieste *bora* (strong wind) often blows. Winds have reached over 100 miles per hour (this is rare), and may blow for three to four days at a time, intensifying the cold. They are usually followed by crisp, sunny days.

TURIN has a long and interesting history dating back to ancient Rome, and including a brief period (1861–65) as the first capital of unified Italy. However, it is better known to the world as a thriving industrial center—particularly in the fields of automobile manufacture and design. During the past two decades it has grown at an astonishing rate, and greater Turin now has a population of over 1.25 million.

The city is the capital of the region of Piedmont (Piemonte), which includes the Provinces of Turin, Asti, Alessandria, Cuneo, Novara, and Vercelli—an area about the size of New Jersey, Delaware, and Rhode Island. The semiautonomous Val D'Aosta region, north of Turin on the French and Swiss borders, is not included in the Region of Piedmont, although it forms a part of the U.S. consular district. Turin is by far the largest city in the district and is the financial, economic, and cultural capital. It is a most important industrial city, but one wouldn't guess it from its architecture.

Turin is equidistant from Rome and Paris and, partially due to many years of French rule, newcomers are often surprised by the "un-Italian" appearance of the city. Wide, straight, tree-lined boulevards slice through the central areas, and the architecture is often a hybrid of Italian and French design. On clear days, the city's personalty is radically changed by the awesome beauty of the nearby Alps, which surround it on three sides. On the fourth or eastern side, lush green hills—studded with churches and luxurious villas—rise from the banks of the Po River to overlook the city.

Turin has the highest standard of living in Italy. Unlike many cities, however, there is no focal point for the entertainment and cultural forces in Turin—no "center of town," and the streets of the city are remarkably free of crowds in the evening. Similarly, the important sights of Turin are not always placed in the centers of great piazzas or on main thoroughfares; one must seek them out or be told where to find them. Even getting there is often not enough—a beautiful chapel can be disguised as an office building, or a world-renowned museum can be housed in a structure as nondescript as its neighbors.

At first, friendships can be as difficult to find as the art treasures. The Turinese admit to being different from other Italians, and they take pride in it. In general, they tend to be reserved, courteous, and uninquisitive, and their distinct personalities have helped to create the atmosphere of their city. They prefer to amuse themselves privately; for example, Turin has an extremely limited nightlife for so large a city. American-style bars and adult nightclubs are limited, and the only foreign restaurant is a Chinese one.

This is not a tourist center for Americans. When a traveler arrives in Turin it is usually because of business or traveling en route to another city. This, more than anything, probably has contributed to the fact that Turin has retained much of its distinctive character, despite its rapid growth. On a more personel level, it also has resulted in a novelty: a large Italian city in which practically no one speaks English.

Aside from the charms of the city, however, the tourist misses a great deal when he fails to stop here—pleasures and sights which residents of Turin have come to love. Only a very short distance from the city, for example, are some of the world's most famous ski resorts—Sestriere, Cervinia (Matterhorn), and Courmayeur. The Italian lakes are nearby, as are the French and Italian Rivieras. All of the foregoing can be reached in from one-and-a-half to six hours by car.

A look at the map will be enough to demonstrate that Turin is an excellent starting point for longer trips to much of Europe. On the other hand, there is much to see within the district itself. The countless Roman ruins, castles, medieval towns, and Alpine valleys will keep a traveler busy for many years.

Recreation

Rome

An incredible number and variety of places of historic and artistic interest are in and around Rome. Commercial and cultural organizations arrange a variety of tours and visits daily. Most are conducted in Italian, but many are also in English.

Naples is less than three hours by car, and Florence is almost as close. Rome itself is filled with major monuments and remains from 2,500 years of Western civilizations. These exist in greater richness and variety in Italy than in any other country. Guidebooks to Italy are available both in Italy and in the U.S., giving many details on touring attractions. Many recreation areas, campgrounds, and facilities are found in the countryside. Good, but crowded beaches, with cabanas and some beach equipment for rent, lie within 20 miles on public transportation lines. To the south, about two hours by car, are beautiful, spacious, and uncrowded beaches.

Terminillo, two-and-a-half hours by car or bus, is the nearest ski resort with a tow system and equipment for rent. Some hunting and fishing is available in the countryside around Rome, but hunting is generally limited to private reserves, for which an invitation is needed.

Horses are available from several riding academies in Rome at reasonable prices.

For children's play, Rome has many parks. The large and beautiful Villa Borghese park has a zoo, a small theater where children's movies are shown in Italian, Punch and Judy shows, donkey rides, small bicycles for rent, a lake with boats for rent, and a large playground.

Almost any form of sports activity can be enjoyed in the vicinity of Rome, including golf, tennis, skiing, swimming, riding, boating, bicycling, hunting, and fishing. Spectator sports include soccer, boxing, horse racing, and auto and motorcycle racing.

Much of the sports activity in Rome is organized around private clubs. The Acqua Santa Golf Club, with an 18-hole course, is five miles from the center of the city. The Olgiata Country Club, about 10 miles north of the city, has a 27-hole golf course, swimming pool, tennis courts, horses, and a fine clubhouse. A number of other tennis and swimming clubs are open to Americans. Good sports equipment is available locally.

Rome offers a wide variety of entertainment facilities appropriate to a major capital city. Some knowledge of Italian is, of course, valuable.

Movie theaters show current Italian, American, and other films with Italian soundtracks. One or two cinemas offer French, English, and American films with original soundtracks.

Several theaters present classics, modern plays, and revues, usually in Italian. Rome's formal opera season opens in December and continues through May, with excellent productions and performances by leading Italian artists. During the summer, outdoor opera is performed in the ruins of the Baths of Caracalla. Popular-priced spring and fall performances are also given. Concert performances are given frequently during the winter season; outdoor performances are held in summer, usually in the late afternoon or evening. Prices at all these musical events are reasonable. Visiting theatrical groups, as well as local pageantry, provide additional interest year round.

Rome has relatively few nightclubs, and prices are high; some places feature dancing and musical entertainment. Many good restaurants, some steeped in atmosphere and others featuring famous food specialties, can be found. Many places offer outdoor dining in summer.

Florence

The hills and mountains surrounding Florence are excellent for hiking, picnicking, and camping. Fishing and small game hunting are also popular in this area. In winter, one can ski at nearby Abetone and Vallombrosa.

Seaside resorts and public beaches dot the Tyrrhenian coast within easy weekend distance of Florence. Closest resort areas are concentrated around the towns of Forte dei Marmi, Viareggio, and Tirrenia.

Florence and the surrounding countryside are rich in points of historic and cultural interest. Besides the world-famous museums, churches, and palaces in the city proper, hundreds of charming and historically important villas, monasteries, and churches are within its environs. Siena, Pisa, Lucca, and a number of smaller towns of great cultural interest in Tuscany are within easy driving distance. In addition, excellent *autostrade* link Florence with most major Italian cities, making them accessible for weekend trips.

Ample opportunity exists for sports in the Florence area. Golf, tennis, swimming, riding, bicycling, hunting, and fishing are the most popular participant sports. Spectator sports are limited mostly to horse racing and soccer.

Much sports activity centers around private clubs. The Ugolino Golf Club, about a 30-minute drive from the city, has an excellent 18-hole course and a swimming pool. The Circolo del Tennis, offers good tennis courts and a small swimming pool—children under 10 are not allowed to use the pool. Membership in both clubs is rather expensive.

Public sports facilities are limited to a number of children's playgrounds and a few large public swimming pools. Children under 10 are permitted at the children's pool at Campo di Marte only. Horseback riding is also available in and near Cascine Park.

Each season a number of worthwhile cultural and artistic events are held in Florence. The city's musical life reaches its high point in May and June with the "Maggio Musicale" featuring concerts and operas by world-famous performers and conductors. In addition, the winter operatic season is followed by a concert season, and many other musical events are held throughout the year. Open-air concerts are given at the amphitheater in Fiesole and in the courtyard of the Pitti Palace during summer. Plays are occasionally performed at the city's two theaters, the Pergola and the Verdi, always in Italian.

Movies are popular with Italians,

and the city has many cinemas. Foreign films are shown, but they are dubbed in Italian. A small English-language cinema has an irregular schedule of films.

Florence is the site of a number of important fairs, including a handicrafts fair, a biennial international antiques fair, a shoe and leather goods fair, and others. Florence and other nearby towns have traditional pageants and festivals in medieval costume held in the spring, summer, or fall. Among the most important are the Scoppio del Carro and Calcio in costume in Florence, the Palio (a spectacular medieval-style horse race) in Siena, and the Giostra del Saraceno in Arezzo.

Florence and the other cities of Tuscany and Emilia have many good restaurants ranging from high-price deluxe restaurants to inexpensive, simple establishments called *trattorie*. The nightclubs of Florence are inadequate and expensive.

Genoa

The Genoa area offers opportunities for swimming, hiking, tennis, golf, roller skating, sailing, and rowing. Many beaches are only a short bus trip from the center of town, but they are of rocky rather than natural sand, and are polluted. The most popular and famous beaches and resorts along the Riviera (Santa Margherita, Rapallo, Portofino) are about 45 minutes from Genoa. Most beaches are privately operated concessions and charge a rather stiff entrance fee. The city itself has an excellent outdoor swimming pool in Albaro which is heated in the winter. Numerous other pool facilities exist, although most are private. One 18-hole golf course (in Rapallo) and one nine-hole course (Arenzano) are within an hour's drive of Genoa. A few public and private tennis courts are available.

Soccer *(calcio)* is the national sport; Genoa has two teams in the Italian league. During the season, which extends from early fall to late spring, a game is usually played every Sunday in the Genoa stadium.

Narrow, congested streets and a hilly terrain make bicycling difficult in Genoa. However, flat stretches of road along the sea can be used by bicycling enthusiasts.

Hunting in the surrounding area is poor. Many private reserves are beyond the Apennines, but with access by invitation only.

Biking enthusiasts will find many pleasant walks near the sea or in the hills. Numerous points of scenic interest along the Italian Riviera are available for sight-seeing by bus or car. The Italian Yacht Club has a clubhouse and yacht basin in the port of Genoa, and sailing is popular throughout Liguria.

Several ski resorts, in the nearby mountains about a two-hour drive from Genoa, are open five months a year. Special excursions at group fares are organized each weekend during the season.

Entertainment facilities in Genoa include cinemas and theaters. Films shown in commercial theaters are dubbed in Italian. The Italo-Britannica and Italo-American Associations sponsor a film club which has biweekly showings during the winter months of English-language films with original soundtracks. Film Story, an association interested in the history of the cinema, shows films in English about once a week. Occasionally, local theaters will

sponsor a series of recent American and British films.

An excellent local theatrical stock company performs throughout the winter season. Visiting companies from other cities present musical reviews, plays, and operettas. The annual concert season runs from October until February. A chamber music series also takes place during the winter months. A short opera season occurs in fall and in spring. Occasionally, a ballet will be performed during the opera seasons, and an outdoor ballet series is held in Nervi every two years.

Milan

While Milan has some outdoor sports facilities, most are on the outskirts or beyond. Milan's private clubs are exclusive and expensive, and few Americans join. Within the city are public indoor and outdoor swimming pools, but they are quite crowded on holidays and during summer weekends.

A number of riding schools and clubs are located in the city and in the suburbs. Private and group riding lessons may be arranged.

The nearest golf courses are private clubs at Monza, Barlassina, Carimate, and Montorfano, all within reasonable driving distances of Milan. However, large nonrefundable initiation fees (several thousand dollars) usually are required. Others, with smaller initiation fees, rarely have enough turnover in membership to accept new members. There are no public golf courses in the area.

The city's Ice Palace is open for ice skating from October to April. A number of American-style bowling alleys also are in Milan and the near suburbs.

In summer, boating and swimming in the nearby lakes (Como, Maggiore, Garda, Lugano) and picnicking in the vicinity are popular. Swimming areas at the lakes usually have rock or gravel beaches, and in some areas swimming is only possible by diving from rocks. The nearest ocean beaches are around Genoa (two hours by *autostrada* or one and three-quarter hours by *rapido* train).

Many ski areas are within an easy drive from Milan, including several within two hours of the city. The ski season usually runs from November or December through April or May. Resorts provide accommodations in all price ranges, and slopes range from very easy to very difficult, with all types of lift facilities. The lower Alpine areas are popular with mountain climbers during summer, and climbing areas are available for the beginner and the expert.

Baseball has a small following in Italy, and a number of amateur teams compete in summer in the Milan area. Basketball is becoming increasingly popular; four major professional and semiprofessional teams are in the area. A racetrack on the outskirts of Milan has horse races five days a week from spring through fall, and three days a week in winter. Italy's principal spectator sport is soccer, which is played almost year round. Milan has two class A teams, and their matches at the San Siro Stadium draw crowds of up to 80,000 persons.

Hunting and fishing in season are popular among Italians.

In addition to the participation and spectator sports described above, northern Italy and neighboring France and Switzerland have much to offer the sightseer. Many points of historic and artistic interest are easily reached on one-day trips.

The opera season at La Scala begins early in December and runs through May. During late spring and fall, orchestral and solo concerts featuring outstanding artists and orchestras are held in the opera house. Milan offers rich fare for the music lover. A large number of concert and recital series are held throughout the winter, many presenting world famous artists, orchestras, and chamber music groups, and featuring music from all periods.

Eight or nine theaters in Milan present legitimate stage productions (all in Italian), ranging from Shakespeare and Chekhov to works of contemporary Italian and foreign playwrights, to musical revues, operettas, and the like. Milan has as many cinemas as any large American city, presenting foreign as well as Italian films, but only one movie theater presents foreign films in the original version. Most American and British films shown here are at least a year old.

Naples

During the long summer season, Naples offers ample opportunities for sports and outdoor recreation. The Bay of Naples is ideal for sailing and fishing, and several clean beaches for swimming are within an hour's drive.

In the winter, Roccaraso, a mountain ski resort about four hours from Naples by car or bus, offers trails for beginners as well as experienced skiers. Skis and other equipment can be rented locally or at the resort for reasonable prices.

The city has a zoo, an aquarium, and a small amusement park appealing especially to the youngsters. The Naples area also contains many interesting possibilities for hiking and sightseeing. Among the nearby places of interest are Capri, Ischia, Sorrento, Pompeii, Cumae, Paestum, Amalfi, Herculaneum, and Ravello.

A reasonably full concert and opera schedule is headed by the famous San Carlo Opera during winter. None of the many first-run Neapolitan movie theaters offers films in English.

In addition to plays and variety shows presented in the five legitimate theaters in Naples, numerous spectator sports events are held. The city has several excellent museums and art galleries, and many historical landmarks.

Palermo

Touring is one of the real delights of a stay in Palermo. Even the casual observer is impressed by the grandeur of Sicily's monuments and the beauty of the countryside. The National Museum of Palermo contains priceless relics dating from prehistoric Greek and Roman periods. Museums in such cities as Gela, Agrigento, and Siracusa have artifacts which testify to the diverse and rich cultural history of the region.

Colorful local festivals and religious ceremonies, especially at Easter and on other church holidays, are all profitable subjects for study and photography. One of the most interesting is the Siracusa theater festival in May and June.

Palermo offers a wide range of spectator sports; soccer is the most popular. The city has a team in the major Italian league. Horse and harness racing and an annual horse show are held. A local tennis club has excellent courts where stars from Europe and the Western Hemisphere compete at the annual invitational tournament. The "Targa Florio," which takes place every spring in Sicily, is one of the most grueling European auto races.

Sports and outdoor life flourish year round, but particularly in summer. The centers for water sports are the nearby beaches and clubs of Mondello, a 15-minute drive from the main part of the city.

Swimming, boating, sailing, fishing, waterskiing, and skin diving are popular. Small open beaches and rocky coves, which are usually crowded, offer the swimmer and skin diver a chance to discover the wonders of the Mediterranean. Sailing is popular, and several private sailing clubs are in the Palermo area. In addition, a number of enchanting islands off the coast offer the opportunity for most water sports.

The city has a modern bowling alley and several modestly equipped gymnasiums offering lessons in judo and karate, with facilities for men and women. The scarcity of wild game (except rabbits and small birds) and the strict regulations governing the import and purchase of guns discourage most would-be hunters. However, a target range, using clay and live pigeons, is available for the enthusiastic marksman. Sicily has no golf courses. Skiing is done in the Madonie Mountains, three hours away. Camping facilities are available at various places throughout the island.

The city has many cinemas, but films are shown mostly with Italian soundtracks. American films, dubbed in Italian, are sometimes featured, and are usually quite recent when released here.

Palermo has two opera seasons; the principal one begins before Christmas in the Massimo Theater, one of the finest in Italy. Operas, operettas, and ballets are given in summer in an attractive amphitheater. Winter performances are usually excellent, with skillful and elaborate staging.

During winter, good concerts are frequent, and some of Europe's best instrumental artists include Palermo in their tours. Tickets are inexpensive. Theatrical companies with some of the best Italian actors occasionally visit the city with repertoires of national and foreign plays. Musical variety shows are given often throughout the year, although usually in winter. These theater and variety performances are all in Italian.

Sicily is famous for its puppet shows, which are given in tiny, family-owned theaters. The performances are not polished, but they are interesting entertainment, particularly for children.

Palermo has several nightclubs, but only one or two with floor shows. The others have small bands where the music ranges from soft and slow to the latest and loudest beat. Discotheques are also popular.

Trieste

The most popular spectator sports in Trieste are soccer, trotting races, and basketball. Others include water polo, swim meets, sailing, rowing, horse shows, boxing, hunting, and fishing. Tennis and golf are available for those who wish to join the respective clubs. Riding facilities exist, and extensive areas of the countryside are suitable for hiking. Excellent skiing and mountain climbing are found in the nearby mountains of Italy and Austria.

Venice is about 100 miles away, some two hours by car or express train. Padova, Vicenza, and Verona—20, 45, and 75 miles to the west of Venice respectively—are also of considerable historic and cultural interest, and are connected with Trieste by express trains. Cortina d'Ampezzo, the well-known Italian mountain resort in the Dolomites, about 130 miles by car from Trieste, offers sports (especially skiing) in winter, and beautiful scenery at all times.

Only 30 miles from Trieste are the ancient Roman ruins of Aquileia, with important early Christian mosaics. The seaside resorts of Grado and Lignano, with long sandy beaches and swimming and wading areas, are also close by. Yugoslavia is easily accessible from the city, and its increasingly popular Dalmatian coast is within weekend range.

Trieste offers a wide range of entertainment for a city of its size. The local opera company's season runs from November to March. The Trieste Symphony's concert series, which takes place in the fall and spring, is extensive. Recitals, concerts, and miscellaneous musical events are also held. During summer, theatrical presentations are staged in the open-air Roman theater, and in winter, the local repertory theater offers a series of presentations, all in Italian.

Turin

Some of the world's most spectacular scenery is visible just outside the city of Turin. The Aosta Valley begins 40 miles to the north. It runs straight into Mt. Blanc, Europe's highest peak, after figuratively glancing off Mt. Rosa and Mt. Cervinia (Matterhorn), which are the second and third highest European peaks. All around those famed peaks, as well as in the west and Maritime Alps, valleys are begging to be explored by car. The roads are not always the widest and straightest, but they are quite adequate.

The Mt. Cenisio Pass into France is just west of Turin at an elevation of 6,000 feet, and Geneva is a four-hour drive via the Mt. Blanc tunnel. Lake Como and the other attractions of the famed Italian lake country are available by public transportation or by a two-to three-hour car drive, as are all the other delightful attractions of Italy.

Whether by car or public transportation, the visitor will enjoy touring in the Alps, in the picturesque wine country south of Turin, or in the nearby countries. Italy is one of the world's truly romantic and interesting countries.

Travel time by car to the nearest point in France is one-and-a-half hours; Austria (except in the dead of winter), five-and-a-half hours; Liechtenstein, seven hours; and Spain, 14 hours.

The most popular participant sport in northern Italy is skiing. A dozen ski resorts are within easy reach of Turin, even for day trips. All these areas have lifts, instruction, and boots and skis for rent. If a skier gets tired of one side of the Alps, in an hour he can reach Chamonix just over the French border, or Zermatt, by cable car, on the Swiss side of the Matterhorn from Cervinia.

Hunting is popular. Quail and pheasant are the most common quarry, but some deer, chaomois, and even ibex can be found.

The Circolo della Stampa Sports Club of Turin has 20 good tennis courts and a huge swimming pool.

Other courts and pools are around town. An excellent 27-hole golf course is just outside the city, and there is a nine-hole, free course in the city. It is difficult to join both golf clubs, but arrangements can usually be made for nonmembers to play both courses for a limited time.

Public swimming pools, available year round, are inexpensive. Mountain climbing, hiking, fishing (rainbow trout), rowing, skin diving, bowling, and even baseball are all practiced with great enthusiasm in this part of Italy.

Soccer (*calcio*) is by far the most popular spectator sport. Attendance at basketball games grows every year, especially since the major teams have begun to import American stars.

The theater is active in Turin, but performances are almost exclusively in Italian. The local repertory company (Teatro Stabile Torino) offers plays of high caliber and professional polish.

During winter, at least three productions are always in town at any one time. Movie theaters abound. Most of the better, and some not so good, American films are shown here, usually dubbed in Italian, as are British and continental films. Some movie clubs show a limited selection of films in the original versions.

Turin is the home of a symphony orchestra which broadcasts under the auspices of the Italian radio and television system each Friday during the season. A second organization, the Union Musical, presents a concert season, normally at least two programs a week. The Turin opera season, while not matching the glitter and polish of neighboring La Scala's, is thoroughly professional, and relatively inexpensive for the best seats in the house. Turinese audiences are not inclined to be demonstrative, but they do appreciate good music.

Notes for Travelers

Numerous major international airlines serve the large cities of Italy on a regular basis. Scheduled passenger ship service from the U.S. to Europe no longer exists, but some cargo ships can accommodate passengers.

No personal documentation is needed for Americans to enter Italy, other than a passport. Certificates of vaccination against smallpox, cholera, or yellow fever are required only for travelers arriving from countries where those diseases are endemic.

Firearms must be registered with the Italian Government upon arrival. Pistols may not exceed a bore of 7.65 millimeters (.30 caliber).

The following holidays are generally observed in Italy: New Year's Day, Easter Monday, April 25, May 1, first Sunday in June, August 15, November 1, first Sunday in November, December 8, Christmas, and December 26. In addition, each city observes the local patron saint's day, and most businesses close for a week or two around the middle of August.

Churches in Rome with English-language services include Catholic, American Protestant, Episcopal, Church of England, Methodist, Presbyterian, Evangelical Assembly of God, Baptist, and Christian Scientist. In Florence, churches holding English services are St. James American (Protestant Episcopal), St. Mark's (Anglican), and Convento Ognissanti (Catholic). In Genoa, the only service in English is a monthly Church of England service; occasionally, however,

a Roman Catholic mass in English is offered by Stella Maris, an international merchant marine association. The Catholic church at Via Fratelli Gabba 7 in Milan holds Sunday services in English, as do the Methodist church at Via Porro Lambertenghi 30, All Saints Episcopal at Via Solferino 17, Church of Christ at Via del Bollo 5, the Christian Science church at 16 Via Bigli, and the Church of Jesus Christ of Latter-Day Saints at Via Carlo Porta 5. There is a Jewish synagogue at Via Guastalla 19 in Milan.

In Naples, the numerous churches offering English services include the U.S. Armed Forces and Naval Facility chapels, Christ Church, Latter-Day Saints, Baptist, Christian Science, and Church of Christ. A synagogue is located in Naples, but foreign attendance is rare. In Palermo and Trieste, the only churches offering English services are the Anglican congregations; and in Turin, one Catholic church and the Waldensian congregation (the principal Protestant church, with world headquarters in Piedmont) conduct services in English.

The official unit of currency in Italy is the *lire*. Its value against the U.S. dollar has fluctuated widely in recent years.

Italy uses the metric system of weights and measures.

The U.S. Embassy in Italy is located at Via Veneto 119a, and is known as the Palazzo Margherita. Consulate offices in Florence are at Lungarno Amerigo Vespucci 38; in Genoa, at Piazzo Portello No. 6; in Milan, at Piazza della Republica 32; in Naples (one of the largest establishments in the U.S. Foreign Service), in the Piazza della Republica; in Palermo, at Via Vaccarini 1; in Trieste, at Via Valdirivo 19; and in Turin, at Via Alfieri 17.

Jordan

The territory which is now the Hashemite Kingdom of **JORDAN** corresponds roughly to the Biblical lands of Ammon, Bashan, Edom, and Moab. Its renowned archeological site at Madaba, dating from the middle Bronze Age, is mentioned in the Bible as a Moabite town. Jordon has been a home to many civilizations, and each one introduced new elements into its culture—influences that are still seen today.

Except for the Crusader Kingdom (1099 to 1187), Jordan remained under Arab rule from the seventh century until the beginning of the 16th century, when the Turkish Ottoman Empire included all Arab Middle Eastern countries. In 1915, Sharif Hussein of Mecca led the Arab revolt against Ottoman rule. By 1918, British and Arab Forces had driven Turkish armies into Syria, and Abdullah, a son of Hussein, became ruler of Trans-Jordan.

The Arab-controlled part of Palestine (West Bank) joined the Kingdom following the 1948 Arab-Israeli War. In 1950, the union of Trans-Jordan and central Arab Palestine was confirmed, and the country name became the Hashemite Kingdom of Jordan. In 1955, the Kingdom joined the United Nations.

Area, Geography, Climate

Jordan, with an area of 37,500 square miles (about the size of Indiana), occupies a central place in the eastern Arab world. It is bounded on the north by Syria, on the east by Saudi Arabia and Iraq, on the south by Saudi Arabia and the Gulf of Aqaba, and on the west by Israel.

Since the six-day war in June 1967, Israel has occupied the 2,000-square mile territory west of the Jordan River known as the West Bank. Today, Jordan controls the East Bank—the area of the former mandate of Trans-Jordan.

The country's terrain varies. On the eastern desert plateau, the average height is 3,000 feet; in the west, mountains rise in places to 5,700 feet; and at the Dead Sea, the terrain drops to Earth's lowest land point of nearly 1,300 feet below sea level. Jordan has a seaport on the Gulf of Aqaba, and good road connections with Syria, Iraq, and Saudi Arabia.

Jordan's East Bank offers a diversity of climate and scenery. A one- or two-day drive includes Irbid's temperate highlands, Ajlun's hills, the tropical Jordan Valley, the southern sandstone mountains, and the arid desert of the eastern plateau.

Inadequate rainfall is a chronic problem, although Jordan is located at the southern tip of the Fertile Crescent. Rainfall occurs from November to April; the rest of the year has bright sunshine daily and little humidity. Daytime summer temperatures can be hot, but nights are usually pleasant, cool, and dry. In the spring, a desert wind can blow in unseasonably hot air. Autumn is long and pleasant; winter often brings light snow to the mountains and to Amman (the capital); and spring carpets the country's grazing lands with beautiful wild flowers.

Population

Predominantly Arab and Moslem, the 1981 population was about 3.1 million: 814,000 on the West Bank and the rest on the East Bank. The 1948 influx of 500,000 Palestinian Arab refugees and the post-1967 war waves of displaced persons from across the Jordan River have divided the East Bank population evenly between indigenous Transjordanians and Palestinian refugees. All are Jordanians; Palestinians are given Jordanian citizenship, and many of them have prominent governmental, commercial, and professional positions. About 200,000 others live in camps run by the U.N. Relief and Works Agency (UNRWA) and have not been fully assimilated into the Jordanian economy.

The population represents a mixture of traditions. The Bedouin origins and values of many inhabitants are still strongly felt. Austere nomadic life produced men of strong personality, self-reliance, and a deep sense of familial and tribal pride. Harsh desert conditions spawned a well-developed code of hospitality still expressed toward each other and toward foreigners. Sophisticated townsmen will visit kinsmen in their tents, sharing a *mensaf* of great rice mounds, embellished with pine nuts, yogurt, and chunks of boiled mutton.

While the eastern desert has been the Bedouin Arab's domain, the well-watered and more fertile hills have been cultivated for centuries by Arabs of diverse origins. Modern Jordan, however, is an increasingly urban society. Most of the East Bank population now live in the three main cities of Amman, Zerka, and Irbid. Population growth is estimated at 3.5 percent, one of the highest in the world. Catholic and Orthodox Christians comprise about one-tenth of the total population. Although some villages are entirely Christian, the Arab desert traditions and strong attachment to the soil persist throughout the country.

One hundred years ago, Amman was a small village of a few hundred Circassian Moslems who had originally fled from the Caucasus area of Tsarist, Christian Russia. Since then, the city's population has doubled each decade as a result of the high birth rate, and an influx of Arab traders, Bedouin followers of the Hashemite Kings, and Palestinian refugees. Amman is still a new city of immigrants linked to their Bedouin and rural village traditions. Black goat hair tents, herds of camels, and flocks of sheep are still part of the rural Jordanian scene. Underneath the city's noise and bustle, life is unhurried; family relationships and traditional hospitality remain strong. Although most city dwellers have adopted Western dress, many men still wear the *kuffiya* or Arab headdress, and some older women wear a black face veil.

Jordanians are courteous, friendly, and dignified in their relations with Westerners. Many speak excellent English and are well-educated, often having studied in the United States or at American institutions such as the American University of Beirut. Although critical of our Israeli policy, Jordanians like Americans. The present monarch, King Hussein I, is married to an American, the former Lisa Halaby.

Government

Jordan is a constitutional monarchy whose legal system is based on Islamic law and French codes. However, as a result of events following the 1967 war, Parliament was dissolved, and there have been no elections since that time. The King appoints Senate members on Cabinet recommendation. The appointed Prime Minister selects the Cabinet and submits the list of Ministers to the King for final ratification. Government organization is centralized, with authority almost entirely in the hands of the national government. National government ministries regulate, supervise, and provide public services. Local autonomy and self-government is not highly developed, although many municipalities and villages have elected councils. The central government appoints the mayor or village chief (*mukhtar*), usually from the elected council.

Municipalities are organized into geographical areas called governorates. The kingdom is divided into eight of these major administrative districts— three on the West Bank. They are headed by a *muhafiz* or governor appointed by the King and Cabinet. In some cases, the governorates are divided into the subdistricts, overseen by appointed deputy governors who have power to supervise and regulate affairs, and who report to the national Minis-

try of Interior for Municipal and Rural Affairs.

Jordan is a member of the Arab League and the U.N. At the Rabat Arab Summit Conference held in October 1974, King Hussein recognized the Palestine Liberation Organization as the sole, legitimate representative of the Palestinians, and thus responsible for the West Bank. Jordan remains a confrontation state vis-a-vis Israel, with the longest common border with Israel of any Arab state.

The traditional political role of the tribe, family, and clan remains an important force in the nation. No political parties and political organizations exist in the Western pattern. Professional organizations and labor unions have been formed, however, and the latter are representative of the working class society, although closely supervised and regulated by the Ministry of Labor.

Quasi-public, social, philanthropic, and commercial organizations and cooperatives have been organized: the Red Crescent Society, Chambers of Commerce and Industry, Youth Care Corporation, and the YWCA.

Arts, Science, Education

Jordanians believe educational opportunities for their children are a means of self-improvement, and a way to develop a responsible citizenry capable of earning a fair income and pursuing a free and decent life. Parents will undergo exceptionally heavy sacrifices to enable their children to receive an education.

Public education is free and compulsory for all children until ninth grade. One person out of five in Jordan is a student, and about 80 percent of the children ages six through 14 are in school. Secondary education through the 12th grade is provided by both academic and vocational high schools for those primary school graduates with the highest scholastic achievement.

At the postsecondary level, Jordan has five two-year teacher training colleges, and a number of specialized higher educational institutes such as the Princess Muna School of Nursing and the King Hussein Agricultural College. The kingdom opened its first university in 1962. The University of Jordan is located on a beautiful campus in the Amman suburbs and has a growing curriculum, including agriculture, arts, science, medicine, and economics and business. Enrollment was 5,500 students in 1977. A second university, Yarmouk, opened in Irbid in 1976 with 650 students.

The UNRWA operates a school system for the children of refugees. There is also a well-developed system of private schools in addition to government-operated and financed schools.

Jordan has a high proportion of university graduates in the professions, sciences, and arts for a developing nation. About 30,000 young Jordanian men and women are studying in colleges and universities abroad. Educated Jordanians at all levels, from those with vocational training to those with advanced degrees, particularly teachers, find a ready market in neighboring Arab countries for their skills. Their remittances to their families in Jordan are an important source of foreign exchange earnings.

Commerce and Industry

Jordan's economy has recovered from disruptions and insecurity caused by the 1967 war and the 1970–71 civil disturbances. Assistance has been provided by Saudi Arabia, Kuwait, the U.S., and others. This assistance represents a major source of government revenue and foreign exchange, sustaining private demand and a high level of imports.

Jordan's important economic sectors are services and mining and manufacturing. The previous dominant role of agriculture has steadily diminished in relative importance in recent years. About 13 percent of the East Bank is arable, although this varies according to annual rainfall. Important crops are wheat (which exceeds 150,000 tons in a good year), barley, citrus fruits, tomatoes, olives, melons, and a wide variety of other fruits and vegetables. Jordan is a net importer of agricultural products, particularly grains, meat, and animal products.

Major Jordanian industries are phosphate mining, cement production, petroleum refining, and steel rerolling. Jordan produces consumer goods such as cloth, cigarettes, beer, soap, handicraft items, and processed foods; but more sophisticated consumer products must be imported. Tourism, a major money-earner until the war of 1967, is steadily growing, and has high potential for the future.

Jordan continues to have a large trade deficit. Phosphates and agricultural produce account for the major part of the country's export revenues, which approached $410 million in 1979.

Imports in 1979 were about $1,998 million. The U.S. is among the main import sources; trade has traditionally been unrestricted by the government. Jordan is a member of the Arab Common Market. Trade with other Arab countries accounts for more than 20 percent of Jordan's total.

Labor-management relations are governed by the Labor Law of 1965. All aspects of Jordanian Labor are closely observed by the government, a conciliator in dispute cases. Collective bargaining is permitted, but under the law, strikes are allowed only after total breakdown of negotiations and under specific conditions. Few strikes have succeeded. Some 40 trade unions operate in Jordan, and most belong to the Jordan General Federation of Trade Unions.

Foreign investment is encouraged, particularly in the "productive" sectors. To aid investors, a variety of concessions, including tax holidays, are obtainable.

Transportation

Alia, the Royal Jordanian Airlines, is the national air carrier. With a small fleet of modern planes, it maintains scheduled flights to Cairo, Tehran, the Gulf, Athens, Rome, Paris, London, Bangkok, and other world capitals. Other Arab airlines, as well as British Airways, Air France, KLM, Alitalia, Lufthansa, and Aeroflot operate to and from Amman. No American airline flies directly to Jordan at this time, but connections with TWA or Pan Am can be made via Athens, Cairo, Frankfurt, Rome, and other cities. Regular flights to and from Beirut have been resumed.

Taxis are available for local travel; however, they are not always easy to obtain. Buses are inexpensive, but they often are overcrowded, with routings and destinations difficult for outsiders to ascertain. There are regular taxis and *servees* operating to other points within the country, and there is a constant flow to Damascus as well. Costs are moderate. Rental vehicles are available for private use.

A Jordanian license is required for resident drivers.

Communications

Telephone service to Arab cities outside Jordan (Beirut, Cairo, and Damascus) is somewhat erratic, but a satellite link is excellent for calls to the U.S. and most European cities. Local telephones are frequently out of order, particularly after rainstorms or other atmospheric disturbances. Telegraph and international mail facilities are satisfactory, with the average letter transit time to the U.S. being about one week.

Radio Jordan broadcasts in English on AM and FM medium wave, as well as shortwave for about nine hours a day. Western music, mostly popular, and newscasts are featured. FM reception of classical music programs from Jerusalem is possible for much of the day. Voice of America and BBC broadcasts in English are available on medium wave during part of the day; at other times shortwave reception is best.

Jordan has one government-owned TV station with two channels, one for Arabic programming and one for English and other foreign language programs. American and British movies and TV serials are often featured, and many programs are in color.

An English-language newspaper, the Jordan Times, is published in Amman daily except Mondays. The International Herald Tribune and the main British dailies are for sale locally one or two days late. Time and Newsweek, as well as British and other European magazines, are on sale locally at rather high prices.

A fairly broad selection of paperbacks is available locally at more than double U.S. prices. The selection of hardcover books is limited. The British Council maintains a library open to the public for a modest membership fee.

Health

King Hussein Medical Center (KHMC), a 450-bed military hospital, is recommended for day-to-day medical problems and for emergency requirements. It is well staffed and has excellent equipment. Local nonmilitary physicians cannot have patients admitted to KHMC, but referrals are accepted. Other hospitals are lacking in some areas, such as laboratory facilities and nursing care. Muashir Hospital, an 80-bed private hospital, is used by Americans for some routine work or emergencies when KHMC cannot be reached.

Physicians are available for medical and surgical care, including obstetrics and pediatrics. They are generally trained either in the U.K. or U.S. Dental care is adequate and some orthodontic treatment is available.

Endemic communicable diseases, including infectious hepatitis and typhoid, are found among the local population, but can be controlled among immunized American visitors who take practical precautions. Gamma globulin shots are advised, and water should be boiled. Only carefully washed fruits and vegetables should be eaten.

Even the cautious, however, occasionally suffer intestinal disorders such as amoebic dysentery. Cholera outbreaks frequently occur in the late summer season, but are generally brought under control within several weeks by the Public Health Department. Malaria has been eradicated throughout Jordan. Dry, dusty weather complicates lung, sinus, and other respiratory problems.

Medical supplies are good. Vitamin preparations come from the U.S., Britain, France, Germany, and Switzerland. With the exception of American brands, medicines are less expensive than in the U.S.

Major City

AMMAN, capital of Jordan, is spread out over many steep hills. With an elevation ranging from about 2,450 to 2,950 feet above sea level, the city has a growing population somewhere near 700,000. Here, in Biblical times, was Rabbath Ammon, capital of the Ammonites, descendants of Lot. The Pharaoh, Ptolemy II, Philadelphus of Egypt (285-247 B.C.), ruled the city; he rebuilt it and renamed it Philadelphia.

Beginning in 63 B.C., the city fell under Roman rule. Before that time, it had flourished as a member of the league of free cities known as the Decapolis. Briefly revived in the eighth century under the Ummayyad Arabs, the whole country deteriorated in the ninth century when the Arab capital moved from Damscus to Baghdad. During the Middle Ages, Amman was no more than a tiny village. In 1921, Amman became the capital of Jordan.

Most city activity centers around the government. Amman is Jordan's principal trading center, the main clearing point for commercial goods, and the center of import activity. The city grew rapidly after the Arab-Israeli wars of 1948 and 1967, after which large numbers of Palestinian Arab refugees and displaced persons from the West Bank became residents.

Amman's climate is moderate. Summer temperatures on the residential *jebels* (hills) rarely exceed 100°F; the atmosphere is dry and even the summer evenings are usually cool. Many days are windy, and dust clouds occasionally blow in from the dry hillsides and nearby desert. Little rain falls from mid-April to mid-November. In winter, temperatures seldom go below 32°F; but the cold is penetrating, the wind frequently strong, and houses are difficult to heat. Rain falls often in January and February. Snow is rare, although during past winters snow has been heavy enough to temporarily disrupt traffic and communications.

In the city, a wide variety of basic services is available, and although they are expensive by U.S. standards, most supplies can be readily obtained.

Recreation

Jordan has a good network of main and secondary roads and a sufficient number of gasoline stations. For long car trips, tourists should fill gas tanks and take plenty of boiled drinking water. Travel to areas not on or near the main highways is difficult, but not impossible. Good places to visit include:

Ajlun, with the forest and medieval ruins of the fort of Qual'at Er-Rabad.

Aqaba, Jordan's only seaport, which has good swimming, scuba diving, and waterskiing. Hotel accommodations are available.

Cairo, the capital of Egypt, two-and-a-half hours by plane from Amman. An excellent museum includes vast treasures taken from King Tut's tomb. The Valley of the Kings is in Luxor.

Damascus, a colorful city with a rich history, a three to four-hour drive from Amman, including stops at the Jordanian-Syrian border. It has a wonderful, inexpensive bazaar and an excellent museum. In the late summer of each year, an international fair is held. Hotels are adequate, but rooms are in short supply.

Jerash, famous for its extremely fine remains of a provincial Roman city.

Jersualem, where permission may be obtained, with 10 days' prior notice, to cross to the West Bank of Jordan and Israel and to return to Jordan. However, transportation must be arranged, since private vehicles are not permitted to cross the Jordan River.

Karak, a Moabite town having one of the finest Crusader castles in the Middle East.

Madaba, where a sixth-century mosaic map of Palestine can be found in the Greek Orthodox Church.

Mount Nebo, from where, overlooking the Dead Sea, Moses allegedly viewed the Promised Land. Mosaic pavements are excellent.

Petra, a unique city carved by the Nabateans out of sheer red sandstone cliffs. Visitors ride on horseback through the Siq, the Silent City's mysterious approach, for about 45 minutes.

Qasr el-Amra, where a castle near Azrak was used by Umayyad caliphs, and has early frescoes recently restored.

There are many opportunties for active sports in Jordan, and some sports clubs offer memberships to foreigners. Scuba diving, snorkeling, and deep-sea fishing facilities are available at Aqaba, and there is freshwater fishing at Wadi Ziglab and Azraq. A limited supply of quail, bustard, rabbit, hare, desert sand grouse, partridge, pigeon, dove, duck, and snipe can be hunted. Among other regulations, hunting and gun licenses are required.

Entertainment in Jordan is somewhat limited. There is no legitimate theater in Amman, and concerts are few and far between, usually presented by one of the foreign cultural centers such as the British Council, the American Center, or the Goethe Institute. Local cinemas show mostly Arabic films or films dubbed in Arabic, although some are occasionally shown with English, Italian, or French soundtracks.

The restaurants most frequented by foreigners serve either continental, Chinese, or Middle Eastern food. Music for dancing and even floor shows are available at the Hotel Intercontinental and at a nightclub or two. The sports clubs maintain restaurants for members and their guests.

Notes for Travelers

TWA and Pan Am provide flights to several European and Middle Eastern cities for connections to Amman.

Many international carriers fly into Jordan.

Passports and visas are necessary for entry. Persons whose passports contain Israeli visas or entry stamps are admitted only under special circumstances, and with great difficulty.

Smallpox immunization is required, and other health recommendations include boosters against tetanus, cholera, typhoid, and hepatitis.

Only nonautomatic firearms may be imported, in the following quantities: pistols (1), rifles (2), shotguns (2), plus 1,000 rounds of ammunition.

Roman Catholic, Anglican, and nondenominational Protestant services are available in Amman in English, as are Roman Catholic, Greek Orthodox, and Greek Catholic services in Arabic.

Local currency is the Jordanian *dinar* (JD) or "pound," divided into 1,000 *fils*. The rate of exchange is JD1 = U.S.$3.36 (February, 1979).

Jordan uses the standard metric system of weights and measures.

Special note:

Jordan is a Moslem country and many Moslems object to having their pictures taken. Discretion should be used in taking pictures of women, or of scenes that could be interpreted as showing poverty. Military installations (bridges included) cannot be photographed.

The U.S. Embassy in Jordan is located on Jebel Amman, in Amman.

Lebanon

LEBANON'S geography has determined much of its history. Located at the easternmost end of the Mediterranean, it serves as a link between East and West, both culturally and commercially. Excavations and restoration works presently being carried on throughout the country reveal traces of great empires that have come and gone, and students of history can bridge the past and present by studying Lebanon's role in these empires.

The Lebanese are known as the traders of the world in the tradition of their Phoenician ancestors. Migrants from this small republic have established colonies in 65 other countries around the globe, engaging mainly in commercial enterprises. More than a half-million Americans of Lebanese descent live in the United States, a fact which enhances ties between the two countries.

Area, Geography, Climate

Scenic beauty in the small area of Lebanon is varied—from the bright blue of the Mediterranean with its beaches, bays and headlands, banana plantations, and citrus and olive groves along the coast, to rugged mountains rising dramatically 9,000 feet behind the capital city of Beirut. Many of the mountains have been terraced, cleared, and irrigated for cultivation. Pine forests abound, although the famed Cedars of Lebanon have long since disappeared except for a few small groves preserved in the north and central regions.

Like most Mediterranean climates, Beirut's can be compared with that of southern California. From May to October, sunny weather prevails and rain rarely falls. Temperatures seldom go above 85°F during the hottest months (the average in August is 80°F), but high humidity makes summers debilitating. Many Lebanese city dwellers move to the mountains in summer, but Americans, unwilling to cope with the frequently primitive comforts of the mountains and with commuting problems, are more drawn to the beaches.

Mountain and sea breezes offset the summer heat to an extent, but one must live on an upper floor to benefit, in which case the wind frequently becomes a problem, particularly in spring.

Fall and spring are relatively short. Winter is chilly and damp. Most of the country's annual rainfall (36 inches) occurs from December through March. Even the most modern apartments are not designed for cold weather, and little or no insulation is used. Glass doors open onto balconies,

189

which are ideal in summer; in winter the wind sweeps through and around door frames, and rain frequently washes in beneath doors. In the city, winter temperatures rarely drop below 50°F. Most of the newer apartment buildings now have adequate central-heating plants, although landlords are often reluctant to use them as early in the winter as Americans might wish.

Beirut has no great dust problem compared with other Middle Eastern cities. Most buildings have insects to some extent, but insecticides and professional exterminators are available. Flies and mosquitoes are not excessively bothersome in the city proper. No buildings are screened, and few people use mosquito netting, which is expensive. Ants are ever present in hot weather. Normal precautions are taken against moths and mildew. To summarize, no particular problems arise from the climate that do not exist in many American cities.

Population

Thousands of small villages dot the mountains and plains of Lebanon. Few Lebanese, even those in the cities, fail to identify themselves by mentioning the family village. Of Lebanon's population of 3.1 million (January 1981), nearly half are found in Beirut (1.3 million). The other population centers are Tripoli (180,000), Zahle (34,000), Sidon (40,000), and Tyre (20,000).

The Lebanese are a mixture of many ancient strains, but are predominantly Arab. The country contains many Armenians, sizable colonies of Syrians, Egyptians, and Palestinians, and an increasing number of Sudanese. In addition to native Arabic, French is widely spoken as a result of long years of French influence, dating back to the Crusades and renewed during the period of French mandate over Lebanon and Syria between the two World Wars.

Some say that to the Lebanese, French is the cultural language and English is the commercial. Hence, knowledge of English has grown in importance as a necessary adjunct to business success. The influence of American University, founded by Protestant missionaries in 1866, is strong. The presence of British and Commonwealth troops during World War II helped to spread a working knowledge of English, at least in the cities. The use of English also was extended by the influx of large numbers of Americans employed by oil companies and other business firms, educational and missionary groups, and U.S. Government agencies. Many Lebanese are trilingual and frequently speak languages other than Arabic in their own homes. They are justly proud of the ability to learn languages, and the knowledge of Italian, German, Spanish, and Turkish is widespread.

Government

In Lebanon, separating the religious and ethnic-tribal-national groupings from the governmental and social organizations of the country is impossible. Whereas most of the Middle East is Muslim, Lebanon's population is about half-Christian and half-Muslim. The Muslim faction is divided into Shia and Sunni, and an influential segment of Druze exists, whereas the larger segments of the Christian doctrine are represented by the Maronite, Greek Orthodox, Armenian (both Orthodox and Catholic), Greek Catholic, Latin (Roman Catholic), and Protestant faiths. To the student of politics today, Lebanon thus presents a unique system of government based on religious proportional representation, including 14 confessions.

Lebanon is a republic with a democratic, parliamentary regime, and the composition of the government, the Parliament, and the civil service is based on a system of proportional representation by religious sect. By unwritten law, the President of the Republic must be a Maronite Christian, the Prime Minister a Sunni Muslim, and the Speaker of the House a Shia Muslim; the Deputy Prime Minister is usually Greek Orthodox. Remaining Cabinet positions are distributed among Lebanon's other religious groups.

The civil and criminal codes of Lebanon are based on the French legal system. However, property, inheritance, marriage, and family relations come under the jurisdiction of the religious communities.

Arts, Science, Education

Lebanon has the highest literacy rate (86 percent) in the Arab world. It has six universities: the American University of Beirut (AUB), 100 years old in 1966; St. Joseph University, founded by the Jesuits, also almost 100 years old; the Beirut College for Women, founded by American Presbyterians in 1924; the recently founded Lebanese National University; the Arab University, run by Egyptians; and Haigazian, an Armenian College. It is also one of the most important publishing centers in the Middle East. Lebanese scientists abound in the fields of chemistry, biology, sociology, mathematics, and statistics. Lebanon is also the area's leading country for

trained technicians in the fields of medicine, public health, and engineering.

Although Beirut is not a recognized center for painting or literature, a number of small galleries exhibit shows of local artists. Now that the excellent natural resources and traditional methods have been fused with newly imported ideas, pottery is becoming the art form of the area.

Commerce and Industry

Lebanon is traditionally a country of merchants and traders—of middlemen rather than entrepreneurs—and the reactions and attitudes of its people are strongly conditioned by their centuries-old preeminence in these skills. Beirut is a modern "trading post" for the Arab world.

Lebanon's major crops are cereals (wheat and barley), citrus fruits, all kinds of vegetables, apples, bananas, olives, grapes, dates, and figs. The industries that exist are mostly concerned with processing locally produced agricultural products, such as olive and vegetable oils (with a resultant subsidiary enterprise of soapmaking). Cement, glass, and textiles are produced; other manufacturing includes silk, cigarettes, printing, and pottery. Pepsi-Cola and Seven-Up, among others, have local bottling plants. Good wines and beers are also produced.

Transportation

Air and sea connections are available from Lebanon to all points in the Mediterranean, offering a choice of trips to Athens, Istanbul, Rome, Naples, Cyprus, and many other places. Khalde Airport, located on the outskirts of Beirut, is an international air transport center. The airport services all major points.

Beirut's public transportation system no longer functions, as all buses have either been destroyed or sequestered for use as movable roadblocks. Taxis are plentiful and consist of two types—legal licensed cabs and private vehicles employed as cabs. The former are identified by official red license plates. The latter usually carry a card in the window indicating availability for hire.

Most parts of Lebanon and the Middle East are connected by good, but narrow, roads. Adequate roads connect Lebanon with Western Europe by way of Turkey and Greece. One may drive, for instance, from Beirut to Athens in about four days.

All vehicles must be licensed and registered with the Lebanese Ministry of Public Works. A foreign country drivers license (provided the expiration date is clearly shown) may be endorsed by the Lebanese Automobile Registration Service for use in Lebanon for as long as it remains valid where issued. A Lebanese license may be obtained only after passing a difficult test. An international drivers license may also be endorsed by the Lebanese authorities without a test for the period of its validity (one year from date of issue).

Automobile insurance, including liability, is not mandatory under Lebanese law; however, public liability and property damage insurance coverage on personally operated automobiles is recommended. This insurance can be obtained through local agents at about the same rates as in the U.S. Some of these agents are representatives of American insurance companies.

Certain makes of cars may not be imported into Lebanon. This edict includes all Ford products. Therefore, one should seek current information from the American Embassy in Beirut (general services officer) before shipping a car to Lebanon. No passenger cars with diesel engines may be imported into Lebanon.

Repair facilities of varying quality exist at local garages, and an adequate supply of spare parts is available for most European and American models. Automatic transmission parts are available. Six-ply tires hold up best on the frequently under-repair or out-of-repair streets in Beirut.

Communications

In addition to telephone lines linking towns within Lebanon, there are lines between Beirut and most of the large cities in the area—Damascus, Baghdad, Aleppo, and Amman. Telephone calls to and from Lebanon's other cities must be booked, and waits of 15 to 30 minutes often occur when calling towns only a half hour away. Service between Beirut and the U.S. varies according to traffic and atmospheric conditions.

Telegrams are sent from the main post office and one branch in the same area. They can also be sent from hotels for an additional charge, but sometimes there is a delay in transmission.

Postal service is satisfactory. Transit time to the U.S. is about eight days.

Lebanon has two medium wave radio stations, one broadcasting chiefly in Arabic; the other in French and English, with frequent programs of Western popular and classical music.

There are daily broadcasts in English from BBC, and reception is excellent. Both AM and FM reception are good. A shortwave radio is useful, since VOA broadcasts in English throughout most of the afternoon and evening, and BBC and other European stations broadcast shortwave continuously. Reception is good.

Four television channels in Beirut offer programs in French, English, and Arabic. A number of American shows, old TV series, and old American movies are shown several times a week, as well as nightly news in French. The stations are on only from about 6 p.m. to midnight.

Radios and TV sets of most American makes are available in Beirut at slightly higher prices than in the U.S., but duty must be paid by nondiplomatic personnel. Sets made in the U.S. must be converted to Lebanese transmission. They can be converted in Lebanon if the owner provides a wiring diagram. However, once converted, a set cannot be reconverted. As RCA and Zenith products are on the boycott list, repair and adaption facilities are limited.

American, British, French, and German newspapers and periodicals are readily available in Beirut. The European editions of Time and Newsweek appear on about the same date as U.S. editions. Other magazines and technical journals are much more expensive than in the U.S.

One local morning newspaper in English and two in French are for sale, as is the International Herald Tribune which appears in Beirut one day after issue. Books, including paperbacks, are readily available in both English and French. Prices are higher, however, than in the U.S.

Several good collections of books are available in Beirut, the largest being the library at American University, where books may be borrowed on payment of a small deposit. Many excellent bookstores stock a wide variety of fiction, nonfiction, children's books, and an enormous assortment of pocket books (American editions in these, however, are often more than twice the U.S. price). Large stocks of recordings can be found in Beirut record shops.

Health

The practice of medicine and surgery in Beirut is conducted on a highly professional level. The number of physicians in practice is sufficient to allow a wide range of choice in the major specialties and subspecialties, all of which are represented. Fees for office visits are reasonable. House calls and night calls are proportionately higher. Emergency service at American University Hospital is similar to that obtainable in the U.S. Ambulance service is available.

Beirut has numerous hospitals. Those most frequently used by the official American community are the American University Hospital and the Dr. Fuad Khoury Hospital. The former is associated with the American University Medical School. It is a modern, 400-bed, well-equipped general hospital. Its clinical departments, constant care unit, radiology, and laboratories are operated at U.S. standards. Khoury Hospital, a small, well-equipped private hospital which also provides excellent care, is located near AUH. Both hospitals are staffed almost completely by American-trained faculties of the medical school.

A number of competent dentists practice general dentistry, and specialties such as orthodontics and oral surgery.

Beirut has air pollution resulting from burning garbage, incompletely burned petroleum products (automobile and aircraft), manufacturing plants, and dust. The municipal water supply is frequently contaminated, as this is an inherent characteristic of gravity flow supply systems. Water should be boiled for internal consumption. Locally bottled spring water is available.

Gastroenteritis occurs frequently, particularly in newly arrived visitors in Beirut. Other enteric diseases such as infectious hepatitis, typhoid and paratyphoid fever, amoebiasis, and giardia lamblia are endemic, but occur less frequently. Upper respiratory infections are common. Bronchitis and pneumonia are not an unusual threat.

Careful sanitary measures in food handling and drinking water can obviate many gastrointestinal problems. All fresh fruits and vegetables should be thoroughly washed and rinsed before storage. Incomplete cleaning of vegetables used in preparation of green salads is a frequent cause of illness. Meat—including beef, pork, and lamb—should be cooked thoroughly.

Pasteurized and homogenized milk is available. Since control of milk may at times be lax after leaving the dairy, milk should be purchased from retail outlets with a rapid turnover of stock.

Immunizations which should be kept current include smallpox, cholera, typhoid, paratyphoid, poliomyelitis, and gamma globulin. Malaria suppres-sives are not needed in Lebanon, but are indicated in a number of surrounding countries.

Major City

Bounded by Syria on the north and east and by Israel on the south, Lebanon forms a strip about 120 miles long and 35 miles wide. BEIRUT, the capital, is situated on a partially elevated head of land projecting into the Mediterranean. The city lies just below the 34th parallel, north latitude. It is slightly south of Los Angeles, about on a line with Atlanta, and covers an area of some three square miles.

Beirut is an amazingly Westernized Middle Eastern capital. Visitors are impressed by the beauty of the city's setting and grateful for its modern facilities.

Unfortunately, some parts of the city, particularly East Beirut and the luxury hotel district adjacent to the port, were heavily damaged during the fighting in 1975 and 1976. However, West Beirut, where many Americans live and work, has escaped relatively unscathed. Somewhat surprisingly, essential services to the public continue to be maintained at a relatively high level. Commerce and business also have continued to flourish in many areas in spite of adverse conditions and uncertainty of the times.

Despite the destruction and damage to such luxury hotel landmarks as the Phoenicia, St. George, and the Holiday Inn during the fighting in the city in the mid-70s, Beirut still has many good hotels. A number of these are located in West Beirut within a short distance of the U.S. Embassy. They include the Riviera, the Commodore, the Cadmos, and the Charles.

*Israeli planes bombed densely popu-
lated areas of Beirut on July 17, 1981, for
the first time in seven years. Hundreds of
civilian casualties were reported. There
were simultaneous sea and air attacks in
southern Lebanon.*.

Recreation

North of Beirut lie the ancient
ruins of Byblos, and to the south are
the fabled cities of Sidon and Tyre; to
the east is Baalbek (ruins of the greatest Roman temple in the ancient
world). All are within easy driving
distance, as are a number of Crusader
castles. Neighboring countries are also
rich in archaeological and historical
sites. Good roads for traveling by automobile are available, and local tourist
agencies offer scheduled trips.

Lebanon's National Museum is
worth particular attention. It holds
some of the world's oldest archaeological finds, including sarcophagi, glass,
mosaics, coins of various eras, and gold
objects from the ancient Phoenician
city of Byblos.

Because of Lebanon's small size,
all parts are accessible in one day's
drive. Within a half hour's drive are
resort towns (such as Bhamdoun and
Aley), some with modern hotels and
nightclubs, where one can retreat during the summer heat from July to
October.

Hiking in the mountains is good,
pleasant, and not too difficult. Camping, although somewhat limited, is
enjoyed by many visitors, particularly
the younger set. Camping and picnicking gear, European and American, is
sold in Beirut. However, there is limited stock. Picnicking is popular in
Lebanon throughout the year, and
there are many delightful spots in the
mountains and by the sea.

Except for a limited amount of
bird hunting, game pursuit is not good
in Lebanon. Dynamiting has ruined
fishing around Beirut, and little deep-
sea fishing is available. Spearfishing
outside of Beirut is good, and some
trout can be found in the Orontes.

Several of Beirut's beaches, like
those in so many other areas of the
world, are becoming polluted. However, swimming is still enjoyable. Private beach clubs abound in the Beirut
area, most offering both pool and sea
swimming. Annual membership fees
are moderate by U.S. standards. Most
clubs require a daily entrance fee. At
many of the clubs, cabana-type cabins
may be rented by the year; the cabins
include plumbing, electricity, and water. They are fairly expensive and are,
therefore, frequently shared. Several
hotels have freshwater swimming
pools which may be used for a small
charge.

Waterskiing is an increasingly
popular sport in the Beirut area, and
skis and tows can be rented. Skin
diving equipment also is available.

The Cedars, a ski resort about
three hours from Beirut, offers first-
class hotel accomodations, chalets to
rent for the season, five lifts, and
slopes ranging from beginner to expert
class.

Laklouk, two hours from Beirut,
has easy beginner slopes with several
T-bars and very modern, fully
equipped family chalets to rent on a
daily or weekly basis, plus a good
hotel. All are within walking distance
of the slopes.

Faraya, the most popular ski area,
only an hour from Beirut, offers several hotels, a wide assortment of cha-

lets to rent for the season, and one chair lift with five interesting runs, four T-bars, and a beginners' area with rope tow. Most sporting goods stores in Beirut rent new or first-class equipment by the day, week, or season at very moderate prices. During the season, both the American School and the YMCA offer inexpensive day-long skiing trips.

Beirut has several good tennis courts and clubs; membership fees are reasonable, and instruction is available. International tennis stars compete in many tournaments. Two nine-hole golf clubs offer swimming pools, tennis, squash, children's playgrounds, and restaurant/bar facilities. Membership fees are moderate.

Before the 1975–76 conflict, Beirut offered many amateur and professional sports. Some are still available to lesser degrees because of travel restrictions and security considerations. This caveat also applies to all other recreational activities in general.

Entertainment is limited in Lebanon. There is no opportunity to attend regular performances of opera, concert, or legitimate theater. However, American and foreign films are shown at several local cinemas, with English soundtracks supplemented by subtitles in French and Arabic. Most theaters are air-conditioned.

Notes for Travelers

The most direct route to Beirut from the U.S. is via TWA through Rome and/or Athens. No American passenger ships call at Beirut, but U.S.

freighters (American Export Lines and Lykes Brothers Lines) carrying a maximum of 10 to 12 passengers, sometimes stop.

Entry requirements include visas and international health cards with smallpox inoculation certificates. Since Lebanese (and most Arab country) regulations prohibit entry to anyone except a foreign diplomat with indication of travel to Israel, passports should not bear Israeli stamps.

Rifles and pistols are not available in Lebanon, nor may they be imported. If they are found in personal effects, they will be confiscated.

In Beirut, English-language religious services are held at the following churches: Adventist, All Saints (Anglican), Christian Science, Church of Christ, Church of Jesus Christ of the Latter-Day Saints (Mormon), Community (International), First Baptist Bible (Fundamental), University Baptist (Southern), Salesian School Chapel, and St. Francois. Other denominations offer services in other languages.

Lebanon's monetary unit is the pound (LL), which is divided into 100 *piasters.* Beirut is a "free money" market (currencies of other countries are freely bought and sold in the open market; no black market exists in currencies). Exchange rates fluctuate considerably.

The metric system of weights and measures is used.

The U.S. Embassy in Lebanon is located on the Corniche at Ain Mreisseh, Beirut.

Luxembourg

The Grand Duchy of **LUXEM-BOURG,** a tiny country surrounded by France, Germany, and Belgium, existed for 400 years under the rule of various European nations. From the end of the Middle Ages, it was dominated in turn by Burgundy, Spain, Austria, and France, and it was not until 1839 that it was granted political autonomy by King William I of The Netherlands. In 1890, upon the death of William III, Luxembourg became totally independent.

The country was invaded and occupied by Germany in both World Wars, but established, in the latter case, a government in exile in England under the Grand Duchess Charlotte. The present sovereign, Grand Duke Jean, succeeded his mother in 1964, when she voluntarily abdicated after a 45-year reign.

Area, Geography, Climate

Luxembourg lies between 49°27' and 50°11' north latitude, and 5°40' to 6°32' east longtitude. Fifty miles long and 36 miles wide, the country is bordered on the north and west by Belgium, on the south by France, and on the east by Germany. Its 1,000 square mile area is somewhat less than that of Rhode Island.

The forested and slightly moun-tainous northern half of the country is a continuation of the Belgian Ardennes. The Lorraine Plateau gives an average elevation of 1,000 feet to Luxembourg's southern region of rolling, open countryside. The Our, Sure, and Moselle Rivers flow north-south along the frontier between Luxembourg and Germany.

Temperatures range from 0°F to 90°F, with a mean annual termperature of 47°F. July and August are the warmest months; January and February the coldest. Northwesterly winds traverse the western, lower portion of the Belgian Ardennes and cause abundant precipitation. Average annual rainfall is 30 inches; some rain falls 50 percent of the year. Climate is typical of countries in northwestern Europe: fog, rain, and generally overcast weather prevail over warm sunshine or bright, clear, cold weather. Most Americans do not find the climate agreeable; it resembles the northeastern U.S. coast in March or November.

Population

The Grand Duchy had a 1981 population of nearly 365,000. Exclusive of city population (77,500), densest distribution is in the country's industrial southwest. About 700 Americans reside in the Grand Duchy.

European Community employees number about 1,500.

French, German, and Luxembourgish are spoken in Luxembourg. French and German are both official langauges. French is used in diplomatic exchanges and in drafting decrees and legislation. Local newspapers are published in German; this language is more generally used in stores and lower courts. Luxembourgers invariably speak Luxembourgish among themselves. Related to the old Moselle Frankish language of Western Germany, it is basically a German language enriched largely by French words and expressions. It varies somewhat from region to region, and is seldom written. Many Luxembourgers are fluent in English, and most of those in regular official contact with American and British know some English.

Luxembourg is predominantly Roman Catholic, but also has small Protestant and Jewish communities.

Government

The Grand Duchy of Luxembourg is a constitutional monarchy with a unicameral legislature. The 50-member Chamber of Deputies is elected directly by universal suffrage through a system of proportional representation. Grand Duke Jean, the Chief of State, has ruled since 1964. However, the head of government is the President of the Council of Government, usually known as the Prime Minister.

The Council of Government (President, Vice President, and currently five other Ministers) is responsible to the Chamber of Deputies. Executive power is exercised in the name of the Grand Duke, and legisla-

tion must be signed by him and countersigned by a responsible government official to become effective. The Council of State (a body of elder statesmen) exercises some of the functions of an Upper House. While the Council of State cites opinions on legislation, its recommendations are not binding on the Chamber of Deputies.

Judicial power is exercised by a series of courts headed by a Supreme Court. The law system in Luxembourg is a modified Napoleonic code.

The three major political parties are the Christian-Social Party, the Socialist Party, and the Democratic Party. Two others, the Social-Democrats and the Communist Party, also are represented in the Chamber of Deputies. Proportional representation gives smaller parties more prominence in the Chamber than under a nonproportional system. Since any one party cannot obtain an absolute majority in the Chamber, a coalition government is needed.

In addition to the government, the three principal organizing forces are the Catholic Church, labor unions, and the ARBED, the primary steel producers' association.

Luxembourg has been linked economically to Belgium since 1921 and is one of three partners in the Benelux Customs Union. It is also a member of the United Nations, NATO, Western European Union, and European Economic Community.

Luxembourg city is the seat of the European Court of Justice, European Investment Bank, and Secretariat of the European Parliament. Component organizations of the European Community meet in Luxembourg's European Center during specified months of the year.

Arts, Science, Education

The cultural influences upon Luxembourg life have varied greatly over the ages. Until the 19th century, Luxembourg was dominated by various European powers: France, Spain, Prussia, Austria, and the Netherlands. The strongest influences have been those of its immediate neighbors: France, Belgium, and Germany. Luxembourg's technology is primarily German-influenced. Many Luxembourg engineering students train in Germany, although Belgium is becoming increasingly popular. The French and, to a lesser degree, the Belgians are the strongest cultural influences. Luxembourgers, however, are appreciative of many other cultures as well, including those of the U.K., Italy, and the U.S.

Commerce and Industry

Luxembourg is aptly described in tourist literature as the "Green Heart of Europe." Despite its pastoral scenery, Luxembourg is, however, a highly industrialized and export-intensive country with its key industry—steel—located along its border with France. Indicative of its highly developed economy is the fact that services now surpass industry in total employment. Luxembourg has one of Western Europe's highest standards of living, with a per capita income of some $12,300. In 1978–79 the country's GDP growth rate in real terms was about three percent, somewhat below the 1970–74 average of 4.1 percent, but nonetheless a recovery from the −7.7 percent GDP growth in 1975 when the general recession struck Luxembourg.

Although Luxembourg has been successful in diversifying its economy away from nearly exclusive reliance on iron and steel, this industry still represents the most important economic sector in the Grand Duchy, accounting for 29 percent of the GDP and employing one-third of the industrial labor force. After an all-time high annual production record of 6.4 million metric tons in 1974, steel production fell sharply in 1975 and 1976 to about 4.6 million tons. It recovered partially in 1978 and 1979 due to a cutback in employment, the retirement of an obsolete plant, the initiation of a major modernization effort, and an upswing in market demand. The Luxembourg steel industry plans to modernize its operations fully by 1983.

Luxembourg has a growing number of medium and light industries which have been encouraged as part of the effort to broaden the country's industrial base. These "new industries," in which U.S. multinational firms in the rubber, chemical, and metal fabrication sectors predominate, account for one-fifth of industrial production. Luxembourg continues to offer a favorable climate for foreign investment, and the Government of Luxembourg is actively seeking new investment by means of tax and infrastructure (construction and equipment) incentives. The original value of U.S. direct investment stands at about $375 million (with a current market value of about $600 million). At a per capita level of over $1,000, this is believed to be the highest level of U.S. direct investment outside North America. The largest American firms are Goodyear, DuPont, and General Motors.

Luxembourg has a small but productive agricultural sector, which provides employment for about six percent of the labor force. Most farmers are engaged in animal husbandry, and the principal products are dairy and meat. Vineyards of the Moselle valley produce annually about 3,698,410 gallons (14 million liters) of dry white wine.

In recent years, banking and related financial activities have grown rapidly, and Luxembourg has become one of Europe's financial centers. The country has nine Luxembourg banks and branches of 100 foreign banks from Germany, the U.S., Scandinavia, Switzerland, France, Belgium, Japan, China, the U.S.S.R., and other countries. The volume of financial activities has grown steadily, and total assets of banks and savings institutions in Luxembourg now exceed $90 billion, of which 85 percent is denominated in foreign currencies, primarily American dollars and German marks. Some 5,000 holding companies are established in Luxembourg. The European Investment Bank, the financial institution of the Common Market, is also in Luxembourg.

The general recession in the industrialized world, which began in 1974, struck the Luxembourg economy with severity in 1975. Steel, which still dominates Luxembourg's economy, was a major victim of the sharp economic downturn in Europe. A 28.3 percent drop in steel output was the prime cause of a 7.7 percent fall in the Luxembourg GDP in 1975. Although the former GDP level was reattained in 1977, the steel industry began to recover only in 1978. A restructuring of the European Common Market steel industries is being developed which will reduce excess capacity (and employment) and modernize plant facilities for greater competitiveness.

The Luxembourg steel group—ARBED—more than doubled its annual investment schedule of prior years, and is also committed to reduce its former work force of 25,000 to 16,000 by 1983 in order to assure full competitiveness.

A tripartite conference of government, employer, and labor union representatives has produced a three-year action plan for economic stimulus, full employment, and continued labor peace, which Luxembourg has enjoyed since the 1930s. The creation of a National Society for Credit and Investment (SNCI) is also included in the action plan. The SNCI will enable the government to seek new foreign investment more actively, and to encourage expansion by established firms by means of increased incentives, as well as to assist in export financing.

Fortunately, Luxembourg's industries, apart from steel, construction, and synthetic fibers, have registered definite progress since 1976, with a 10 percent average growth rate. With the mild recovery of the steel industry in 1978 and the increased introduction of new industries, the Luxembourg economy was considerably revitalized. This upswing in steel production continued through mid-1979. However, the Luxembourg Government, faced with predictions of a worldwide growth slowdown, rising inflation, and a reduction in world demand for steel, forecasts a reduced real growth of GDP to about two percent coupled with an increased inflation rate of five percent for 1980, up from three percent for 1977 and 1978. Despite these portents, the improvement in the Luxembourg economy begun in 1977 continues to boost the economic situation; the rate of improvement simply has tapered off.

Transportation

From its modern airport, Findel, Luxembourg has daily service to Paris and Frankfurt, and flights to London on weekdays. A wide variety of connecting points are available at Paris, Brussels, and Frankfurt. Loftleider, Icelandic Airlines, and International Air Bahamas also maintain direct service.

Paris is accessible by car in less than five hours, Brussels in two-and-a-half, Le Havre in 10, Frankfurt in four, and Amsterdam in six. Trains travel frequently to Brussels and Paris, but are inconvenient to points in Germany.

In Luxembourg city, taxis are plentiful and medium-priced. However, they do not cruise the streets. Buses, geared to shopping and office hours, are inexpensive, but slow.

Luxembourg has excellent paved highways and secondary roads, and driving is on the right, with "priority to the right" (the driver to the right has the right of way, and exercises it). Cars for hire are expensive. Private automobiles imported into Luxembourg should be small American or European cars, as the roadways throughout Europe often are narrow and winding. A medical examination is required with the registration of a car.

Communications

Telephone and telegraph facilities are like those in the U.S. There is direct-dial service to most of the Western European countries and to the U.S.

International airmail between Luxembourg and America takes three to six days, and sea mail about a month.

Radio reception is adequate to receive stations throughout Western Europe. Luxembourg receives American programs from the Armed Forces stations in Germany. Radio Luxembourg has daily programs of light music in English; however, certain areas require an aerial.

Radio FM and television programs from West Germany, Belgium, and France are received in Luxembourg. Radio Luxembourg also has daily television programs in French. German television programs come in on a modified American set.

The leading newspapers of Luxembourg are in German or French (Luxemburger Wort and Republican Lorrain). The main newsstands in Luxembourg carry a wide selection of European newspapers as well as French, Belgian, and German magazines. The international edition of the New York Herald Tribune is available at local newsstands or by subscription. American periodicals sent via regular mails usually arrive five to six weeks after publication.

Health

Ordinary medical and surgical attention in Luxembourg is good, but not as modern as in the U.S. All Luxembourg physicians and surgeons receive their medical education abroad. Several local doctors, including pediatricians, have trained in America. The profession, as a whole, appears to keep reasonably informed of modern developments. The hospitals, including maternity hospitals, are clean and well kept, and are usually well staffed by Catholic nursing sisters.

Competent dentists practice in Luxembourg, but many Americans do not consider them equal to the best American dentists. Their fees are comparably lower also. Americans are usually satisfied with minor dental work done here. Local ophthalmologists and opticians are dependable. Pharmacies are well supplied with most general medicines.

Luxembourg enjoys a high standard of living. Sewage and garbage disposal are no problem; the public water supply is potable. Prevalence of disease is comparable to that in the New England states, except for a slightly higher incidence of tuberculosis and respiratory diseases. Several outbreaks of typhoid, influenza, and infantile paralysis have occurred since World War II; however, none has assumed serious proportions, and statistics reflect a steady downward curve. The last recorded case of infantile paralysis was in 1963. Ordinary colds and bronchial coughs from the damp climate are the most common ailments. Humidity increases sinus trouble, rheumatism, arthritis, catarrh, and asthma.

Pasteurized milk is sold in cartons and is considered safe by U.S. Armed Forces standards. Glass-bottled or plastic-bagged milk is pasteurized, but does not meet U.S. sanitary standards. No special treatment is required for milk, water, or fresh vegetables. Local water supply is hard.

Major City

The southern central city of **LUXEMBOURG** is the capital of the Grand Duchy. Built on ridges overlooking the confluence of the Alzette and Petrusse Rivers, the city has lovely park areas along both streams. The

Court of Justice of the European Community, the general secretariat of the European Parliament, the European Investment Bank, the Office of Statistics, and the European Monetary Fund all are based here.

In 1963, the city celebrated its 1,000th anniversary. For centuries, Luxembourg was one of the most powerful fortresses in the world, earning the name of the "Gibraltar of the North." Although the fortress was dismantled during the years 1867 to 1883, the many remnants of these ancient fortifications, the medieval towers and ramparts, are of great interest. The Casemates are a 23-kilometer network of underground passages, hewn from solid rock. The Grand Ducal Palace, built during the 16th and 18th centuries, is nestled among the narrow, winding streets of the old city.

Within the Cathedral of Notre Dame are the Grand Ducal Mausoleum and the tomb of Luxembourg's national hero, John the Blind, who was killed in 1346 at the Battle of Crecy.

Luxembourg offers the advantage of life in a medium-sized Western European town, coupled with many of the social and cultural aspects of a modern capital. Its central location in Western Europe, and its lovely and varied countryside, provide many opportunities for excursions. Basic services are nearly always available, either in Luxembourg itself, or in nearby Germany. Most supplies can be obtained locally.

Recreation

The Luxembourg countryside is beautiful in the spring, summer, and early fall. Tourists and hikers from all over Europe enjoy the unspoiled natural attractions of "Little Switzerland," the Sure and Moselle Valleys, and the thick forests of the Ardennes Mountains. More than 30 old castles dot the country at Vianden, Clervaux, Borscheid, Beaufort, and Esch-sur-Sure. Grape and wine festivals and tastings are held in towns and villages along the Moselle in the fall and spring when the grapes are gathered and the wine is bottled.

Trier, a former provincial capital of the Roman Empire and an important German town in medieval days, is 30 miles from Luxembourg city and an interesting day's excursion. North from Trier along the German Moselle, a series of picturesque wine towns and ruined castles extend to Coblenz, where the Moselle joins the Rhine. To the south near Luxembourg, the Verdun battlefield in France is well worth a visit. Paris and Brussels are fun for a weekend visit. Reims, Cologne, Aachen, and Strasbourg are within easy reach of the Grand Duchy. Spring trips to Holland's tulip fields are popular.

Sailing, canoeing, kayaking, water skiing, and fencing are available in Luxembourg city and there are also several swimming pools. The Mondorf twin modern pools are attractive and clean, but some open-air pools fail to meet American sanitary standards. River bathing is possible in several places. A private tennis club with excellent courts is available, as are a few well-kept municipal courts. Two riding academies and many riding trails are located in the surrounding countryside. Lessons are available at local academies. Several excellent ice skating rinks are available a short distance from the city.

Although unlike American golf courses, the Grand Ducal Golf Club has an excellent 18-hole course and a small, attractive clubhouse where meals are available. The course, considered to be among the most challenging and beautiful in Europe, attracts golfers from all over the continent.

Gym classes for men and women are available. Soccer, cross-country bicycle racing, and occasional boxing and fencing matches are the principal spectator sports.

A permit from the Ministry of Justice is required for possessing a hunting weapon, and hunters and fishermen must also pay annually for licenses. Wild boar, deer, and pheasant hunting is excellent and popular in Luxembourg. Many wooded streams provide fine fishing. However, hunting and fishing rights are privately owned, so one is usually dependent on invitations from Luxembourgers.

Luxembourg has several motion picture theaters where American, English, French, German, Italian, and other films are shown. American films are usually six months to one year old, but in their original English version. In winter, the New Municipal Theater presents a series of plays in French and German by excellent touring companies. Also, touring companies perform operatic and ballet series each season. Radio-Television-Luxembourg has an excellent symphony orchestra.

Luxembourg city's cultural center is the New Municipal Theater, which opened in April 1964. It offers opera, drama, symphonic concerts, and solo recitals, and profoundly enriches the country's cultural life. The annual open-air International Festival of Theater at Wiltz Castle in northern Luxembourg also provides a well-rounded selection of musical events, theater, and ballet.

A number of small nightclubs are further diversions. Apart from private social activity, Luxembourg is unusually quiet.

During three weeks in May, pilgrimages are made from all parts of the country to the Cathedral, culminating in a procession of the statue of "Our Lady of Luxembourg" through the city streets. The *Schobermess* comes to town at the end of August. This annual fair has all the usual attractions loved by children—bumper cars, carousels, shooting ranges—plus many temporary restaurants and two dance halls. European commercial companies display their products at an annual International Fair.

Notes for Travelers

Most travelers to Luxembourg arrive via London, Paris, or Frankfurt. Flying time from New York is approximately 12 hours.

No visas are required for Luxembourg or any of the surrounding countries.

The quantities and types of non-automatic firearms which may be taken into Luxembourg are: pistols and revolvers (2), rifles (4), shotguns (4), and ammunition (1,000 rounds).

The population is 97 percent Roman Catholic. However, a French Protestant church and a synagogue are located in the city of Luxembourg. Most services are held in German, but sermons are given in French in several Catholic churches. A small English-speaking Protestant community and an English-speaking Catholic church also hold services.

Under the terms of the Belgium-Luxembourg Economic Union, the Luxembourg franc is equal to the Belgian franc. Both circulate in Luxembourg, but the Luxembourg franc is not generally accepted in Belgium. Banks in other countries do not carry Luxembourg francs.

The metric system is used for weights and measures.

The U.S. Embassy is located at 22 Boulevard Emmanuel Servais, Luxembourg city.

Malta

MALTA, whose first known inhabitants were the Phoenicians, is the product of a long and interesting history. Its story spans thousands of years, ranging from Copper and Bronze Age temples, through Roman and early Christian sites, to the 16th- and 17th-century architecture of the Knights of the Order of St. John of Jerusalem. Folk patterns of the past prevail in parts of the islands alongside modern trends of living. It is a true collage of Mediterranean cultures.

Area, Geography, Climate

The Maltese Islands are a small archipelago of six islands and islets in the middle of the Mediterranean Sea. Malta (95 square miles) is the largest island of the group, followed by Gozo (26 square miles) and Comino (one square mile). Cominotto, Filfla, and St. Paul's are small uninhabited islets.

The longest distance on Malta is about 17 miles, from southeast to northwest; the widest part is nine miles in an east-west direction. The same figures for Gozo are nine miles and four-and-a-half miles. Gozo lies northwest of Malta across a narrow channel; Comino is in this channel. Malta's shoreline is 85 miles; Gozo's is 27 miles.

A number of hills, valleys, and plains intersperse the island. Some of Malta's and most of Gozo's villages are situated on hilltops overlooking the terraced fields that characterize the islands. The northern part of Malta is a series of ridges, valleys, bays, and promontories. The western side is dominated by 800-foot-high cliffs. Shorelines are quite rocky, but a few sandy beaches can be found.

The islands are bare and rocky, with scattered fertile patches. Gozo has less high ground and more arable land than Malta, while Comino is almost completely barren. In summer, the landscape is brown and arid, but soon after the fall rains begin, the countryside becomes green.

Malta lies about 60 miles south of Sicily, near the center of the Mediterranean Sea, with Gibraltar 1,141 miles to the west and Alexandria 944 miles to the east.

Annual rainfall averages 19 to 22 inches, but may vary from 40 to less than 10 inches. Temperatures range from 40°F in winter to 90°F in summer. The climate is temperate. First rains come in September, are heaviest from November to January, and ease off slightly in February and March. Beginning in March, rainfall diminishes until it stops in May, which, next to July, is the driest month.

Summer is hot and dry with almost cloudless skies. The *scirocco,* a warm, humid southeast wind, occurs in spring and from mid-September to mid-October. The *gregale,* a cold Greek wind, blows from the east and northeast in winter, occasionally reaching gale force. Winter is chilly to cold with occasional heavy downpours. Nonetheless, winter has many fine days.

Population

Malta is one of the world's most densely populated countries. The population of the Maltese Islands is estimated at 348,000. Population density is about 2,852 persons per square mile, compared to 56 per square mile in the U.S. A high percentage of Maltese live around the capital, Valletta, and the harbor area.

The first known inhabitants of Malta and Gozo, the Phoenicians, were followed by the Carthaginians. Later came the Romans, Arabs, Normans, Spanish, Italians, French, and British. The present population derives from this amalgam.

The Maltese remained a distinct ethnic group through the centuries, despite considerable intermarriage with the people who controlled the islands. Today's Maltese language incorporates Italian and English words, but is more like Arabic than any other language; Arabic speakers can understand Maltese and be understood. Arabic influence is also somewhat apparent in the island's architecture, folklore, and proverbs.

Knowledge of English is widespread among urban dwellers, and many young educated adults, students, and the upper-class older generation also know Italian and French. However, Maltese is spoken throughout the island by all for daily use. Since the early 1930s, both Maltese and English have been taught in the schools.

Maltese did not develop as a written language until the 20th century. Throughout the 19th and early 20th centuries, Italian was the language of the schools, law courts, and Maltese society. Despite Malta's small size, several variations of Maltese are spoken. Villagers at distant points on the islands use variations in idiom and pronunciation, and none speaks the "pure" Maltese taught in the schools.

The 1964 Constitution established Roman Catholicism as the religion of the country, but also guaranteed freedom of worship. Religion is a required subject in all government schools. Malta has traditionally been almost 100 percent Roman Catholic. Over 300 Roman Catholic churches are on the islands, about one for every 1,000 Maltese. No other religion has gained ground among the people, but a significant decrease has occurred in the strict observance of religious duties by urban dwellers. However, in the villages, and to a slightly lesser extent in towns, the parish church remains the focal point of community life. The annual *festa* of each town or village parish, in honor of the patron saint on his name day, is still the most important day of the year for the inhabitants. The people contribute substantially for church and street decorations, lights, floats, and fireworks, all essential to local observance of this ostensibly religious event.

In the absence of local or regional government authority, the village church was and, in some ways, continues to be the people's spokesman to secular authorities. The parish priest reads government notices from his pulpit, serves as legal adviser, banker, and letterwriter for his parishioners, and retains his traditional role as the people's "patron" or spokesman to the government. This role, however, is rapidly diminishing.

More than 25 percent of Malta's population lives in essentially rural areas. The urban Maltese resembles, in outlook and sophistication, other Europeans of the same educational background and employment level. However, the typical rural Maltese is a very provincial person whose life centers around the village. Many older villagers have not visited Valletta for years. In fact, thousands of Maltese have never left the main island, even to visit Gozo.

Italian, English, and American films and TV programs have had a great impact in broadening the Maltese viewpoint, but all cultural imports (films, TV programs, books, etc.) are subject to censorship board evaluation and control.

Government

Malta's location has for centuries given it political and military importance out of proportion to its size and natural resources. The islands have been occupied and ruled by alien peoples from time immemorial until independence from the United Kingdom was granted in 1964. In recent history the two longest and most significant periods of occupation were by the Knights of the Order of St. John of Jerusalem from 1530 (after their ejection from Rhodes by the Turks) to 1798, and by the British from 1814 to 1964.

Almost equally famous was the prolonged and intense air bombing during World War II. The islands' population and defenders were close to starvation when a relief convoy of four surviving ships reached them on August 15, 1942. The danger of starvation did not abate until spring of 1943, when control of the Mediterranean passed to Allied hands. In April 1942, Malta was awarded the George Cross for "a heroism and devotion that will long be famous in history."

Malta, a self-governing republic, gained its independence from the U.K. in 1964. The Head of State is the President, Dr. Anton Buttigieg. Malta's parliamentary system of government is led by Prime Minister Dominic Mintoff, leader of the Malta Labor Party, who has held this office since 1971. Parliament consists of a unicameral House of Representatives with 65 members. The present Parliament has 34 Labor Party members and 31 members of the opposition Nationalist Party led by Dr. Edward Fenech Adami.

The judiciary consists of eight judges who sit in the superior courts and 10 magistrates who sit in the inferior courts. The legislative and judicial systems are closely related to the British systems, but the judiciary also owes much to French law and the Napoleonic Code, as well as to the Italian judicial system.

Italian was, by default, the written language of the government (including the law courts) and the spoken language of society throughout the 19th century to the early 1930s. Precedent law of this period is all in Italian. Since 1934, Maltese and English have been the official languages of government, including the legislature and courts. Government officials at all levels must have a minimum tested level of competence in both languages.

Arts, Science, Education

Malta's opera house, destroyed in the World War II bombing, has not been rebuilt. The Manoel Theater, a charming 18th-century structure, is used for local and visiting cultural attractions. During the winter season, a number of orchestral, choral, and chamber music concerts are presented by visiting groups. The Malta Amateur Dramatic Club, Atturi Theater, and other groups present plays and musicals in English at the Manoel Theater, Phoenicia Theater, San Anton Gardens, and other locales in winter and spring.

Malta has a number of architecturally interesting churches, mostly of the baroque or rococo periods. Other architectural classics are the fortifications of the "Three Cities," built during the 16th century by the Order of St. John of Jerusalem, and several 17th-century forts and secular architecture (principally the Auberges) of Valletta, also built by them. The old walled town of Mdina is lovely.

The principal Maltese art collections are at St. John's Co-Cathedral in Valletta, the Cathedral of Sts. Peter and Paul in Mdina, the National Museum, and the Grant Master's Palace in Valletta. All four contain works of interest.

Local branches of the Alliance-Francaise, British Council, Dante Alighieri Society, and German-Maltese Circle (each affiliated with the Embassy or High Commission of its respective country) all operate in Malta. The British Council frequently sponsors concerts and other cultural events.

American, English, Italian, and other foreign films are shown at the 40 movie houses in Malta. Charitable groups customarily arrange a benefit performance for the premiere of an exceptionally good film, and this is a major social event.

During the 1977–78 academic year, the Government of Malta began a reform of higher education with the stated aim of making it more practical and job-oriented. The final shape of these reforms might take several years to evolve, but the following features of Maltese higher education applied as of November 1978:

The University of Malta (Old University), which traces its origin back to 1592, conducts programs leading to bachelor's degrees in arts and sciences and to a doctorate in law.

A "New University" is being established from the former College of Arts, Sciences, and Technology (MCAST). Degree programs in medicine, dentistry, pharmacy, and architecture have recently been transferred from the University of Malta to the New University. In addition, the New University is organizing degree programs in engineering, business studies, and education.

Both insitutions are geared to full-time day students but give occasional short-term evening courses in such subjects as banking, accounting, journalism, and social work.

Preference is given to student applicants who are accepted by employers for a work-study program. These students spend half the year studying and half the year working and receive a small salary and free tuition. Nonsponsored students are admitted on a space-available and fee-paying basis. Foreign students wishing to enroll at either institution might have some difficulties until the reform of higher education has been completed.

Commerce and Industry

Over the centuries Malta's economy has been a "fortress" economy, dependent on various occupying powers for the greater part of its national income. Malta's excellent harbors and strategic location made it an important naval base and bunkering station. Today, Malta Drydocks Corporation (formerly a Royal Navy shipyard turned over to the Malta Government) is still the largest industrial enterprise, employing about 5,500.

On attaining independence, Malta remained heavily dependent on the expenditures of British forces on the islands and loans and grants from the U.K. Malta had only one first-class hotel and little industry other than the drydocks. Most Maltese were directly or indirectly employed in providing goods and services for British forces, or in trade.

Over the past 14 years, however, Malta experienced an economic boom of substantial proportions. Tourist facilities expanded rapidly, and new foreign and domestic industrial investments created export-oriented and import-substituting industries. In 1972, Malta's base agreement with the U.K. was renegotiated. The new pact provided for 14 million pounds sterling in annual payments from the U.K. and NATO, almost three times greater than previous levels, and was in effect until March 1979.

Exports have more than doubled in recent years. Until 1976, the U.K.

had been Malta's most important export market; the Federal Republic of Germany has since occupied this position. Clothing, textiles, rubber articles, vegetables, and animal feeds are among the major export commodities.

Since Malta has no natural resources, it must import most of its food requirements, as well as raw materials and semi-manufactured goods for its export industries. As a result, Malta constantly runs an overall trade deficit. In 1977, Malta's exports to the U.S. were valued at 1.5 million Malta pounds (£M).

The major U.S. manufacturing firm in Malta is Blue Bell (Wrangler jeans). It employs about 1,500 workers in its plants in Malta and Gozo and exports about U.S. $60 million worth of goods. Other U.S. manufacturing concerns include General Instruments Europe (electronic components) and Malta Industrial Clothing (workclothes). Recently, a large number of U.S. offshore-drilling companies have set up an operational base in Malta. These firms include Reading and Bates (1,200 employees and dependents) and Offshore International (600 employees and dependents).

Tourism is a major source of income and has nearly doubled since 1974, when there were 272,000 visitors. Most tourists are from the U.K., but increasing numbers are coming from Western Europe and the U.S.

Malta's income from tourism, direct payments under the base agreement, and other capital inflows have resulted in an overall balance-of-payments surplus over the years.

Despite substantial economic progress, unemployment remains one of

Malta's principal problems. Total employment now stands at 114,400. Over 27,700 are employed by the Malta Government, including 6,500 members of the Labor Corps, which was formed to alleviate unemployment, to provide useful work, and to train volunteers for employment in industry. About 7,400 are employed in fishing and agriculture, and 76,500 in industry, services, commerce, and other private employment. The British forces employed over 11,000 Maltese in 1964, but by 1978 successive reductions had brought the total to under 2,600.

Malta's major economic objective is to create sufficient employment and to expand export earnings, so that the country will no longer be dependent on the jobs and income arising from a foreign military presence. Besides promoting direct foreign investment in the industrial sector, Malta has sought assistance from many foreign governments, both Communist and non-Communist.

Transportation

Malta is 58 miles from the nearest point in Sicily and 180 miles from the nearest point on the North African mainland. Air service is frequent to Frankfurt, Paris, Tripoli, Rome, and London. Daily flights to Rome and London are offered throughout the year, and to other points mentioned several times weekly. The airlines operating from Malta are Air Malta, the national airline, British Airways, Alitalia, Libyan Airlines, and Universal Travel Agency (UTA).

Throughout the year, the Tirrenia Line sails round trip from Malta to Syracuse, Catania, and Reggio Calabria. The ship serving this route carries passenger cars. Departure from Malta

and Italy is three times weekly. The run from Malta takes four hours to Syracuse, eight hours to Catania, and twelve-and-a-half hours to Reggio Calabria. Ships on this line are far from luxurious, but provide the only satisfactory way of taking passengers with private cars from Italy to Malta.

In Malta, transportation is by private or rented car, taxi, or public bus. Paved roads, even to remote villages, are common, but their condition is less than satisfactory. Few roads have shoulders. Children, unlit horse-drawn or antique motor-driven vehicles, and animals abound, both in villages and on the highways. In summer, tourist-driven cars add to the confusion, and minor fender-bender accidents often occur.

Traffic is on the left. However, left-hand-drive cars are permitted and the "LHD" emblem on the rear is not mandatory. Many road signs indicate which of two intersecting roads has the right-of-way. Fortunately, driving speeds are relatively low due to the poor condition of most roads.

Public buses go to all parts of the island, but one or more transfers may be needed to reach remote areas. Fares are low, but buses are fairly crowded during morning and evening rush hours. Bus service on most lines stops early in the evening or else runs only infrequently after the evening rush. Use of public buses is not practical for evening social engagements.

Some garages operate taxi services. One must call for a cab, since they do not cruise looking for fares, and the fare should be negotiated in advance. Car rentals vary according to season, model, type of insurance, and individual garages.

Those planning to arrive in Malta with a private car must have valid auto tags of some foreign country, proof of ownership, and auto insurance valid for driving in Malta. There is no vehicle inspection or published traffic code. Automobile repair is only fair, but usually costs far less than in the U.S. Parts are difficult to obtain.

Communications

International phone service is available to Europe, parts of North Africa, and the U.S. Reversed-charge (collect) calls can be made to the U.S. International calls should be placed as early as possible. A direct-dialing service links Malta to the U.K., Italy, and Libya. Commercial cable service is available worldwide. International postal service is adequate for letters, but inconvenient for outgoing packages because of customs formalities.

News coverage on Malta radio and TV is in Maltese, and Italian TV news coverage is in Italian. No English-language news is broadcast on the island.

A variety of periodicals are published both in Maltese and English. Many are affiliated with churches or political parties and have small circulations, parochial themes, and poor journalism. The local daily newspapers most widely read by foreigners are The Times, published by the Strickland family, which generally supports the position of the Nationalist Party, and The News, which expresses the views of the General Workers Union and the Malta Labor Party.

Time and Newsweek (international editions) are sold on newsstands the day after publication. British daily newspapers and weekly periodicals are usually available on newsstands the same afternoon as publication.

Health

Malta's health-care system is undergoing a rather drastic change. The government is setting up a national health service similar to that in the U.K. Unfortunately, a number of private physicians who refuse to accept the government's requirements have been banned from all hospital privileges. Some doctors have left the country, and others maintain a private practice without access to public or private hospitals. Considerable uncertainty in medical-care practice remains to be resolved.

Fortunately, several good generalists and specialists are available to the American community. They are quite capable of dealing with most typical health problems.

Malta has two major private hospitals, Blue Sisters Hospital and St. Catherine's Hospital. These excellent and well-staffed, well-operated general hospitals provide comfortable and dependable care. For major emergencies, the government-run or public hospital, St. Luke's, has a record of round-the-clock care which has proven to be highly effective.

Maltese physicians and nurses are well trained and fluent in English. Dental care is generally good, and several dentists have British and American experience.

No unusual health hazards exist in Malta that are not present in the U.S. Sanitation is generally good. Tapwater, however, has a high saline content, so it is wise to boil and filter it to improve its taste.

Regular TB screenings and routine immunizations for polio, diphtheria, tetanus, whooping cough, and measles are necessary, as they would be in the U.S. Illnesses contracted in Malta are predominantly virus infections. Common-sense care and attention to good health practices are urged. Homes should be screened to keep flies and mosquitoes out. During winter, heating is needed. Homes do not have central heating.

Major City

The capital city of **VALLETTA** is located on a peninsula with deepwater harbors on two sides and the open sea on a third. The city is one mile long and several hundred yards wide. Its narrow streets are lined with buildings dating from the 16th, 17th, and 18th centuries. Pedestrians throng the streets during the day, and parking space inside the city is very limited. Modern office buildings are few, since new construction is limited by many national monuments that cannot be razed or radically altered.

More than half of the 300,000 residents on the Island of Malta live in the central urban Valletta-Floriana-Sliema area, where nearly all major commercial firms and government offices are located. A number of British have retired here or have come to Malta to reside and invest in the island's development. Thus, urban Malta has a British flavor and is strongly British-oriented. Shops carry English and European goods of all types. Most tourists are British, but European and American tourists are increasing in number.

Most basic services and supplies are available in the urban area, but generally speaking, are less adequate

than those in the major cities of Western Europe.

Recreation

Hiking in the rural areas of Malta, particularly the thinly populated north and northwest, can be pleasant and interesting. A number of picnic spots, many accessible only by foot, provide lovely sea vistas. Malta has a medium-sized botanical garden.

Much interesting sight-seeing can be done. Perhaps most interesting are buildings from the period of the Knights and prehistoric sites, some of which are still being excavated. Nonetheless, a week of concentrated sightseeing would exhaust the principal attractions, including the most important architectural monuments and museums.

Despite Malta's relative proximity to a number of other Mediterranean ports (e.g., Greece), neither direct ship nor air service exists to points other than those already indicated. Therefore, travel to other areas in the Mediterranean basin must be via Italy.

Swimming, sailing, waterskiing, and skin diving are available about six months of the year. The one golf course is also used throughout winter. Tennis is played year round at the Union Club and Marsa Sports Club, which also have squash courts. Two riding stables have good horses.

Water polo is a popular spectator sport in summer. Soccer, the favorite Maltese spectator sport, is played year round except during the hottest summer months. A surprising number of fine trotting horses are on the island. Trotting races start when it begins to cool in the fall, and last until spring.

Races are held on Sundays and holidays, and betting for small stakes is permitted.

Fishing from small boats or the shore may be readily undertaken. No facilities exist, however, for deep-sea fishing from chartered boats equipped with heavy gear. In winter, hunting (small birds) is popular with Maltese men, who use both net and gun.

Malta offers little in the way of live concerts, theater, or opera comparable to first-class attractions in major American or European cities. Most major American and foreign films eventually arrive in Malta about a year after their premieres abroad. All are censored by a government-appointed board, which includes a church representative. Objectionable dialogue or scenes are removed, and some films are not shown at all. English-language films are shown in the original version, and most foreign films have English subtitles. Movie prices are inexpensive. Most movie theaters are not air-conditioned, thus limiting attendance during the hot summer.

A government-licensed casino operates year round, offering roulette, blackjack, and chemin de fer (a variation of baccarat).

In terms of local folklore, the village *festa,* held mostly between May and October, holds some interest. *Festas* combine religious processions and ceremonies with elaborate street lighting, band parades, and fireworks displays. Similar celebrations take place at carnival season.

Notes for Travelers

Daily flights to Malta arrive from London and Rome, and most travelers from the U.S. use one of these routes.

No evidence of immunization is required of visitors, except those arriving from Africa, Asia, or South America, and they must have proof of current smallpox vaccination. However, when a contagious disease reaches epidemic proportions in any part of the world, persons arriving from infected areas are subject to isolation and surveillance.

The Government of Malta permits no cats or dogs to be imported into the islands at any time.

Local law requires that all firearms taken into Malta be licensed with the police department.

Malta has about 313 Roman Catholic churches. Masses are held in Maltese. One Catholic church in Velletta offers masses on Sundays in other languages—one service in English, one in French, and one in German. Several Anglican churches are found here, as well as a Greek Orthodox church, a Greek Catholic church, a Gospel Hall, a Jewish synagogue, and the Salvation Army. Services are held in English at these places of worship, except for the Jewish synagogue and Greek churches.

Malta has its own currency, of which the Maltese pound (£M) is the main unit. It is divided into 100 cents (c), and each cent into 10 mils (m). There are no American banking firms on Malta.

The British (imperial) gallon is used as the measure for gasoline (one gallon equals 4.8 U.S. quarts). For food purchases, the *ratal* (equal to 28 ounces) is used.

The U.S. Embassy in Malta is located in Development House, St. Anne Street, Floriana, just outside Valletta.

Netherlands

The **NETHERLANDS** had no history of unity before the late 16th century. It was ruled by Romans, Franks, Burgundians, English, Spanish, French, and Germans—all the while continuing its endless struggle against the relentless sea. Its name means "low countries," and in fact, half of its area has been reclaimed from the waters of the North Sea.

History

Julius Caesar found the Netherlands inhabited by Germanic tribes, one of which, the Batavi, did not submit to Rome until 13 B.C., and then only as an ally. The area was part of Charlemagne's empire in the eighth century, later passed into the hands of the House of Burgundy and the Austrian Hapsburgs, and eventually fell under harsh Spanish rule in the 16th century. The Dutch revolted in 1568 under William of Orange, and 11 years later, the seven northern provinces formed the Union of Utrecht and became the Republic of the United Netherlands.

During the 17th century, the "Golden Era," the Netherlands became a great sea and colonial power. Its importance declined, however, during the 18th-century wars with Spain and France. In 1795, French troops ousted William V.

Following Napoleon's defeat, the Netherlands and Belgium became the "Kingdom of the United Netherlands" under William I, son of William V and head of the House of Orange. The Belgians withdrew from the Union in 1830 to form their own kingdom. In 1840, William I abdicated in favor of William II, who was largely responsible for the liberal revision of the Constitution in 1848. During the long reign of William III from 1849 to 1890, the Netherlands prospered. Wilhelmina, William III's 10-year old daughter, succeeded her father in 1898.

The Netherlands was neutral during World War I and again proclaimed neutrality at the start of World War II. Nonetheless, German troops overran the country in May 1940. Queen Wilhelmina and Crown Princess (later Queen) Juliana then fled to London, where a government-in-exile was established. They later moved to Canada. The German Army in the Netherlands capitulated May 5, 1945.

Juliana's daughter, Beatrix, is the present Queen.

Area, Geography, Climate

The Netherlands is bordered on the north and west by the North Sea, on the south by Belgium, and on the east by the Federal Republic of Germany. It covers about 14,000 square miles, and is almost one-third the size of Virginia.The land is low and flat except in the southeast, where some hills rise to 1,000 feet. About one-third of its area is below sea level, making the famous Dutch dikes a requisite to land use. Continuing reclamation of land from the sea into new areas (polders) provides fertile land for this densely populated country.

The warmest period falls between June and September; the other months are cool or cold. Despite an occasional warm spell in summer, temperatures rarely exceed 75°F. Winter is long, often dreary, and the damp cold is penetrating.

Population

The Netherlands has a population of 14,182,000 (January 1981). The Dutch are mostly of Germanic stock with some Gallo-Celtic mixture. A proud people, they have clung tenaciously to their small homeland against the constant threat of destruction by the North Sea and the recurrent danger of extinction at the hands of the great European powers.

Religion influences Dutch history, institutions, and attitudes. It is closely interrelated with social and political life, but in a diminishing degree. The right of every individual to profess his religion is guaranteed by the Constitution. Although church and state are separate, a few historical ties remain, such as the royal family belonging to the Dutch Reformed Church (Protestant). According to the 1971 census, as adjusted, 40 percent of the population are Roman Catholic, 23.5 percent Protestant Reformed, 7.2 percent Protestant Calvinist, 5.3 percent other denominations (mainly Protestant), and 23.6 percent have no religious affiliation.

Government

The Netherlands Government is based on the principles of ministerial responsibility and parliamentary government common to most constitutional monarchies in Western Europe. It is composed of three basic institutions: (a) the Crown (the Monarch, Council of Ministers, and Council of State); (b) the States General (Parliament); and (c) the Courts.

Although her functions are largely ceremonial, the Queen still maintains an influence in the government. The Queen's influence derives from the traditional veneration for the House of Orange, her personal qualities, and the Dutch political party system, wherein it is difficult to obtain a parliamentary majority. This influence enables her to designate the individual charged with forming a coalition Council of Ministers.

Ministers have two general functions. Except for the Ministers without portfolio, they head ministries or departments. Collectively they form the Council of Ministers, which formulates and carries out government policies and initiates legislation. The Ministers collectively and individually are responsible to the States General.

The States General (Parliament) consists of the First Chamber (Upper House) and the Second Chamber (Lower House), which meet separately, except for ceremonial occasions. In addition to their legislative authority, both chambers exercise a check on the Council of Ministers through questioning and investigation. The Second

Chamber is far more important, for it alone has the right to initiate legislation and amend bills submitted by the Council of Ministers. The First Chamber has 75 members chosen for a six-year term by the 11 provincial legislatures. Half its membership is renewed every three years. The Second Chamber has 150 members elected directly for four-year terms on the basis of proportional representation.

Of the Netherlands' overseas territories, Indonesia gained its independence in 1949 and Surinam became independent in 1975. The six islands of the Netherlands Antilles (Aruba, Curaçao, Bonaire, Saba, St. Eustatius, and a part of St. Maarten) are integral parts of the Netherlands realm, but are increasingly autonomous.

Arts, Science, Education

Education in the Netherlands is of excellent quality, and many foreign students are enrolled in the 13 schools of higher education. Of these, the University of Leiden, the School of Economics of the Erasmus University at Rotterdam, and the Technical University at Delft are outstanding schools which have played an important role in the development of European universities. The International Court of Justice in The Hague and the Universities of Leiden and Amsterdam offer summer courses in international law which are attended by many Americans. Music schools and art academies enjoy a good reputation as well.

With the upheavals of the 1960s, legislation was enacted to liberalize the university system. This stimulated the democratization of the universities and has brought about profound changes in their structure. Students, profes-

sors, assistants, and staffs have a voice in the administration of the schools. Not all the results have been positive, and the process has caused some concern throughout the country.

Of the more than 450 Dutch museums, the Rijksmuseum, the Stedelijk Museum, and the Van Gogh Museum in Amsterdam are world famous. Boymans-van Beuningen Museum in Rotterdam and the Kroller-Muller Museum in Otterloo have excellent collections of modern art. The small, but exquisite, Mauritshuis in The Hague displays mostly 17th-century Dutch and Flemish paintings.

The performing arts in the Netherlands have always has a good international reputation. The two major ballet companies, Het Nationale Ballet and The Netherlands Dance Theater, have frequently toured the U.S. and Europe. This is also true for the three major symphony orchestras, the Concertgebouw Orchestra, the Residentie Orchestra and the Rotterdam Philharmonic. The yearly Holland Festival features many American artists. In addition to the repertory companies, the Netherlands houses many avant-garde theater groups which often perform off-Broadway plays.

Commerce and Industry

The economy is based on private enterprise, but both labor unions and government have recently moved toward acquiring substantially increased control over the operation of enterprises. This trend, combined with increasingly higher government and social security expenditures (65 percent of national income), has caused investment to decline in recent years. As a result, growth in gross national product has moved toward a lower long-term trend and unemployment has risen substantially. Dutch financial authorities continue to assign a high priority to fighting inflation which has been, at five to six percent, one of the lowest rates in Europe.

The government has been aided in its fight against recent economic difficulties by extensive revenues from the production and export of natural gas from fields in the northern part of the country and the North Sea. However, gas exports have been unable to prevent a deterioration in the Dutch balance of payments from a position of surplus during the mid-1970s to deficits in the last few years. Nevertheless, the guilder remains strong within the European Monetary System (EMS), in which it is linked with the German mark and several other European currencies.

Industry is concentrated in the western coastal areas, particularly around Rotterdam, the world's largest port. However, efforts to disperse industry continue and the government promotes industrialization in the eastern, northern, and southern districts. Nevertheless, the structure of industry tends toward centralization through mergers to realize economies of scale, to improve competitive positions, and to exchange technology. Principal industries include oil refining, metal fabrication, chemicals, electronics, and textiles.

Over 1,000 Dutch firms are either wholly or partly American-owned, and represent a total direct U.S. investment of nearly $5 billion. In addition, Dutch investments in the U.S. exceed $10 billion, making the Netherlands the largest foreign investor in America.

Due to a lack of natural resources

but a favorable geographical location, the Netherlands has traditionally been a trading nation. In 1979, total Dutch exports reached $63.8 billion, or close to 42 percent of GNP, while imports rose by 18 percent to $67.4 billion. Total imports from the U.S. of $6.9 billion in 1979 make the Netherlands the sixth major customer for U.S. exports. The main components of these exports are agricultural products along with industrial machinery, transportation equipment, and office and data processing machines. American imports from the Netherlands in 1979 amounted to $1.9 billion, thus giving the U.S. a favorable bilateral trade balance of $5 billion.

Holland is the country which added the windmill to the landscape and the "polder" to the vocabulary. Dutch agriculture, due to severely limited availability of farmland (5.1 million acres), is primarily a conversion industry. It utilizes imported feedstuffs, managerial efficiency, and proximity of markets for its exports. Livestock production accounts for 68 percent of total production by value, with horticulture (20 percent) and arable crops (12 percent) next in importance. Wheat and barley are chief grains. Production of milk and milk products, slaughter hogs, and vegetables are of greatest value.

In 1975, Holland's import of agricultural products from the U.S. totaled $1.5 billion or 26 percent of the $5.6 billion of its total imports. Major imports from the U.S. in order of importance were: soybeans, feed grains, wheat, tobacco, vegetable fats and oils, and fresh citrus. Exports of $261 million to the U.S. consisted mostly of canned hams, dairy products and flower bulbs. The Netherlands is the world's largest exporter of poultry meat. Neighboring countries of the nine-member European Community are by far the largest market (78 percent) for the Netherlands agricultural exports.

Transportation

Many airlines serve Schipol (the international airport) near Amsterdam, and provide worldwide connections. American flag service also is available. The Rotterdam airport has daily flights to and from London.

Most Dutch cities are connected by rail, and almost all regions are accessible by other public transportation. Similar transportation and flights to principal European cities are available. There is daily express rail service between The Hague, Amsterdam, Rotterdam, Antwerp, Brussels, and Paris at a small supplementary charge.

Good public transportation is available in the cities by bus and streetcar, which serve the principal sections of the city as well as the suburbs. Savings can be made by buying multiple ride tickets. Trams and buses do not run between 1 and 5 a.m. Taxicabs, plentiful and available by night or day, do not cruise and are expensive. One must either phone for one or walk to a cabstand.

Most people ride bicycles or motorbikes, causing a formidable traffic problem during rush hours. The newer Netherlands bicycles are excellent but expensive. They weigh less than American bicycles. English and Italian bicycles are also available, as well as motor scooters.

Driving in the Netherlands is on the right, with roads ranging from good to excellent. Newcomers may find driving in town a little disconcerting because of many cyclists, who often make unexpected turns or must be passed at close range. Many persons own low-priced American cars, but smaller European cars are also popular. General Motors, Ford, and American Motors products are sold here. Repair services and spare parts are available for practically any make of car, but often work is very expensive. A waiting time of up to three months may be required for the delivery and licensing of a new car bought in the Netherlands.

Communications

Telephone and telegraph facilities for local and long-distance use are good. Direct-dial telephone service is available to the U.S. and most parts of Europe, or calls can be booked through the long-distance operator. Many phone operators speak English, and information operators are multilingual. International postal service is fast and reliable.

Radio reception is good, and programs from a number of neighboring countries can be heard on an ordinary set. English programs can be heard via the BBC and VOA; Radio Luxembourg also has good reception. The U.S. Armed Forces Network (AFRS) in Germany can generally be received only at night on the standard broadcast band. Its reception ranges from fair to good. Several FM channels, as well as FM stereo, transmit at certain times during the day.

TV is on from about 7 to 11 p.m., seven days a week, with occasional morning programs or special events coverage. English TV shows are broadcast in English with Dutch subtitles. TV commercials are few. Two channels are available.

Many excellent bookstores offer a variety of books in English. International editions of Time, Newsweek, Life, and the Herald Tribune are sold locally. Popular U.S. magazines also are sold at local newsstands. English-language children's books are scarce. The Royal Library in The Hague has an English section, and some Dutch public libraries have selections of books in English.

The American Women's Club of The Hague maintains a library in the American Protestant Church. It contains about 3,000 volumes, with a special children's book section. The community library in Wassenaar contains a small but good range of fiction and nonfiction. The American-Netherlands Club of Rotterdam maintains a small library which carries a good selection of new fiction and nonfiction books. One private library, the Rotterdamsch Leeskabinet, has some English-language fiction in its collection.

Health

In general, medical training in the Netherlands is good. Although dental training and techniques differ somewhat from U.S. standards, dental work also is good. In addition to competent oculists and opticians, well-trained specialists of many types are available. Several large, well-equipped hospitals are considered satisfactory. Diagnostic clinics and lab facilities are good. Common medical supplies also are immediately available and any special supplies may be obtained on fairly short notice.

Community sanitation is comparable to standards maintained in U.S. urban areas. Dutch cities are as clean as the cleanest American cities. Garbage is collected twice a week and the water supply is good. Public eating places, butcher shops, and dairies are regularly inspected.

The Netherlands has one of the lowest death rates in the world. Although most temperate-zone diseases appear, no particular ailment is peculiar to this area. Sporadic cases of typhoid and mild epidemics of influenza occur. Some jaundice, sinusitis, and poliomyelitis exist here, as in other European countries and the U.S.

Major Cities

THE HAGUE is the seat of the government, court, and Parliament (States General), although Amsterdam is the capital. With 479,000 inhabitants, The Hague is the country's third largest city. A most attractive urban center, it is clean and well maintained with a relaxed, small city atmosphere.

The city takes its name from the older and longer version, 's-Gravenhage, meaning "The Count's (Graven's) Hedge." This hedge surrounded the original hunting lodge of Count Willem II of Holland. After 1248, he erected a stronghold of which the present "Hall of the Knights" forms a part. It included the site of the present Parliament buildings. These, together with the inner and outer courtyards and the Hofvijver (artificial lake), form the medieval heart of the town.

Nearby is the Voorhout, a park-lined avenue where the American Embassy is located. A mile away is the Peace Palace which houses the International Court of Justice and the Permanent Court of Arbitration. It was built in 1913 from funds donated principally by the American steel millionaire, Andrew Carnegie.

Most people live in suburbs of endless apartments and rowhouses. An exception is the expensive suburb of Wassenaar, which is landscaped and spacious, with large, attractive houses.

The Hague has no large industries. Many U.S. firms, including Aramco, Chevron, Esso, Goodrich, and Goodyear, are represented here. As a result, the American community numbers in the hundreds. Some 60 foreign missions are located here.

Most basic services and repairs are available, and vary in quality from good to poor. Prices are higher than in the U.S.

AMSTERDAM, the capital of the Netherlands, also is its largest city and most important financial and commercial center. It is the city nearest Schipol, one of Europe's busiest airports. Amsterdam is a charming city with a population of about 800,000. It is located at the junction of the Amstel and IJ Rivers near the IJsselmeer (formerly the Zuider Zee).

The earliest recorded date in Amsterdam's history is 1275, the date of a document granting certain tax exemptions to the city's people. During the later Middle Ages, the city grew in importance. It reached its Golden Age in the 17th century when it was practically the financial and commercial center of the Western World. The 18th and early 19th centuries were a period of retrogression. Completion of the North Sea Canal reversed this process and in 1876, restored the city's position as a major seaport.

Although many modern buildings can be seen on the outskirts, the center of Amsterdam retains the character of the Golden Age. This is due to the city's policy of preserving the facades of the stately houses, warehouses, churches, and other fine buildings of that period. Elsewhere, the city consists principally of three-, four-, and five-story rowhouses and apartment buildings. While Amsterdam does have some impressive buildings (the Palace, the Stadsschouwburg, the Rijksmuseum, the Concertgebouw), it has few of the palaces and huge public areas that mark many other major cities. Its charm and unique character are due to its 17th-century buildings, its many canals, and hundreds of bridges which make Amsterdam a fascinating "walking city."

ROTTERDAM is 18 miles up the River Maas (the mouth of the Rhine) from the North Sea. It is about 15 miles from The Hague, 45 miles from Amsterdam, and only 90 miles from the German border. The surrounding countryside is low and flat, with much of the area below sea level.

Because its downtown section was destroyed by bombs during World War II, Rotterdam is a new and modern city. Much of its architecture is functional, and the city's most distinctive feature is its dynamism. It is the Netherlands' second largest city, with a population of 590,000.

The burgomaster and city fathers describe Rotterdam as a port with an attached city. Life revolves around the port, its man-made waterway (the Nieuwe Waterweg), and industrial appendages. The city is the home port for several major shipping lines, including the Holland-Amerika Line. It is also an important center for a number of American lines, such as Lykes, Sea Land, Sea Train, and United States Lines. It is frequently visited by units of the U.S. Navy.

In terms of geography and tonnage handled, Rotterdam is the

world's largest port. More than 30,000 oceangoing vessels transport goods to Rotterdam each year, and 200,000 barges and vessels carry most of the goods to other destinations.

Much heavy industry has moved into the port area in the past 25 years. With the construction of Europoort, a 3,875-acre extension of the port facilities and industrial area, the expansion can be expected to continue. Europoort began June 11, 1958, and will be a continuing development for at least the next five years.

The largest industries in Rotterdam are petroleum and petrochemical firms. The port contains tank farms and refineries of Shell (the largest in the world), Chevron, Esso, Gulf, and British Petroleum. It has also become the largest transshipment port in Europe for grain and metal ores.

American companies with plants and establishments in the district include Du Pont, Dow Chemical, Cincinnati Milling Machine, Continental Carbon, Esso, Chevron, Gulf, Oxirane, Nicholson File, Quaker Oats, Alcoa Aluminum, Chicago Bridge International, and Cyanimid.

Recreation

Sight-seeing in the Netherlands is a pleasant, popular, and relatively inexpensive pastime on foot, bicycle, or by car or bus. Separate bicycle lanes are provided in many areas, adding to the safety and enjoyment of this type of touring. Bicycle lanes often run parallel and adjacent to the sidewalk, so the pedestrian must be wary of inadvertently walking in bicycle territory.

Since this is a small country, most points of interest are easily reached. For a major change of scenery, one

must travel to the southeastern part of Holland or to a neighboring country, since the Netherlands' topography is generally flat or only slightly rolling. Short trips can easily be taken to nearby beaches, lakes, dunes, and woods.

The many lakes, canals, and rivers provide ample opportunity for sailing and motorboating. Sailboats, rowboats, and canoes can be rented at various places on the banks of these waterways. Boating and sailing are popular sports, and membership in one of the numerous yacht clubs can usually be arranged without much difficulty.

Since the climate is quite healthy, there is no need for the long-term visitor to seek relief except to escape the monotony of the cloudy and rainy winter months. As the weather in countries in this part of Europe is similar, the nearest place to find a change is southern France. In general, Americans visiting or working in the Netherlands use their weekends and holidays to take short trips within the country, holding their local leave time for tours to other European countries.

Facilities are available for most popular sports. However, organized activities for children under eight are mainly dependent on the parents. The Hague offers several unsupervised play gardens for children, local zoos, and a children's museum and theater.

The Hague Country Club at Wassenaar is excellent for golf, but unfortunately is expensive. The area has no public courses. Members of golf clubs which are recognized by the Netherlands Golf Club Association may play at other clubs in Holland. With a few exceptions, such clubs charge nominal greens fees.

Outdoor tennis courts are inexpensive. Several indoor tennis facilities also exist. It is customary to wear whites on courts here.

Several attractive and well-maintained public beaches are close to the major cities, but they are seldom used for swimming due to cool summer temperatures and treacherous currents. For serious swimming, large public and private indoor pools offer swimming lessons at moderate prices.

The American Baseball Foundation offers opportunities for youngsters to participate in baseball, basketball, and flag-football programs. Adults may play on a baseball team which competes in one of the many Dutch leagues. The Foundation, a private organization with headquarters and playing fields in The Hague area, concentrates its efforts on providing practically the same extracurricular athletic environment that exists in the U.S. Its programs are well organized and an integral feature of American community life. It should be noted that baseball is a popular sport among the Dutch; many follow the American baseball scene with great interest.

Fishing is popular here and licenses are easy to obtain. However, one can obtain hunting licenses only with an invitation to hunt. The license is valid from April 1 until March 31. Guns cannot be kept without a hunting license.

An indoor and an outdoor ice skating rink is open in The Hague from October to March, and inexpensive lessons can be arranged. The canals are seldom frozen long enough for much outdoor skating. Locally made and imported ice skates are inexpensive.

Facilities in Amsterdam for popular U.S. sports are somewhat limited. Amsterdam has no public tennis or golf facilities; all are operated on a commercial basis or by private clubs.

Soccer is the national and major spectator sport. Amsterdam boasts a championship team, Ajax, and has numerous soccer clubs with a full schedule of games from September through June. Foreign boys may be admitted to membership in the amateur clubs. Teams play every Sunday, weather permitting.

Baseball enjoys some popularity, and several Dutch amateur clubs in and around Amsterdam accept foreign boys. Games are regularly scheduled on Saturdays. Some clubs also have girls' softball teams. Amsterdam has no American-style football teams.

Entertainment

Movies are presented in the original language, with Dutch subtitles. American movies are shown throughout the country, but some time after their U.S. release. Plays are presented in Dutch, except for occasional performances by English, French, German, or Italian companies. The country has several excellent acting companies.

The Netherlands Opera Company performs year round in The Hague, Amsterdam, and Rotterdam. Each year several foreign and three well-known Dutch ballet companies perform. Many concerts are presented annually by foreign and local talent.

Tickets for the theater, operas, concerts, and other events are somewhat cheaper than in the U.S. and are usually available not more than two days in advance of a performance. When special attractions are offered, such as the Holland Festival, advance reservations are essential. The Holland Festival, held during early summer, offers cultural attractions, especially in music and theater.

Holland has many restaurants. Meals in hotels and restaurants are usually more expensive than in America, but the servings are large. Places serving national specialties such as pea soup, pancakes, and Indonesian food, are popular. Nightclubs are found in the larger cities. Whiskey and wine are expensive. Good beer and locally produced spirits are available at every bar.

Three events of special interest are the colorful ceremony opening Parliament on the third Tuesday of September, the celebration of the Queen's birthday, and the ceremony opening the herring fishing season at Scheveningen sometime in late May.

As the cultural and entertainment center of the Netherlands, Amsterdam offers a wide variety of entertainment. The city has many movie theaters where American films, as well as those of other countries, may be seen. The Municipal Theater, the home of the Netherlands Opera Company, also boasts an excellent ballet company. The outstanding Concertgebouw Orchestra is world famous. Subscriptions series and other concerts are presented by this orchestra, as well as by others. Art lovers will find a wealth of museums, of which the most famous is the Rijksmuseum, and now also the newly opened Van Gogh Museum. For those seeking lighter entertainment, there is a variety of nightclubs and theaters.

At the modern Doelen Concert Hall in Rotterdam, most of the world's name artists appear with the Rotterdam Philharmonic Orchestra. There are also excellent opera, ballet, modern dance, and theater productions, as well as outstanding sports events at the Ahoy Hall and Feyenoord Stadium.

Notes for Travelers

During the summer months, there are direct daily flights from New York to Schipol Airport in Amsterdam, but during winter only two direct flights weekly are available. Other major international airlines serve Amsterdam with either direct or connecting flights.

A valid passport is required for entry.

An import permit must be obtained to take guns into the Netherlands, and a hunting license is necessary to keep firearms in one's residence.

Religious denominations conducting services in The Hague include Roman Catholic, Protestant, Episcopal, Mormon, Jewish, Christian Science, Quaker, and Orthodox. American Protestant and Episcopal services are in English, and the International Catholic Chapel has both English and French services. In Rotterdam, several churches and a synagogue provide English services.

The official currency unit is the Netherlands guilder (*florin*), based on the decimal system. Payments may be made in cash, by personal checks drawn on Netherlands banks, or through the Netherlands post office "Giro" system.

The Netherlands uses the metric system of weights and measures.

The U.S. Embassy is located at 102 Lange Voorhout, The Hague. Consulates General are at Museumplein 19, Amsterdam; and at Vlasmarkt 1, Rotterdam.

Norway

NORWAY's fjords, mountains, forests, and lakes make it one of the most beautiful countries in the world. Bascially a nature-loving people, the Norwegians are acutely aware of their national heritage, and are intent on keeping their country's natural resources unspoiled for future generations.

Norway has recently gone through a period of rapid industrialization, and in moving to the forefront as an oil-producing nation, now has one of the highest standards (and highest costs) of living in the world. The economy is foreign-trade oriented, and the cooperation is good between government and industry. During the past few years, however, Norway has begun to experience the problems suffered by other countries of comparable economic development, such as price and wage inflation, and taxes for welfare programs.

Area, Geography, Climate

Norway, located in northwestern Europe on the Scandinavian Peninsula, is bounded on the west by a 2,125-mile jagged coastline along the North, Norwegian, and Barents Seas. Sweden, Finland, and the Soviet Union are its eastern neighbors. With about 125,000 square miles, excluding Spitzbergen and Jan Mayen Islands, Norway is slightly larger than New Mexico.

Norway is a rugged mountainous country with high plateaus. Fertile valleys and many lakes break up the highlands. One-fourth of the land is forested; only three percent is arable. Most of the country lies latitudinally north of Canada. The Gulf Stream, flowing past most of the Norwegian coast, and warm westerly winds moderate Norway's climate.

Summer lasts from June 1 to September 1 in the south, with long daylight hours. In June and July only two to three hours of twilight separate sunset and sunrise. Farther north, the mid-summer sun shines for 60 days. Winter is long with little daylight. However, Oslo, the capital, is warmer than New England or Chicago, and usually has less snow. Oslo is generally dry and heathy with little pollution.

Population

Norway's 1981 population was 4.1 million, with an annual growth rate of 0.3 percent. Averaging 33 persons per square mile, Norway has the lowest mean population density in Europe. Some 65 percent live in the south and along the coast. Americans living in Norway total about 10,000.

224

Major cities are Oslo, Bergen, and Trondheim.

Most Norwegians are of mixed Germanic (Nordic, Alpine, and Baltic) and indigenous Norwegian, Finn, and Lapp ancestry. About 20,000 Lapps, following a traditional reindeer culture, live in the north.

The official language is Norwegian. Most people in the larger cities speak some English, and many are bilingual. Lapps still speak their ancient Lappish tongue. Norwegians appreciate any foreigner's effort to learn their language, and knowledge of Norwegian is often necessary for social and business contacts, particularly in remote areas. Almost 94 percent of the population attends the state church, the Evangelical Lutheran Church.

Government

The Viking era was one of national unification and expansion. The Norwegian royal line ended in 1319, and Norway, weakened by the Black Plague, united with Denmark. Denmark lost Norway to Sweden in 1814 during the Napoleonic wars. Struggling for independence, a constitution was written in 1814; however, Sweden did not recognize Norwegian independence until 1905.

That year, the Norwegian Government offered the throne of Norway to Danish Prince Carl, who took the name of Haakon VII in tribute to the kings of independent Norway. He reigned until his death in 1957, and was succeeded by his son, Olav V. Olav's 44-year-old son, Harald, is the Crown Prince and heir apparent. Norway is a constitutional monarchy. The functions of the King (Chief of State) are mainly ceremonial, but his influence is felt as the symbol of national unity.

The Storting (Parliament) is a modified unicameral parliamentary structure, with 155 members elected from 19 electoral districts for four-year terms. Norway has universal suffrage for those 20 or older. The judicial structure is similar to that in the U.S., but Norway's penal system places greater emphasis on rehabilitation.

Norway is divided into 18 provinces or counties, plus the city of Oslo, each headed by a governor.

The dominant force in Norwegian political and social economic life is the Norwegian Labor Movement. Successive Labor Party governments have created a social democratic welfare state with full employment and public welfare, health insurance, and pension coverage. Non-Socialist governments have also supported the evolving system. The result is an egalitarian and prosperous society. Although few are in need, many complain of high prices, taxes, and too much government involvement in their daily lives.

Arts, Science, Education

Norway, in spite of its small population, has made impressive contributions to Western culture. Native sons include composer Edvard Grieg, whose music is honored during the spring Bergen International Music Festival; playwright Henrik Ibsen; artist Edvard Munch, represented in Oslo's Munch Museum; and sculptor Gustav Vigeland, whose work is displayed in Oslo's Frogner Park. Norway also boasts the impressive medieval wooden "stave" churches. An example of a stave church has been relocated to the Oslo outdoor Folk Museum.

Free education in Norway is compulsory through age 15. Norway has almost 100 percent literacy, and many Norwegians are also literate in other Scandinavian languages, English, and some German. More than 41,000 students attend Norway's four universities or other institutes of higher learning.

The level of scientific and technical education is high, and Norwegians have made significant contributions to many fields of study. Thor Heyerdahl of *Kon-Tiki* fame has followed in the footsteps of the famous Norwegian explorer Fridtjof Nansen. Although Sweden awards Nobel prizes for contributions to humanity in the fields of science, medicine, and the like, Norway awards the Nobel Peace Prize.

Commerce and Industry

Norway's economy is progressive, prosperous, and diversified. Major industries include offshore oil and gas exploration and exploitation, shipbuilding, metals, pulp and paper products, chemicals, fishing, and forestry. Norway's merchant fleet is the world's fourth largest and the country's largest foreign exchange earner. Large offshore oil and gas reserves and the abundance of hydroelectric power will fuel Norway's future economic expansion.

A member of the European Free Trade Association, Norway also enjoys duty-free trade in manufactured products with the EEC. However, Norway decided in 1972 not to enter the EEC, and the fisheries, aluminum, and pulp and paper industries have suffered somewhat from the Common Market trade barriers. Since Norway's total exports of goods and services, including shipping, equals nearly half of its

GNP, the economy is heavily influenced by world trade levels. The eventual export of offshore oil and gas should insure Norway a surplus balance of trade during the next several years.

Due to an unprecedented economic expansion since 1960, Norwegian GNP per capita was $11,360 in 1979. However, the Norwegian consumer and wage earner faces significant inflation, high taxes (often half of salary), and high prices.

The U.S. ranks fifth among Norway's trading partners, supplying principally transportation equipment, machinery, alumina, coal, oil, seeds, scientific and technical instruments, fruits, and vegetables. America imports Norway's aluminum, nickel, furs, fish, ferroalloys, machinery, and fertilizers.

Transportation

Oslo is connected to all major European centers by rail and air. Scandinavian Airlines (SAS) flies directly between Oslo and major U.S. cities. Train stations are within 10 minutes of the city center by car and Fornebu Airport is within 20 minutes. Various ferries are available from Oslo to Copenhagen, Kiel, and England, and from Kristiansand to Amsterdam. Well-organized charter flights provide excellent, inexpensive vacations worldwide.

Transportation within Norway includes car, bus, train, ferry, and various other feeder airlines and charter services.

Oslo's municipal travel system includes electric trains, buses, subways, and suburban train services. Buses provide good service within all of Oslo, and buses and commuter trains service the suburbs; however, almost no public transportation is available between midnight and 5 a.m. Taxis (*drosje*) operate 24 hours a day and are plentiful, but they do not stop on signal; one must catch or call one from various taxi stands in the city. During rush hours, transportation is crowded and traffic is heavy.

Norwegian roads are generally good, if somewhat narrow, for American cars. Most highways are dual lane. Persons driving automobiles to Norway should have proper international insurance coverage (green card). A Norwegian drivers license is not necessary for nonresidents with a valid U.S. license. Those without valid licenses must take a test to obtain a Norwegian license. An international drivers license, valid in all Western European countries, can be obtained from the Royal Norwegian Automobile Club on presentation of a valid license and three passport-sized photos.

Driving under the influence of even moderate quantities of alcoholic beverages is a serious offense in Norway, usually punishable by imprisonment.

Communications

Telephone and telegraph facilities are provided by Televerket, a government service. International mail is reliable, with airmail delivery to the U.S. taking only three to four days, and surface mail about a month to six weeks.

The Norwegian Government operates one national radio network and one television station. In recent years, TV programming has included more American and British shows and movies televised with original soundtracks. Some apartments and houses are equipped with antennas to receive Swedish TV. Radio programs are limited in variety. Shortwave reception of English-language programs is also limited, requiring a good shortwave radio.

Use of voice radio equipment, such as CB transceivers/transmitters, is illegal in Norway. Norway manufactures excellent radios.

Many bookstores in Oslo carry recent American and British hardcover and paperback books, but at higher-than-retail prices. Current English newspapers, and English and U.S. publications are available at newsstands, as is the Paris edition of the Herald Tribune.

Health

Access to the extensive public health and medical care facilities in Oslo is readily available, at reasonable cost. Emergency treatment is good, but Norwegian physician care is variable and may lack bedside manner. Oculists and optometrists are competent; opticians fill prescriptions promptly. Norwegian dentists generally are good; prices are reasonable, especially for orthodontia.

Drugstores are open weekdays from 9 a.m. to 5 p.m. Eight pharmacies are open nights and Sundays. Drug quality and prices are strictly controlled by the State Control Laboratory, and government subsidies lower some drug prices. Only centigrade thermometers can be purchased locally.

Sanitary conditions in Norway are about average. Strict laws govern commercial processing, cooking, handling, and serving foods. The state-owned water supply system is excellent. Pasteurized milk is available and dairy products are pure; in fact, Oslo is cleaner than most U.S. cities of this size.

Norway has not had any serious epidemics in years. Colds, influenza, and throat infections may be aggravated by a lack of sunshine and the long, cold, winter season. Oslo is one of the drier areas of the country and can be uncomfortable for some.

Norway's climate is generally healthy, but upper respiratory infections are common during winter. To compensate for the lack of winter sunshine, Norwegians consider vitamin pills or cod liver oil, or both, essential. A good assortment of inexpensive vitamin pills and cod liver oil concoctions are available locally.

The risk of contagious disease infection is probably the same, or less than in the U.S. To combat tuberculosis, the state gives free tests annually to all school children, including those in the American School. Mumps, measles, and whooping cough are the most common children's diseases. Children with these diseases are not quarantined, however, on the theory that after the age of two, the sooner children are naturally immunized, the better.

Major Cities

OSLO lies in the shape of a horseshoe at the head of the Oslo fjord, covering 167 square miles between the shoreline and the surrounding hills. The horseshoe faces a fjord stretching some 60 miles between forested hills and farmlands down to the open sea. The city is spectacular during spring and summer when flowers blossom in parks, around public buildings, and on almost every window ledge.

Oslo, the seat of the Nobel Institute, is the nation's largest city and its chief commercial and cultural center. A modern city in design and construction, the Oslo government has encouraged contemporary art in many public projects. Among these are 150 sculptural groups by Gustav Vigeland in Frogner Park. A national theater and gallery are there, as well as a university and several schools and colleges. The city has preserved some 12th and 13th century buildings. Each year, the famous Holmenkollen Ski Meet attracts skiers from all over the world.

TROMSØ is a city of 43,000, on an island joined by a bridge to Norway's mainland. The island is in a spectacular fjord area of northwestern Norway on the same latitude as northern Alaska. However, the Gulfstream tempers its climate.

As the chief city of arctic Norway, Tromsø is a base for seal hunters and has large herring fisheries. Ships and rope are manufactured there and the seaport is a starting point for many cruise ships.

STAVANGER, the oil capital of Norway, has an American population of more than 3,000. It was founded in the eighth century and occupied by the Germans during World War II on April 9, 1940. Stavanger is important commercially and industrially for shipbuilding and fish processing. There are noteworthy ethnological, ornithological, and archaeological collections at the museum, and a 12th-century Utstein monastery nearby.

Recreation

Norway offers outstanding opportunities for the tourist and outdoorsman. The spectacularly beautiful western fjord country can be reached daily by trains connecting Oslo year round with Trondheim and Bergen. Both routes traverse high mountain ranges and narrow valleys. Coastal steamers sail from Bergen to the northern tip of the country at Kirkenes on the Soviet border. The trip lasts two weeks, but many stops along the coast allow shorter side trips. The North Cape and Finnmark, Norway's northernmost areas—the land of the Midnight Sun and Northern Lights—are also accessible by air (three to seven hours one way). During winter, main roads are open for auto traffic except over the high mountain passes which are snowbound from October to June.

Interesting sights can be found in and around Oslo, from parks and museums to ancient rock carvings, old stave churches, and lovely countryside. Only a few hours by rail or automobile from Oslo are popular seaside towns along the outer fjord's west coast (Vestfold). Buses supplement train service from Oslo to many towns and to popular ski centers. A five to seven-hour train ride takes one to the highest mountain ranges for skiing in winter, and fishing, hiking, or mountain climbing in summer.

Every Norwegian dreams of owning a *hytte* (cabin) in the mountains and one by the sea, where he and his family can relax and enjoy nature in winter and summer. For those tourists without *hyttes*, Norway has some 200 reasonably priced hotels, private log cabins, or camping sites available. Hotels are quite expensive and generally crowded. For the hiker, the Norwegian Tourist Association operates inexpensive huts in all the principal mountain ranges. The huts, situated a day's walk apart along well-marked trails, offer meal facilities and overnight accommodations.

Norway offers excellent and varied recreational opportunities. Sports and outdoor activities can be found to fit almost any purse or interest. Practically all sports equipment is available in Oslo, but is quite expensive.

Cross-country skiing is not only the country's first winter sport, but almost a way of life. Slalom skiing is becoming more popular. The number of lifts is increasing, and ski resorts like Geilo and Voss are packed during Christmas and Easter holidays. Slopes and trails for cross-country skiing, many illuminated at night, are easily reached by car or public transportation from Oslo. Bilingual instructors are available for beginners. Many comfortable hotels, cabins, and lodges in the mountains cater to winter sports enthusiasts. The American Ski Club has an active program.

Next to hiking, fishing is probably the most popular summer sport. First-class trout and salmon fishing is at least a day away from Oslo. Fishing can be expensive, as hotels or landowners control some of the best streams, and charge high fees for fishing rights. But inexpensive streams can be found. Fishing for cod or other saltwater fish in the Oslo Fjord or on the west coast is quite reasonable. Good equipment is available in Oslo, and fishing licenses are inexpensive.

September and October is the hunting season for game birds such as grouse, duck, and ptarmigan, as well as for hunting moose, deer, and reindeer.

Sailing and rowing are popular summer sports. By four o'clock on summer afternoons the Oslo Fjord is white with sailboats. Boat rentals and sailing lessons are available. Golf courses are open from May 17 through November, weather permitting.

Summer is usually warm enough for swimming in the fjords and nearby lakes, and indoor pools are available during winter. A heated outdoor pool at Frogner Park in Oslo is open from May to mid-September, and children's swimming instruction is offered in July and August. Oslo has good indoor and outdoor tennis courts, but they are often crowded and difficult to rent. Badminton courts are also available.

Spectator sport enthusiasts enjoy soccer, track and field competitions, horse races, figure and speed skating competitions, and the internationally known ski-jumping competitions at Holmenkollen.

Entertainment

Oslo is a pleasant, family town rather than a bustling metropolis. Most Norwegians spend weekends relaxing outdoors at their *hyttes*, with their families, or skiing, or hiking. It is therefore difficult to entertain Norwegians on weekends except for important occasions. Nevertheless, Oslo offers various things to do and see for those less interested in the outdoors.

Sight-seeing attractions include the striking Viking ships, Thor Heyerdahl's raft Kon-Tiki, Nansen's vessel Fram, and the outdoor Folk Museum. In addition to the Vigeland and Munch Museums, numerous other museums and galleries exhibit work by traditional and contemporary artists. The most attractive is probably the Henie-Onstad Center, which stages concerts and film showings as well as modern art exhibits.

Many musical events take place in the winter, including weekly Oslo Philharmonic Orchestra concerts often with internationally known soloists or guest conductors. Foreign opera and ballet companies visit Oslo, and the Norske Opera presents a series of operas and ballet performances each season. The recently opened Concert Hall has added an extra dimension to Olso's cultural life. An increasing number of internationally recognized artists now perform in Oslo. Outside Oslo, the musical highlights each year are the Bergen International Music Festival, and the annual jazz festivals in Molde and Kongsberg.

Some 20 movie theaters present American, English, and other foreign language films; however, children under seven are not admitted. Films are screened with the original soundtracks and Norwegian subtitles. Three theaters produce modern and classical Norwegian dramas. American and other plays in Norwegian translation are also presented.

Oslo is not noted for its cuisine, and restaurants are expensive. However, some pleasant restaurants have attractive decors and international menus. Interesting Norwegian dishes include reindeer meat and a wide range of fish specialities, such as smoked and pickled herring and various salmon dishes. Norwegian eating habits are different from ours. Breakfast is a full meal; luncheon is often only an openfaced sandwich late in the morning; the main meal of the day is in midafternoon; and supper is a late snack. Oslo has several nightclubs with dance floors, but nightlife is limited by the high cost of drinks, restrictive licensing laws, and early closing hours.

Notes for Travelers

At present, no American airlines provide service to Oslo, but flights are available on several international carriers. Other transportation includes overnight car ferries from England, Copenhagen, and Kiel, as well as a rail link from Sweden.

The borders with neighboring Scandinavian countries are open, and customs and immigration inspection is randomly carried out at these points. The traveler generally makes formal entry at the first Scandinavian location.

The following arms and ammunition may be imported into Norway: rifles (4); shotguns, any gauge (4); and ammunition (1,000 rounds, total). No pistols or automatic weapons may be taken into the country. Registration of firearms with the Norwegian police is required.

The American Community Chapel in Oslo offers a full religious program under the leadership of a U.S. Air Force chaplain. Nondenomina-tional Protestant services are held at the Oslo American School. Roman Catholic and Anglican services are conducted in English. The American Lutheran Church in Oslo accepts members from various Protestant churches. Worship facilities are available for the Jewish community as well as the Quaker, Mormon, Church of Christ, and other faiths.

Norway uses decimal currency; *krone* and *øre*. The rate of exchange is NKr. 5.40 = U.S.$1 (1978). Local banking and exchange facilities throughout the country are excellent.

Norway uses the metric system of weights and measures, but travelers should note that one Norwegian mile is equivalent to ten kilometers. American miles are not used.

The U.S. Embassy in Norway is located at Drammensveien 18, Oslo. There is an Information Office in Tromsø.

Poland

POLAND's geography, and the national struggles which have marked its history have made it a country of contradictions, ideologically and emotionally torn between East and West. The Polish people, still haunted by a century-and-a-half of partition and the holocaust of the Second World War, are vigorous and patriotic, and eager for a better life.

The government, although Communist-controlled, permits its citizens more individuality and freedom of expression than is the case in most other Eastern European countries. The diplomatic missions which serve in Poland also are allowed more freedom of movement.

Area, Geography, Climate

Postwar Poland, including the lands placed under Polish administration at the Potsdam Conference (1945), covers about 120,000 square miles, an area about the size of New Mexico. Poland ranks seventh in Europe in area and population.

Most of Poland consists of lowland plains. In the north are the Baltic Sea coast and a broad belt of lake land. In the center are broad, low-lying plains and vast forest belts. To the south, the land passes into chains of mountains—the Sudety in the west

and the Carpathians in the east. These mountains combine to form the southern boundary of Poland. The Tatra Mountains, a part of the Carpathian chain, are the highest in Poland. Rysy Mountain rises 8,212 feet above sea level. At the foot of the Tatras lies the town of Zakopane, the winter sports center.

Poland borders the U.S.S.R. on the east, the Baltic Sea on the north, the German Democratic Republic (G.D.R.) on the west, and Czechoslovakia on the south.

One main seaport, Szczecin, is near the G.D.R. border. Poland's two other major port cities, Gdansk and Gdynia, lie about 170 miles farther east at the mouth of the Vistula River. Many summer resorts with beautiful beaches lie along the Baltic coast, which has summer weather from June to August with sea temperatures ranging from 64° to 77°F. About 200 miles north of Warsaw, the capital, is a belt of lakes stretching from Olsztyn to Augustow, and surrounded by the greatest forests in Poland. Good camping and fishing abound.

Main rivers are the Vistula, on which Warsaw and Krakow are situated; the Odra, whose northern course forms a part of the border with the

G.D.R.; the Narew, in northeastern Poland; the Warta, on which Poznan is located; and the Bug, part of which helps form Poland's eastern boundary.

In addition to Warsaw and the port cities, Poland has several other major cities. Krakow, once the capital, is noted for its beautiful medieval architecture. The Wawel, or citadel, in Krakow is the former seat and present burial site of Poland's past kings. Lodz is the center of the Polish light industry. Poznan, an earlier capital of the Polish state, is an industrial and agricultural center and site of the International Poznan Fair. Other major cities are Wroclaw and Katowice.

Poland's climate is continental European. Winters can be severe, with heavy snows possible from December to March. Winter temperatures in Warsaw average about 32°F. The lowest temperature in recent years was −7°F. Spring is usually cold and rainy, and summer relatively cool. The highest temperature recorded recently in Warsaw was 90°F. Autumn is usually cloudy and can be quite cold. Yearly rainfall averages about 23.5 inches.

Poland has no diseases caused by climate, and mildew is not a problem because humidity is usually low. Earthquakes do not occur, and snowslides in the mountains normally are not hazardous.

Population

Poland's population of 35.7 million is 98.7 percent ethnically Polish. Small German, Ukrainian, Byelorussian, and Jewish minorities, and even smaller Lithuanian, Czech, and Slovak colonies exist. Warsaw's population is about 1,475,000.

Ninety-five percent of Poland's population is Roman Catholic. The Church was led by the Polish Primate, Stefan Cardinal Wyszynski, until his death on May 28, 1981. The Vatican has named Archbishop Jozef Glemp as his successor. Church attendance is high, and Catholic holy days are strictly observed by most of the people.

The foreign colony in Warsaw, made up primarily of the diplomatic corps, foreign students, and business representatives, numbers around 1,000. About three-fifths of the diplomatic corps represent missions of non-Communist countries. A small number of nondiplomatic Western residents represent international organizations, private firms, and private welfare organizations. Many American tourists and business representatives visit Poland.

Government

Poland's government is controlled by the Polish United Workers' (Communist) Party (PZPR) whose Politburo, headed by the Party First Secretary Stanislaw Kania, is the policy-making authority. Party members occupy virtually all key government posts, but in landmark secret-ballot elections on July 17, 1981, two members of the Solidarity Trade Union were named to Central Committee seats.

Two other political parties, the United Peasant Party and the Democratic Party, continue to exist and are represented in the national government. Both, however, are completely subordinated to the policy and programs of the Communist Party.

Although controlled by the PZPR, the government is formally organized as a parliamentary democracy.

Nominally, legislative functions are performed by the Sejm (Diet), and executive functions are performed by the Council of Ministers. The Council of State is the executive organ of the Sejm; its chairman is the titular chief of state. The judicial system, outwardly based on the system of Roman law used in most of Europe, also is directed by the Communist Party.

Polish labor and youth organizations as well as the Scout movement and most other social organizations—with the striking exception of the Catholic Church—are closely controlled by the State. However, in recent months, Solidarity and its leader, Lech Walesa, have successfully challenged authority.

Arts, Science, Education

With some exceptions, Polish intellectual and cultural life has preserved much of its traditional vigor under the Communist regime. Culture is still primarily Western-oriented despite sporadic and sometimes intensive government efforts to restructure it along Communist lines. Extensive cultural exchange agreements with countries of different political systems bring performing artists and intellectuals to Poland each year—many to Warsaw, and some to other cities.

Warsaw, Poland's intellectual center, has the country's largest university as well as a symphony orchestra, opera company, and theaters of various types. Poznan University has a prestigious Institute of English. The Institute administers an annual three-week summer course of intensive English for 400 to 500 advanced English-language students from all over Poland. The Polish Ministry of Education asks the U.S. and Great Britain to supply most of the teaching staff for the course.

Commerce and Industry

Poland's economic system is basically socialist. Central government ministries and planners set wages and prices and control input and and output of labor and material. Government-owned enterprises carry out all manufacturing. Most retail and service establishments are government-controlled cooperatives, although some small firms, shops, and restaurants remain in private hands.

In contrast to other East European countries, except Yugoslavia, 85 percent of Poland's arable land is privately owned and tilled. State farms use most of the remaining arable land. Although Poland is a leading European producer of rye, oats, potatoes, sugar beets, and pork, it continues to require some imported grain.

Poland is a major European source of coal, and has begun to exploit its resources of sulphur, copper, and natural gas. Major industries include iron and steel production, machine tools, textiles, shipbuilding, electrical machinery and electronics, petrochemicals, and plastics. The oil-refining and steel industries depend on raw material imports from the Soviet Union.

Poland is a member of the Council for Mutual Economic Assistance (CEMA or COMECON), whose other members include the U.S.S.R., Czechoslovakia, Hungary, the G.D.R., Romania, Bulgaria, Mongolia, and Cuba. About 50 percent of the nation's trade turnover is with other CEMA countries. Industrial products predominate in Poland's exports to

CEMA, and coal, agricultural products, and other basic materials predominate in its exports to the West. Poland imports agricultural goods, machinery and equipment, and other materials from the West.

Poland joined the General Agreement on Tariffs and Trade (GATT) in 1967, after other GATT members agreed to reduce their restrictions on imports from Poland and Poland agreed to increase its imports from GATT members by seven percent a year. Since 1963, Poland has had most-favored-nation status in its trade with the U.S.

Poland's high rate of investment has not been balanced by equal development of the consumer sector. Although that sector is improving, shortages in consumer goods occur. Clothing and household articles are expensive and not always of the highest quality. A severe housing shortage exists, and people often wait years for an apartment. The food supply has been adequate, but recent labor disputes have created shortages.

The government plans to give priority to improved performance in the agricultural, foreign trade, and consumer-goods sectors. Poland also is trying to limit its imports from the West and to increase its exports in order to resolve a chronic balance-of-trade deficit with the non-Communist world.

The Poznan International Technical Trade Fair, one of the largest and most important in Eastern Europe, lasts 10 days each June. In September 1973, the U.S. participated in the first annual International Consumer Goods Fair in Poznan, and has been a major exhibitor for many years. Normally, an American pavilion manager lives in Poznan for three or four months every year. The manager's staff usually includes a number of American employees who are in Poznan on temporary duty, supplemented by a staff of Polish personnel.

Transportation

Warsaw is serviced by a number of airlines—Pan Am, LOT, Swissair, Aeroflot, Sabena, SAS, Air France, KLM, Lufthansa, British Airways, and others—to most European capitals. Airline tickets for international travel must be purchased with hard currency. Pan Am offers twice-weekly air service between Warsaw and New York via Frankfurt during the winter, and more frequent service via Copenhagen in summer.

Polish airlines operate several daily flights from Warsaw to and from Krakow and Poznan. It also is possible to travel by rail or auto directly to Vienna, Prague, and Munich. Travel by car or air between West Berlin and Poland is now allowed if performed in accordance with established procedures. Rail transit between Warsaw and West Berlin is also possible, but involves advance arrangement.

A daily car-ferry service is available between Swinoujscie (about one hour's drive north of Szczecin) and Ystaad, Sweden. The crossing takes about seven hours. Reservations should be made well in advance, especially during the summer tourist season.

Most main roads in Poland are good all-weather roads by European standards. Important towns and places of interest are served by inexpensive trains. Principal cities also are served by Polish Airlines (LOT) at moderate fares. A country-wide network of bus lines exists, but buses are usually crowded and uncomfortable and are rarely used by Americans. Tickets for travel in Poland are reasonable and may be purchased for *zlotys* (the unit of currency).

Motorists must obey signs that close roads to traffic or indicate restricted areas, and should be alert to emergency vehicles with flashing lights, since these vehicles always have the right-of-way. Ambulances are beige with a red or blue cross on the side, fire trucks are red, and police vehicles usually are grey or blue with "MI-LICJA" printed in large letters on the doors.

Warsaw buses and streetcars can be crowded and slow during rush hours. Cabs are available at taxi stands, sometimes by hailing, and with varying degrees of success, by telephoning a request. Official fares are much lower than in Washington, D.C., but many drivers illegally demand payment in dollars.

Buses and streetcars in Poznan and Krakow are scarce and crowded during rush hours. Fares are low, however, and service can be satisfactory, except during rush hours. Good taxi service is available at low cost, and taxis can be summoned by phone with fair reliability.

International drivers licenses obtained outside Poland are valid for one year after entering Poland and are recommended for all new arrivals. Polish drivers licenses are issued based upon valid foreign drivers licenses and an oral examination conducted by the Polish traffic office. International drivers licenses may be obtained in Poland

for a fee of 100 *zlotys*. Traffic moves on the right as in the U.S. Motorists must exercise extreme caution while driving, since numerous horse-drawn carts, tractors with wagons, trucks, and pedestrians are constant hazards on both highways and streets. Night driving is dangerous.

Owning an automobile can be expensive. Rough cobblestone roads subject cars to heavy wear and tear. Vandalism is a problem; foreign cars seem to be prime targets.

Although adequate work can be done on some foreign cars, repair service for American makes is hard to arrange and seldom satisfactory. No parts for American vehicles are available in Poznan or Krakow. American cars must be driven to Western Europe for major maintenance. Poznan has authorized repair facilities for many major Western European makes, but stocks of spare parts are limited. A fully licensed Volkswagen repair shop at Leszno, 50 miles south of Poznan, has a good supply of spare parts, and performs required maintenance and periodic checks.

Polish law requires cars to have directional signals and mud flaps. U.S. officials in Poland recommend export-grade, heavy-duty shock absorbers and springs, snow tires for winter, and an engine that can run on regular gas. Emission controls are not required, and cars appear to run better in Warsaw without such controls. Major repairs to automatic transmissions must be done in West Berlin.

The Polish State Insurance Company (WARTA) sells third-party liability insurance (required in Poland) at nominal cost. WARTA also offers collision, fire, theft, and other special coverage, both inside and outside Poland, but rates for foreign-made cars are high. Insurance is also available from a few American or Western European agencies which insure vehicles in Poland.

Communications

Telephone and telegraph service is available to Western Europe and the U.S. Service is slower and less reliable than in America, but is adequate in emergencies. Rates within Poland are inexpensive; standard world rates usually are charged for international calls.

International mail via Polish (PTT) facilities is unreliable. Bad weather and cancelled flights frequently result in turn-around times of over one month from the date a letter is mailed to Warsaw from the U.S. until a reply is received. Turn-around times for Krakow and Poznan are even longer.

Radio Warsaw, which broadcasts on four frequencies, includes music programs ranging from rock to classical. Commercials are missing, but Radio Warsaw broadcasts a good deal of didactic material. Daytime reception of Western European stations is not possible on most broadcast bands. Night reception is much better. The Voice of America broadcasts in Polish two hours daily, and VOA English broadcasts can usually be heard without difficulty morning and evening. The U.S. Armed Forces radio broadcasts from West Germany cannot be heard most of the time in Warsaw and Krakow, and reception is only slightly better in Poznan.

Although an ordinary table-model AM radio receives broadcasts from Western Europe adequately, a small shortwave set gives much better reception. It is possible to buy a well-made, reasonably-priced Polish short-wave radio. Polish FM broadcasts cannot be received on American-made sets, since a different frequency band is used.

Like most European countries, Poland has a state-owned national TV system which broadcasts on two channels in both color and black-and-white. Polish TV frequently shows British and American films with a Polish-language voice-over, as well as some old American TV series. Programming for children is meager, usually consisting of about 10 minutes daily at 7 p.m. On Sundays this show is expanded to one-half hour.

Polish TV sets can be rented.

Few newspapers, magazines, or current books in English or any Western language are available in Poland. A library, operated in the U.S. Chancery, maintains a selection of American literature and periodicals. Americans are welcome to join the British Institute library. The Sunday editions of the Washington Post or the New York Times can be obtained by subscription, although they arrive weeks late.

Health

Arrangements can be made for medical consultations and for treatment in local hospitals. U.S. officials, however, discourage the practice except in emergencies. Some Americans are satisfied with the available services, but in most cases, go to Western Europe for serious medical problems and major dental work. Eye care can be obtained, but contact lenses are not available in Poland.

Poland's community sanitation is generally satisfactory. Flies are a problem, even through most U.S.-owned and -leased apartments and houses are screened. Restrooms in restaurants, theaters, hotels, and other public places are usually below American standards of sanitation and cleanliness.

Common colds, bronchial ailments, sinusitis, and intestinal flu are common, especially in winter. A form of gastroenteritis is prevalent in spring and summer. Poland is considered a "jaundice area." Inoculation against typhoid is desirable, especially for those who plan to travel to remote parts of the continent. Gamma globulin and polio vaccine are recommended.

Raw fruits and vegetables require careful washing or peeling. The water purity is sometimes questionable, and it is recommended that all water for human consumption be boiled for 20 minutes. Some Americans drink one brand of locally pasteurized milk, which is considered safe but which often sours within a day or two.

Major Cities

WARSAW, with a population of about 1,475,000, is in eastern Poland on the banks of the Vistula River. More than 80 percent of the city was destroyed during World War II, and the extent to which it has recovered from the holocaust is a tribute to the vigor and patriotism of the Polish people. Many old sections of the city have been rebuilt in styles reminiscent not only of the prewar period, but also of earlier eras, and a remarkable amount of new construction has taken place. Few ruined buildings or rubble remain. In winter, the lack of sunshine and the smoke from the soft coal burned for heat combine to make Warsaw somewhat drab. But in spring and summer the many parks, squares, and tree-lined boulevards come alive and give the city a cheerful appearance.

Postwar Warsaw is characterized by a profusion of large buildings housing government ministries and enterpises. Many new apartment blocks have been built, but housing still is short. Hotel space remains insufficient in spite of several good, new hotels. A new highway and bridge were completed in 1975 to provide additional access for the growing population on the east bank of the Vistula. Buses and streetcars remain the principal means of public transport around Warsaw. Service is frequent and routes extensive.

The Old Town, with its famous market square, was almost totally destroyed during World War II. It has been painstakingly reconstructed in 17th- and 18th-century style. On the south side of Old Town is Castle Square, dominated by a granite column with a statue of King Sigismund III. The Royal Castle, which stood on the east side of this square, has been rebuilt by the voluntary contributions of millions of Poles as a symbol of Polish nationhood.

Many Poles are learning English. English, French, and German are widely spoken in the foreign colony. Russian is mandatory for secondary school students.

In general, most basic services are available and satisfactory in Warsaw. Prices are relatively inexpensive for these services.

The name KRAKOW first appeared in written records in 965, when the town was already an active east-west trade center. Despite the Tatar invasions, one of which destroyed the city, Krakow continued to grow, and became the capital of Poland in 1320. At about this time, King Casimir the Great opened his realm to Jews and founded the city's university, the second oldest in Central Europe.

Krakow's golden age was during the 15th and 16th centuries, when the Jagiellonian dynasty rejuvenated the university and encouraged the arts and sciences. While Copernicus studied at the university, Polish and Italian artists were giving the city the Renaissance flavor which characterizes it even today.

After the capital moved to Warsaw in 1596, Sweden twice invaded and burned Krakow. Following the first partition of Poland in 1772, hard times continued for the city. For the next 150 years, first the Prussians and then the Austrians occupied Krakow. Tadeusz Kosciuszko, hero of the American Revolution's turning-point Battle of Saratoga in 1777, returned to Poland in 1784. During the next five years he became increasingly involved in Poland's struggle to save itself from the Russian invaders. In 1794, Kosciuszko took an oath in Krakow's Great Square, swearing to lead the nation to the end in the fight for liberty, integrity, and independence. His heroic efforts ended in October of that year when, betrayed by Prussian entry into the conflict, he was wounded and captured by the Russians. Thomas Jefferson wrote of Kosciuszko, "He is as pure a son of liberty as I have ever known, and of that liberty which is to go to all, and not to the few or the rich alone." Kosciuszko is buried in Krakow's Wawel Cathedral.

For a short period of oppression and revolts (1815–1846), the Austrians shared their rule of the "Republic of Krakow" with the Prussians and the Russians. Under the relatively mild Austrian rule in the latter part of the 19th century, however, Krakow flourished as a center of Polish culture, the only place in Europe where Polish civil rights were recognized. The governor-general was a Pole and the Polish language was used in schools, courts, and government offices. In this fertile atmosphere, Matejko, Wyspianski, Helena Modjeska (Modrzejewska), and other outstanding artists flourished.

The Nazis made Krakow the capital of their general government. Prominent Cracovians were arrested and sent to concentration camps, the largest of which, Auschwitz-Birkenau (Oswiecim), stands 40 kilometers west of the city. Four million people, including Krakow's entire Jewish population, perished there.

Krakow escaped the destruction suffered by other Polish cities. Although Krakow received only a small share of postwar reconstruction funds, a new town, Nowa Huta, was built around the Lenin Steel Works in 1947 and eventually was incorporated within the city limits. This plant, until recently the largest of its kind in Poland, and the city's chemical industry have changed the face of Krakow, adding an aspect of bustling, grimy, 20th-century industrialism to the traditional calm of a thousand-year-old cultural center.

The U.S. consular district, of which Krakow is the center, consists of 10 voivodships (administrative centers), and is in the eastern and central portions of extreme southern Poland. It extends from the Russian border in the east about 300 miles westward, almost to Wroclaw, covering about 55,609 square kilometers or 21,850 square miles, about half the size of the State of Ohio. Much of the area is hilly or mountainous. To the south, on the Czechoslovak border, lie the Beskidy and Bieszczady Mountains, including the high Tatras. These mountains, an extension of the Alps, rise to 8,200 feet in the area directly south of Krakow.

The voivodship of Katowice, the second largest in the consular district, contains about one-third of the district's 10.1 million inhabitants. According to official statistics, almost half of those gainfully employed in the 10 voivodships work in industry, although traditionally areas such as Opole, Rzeszow, and Przemysl have been considered primarily agricultural. In Katowice, the country's most heavily populated voivodship, most workers are employed in the mines and mills. The southeastern provinces of Poland have for many years been centers of emigration to the U.S. and many in the area, especially the *gorale*, or highlanders, have relatives in America.

Krakow lies near the center of the district in a shallow basin on the Vistula River some 80 kilometers east of the Katowice-Gliwice industrial area. A "city voivodship" of 3,254 square kilometers and more than 700,000 inhabitants, it is the meeting place of three geographic regions: the Carpathian Uplands, the Malopolska Highlands, and the Vistula Lowlands.

A point of interest to Americans is Krakow's American Children's Hospital, which was built and organized with U.S. assistance. Facilities and services at this hospital are good, and adults are also treated in emergencies.

Although more than half of the city was destroyed during World War II, POZNAN today shows few signs of war damage. Much new building and rebuilding is in progress. The Opera House, Palace of Culture (formally the Kaiser's Palace), the University, and many impressive public buildings and churches give an elegant appearance to the city. The Old Square and City Hall, destroyed during the war, have been handsomely rebuilt. Apartment houses are going up in the suburbs, but the exteriors of some are left unplastered and give a rough, unfinished appearance to those sections. Most new construction is of apartment complexes rather then detached houses.

Aside from the staff and dependents of the American Consulate, Poznan's foreign colony consists almost entirely of American and British lecturers at Poznan University's Institute of English, exchange students, and personnel of the Soviet Consulate General. The number of Americans and other foreigners in Poznan increases as preparations for the annual spring International Trade Fair get underway. A variety of American official, scientific, and cultural representatives visit throughout the year. A large influx of visiting Americans occurs in August, at the time of the three-week summer seminar in English. The American staff for this seminar usually totals 15 or more.

Poznan has a population of 520,000 and is located about 120 miles east of the Polish-G.D.R. border. The city is 266 feet above sea level and, although generally in the same northern continental climatic zone as Warsaw, seems to have somewhat milder weather. The Warta River, which runs through the city, is Poland's third largest, and carries barge traffic for half its length. The area surrounding Poznan, generally flat with a few rolling hills, contains several large lakes, some narrow streams, and forested areas. Covering the western third of the country, the Poznan consular district contains 17 of Poland's 49 provinces (*wojewodztwa*). The area is about 91,000 square kilometers.

The Baltic provinces of Szczecin, Koszalin, and Slupsk have long coastlines with some fine beaches. The large port city of Szczecin (population 370,000) is at the point where the Odra River flows into Szczecin Bay, about 40 miles inland from the Baltic coast port of Swinoujscie. Szczecin and Swinoujscie together form one large port complex under a single port administration. Koszalin and Slupsk provinces are largely rural and sparsely settled. With gently rolling terrain, many lakes, and large areas of mixed coniferous and deciduous forests, the region generally is reminiscent of northern Minnesota or Wisconsin.

The provinces surrounding Poznan comprise a rich agricultural area of flat to gently rolling terrain with many small lakes and forests. The area to the south, which includes the important industrial, academic, and cultural center of Wroclaw (population 575,000) ranges from flat and rolling plains to the Sudeten Mountains along the Czech border.

Altitudes in the district vary from 75 feet above sea level in Szczecin to 1,100 feet in the southwestern city of Jelenia Gora. A few miles south of Jelenia Gora is 5,200-foot Sniezka Mountain, the highest point in the consular district.

Recreation

Warsaw

Citizens of Warsaw are justly proud of their many large, open parks which afford extensive opportunity for rest and relaxation. A variety of tame animal life abounds in the woods and ponds of the Warsaw parks. Children can play in a number of playgrounds and fields while their parents hike along miles of fine paths, enjoy an open-air concert, lunch at a restaurant in the park, or just relax on a convenient park bench.

Fishing is possible in many rivers and lakes. Tackle, boats, and related items can be bought locally at moderate prices. Licenses are required, but membership in a group or club is not necessary.

Camping is growing in popularity, especially with families. Many excellent campsites are near Warsaw and in other parts of the country. The most beautiful are in the lake region near Augustow, about 155 miles northeast of Warsaw, and in the Mazurian lake region, about 185 miles to the north. These two lake belts, situated in forests, offer many lakeside cottages, boats for rent, and excellent fishing and waterskiing. Camping equipment is available locally, but many Americans consider it expensive.

Tennis and swimming are popular sports during the summer, although swimming in the Vistula River is not recommended because of strong currents and pollution. Many Americans enjoy skating at outdoor rinks or at the Torwar Stadium in the winter. The Torwar management sets aside a special hour on Sunday afternoons for the exclusive use of the diplomatic and foreign business community.

Skiing is excellent at Zakopane and in the Karkonosze Mountains, and skiing and climbing are possible in parts of the Tatra and Beskidy Mountains, about 280 miles from Warsaw. Many of these mountain areas have well-equipped shelter houses, but ski lifts are not always available.

The Baltic coast, 230 to 330 miles from Warsaw, has a wealth of sea resorts with beautiful sandy beaches. The water is much colder than that of the Adriatic or the Mediterranean. The bathing season lasts from the middle of June until the end of August. The most famous of the Polish seaside resorts, Sopot, hosts an annual, internationally famous song festival.

About 150 miles from Warsaw is an interesting nature preserve, Puszcza Bialowieska, which has a herd of rare European bison, a virgin forest with 1,000-year-old oaks, and other attractions.

Entertainment in Warsaw is very good. There are opera, ballet, concerts, theater, movies, and museum exhibitions, as well as many sports events.

The Polish National Philharmonic Concert Orchestra of Warsaw sponsors guest conductors, and the Orkiestra Kameralna is well known outside Poland. In 1965, a new opera house—one of the largest in the world—opened in Warsaw. It has the most modern equipment in Europe. Some 21 theaters present Polish plays as well as adaptations from the classical and modern Western repertory. Several small, popular cabaret reviews also play in Warsaw. Warsaw has three puppet theaters and an operetta theater.

Spectator events—ice shows, soccer, track and field, boxing, cycling,

basketball, horse racing—are held regularly.

Local museums show frequent exhibitions of art, handicrafts, books, and related subjects. Warsaw's National Museum holds international exhibits. A Chopin museum is located at the composer's birthplace in Zelazowa Wola, about 40 miles from Warsaw. Distinguished Polish and foreign pianists give Sunday recitals there and in Lazienki Park in Warsaw during the summer.

In addition to Polish films, Warsaw cinemas show many American and other imports, usually in the original language with Polish subtitles.

Warsaw restraurants are usually state enterprises, and several are very good. Sidewalk and indoor cafes are popular meeting places, and two or three nightclubs offer dancing. Roadside picnics are popular during fair weather. Many picturesque forest and riverside sites are only a short distance from Warsaw.

Krakow

With its beautiful medieval monuments, Krakow is Poland's leading tourist center. The city annually draws hundreds of thousands of foreign and Polish visitors to its historic churches, museums, and palaces. A visit to the Wawel Castle and Cathedral forms part of every Polish child's education in the country's great artistic and political achievements.

Numerous sites are also within an easy drive of the city. Both the Pieskowa Skala National Park and the famous Wieliczka salt mine are close to downtown Krakow. Within an hour of the city is the Dunajec gorge with its well-known raft ride. Farther away are the Czestochowa shrine in Katowice Province and the palaces in Lancut and Baranow in Rzeszow voivodship. Prague, Vienna, and Budapest are within a day's drive of Krakow. Czechoslovak visas may be obtained in Katowice.

Spectator sports are popular in Krakow. Wisla, the city's soccer team, is one of the best in Poland, and the annual Rajd Polski (Polish automobile rally) originates in Krakow.

Swimming, fishing, and camping in the nearby mountains, forests, and national parks are the principal outdoor activities available. Ice skating, tennis, and indoor swimming are also available in the city.

Skiing is the main attraction at mountain resorts just south of Krakow. The most popular of these, Zakopane, is about one-and-a-half hours from the city. It has a good ski lift and many excellent hotels, villas, and restaurants—all set in the breathtaking scenery of the Tatras. Zakopane is usually crowded, particularly at Christmas and in March.

Farther east, about four hours from Krakow, the virgin forests of the Bieszczady offer some of the best camping in Poland, especially around Lake Solina.

Krakow has a good reputation for its theater. In addition to the Old Theater (Stary Teatr) and Slowacki Theater, both of which present innovative stagings, some interesting semiprofessional and student theaters are available.

Krakow has no opera, and the quality of philharmonic concerts is unpredictable. A light opera company

presents Broadway-type musicals. The city's Higher School of Music, under the aegis of Krzysztof Penderecki, is a focal point of a small group of talented avant-garde musicians. Several good rock groups in the area often perform at student clubs.

Katowice, only one-and-a-half hours from Krakow, has a fine symphony orchestra, the Katowice Radio and Television Orchestra.

About 10 American or English films usually are shown at any given time in the city's theaters, most of them in English with Polish subtitles. In early June, Krakow hosts an international short film festival. An art film theater in town features classic films— often American and English.

Krakow is a center for the plastic arts and the home of several world-famous painters and sculptors. Numerous galleries and museums in the city have a constantly changing variety of offerings.

Krakow has some good restaurants, including the Wierzynek, reputedly the best in Poland. The restaurants in the Francuski Hotel, Holiday Inn, and Cracovia Hotel feature international cuisine. The Pod Strzelnica on the airport road has a delightful outdoor garden. In a slightly lower-price category are the Hawalka and Hermitage, featuring Polish dishes, and the Dniepr, a Ukrainian restaurant. The Francuski, Cracovia, Pod Strzelnica, and Dniepr have dancing, and the city's two nightclubs feature floor shows.

Poznan

Several areas of touring interest are near Poznan. Kornik, a town of

5,000 about 10 miles southeast of the city, is the site of a moated 16th-century castle which is now a museum. It contains an unusual picture gallery, beautiful polished floors, fine old furniture, porcelain stoves and appointments, Polish handicrafts, archaeological and nature collections, and a 100,000-volume library, including old manuscripts and prints. The museum contains not only collections from the Dzialynski and Zamojski families who formerly lived in the castle, but also such Polish artistic work as a magnificent collection of embroidered sashes and costumes. The park surrounding the castle-museum is planted in a variety of trees, shrubs, and hedges.

At Rogalin, near Kornik, is an 18th-century palace which is now a museum and gallery containing valuable historical objects and paintings by 19th-century Polish artists. Rogalin also is noted for a stand of 1,000-year-old oak trees.

Other country palaces, recently restored, are within a half-hour's drive of Poznan. Some have restaurants or coffee houses. Gniezno, about 30 miles northeast of Poznan, is Poland's first capital. This 1,100-year-old city contains an ancient cathedral with paintings, scupture, medieval tombs, and a set of bronze doors dating from the 12th century. St. John's Church, in 14th-century Gothic style, is also of unusual interest.

Biskupin, not far from Gniezno, is one of the largest prehistoric settlements in Europe. It dates from 700 to 400 B.C., and Poles assert that it shows the historic predominance of a Slavic culture in the region. The site, excavated and partially restored, includes a museum with a collection of prehistoric ceramics and tools.

Roads to these places of interest are narrow but in good condition. A personal car is the best mode of transportation, although train and bus service is available to most of the cities mentioned. Public transportation generally is crowded.

Large lakes in forest settings near Poznan provide ample opportunities to swim, fish, picnic, or camp. In some cases, these activities can be combined with visits to nearby places of interest. Arrangements also can be made to use good tennis courts.

A large municipal outdoor ice rink in Poznan is available for skating six months of the year. In addition, ice skating on the lakes is possible during the coldest periods of winter. Sledding is possible on a few hills in town and in the nearby countryside. Poznan has two heated indoor swimming pools.

Skiing is good around the tourist centers of Karpacz and Szklarska Poreba in the Sudeten Mountains southwest of Wroclaw. Tow facilities are crowded, but are being expanded each year. A shortage of hotels and restaurants still exists in both places, so reservations should be made well in advance. Depending on winter driving conditions, the area is about five hours from Poznan. Although Zakopane is 300 miles from Poznan, it is a more popular ski area because of its more extensive facilities.

The Baltic coast north and northeast of Szczecin offers excellent beaches and swimming. The resort city of Kolobrzeg has a good hotel, and nearby beaches are wide and sandy. Summer weather is usually sunny and breezy. Lifeguards are on duty during the season, and swimming is good for both children and adults. The drive from Poznan to Kolobrzeg takes about four hours and passes through some scenic countryside.

Poznan has an extensive opera, operetta, concert, and theater season. The opera company is uneven but enjoyable. The Poznan Philharmonic Orchestra, a source of great local pride, has a distinguished record of performance, and often has fine Polish and foreign guest artists. The Struligrosz and Kurczewski Boys' Choirs are outstanding. The ballet troupe is one of the best in the country. The two dramatic theaters present a varied program of Polish and foreign works, and the quality usually is high. Local student theaters often produce experimental works. A puppet theater also is available.

Of the city's 20 movie theaters (two wide-screen), three are excellent. Both Polish and and foreign films, often good ones, are shown. English soundtracks are usually left intact. American movies are popular. Movie tickets, like tickets for opera, concert, and ballet, are not expensive.

Poznan has five fairly good restaurants. Some nightclubs feature floor shows. One discotheque and one cabaret theater also are available.

Notes for Travelers

Several international carriers serve Poland. Pan Am flies from New York to Warsaw, via Frankfurt, twice weekly during the winter, and more often in the summer via Copenhagen. The most frequently traveled auto route is from Frankfurt to Berlin, and from there on Highway E-8 to Poznan and Warsaw. Other routes are from Nuremberg to Prague to Cieszyn (on the Polish border) and north to Warsaw, or from Vienna north through Brno to Warsaw. G.D.R. or Czechoslovak visas are required for these routes. Travel by train through Prague or Vienna also is possible.

A valid Polish visa is essential for entry. Visas cannot be obtained at the border or at any other port of entry, but must be applied for six weeks before departure. Those transiting Czechoslovakia or the G.D.R. must also obtain a transit visa in advance.

Only those holding diplomatic passports may import, buy, or own firearms and ammunition.

Since 1973, Poland has strictly enforced laws and regulations prohibiting the exportation of articles produced (or which may have been produced) before May 9, 1945.

Poland is predominantly Roman Catholic, and churches are numerous throughout the country. In Warsaw, one Catholic church has an English mass every Sunday. The city's Methodists have Sunday services in Polish. The one Jewish synagogue has traditional services year round, and Christian Science and other denominations have regular services except during the summer. An Anglican clergyman visits Warsaw several times a year. Krakow has more than 85 Roman Catholic churches. There also are a Lutheran and a Baptist church (services in Polish), and a synagogue (without a rabbi), as well as a Jewish community center. Poznan has many Catholic churches and four Protestant churches, but no synagogue.

The basic unit of Polish currency is the *zloty*. The rate of exchange fluctuates, but is about Z1.33 = U.S.$1.

Import and export of zlotys is prohibited.

Poland uses the metric system of weights and measures.

The U.S. Embassy in Poland is located at Aleje Ujazdowskie 29/31, Warsaw. The Consulate in Krakow is at 9 Stolarska Street; in Poznan, at Ulica Chopina 4.

Portugal

PORTUGAL is one of Europe's oldest independent nations. It has been a sovereign state since the 12th century, when it became a kingdom following victories over the Castilians and Moors. Before that time, the area had been successively overrun or occupied by the Celts, Romans, and Visigoths. In the 15th and 16th centuries, the young Portuguese nation led the way in overseas exploration and discoveries, founding an empire in America, Africa, and Asia.

Area, Geography, Climate

Portugal, in the southwest corner of Europe, is part of the Iberian Peninsula. The country consists of continental Portugal, which is about the size of the State of Indiana, the Madeira Islands, and the Azores in the eastern Atlantic.

Its climate is temperate, seldom above 90°F (32.2°C), and pleasant. Summers are sunny and generally cool at night. Winds increase in intensity late in the day. At times the prevailing north wind dies down altogether, giving way to short periods of dense fog along the Costa do Sol and in Lisbon, the capital. Spells of intense heat are infrequent, and last only a few days at a time. Summer rainfall is minimal.

From October into May or early June, rain is frequent and sometimes heavy. Atlantic southwesters assail the coast. The average annual rainfall is 30 inches in Lisbon, but annual variations are considerable. Years of relative drought alternate with years of serious nationwide flooding. Snow caps the highest mountain ranges in mid-winter, providing some skiing in the Serra da Estrella. Lisbon's winter temperature seldom drops below 40°F (4.44°C).

Population

Continental Portugal has about 9,915,000 million people. More than 600,000 former residents of Angola, Mozambique, Timor, Cape Verde, and Goa currently live in Portugal. American residents of Portugal are found mainly in the Lisbon area, the Oporto district, and in the Algarve province of southern Portugal. They number about 4,000, with 350 U.S. Government employees and dependents.

Tourism is a major Portuguese industry. More than two million tourists visited Portugal in 1978, and of that number, some 100,000 were Americans. Tourism declined following the 1974 revolution, but is expected to return shortly to the pre-1974 levels, when some 350,000 American tourists per year visited Portugal.

247

English and French are the two most widely spoken foreign languages. Many Portuguese understand Spanish, but few learn to speak it. Tourists who know Spanish find it initially frustrating to learn Portuguese because of the great difference in pronunciation. The two languages are similar in structure and vocabulary, however, and Spanish is helpful in learning Portuguese.

Government

The monarchy, which has been led by the House of Braganca for 270 years, was overthrown in 1910. A republic lasted 16 years before the military took over. Dr. Antonio de Oliveira Salazar, a university professor, held dictatorial powers as Finance Minister and later Prime Minister from 1928 to 1968. Marcello Caetano followed Dr. Salazar as Prime Minister and dictator from 1968 to 1974.

On April 25, 1974, the Armed Forces Movement overthrew the Caetano regime. Although the period which followed was marked by considerable instability, progress was made in restoring individual and political rights. Free elections were held for the Constituent Assembly in April 1975, and for the Legislative Assembly in April 1976. Former Army Chief General Antonio dos Santos Ramalho Eanes was elected President in June 1976 with the backing of three principal parties. Francisco Pinto Balsemão is Prime Minister.

Arts, Science, Education

Portugal's culture reflects its rich historical heritage—a blend of Western European, Mediterranean, and North African values. Portuguese art has found expression in architecture, especially during the Manueline pe-

riod—the 1495-1521 reign of King Manuel—and in epic and lyric poetry rather than in painting, sculpture, or music.

By law, all Portuguese children must attend six years of primary school. The number of public schools is increasing. Students who qualify academically and financially may seek admission to state or private secondary schools and vocational schools. Diplomas from such schools are necessary for admission to one of the three state-run universities, or to the technical institute.

Commerce and Industry

Agriculture and forestry, where productivity tends to be low, are the basic economic activities of the country, engaging about one-third of the population. Some 30 percent of the total area is cultivated. Thousands of vineyards and olive, fig, and almond groves abound. Portugal's Port and Madeira wines are world famous. Other crops are wheat, corn, rye, tomatoes, rice, potatoes, and fruit. The forest area comprises another 35 percent, and includes extensive acres of cork, maritime pine, and eucalyptus. Portugal is the world's foremost cork producer, normally supplying about half of world cork products.

The industrial sector accounts for 35 percent of the GNP, with an annual growth rate of about 12 percent until 1974. It dropped in the following year and was estimated at 2.7 percent in 1980. Sardines, anchovies, and tuna are caught along the 500-mile coastline; a large part of the catch is canned for shipment abroad. An ocean fleet fishes for cod in the North Atlantic.

Among leading exports, cotton textiles are first and wine second. Remittances from Portuguese emigrants and tourism earnings constitute the two major sources of foreign exchange.

Transportation

Railroads and buses reach all parts of Portugal and, despite several recent fare increases, are still inexpensive. Two daily trains, overnight and dayliner, connect Lisbon with Madrid, and there is fair express service daily (28 hours) to Paris. Connections to all of Europe can be made at these two points. Within Portugal, there are several good express trains daily and a triweekly express service to the southern Algarve from Lisbon. "Auto-express" is available on the overnight Lisbon-Oporto passenger train.

TWA has daily flights between New York and Lisbon and weekly flights between Boston and Lisbon via the Azores. A westbound Pan Am flight connects Lisbon and Miami weekly. Various European airlines provide multiple daily flights between Lisbon and Western Europe and North Africa. The national airline company of Portugal—Transportes Aereos Portugueses (TAP)—has daily jet flights between Lisbon, Oporto, and Faro, as well as air-taxi service with small aircraft connecting smaller cities to Lisbon. No American passenger ships call at Lisbon.

Oporto can be reached by private car, rail, or plane. Air travel to Oporto is normally through Lisbon, except for the weekly BEA/TAP flights from London, and two flights a week to Paris. Four daily flights connect Lisbon and Oporto. The commuter train, the most convenient and comfortable rail facility available, operates to and from Lisbon twice a day. One should allow

about five hours from Lisbon to Oporto if traveling by train or car.

SATA, the local airline, flies daily between the islands of Santa Maria, São Miguel, Terceira, and Faial. It also goes to Flores once a week. The other islands can only be reached by ship. A passenger ship goes around the islands every two weeks, docking where weather permits. In winter, bad weather often delays sailings. The ship does not have stabilizers and is recommended only for good sailors. Sea travel can be quite uncomfortable.

TWA flies twice a week between Boston and Santa Maria (about 55 miles from São Miguel); TAP about three times a week. SATA provides the connecting flights to Ponta Delgada, weather permitting.

The CTM Shipping Company has two ships (the Bernardino Carreia and the Pereira d'Eca) traveling monthly from Lisbon to New York, Baltimore, and Philadelphia, stopping in Ponta Delgada only on the way to the U.S.

Lisbon has a good municipal transport system and fares are low. Streetcars, also inexpensive, are old and colorful. Except for the small subway system, public transport is slower than private cars, but using it avoids the impossible parking situation in town. The subway is modern, but covers only a small part of the city. It does not serve most American residential areas. Taxis are inexpensive and usually available except during rush hours and rainstorms. Interurban electric trains serve the Lisbon-Estoril-Cascais coastal area, where many Americans live, as well as Lisbon-Sintra. They are inexpensive and, as might be expected, badly overcrowded during rush hours.

Oporto has good bus service. A wide network of streetcars is reliable but slow. Taxis are plentiful and inexpensive. Trains out of Oporto north to Spain (Galicia) and south to Lisbon provide a pleasant view of the countryside. Taxicabs within the city of Ponta Delgada are inexpensive, but a tip is customary. Night service is available only until midnight and is more expensive. Bus service is also available.

An automobile adds greatly to the enjoyment of the Portuguese countryside. The scenery is beautiful, roads are narrow but fairly good, and distances are relatively short. Compact cars are the most practical to drive, particularly in Ponta Delgada, where the streets are narrow, and most roads are made of cobblestones and are hilly and winding. It is expensive to repair American automobiles in Portugal, as parts generally are unavailable, and must be ordered from the U.S. Auto insurance is not compulsory. A valid foreign drivers licence can be exchanged for a Portuguese license without charge.

Communications

Telephone and telegraph circuits are available to Europe and almost all points in the world. Telephones in the Lisbon area are now automatic, with direct-dial service available to Spain, France, England, and Germany. Airmail to and from the U.S. normally takes eight days. Surface mail is very slow.

Radio reception is fair to good, depending on set and location. U.S. radios can be used with a transformer. Reception of European stations is usually clear at night; French, Spanish, British, and German stations in AM and/or shortwave can be received. Local AM/FM stations operated by the State Broadcasting Service (RDP) and the Catholic station (Radio Renascenca) provide news, local sports coverage, and popular and classical music.

The one state television network, RTP, has two channels. Television is only in black and white. Generally, the first channel operates from 7 p.m. to 11:30 p.m., with some afternoon programming on weekends, and the second (UHF) channel from 8:30 p.m. to 11 p.m., except in summer. All foreign shows, except for a few designed for children, are in the original soundtrack with Portuguese subtitles. On São Miguel, TV operates evenings during the week; weekends include some afternoon shows. About half of the programs are in Portuguese and the rest in English, Spanish, German, and French with Portuguese subtitles.

English-language newspapers— the Paris edition of the Herald Tribune and the Amsterdam edition of the London Times—are available in Lisbon within a day or two of publication. Many newsstands carry American and British news magazines, some at prices much higher than domestic rates. A few local bookstores stock books in English. Most Portugese dailies carry normal wire service news.

Health

Generally speaking, the quality of medical services available in Lisbon is only fair. Most hospitals are underequipped, and in some cases poorly managed. Overcrowding is a serious problem.

Lisbon has several hospitals, including a small British hospital which does not have a resident physician, but staff doctors who call daily. The CUF and Red Cross hospitals have moderately well-equipped operating rooms and laboratory facilities. Santa Maria Hospital, while leaving much to be desired, is well-equipped for cardiac emergencies. Maternity hospitals are questionable, but several American babies have been born in Lisbon during the past years. Hospital costs are moderate. Doctors' and surgeons' fees are not more than those in the U.S.

Leading Oporto medical specialists are good. Several private and public hospitals are satisfactory, but doctors are extremely busy and in short supply. Nevertheless, a number of highly competent physicians and specialists practice in the city.

Good medical and surgical facilities are available in Ponta Delgada. Specialists include pediatricians, obstetricians, and gynecologists. Two clinics have 15 to 30 beds, and the local hospital with 300 beds is adequate. There are three medical laboratories. Local pharmacies stock American, Portuguese, and German drugs.

In Lisbon, certain contagious diseases are fairly common, such as hepatitis, tuberculosis, typhoid, venereal diseases, and undulant fever. Colds are more common than ever during winter because of inadequately heated homes. Foreigners experience stomach and intestinal upsets, usually of short duration. No serious epidemics have occurred in recent years.

Sanitation in Oporto is generally good in residential districts and fair in the city's poorer sections. Tap water is considered safe but not very palatable.

Sanitation in the Azores (Ponta Delgada) is poor. The local public health department guards against the spread of communicable diseases through inspection, quarantine, and fumigation. Garbage is collected at homes regularly by city workers. Meat markets are seldom inspected. Fish, bread, and milk are hawked through the street or delivered to homes with few or no sanitary precautions. Few stores have refrigeration facilities. Much of the transportation is by animal, and the animals are infested with flies and fleas. Homes and stores are not screened. A mild form of typhoid is common, as are dysentery, measles, chicken pox, whooping cough, and flu.

Tap water in Lisbon and the outlying suburbs is safe to drink only during the rainy season. During periods of drought, it is advisable to use boiled water, since pressure often drops low enough to permit seepage. The high mineral content of tap water may cause digestive upsets. Good bottled spring water is available.

Major Cities

LISBON stretches over several hills on the north side of the Tagus River (Portuguese: Tejo). The city faces south across one of Europe's finest bays toward the Arrabida mountain range, about 25 miles. The bay's entrance is spanned by Europe's longest suspension bridge—the April 25 Bridge, with a main span of 1,108 yards.

Lisbon contrasts old, narrow alleyways and tiled buildings that reveal its Moorish heritage, with broad, modern boulevards, new apartment buildings, and beautiful parks. The city's architecture complements the natural beauty of its setting. Social ferment after 1974 brought about a change in Lisbon's former spotless appearance. Political grafitti took the place of the pastel and whitewash that had covered the city's buildings. Subsequent government attempts to clean up the city show promise.

With a population of one-and-a-half million people, Lisbon is the administrative, commercial, and cultural center of the nation. From early morning until mid-evening, traffic is heavy and somewhat disorderly in town, and hazardous at all times along the coastal road which leads to the suburbs.

OPORTO, situated at the mouth of the Douro River, some 213 miles north of Lisbon, is Portugal's second largest city and the seat of an important administrative district. The area has a high concentration of Portuguese commerce, industry, agriculture, educational facilities, and centers of religious thought. It has a great many famous historical sites and cities, artistic monuments, attractive towns and villages, and varied scenery.

The temperature of Oporto's coastal area varies moderately between a mean maximum of 74.5°F (23.6°C) and a minimum of 58°F. In summer it seldom reaches 80°F, and in winter it seldom drops below freezing. Oporto winters, although comparatively mild, call for heating and warm clothing. The dampness is penetrating, as are the north and east winds. Private homes, schools, and public buildings often lack central heating and can be uncomfortably cold.

More than half of Portugal's people live in Oporto's U.S. consular district. According to the last census (1980), the greater Oporto area had close to 850,000 people.

PONTA DELGADA is the largest city and the district center of the Azores archipelago, an autonomous region of the Republic of Portugal. Located in the North Atlantic Ocean about 800 miles west of Lisbon and 2,300 miles east of New York City, the Azores are geographically and culturally isolated. The port city of Ponta Delgada is on São Miguel, one of the nine islands whose total land area is 890 square miles, with an estimated population of 285,000. About half live on São Miguel. The other islands are Santa Maria, Terceria, Graciosa, Sao Jorge, Pico, Faial, Flores, and Corvo. People from Portugal, the Low Countries, France, and Spain were among the first settlers. Present-day inhabitants reflect those physical characteristics.

The islands are of volcanic origin, characterized by steep coastlines with occasional black sand beaches. Inland, the terrain is marked by extinct volcanic craters, some with lakes and picturesque hills rising to 3,000 feet. Lush vegetation and, in season, beautiful flowers cover the countryside.

The Azores are a popular winter resort. The climate is temperate and the Gulf Stream wards off extremes of heat and cold. Temperatures never reach freezing and rarely go above 80°F. June through September is usually good beach weather. The annual rainfall is 34 inches.

In the past, the Azores were an important port of call for ships bound for the New World and those returning from India. Now, except for the cargo ships which link the archipelago with continental Portugal and the rest of the world, ships stop only occasionally for bunkering and emergency repairs. In summer, several cruise ships call for a day at Ponta Delgada. U.S. and other NATO naval vessels refuel at a NATO depot located in Ponta Delgada.

The principal economic activity is agriculture. About two-thirds of the land is devoted to pasture or crops. Dairy products account for about 45 percent of the industrial production. Next in importance are canned fish, milling and feed, bakery products, sugar, tobacco, wood, and meat products. Some pineapple is produced in hothouses, but it is a dying industry. Some Azorean wine and an aperitive called "Pico" are very good, but not enough is grown to permit export.

The Azores maintain a lively trade with Portugal and also import materials, foodstuffs, and manufactured goods from many areas of the world.

According to the Constitution of April 25, 1976, the Azores are an autonomous region of Portugal and have a parliamentary style government consisting of a democratically elected regional assembly and a regional goverment responsible to the assembly. The President is represented by the Minister of the Republic, whom he appoints.

The Regional Government consists of a president, nine regional secretaries, and one regional sub-secretary. The Azores have no capital. Government functions are divided between the three administrative centers— Ponta Delgada, Angra do Heroismo, and Horta. The Azores are represented in the national Assembly of the Republic by six deputies.

A military governor with headquarters in Ponta Delgada oversees military operations throughout the Azores and also is the NATO representative in the archipelago. Under

him, a commodore of the Portuguese Navy supervises the small naval detachment stationed in the islands, and an Air Force brigadier commands the air zone which includes Lajes Air Base. An army brigadier is also in charge of the two training regiments. As a result of a treaty between Portugal and the U.S., an American military establishment has existed on the island of Terceira, at Lajes, since the early 1940s.

Recreation

Sight-seeing trips and organized tours are plentiful and costs are moderate. Portugal operates state inns called *pousadas,* most of which are excellent, fairly inexpensive, and located near places of interest. Lisbon has lovely tree-lined and flower-filled parks, numerous children's playgrounds, a fine small zoo, botanical gardens, an aquarium, museums, galleries, cathedrals, palaces, and castles. The Royal Coach Museum has the finest collection of royal and state coaches in the world.

Camping grounds in the pine-covered hills of Monsanto Park, just outside Lisbon, have tennis courts, a swimming pool, a hockey field, and a clubhouse with a restaurant-snack bar, hot water, and automatic washers. It is open all year. Other campgrounds are at Oeiras, Guincho, Setubal, and Caparica.

The temperature of the Atlantic Ocean from Lisbon north seldom goes above 60°F, and, coupled with a strong north wind, limits the enjoyment of swimming. Carcavelos, Estoril, and Cascais have good protected beaches, but because of nearby sewage disposal systems, bathing there is not recommended. Less pollution and fewer people are found farther to the west and north of Lisbon (Guincho, Praia Grande, Praia das Macas) and five miles southwest across the Tagus River (Caparica). Some beaches have dangerous undertows with cross currents—along with superb surf. Arrabida, 25 miles south of Lisbon, has a protected beach where the temperature rises slightly above 60° as the summer progresses. The Algarve waters in southern Portugal are warmer. Most public beaches in Portugal have lifeguards.

Several hotels on the Costa do Sol near Lisbon have large fresh or saltwater swimming pools which nonguests may use for a fee. Several municipal pools, including one in Monsanto, offer season tickets. The Sheraton Hotel has an outdoor swimming pool, which is open year round.

Although no "country clubs" as such exist, the Belas section of the Lisbon Sports Club (15 miles north of the city) is similar to one. It has a swimming pool, a 14-hole golf course, small clubhouse, fine cricket pitch, and four well-kept tennis courts. In addition, the Carcavelos section of the club has one court opposite the Carcavelos train station. The Estoril Golf Club, formerly one of the best in Europe, has an 18- and a nine-hole course and a pleasant clubhouse. Nonmembers may pay to play at any time.

The Tennis Club of Estoril has seven clay courts. By paying a fee, nonmembers may play if courts are available. The National Stadium has 19 excellent public tennis courts. Monsanto has municipal courts.

A hunt club is located at Santo Estevão in the Ribatejo, about an hour's drive from Lisbon. The club engages in traditional English-style fox hunts, complete with red coats. Lisbon, Estoril, Cascais, and Marinha Grande also have riding stables. Instruction is good.

Some yacht clubs rent ocean-going sailboats, with one or two crewmen. Also, a skeet club is in Estoril, and a public skeet range in Monsanto Park. Tourist agencies arrange excursions to private hunting preserves in the interior.

Skiing is sometimes possible in mid-winter in the Serra da Estrela, about 250 miles northeast of Lisbon. Better skiing is found in the mountains north of Madrid—12 hours by car.

Touring and picnicking in northern Portugal are delightful. Roman or pre-Roman ruins and interesting buildings, museums, and fine scenery abound.

Spectator and participant sports within easy reach of Oporto include soccer, basketball, roller skating, roller hockey, tennis, golf, swimming, riding, boating, fishing, and hunting. Beaches are perhaps more popular for sunbathing than for swimming because of the low water temperatures. Some hotels and private clubs, however, have large pools. There is boating all along the coast.

Trout are fished in some streams. Snipe and quail shooting are fall and winter pastimes. Skeet and trap shooting are also available.

Some bullfights (*touradas*) are held in northern Portugal. The *tourada* during the August Festa da Agonia in Viana do Castelo always draws large crowds. So do the occasional Sunday and holiday bullfights in Povoa do Varzim, a beach resort just north of Oporto.

There is skiing high in the mountains, chiefly in the Serra da Estrela. Better facilities exist in the mountains north of Madrid. Riding is popular and horses are readily available. The Lawn Clube da Foz and the Oporto Cricket and Lawn Tennis Club offer tennis, restaurant, and other facilities to members. Membership is available through normal channels. Two golf courses are near Oporto.

Entertainment

Movies are a favorite form of entertainment among the Portuguese, rivaled only by TV and sports events. Current and not-so-current American, British, French, Italian, German, and Spanish films are shown, usually in the original language with Portuguese subtitles.

Lisbon's opera season starts in mid-winter and runs about 15 weeks. Operas are sung in Italian, German, French, and Portuguese. Professional theater performances are in Portuguese. Usually the revues are original works of Portuguese playwrights, but some plays feature translations of well-known foreign works. The Lisbon Players, an amateur theater group of Britons and Americans, give several performances each year.

Concerts and recitals are performed at the Gulbenkian Foundation, local cinemas, the National Theater, and occasionally in the Cathedral. Music festivals and open-air concerts are sometimes given in parks or historical sites.

The Lisbon ballet company presents classical and modern ballet. A foreign company visits annually. Ballets are given at the Gulbenkian, the Coliseum, and the São Carlos Opera House. The Gulbenkian has its own ballet company.

The bullfight season runs from Easter to about the first of October. Portuguese bullfighting is a demonstration of horsemanship and skill, and differs from the Spanish in that it is mostly on horseback and the bull is not killed. Fights are usually on Thursday nights at the Campo Pequeno bullring in Lisbon. Fights take place as well at the large bullring in Cascais.

In the older sections of Lisbon, the Alfama and Bairro Alto, the *fado* is sung in many little restaurants. The *fado* is to Portugal what the blues is to America. The songs are haunting in tone and tragic in theme.

Nightclubs vary in quality. Discotheques (*boites*) have become popular over the past few years. The Estoril Casino features a floor show and licensed gambling. Hotels and tourist agencies provide a full listing of restaurants (many are very good), nightclubs, and entertainment schedules.

The Rotarians, Lions International, and other similar groups meet regularly in Lisbon. Americans are welcome in these clubs.

The music season in Oporto is getting started again after a two-year slowdown, and is promoted through subscription organizations. Occasionally, the British, German, and French Cultural Institutes and the Ateneu Comercial stage musical events.

Home entertainment centering around close family life is still dominant in this part of Portugal. First-rate restaurants and nightclubs are few.

Movies are a favorite evening entertainment, and many are American films. The best films of most nationalities get to Oporto eventually, normally with the original soundtrack and Portuguese subtitles.

The Azores

A beautiful golf course is located in the hills 28 miles from Ponta Delgada. The weather is usually cloudy, chilly, and windy, so rainwear is advised. Lajes also has a nice golf course.

There is some fishing in São Miguel. Salt water fish include perch, carp, bluefish, amberjack, tuna, and shark. Several world records have been broken by local anglers. There are trout in some streams. It is possible to hunt in the area for quail, ring doves, pigeons, and rabbits about nine months of the year.

A visit to the different islands is worthwhile as each has a distinct personality, different customs, food, and even accent. Throughout the area, there are incredibly beautiful spots for picnics and camping. The islands are a hiker's paradise when it is not raining. Faial, Terceira, and São Miguel have some nice hotels. Flores has a French hotel run for French personnel on the island, but outsiders may be accommodated when space is available. The other islands have only small *pensions*. During summer, nearby beaches are popular for picnics and swimming. Hiking and camping by the lakes or sea are also popular.

Ponta Delgada has four regular motion picture theaters, of which two are of American standard. The films are predominantly American, English, French, Italian, Spanish, and German. Soundtracks are not dubbed, but Portuguese subtitles are used. Practically all films are several years old.

There is one local night club which is open most Saturdays. The few acceptable restaurants serve only Portuguese cuisine.

Notes for Travelers

TWA provides daily nonstop flights between New York and Lisbon, and weekly flights with stops in Boston and the Azores. Pan Am connects Miami and Lisbon, and several European airlines schedule regular flights from Europe and North Africa.

Some Portuguese embassies will issue a visa; others may indicate that it is not necessary. Without a visa, a 60-day permit will be stamped on the visitor's passport upon arrival in Portugal. No vaccinations are required.

Firearms may be imported for hunting or protection, but are subject to customs formalities and registration with appropriate Portuguese authorities. They must be packed and shipped separately. The size of sporting rifles is limited to .22 caliber, and of pistols to .32 caliber.

Irish Dominican priests hold Roman Catholic services in English in Lisbon, Carcavelos, and Cascais. A Scottish Presbyterian church in Lisbon, and an interdenominational American Protestant church in Cascais also hold services in English. An Anglican church in Lisbon and an Anglican-rite church in Estoril sponsor an American Episcopalian Sunday school. Evangelical, Baptist, and Seventh-Day Adventist missionary groups are Portuguese-oriented. There is a Jewish synagogue. In Oporto, the British

Community Church of St. James holds English services regularly. All services in Ponta Delgada are in Portuguese.

Portuguese monetary units are the *centavo* and *escudo*; 100 *centavos* equal one *escudo*. The conversion rate is one *escudo*=U.S.$0.0229 (1978).

The metric system of weights and measures is used.

The U.S. Embassy in Portugal is at Avenida Duque de Loule 39, Lisbon. The Consulate in Oporto is at 826 Rua de Julio Diniz; in Ponta Delgado, on Avenida Infante D. Henrique.

Romania

Although it is surrounded by Slav and Magyar neighbors, **ROMANIA** is mainly a Latin country which traces its origins back to the Roman Empire. It has been a unitary national state for less than a century, and its historical traditions are a source of pride and national sentiment. Romania has a larger proportion of ethnic minorities than most other European countries, and thus has appeal for students and folklorists. In addition, its mountains, beaches, and unusual historical monuments make tourism especially rewarding. The country features a rich and varied cultural life which appeals to those interested in music, the theater, and fine arts. Many sports are available for participants and spectators.

Those whose interests are more political and sociological will observe the continuing efforts to transform a previously agrarian economy into a highly industrialized system. However, one must remember that Romania is a country where the state, and the Communist Party in charge of it, rigorously control all aspects of life in an effort to create a modern Socialist society.

Area, Geography, Climate

The Socialist Republic of Romania extends inland from the Black Sea halfway across the northern part of the Balkan Peninsula and covers an area somewhat less than New York and Pennsylvania combined. It is bound by the Black Sea on the east, the U.S.S.R. on the east and north, Hungary on the west and northwest, Yugoslavia on the west and southwest, and Bulgaria on the south.

Romania has three major geographical areas. A fertile fluvial plain stretches in a crescent from the northeast to the southwest, bounded by the Danube and Prut Rivers. Bordering this plain to the west and north are the Carpathian Mountains and Transylvanian Alps, a number of which reach above 7,000 feet. Most of the rest of the country is comprised of the hilly Transylvanian plateau. Finally, there is the Black Sea shore with its coastal plain, and the Danube River delta.

Due to Romania's geographical and topographical diversity, the climate varies from region to region. It is generally continental, with short springs that quickly give way to long, warm summers, followed by pleasant, prolonged autumns, and moderately cold, but comparatively short, winters. Snowfall in the Bucharest (the capital) area usually is not heavy; however, the mountains have enough snow for skiing. The average daily minimum temperature for Bucharest in February is 28.6°F, and the average daily maximum in August is 95°F. Rainfall is normally heaviest from April through July, with an average of five inches in June. Aside from the relatively low humidity, Bucharest's climate is much like that of Washington, D.C.

Population

Romanians consider themselves descendants of the ancient Dacians and their conquerors, the Romans. After the Roman occupation and colonization (A.D. 106 to 271), the Goths, Huns, Slavs, Magyars, Turks, and other invaders each in turn left their mark on the population. Nevertheless, contemporary Romanians take particular pride in their Roman origins and Latin language and culture, which, they believe, differentiates them from their Slavic and Hungarian neighbors.

Today about 88 percent of the country's estimated 22.3 million inhabitants, are ethnically Romanian. Most of the remaining 12 percent, principally Hungarians (1,715,000) and Germans (347,000), live in Transylvania, which until 1918 was part of the Austro-Hungarian Empire. Jews (40,000) and Gypsies are spread throughout the country, predominantly in Moldavia. The Jewish population was formerly greater, but emigration, primarily to Israel, has greatly reduced its strength. Romania's population has an estimated annual growth rate of about 0.7 percent.

As a result of the country's ethnic diversity, Hungarian and German are important secondary languages, and various other languages are spoken among the smaller minority groups. Religious affiliations tend to follow ethnic lines, with about 80 percent of all Romanian citizens belonging at least nominally to the Romanian Or-

thodox Church. Roman Catholics, mostly Hungarians, constitute about nine percent of the population, and the remaining 11 percent include Calvinists, Lutherans, and Jews. Recognizing the potential of friction among the country's disparate ethnic groups, the government has tried to encourage integration of the minorities and the creation of a higher loyalty to the nation.

Government

Romania was an independent constitutional monarchy until King Michael's abdication in December 1947. The country is now a Socialist Republic with the leading role of the Communist Party written into the Constitution. By far the largest and most important organization in the country, the Communist Party has more than 2.7 million members, making it, per capita, the largest in the European Communist world. It provides direction to institutions and organizations in every area of Romanian life—government, industry, agriculture, education, and culture. The three principal branches of government are the Grand National Assembly with its Council of State, an executive division consisting of the Council of Ministers, and a judiciary.

The chief of state is the President of the Republic who is elected by the Grand National Assembly for a five-year term. He serves concurrently as President of the Council of State and has the power to issue decrees with the force of law.

The unicameral Grand National Assembly has 349 deputies, each elected for five-year terms from among several candidates in their respective electoral precincts. Although in theory the Assembly is the "supreme organ of state power," in actuality it meets only a few days a year, and strictly follows party dictates in the performance of its functions, *inter alia*, the appointing of the Council of State, the Supreme Court, the Chief Public Prosecutor, and the Prime Minister. The bulk of the legislative work is carried out in fact by the 25-member Council of State, which acts when the Assembly is not in session. It issues decrees with the force of law.

The Council of Ministers is headed by the Prime Minister, who is appointed by the Grand National Assembly. Ministers, their deputies, and presidents of other central state bodies are appointed by the President at the proposal of the Prime Minister. The Council of Ministers is subordinate to the Grand National Assembly. The Constitution gives the Council power to carry out the state economic plan, manage the economy, insure public order, defend state interests, protect citizens' rights, run the armed forces, conduct foreign affairs, and suspend decisions by the County (*Judet*) peoples' councils which do not conform to the law.

A new Supreme Court is elected by each Grand National Assembly and is responsible to it and, between sessions, to the Council of State. Each Assembly also appoints a Chief Public Prosecutor who is vested with the "supreme supervisory power to insure the observance of the law."

Romania is administratively divided into 39 Counties (*Judete*) and the city of Bucharest. Each County is governed by a people's council, whose chairman is also First Secretary of the County's Communist Party organization.

Arts, Science, Education

The impact of folklore and tradition has had a strong influence on the evolution of Romanian culture. *Miorita* (*The Ewe Lamb*), an ancient legend about the relationship between man and nature, is considered the masterpiece of Romanian literature. Modern Romanian literature was born in the mid-19th century and boasts such writers as Mihail Eminescu (1850–1889), Ion Creagna (1837–1889), Ion Luca Caragiale (1842–1912), and the poet Tudor Arghezi (1880–1967).

The modern movement in painting and sculpture is rooted in the revolutionary period of 1830 to 1848, when the sons of wealthy Romanian boyars traveled abroad to study in Western schools of art, particularly in Paris and Rome. Such painters as Theodor Aman (1831–1891) and Nicolae Grigorescu (1838–1907) found their themes and subjects in peasant life. Constantin Brancusi produced sculpture of first rank. In music, George Enescu and Dinu Lipatti are well known.

In contemporary Romania, the arts are subject to ideological discipline, and individual artists receive government subsidies to carry on their work through the various artists' unions. Serious literature is widely read, and mid-city Bucharest is sprinkled with galleries exhibiting the work of both Romanian and foreign artists. Several concerts and recitals are held weekly in season, in addition to regular performances of the Romanian opera and ballet. Theater in Romania is extremely active, and a wide selection of plays from Romania, the U.S., and other countries is presented. The large, modern National Theater, opened in

December 1973, symbolizes the importance assigned to the arts by the state.

Science and technology in Romania are closely connected with contemporary efforts to modernize the nation and create an industrial state. The most prestigious of the "scientific societies" founded in the last century is the Romanian Academy, founded in 1866. Today, applied science and technology represent important areas of official emphasis, particularly in the educational and research institutions. Research work in scientific fields is directed by the National Council for Science and Technology and the Academy of Social and Political Sciences.

Education in Romania is state supported and fully state controlled. Elementary education and the first two levels of secondary school are compulsory for all students. Secondary schools, called *licee,* are available for students who have passed national examinations and are preparing for advanced study at universities. Competition for entrance into the universities and for postgraduate study is intense. Major university centers include Bucharest, Cluj, Iasi, Timisoara, and Craiova. Half of the students receive state scholarships.

Commerce and Industry

Possessing considerable natural wealth, Romania's resources include petroleum, timber, methane gas, soft coal, waterpower, uranium ore, bauxite, salt, and pyrites. About 25 million acres of agricultural land are arable, the greatest percentage of which is planted in feed grains, mostly corn. Romania is a net agricultural exporting country, but recently, due to emphasis on the livestock sector, a shift away from wheat production has been effected.

Romania is now placing more emphasis on industrial production, but needs its agriculture to help support its expansion program. More land is under irrigation and more vegetable production is being accomplished through glasshouse farming.

The Romanian economy is centrally controlled by a national economic development plan regulating most aspects of the country's commerce and industry. Emphasis is on industrial growth, with less attention given to consumer goods production and agriculture. A rich base of natural resources includes oil and gas reserves, and most productive farmland is devoted to wheat and corn. To supply its expanding industry, Romania imports capital goods and raw materials. It exports agricultural commodities and processed goods. About half of its trade is currently with non-Communist countries. De-emphasis on production of consumer goods and agricultural products for domestic use, and the export of many of these goods, accounts in large part for the limited availability of consumer and food products on the local market. Private property and production ownership generally are not allowed. However, recent changes in housing laws are leading to increased private-housing ownership.

Romania maintains economic and commercial relations with both Communist and non-Communist states among the industrialized, developing, and less developed countries. It is the first COMECON country to allow foreign direct investment and partial foreign ownership of producing enterprises. One American electronics company has formed a joint company with a Romanian organization, and other U.S. commercial interests are trying to open activities here. Romania belongs to the General Agreement on Tariffs and Trade (GATT), the International Monetary Fund (IMF), and the International Bank for Reconstruction and Development (IBRD). It is also developing a relationship with the European Economic Community.

Transportation

Bucharest's Baneasa Airport provides domestic air service on TAROM, the state airline. Foreigners frequently use the inexpensive rail system for official and personal trips within Romania. Intercity buses exist, but are rarely used by foreigners.

The national road system is generally good. Most roads are two-lane and asphalt-surfaced, but dirt roads are common. A four-lane highway goes from the northern city limits of Bucharest to Ploiesti, and a limited access superhighway goes to Pitesti.

Buses and trolleys in Bucharest are plentiful and cheap, but are often crowded and breakdowns are common. Reasonably priced taxis are difficult to obtain. Streets in Bucharest are hardsurfaced but of varying quality, with bumpy and cobblestone streets still common in many sectors. Streets become slippery when wet, particularly cobblestone routes.

Left-hand-drive automobiles are used in Romania. The lack of foreign car parts is a major inconvenience. European car parts are obtained more quickly from abroad, but most American car parts must be imported from the U.S., which takes several weeks. The most conveniently serviced automobiles are those of European manufacture.

Communications

Romania has reasonably good telephone service. Dial telephones are used. Long-distance domestic service is available, but 30-minute waits and bad connections are common. International service is often faster and of better quality than domestic service. Calls from the U.S. to Romania are about half the cost of calls from Romania to the U.S. International telegraph services are not always reliable.

Delivery time for mail between the U.S. and Bucharest is approximately two weeks, except for parcels, which usually take three to five weeks. Both incoming and outgoing parcels require a customs declaration.

Although Romanian radio carries music and news programs, it is not a common source of information and entertainment for visitors. Two local TV channels make a TV set worthwhile, but no color programming is broadcast yet. Romanian television carries international news, Western movies (many of them American of varying vintage), American television reruns, international sports events, children's cartoon shows, and international events by satellite. For those who are interested in and understand the Romanian language, local television is a good way to learn more about Romanian politics, economics, culture, and sports.

Except for official purposes, local publications have little interest for visiting foreigners. International newspapers and magazines are seldom found even in international-class hotels.

Health

Generally, local medical care is below U.S. standards. The Romanian

Government expects members of the diplomatic corps and certain other foreign residents to the use the services of the Diplomatic Polyclinic in Bucharest for medical examinations and treatment. Personnel ordinarily receive good attention at the Polyclinic for routine ailments. Local pharmacies usually do not stock Western medical and health supplies, but the Polyclinic sometimes stocks limited amounts.

Weather and local sanitation present no unusual health hazards. Garbage is picked up once or twice a week. In winter, soot from wood burning and soft coal aggravates some sinus problems and allergies.

Although tapwater meets U.S. standards, drinking water is commonly boiled. Streets are regularly swept and sprinkled by the city sanitation department, and sewage disposal is adequate. Bottled drinks are considered safe, even for children. The Romanian Government deals quickly with possible epidemics by closing borders and implementing inoculations.

Major City

BUCHAREST, Romania's largest city and political, economic, and administrative center, has a population of nearly 1.9 million. It is located on a wide agricultural plain in the southeastern part of the country, 40 miles north of the Danube and 156 miles west of the Black Sea.

The city is at an altitude of 265 feet and enjoys a temperate climate. Except for the 22-story Intercontinental Hotel, Bucharest has a low skyline. Many attractive parks and drives add beauty to the city. A large part of Bucharest architecture dates to the pre-World War II era and consists of old baroque and Renaissance-style structures. Many of these are former homes of the old aristocracy taken over as offices for state enterprises or by foreign diplomatic missions. New construction is limited to apartment buildings.

With the expansion of Romania's foreign relations, Bucharest has become an international crossroads with a growing stream of tourists, business representatives, and various government officials. International cultural attractions, scientific conferences, and trade fairs are increasing. Fashion trends are only slightly behind those in the West, and an awareness of Western culture is apparent.

French and German are spoken in Bucharest. English is spoken by a number of official contacts and is fast replacing French as a second language among Romanian youth. Russian is no longer required in schools and is rapidly declining in use, although it can be useful in contacts with Eastern European diplomats.

Traffic in Bucharest is moderate by Western standards. Residents enjoy walking, and pedestrian traffic is sometimes heavy, particularly from 4 to 10 p.m. on weekdays. Parks and recreation facilities are crowded on weekends. Romanians usually take to the highways on weekends, beginning around noon on Saturday.

In general, visitors requiring basic services and supplies in Bucharest find them expensive and either unavailable or irregularly available. Personal service facilities, such as barbershops and beauty salons, however, are satisfactory.

Recreation

Romania has many natural and historical points of interest and beauty. Travel restrictions, commonplace in Communist countries, no longer exist in Romania. Signs designate certain areas as "off limits" for photography, but in general, unlimited and irresistible photo opportunities abound.

Among the many interesting places to visit in Romania are the Black Sea coast, the Danube delta, the Moldavian monasteries, Maramures and its wooden churches, the scenic Retezat Mountains in western Romania, and the medieval cities of Sibiu and Sighisoara. A few locations in southern Romania, from the west to the Black Sea coast (e.g., Sarmizegetusa, Adamclisi, and Histria), have ruins from Greco-Roman times. Camping enthusiasts find many sites, either in commercial cabins or by pitching tents, in attractive surroundings. Mountain climbing possibilities abound, and fishing for trout in the mountains or for a variety of game fish in the delta can be arranged. Hunting can be productive but expensive.

Bucharest and vicinity have a few tourist spots. Just outside the city limits is a small but growing zoo. North on the road to Ploiesti are Lake Snagov and the Caldarusani Monastery (where Vlad Tepes—the historical prince identified by many as Dracula—was reportedly buried). To the northwest is the town of Tirgoviste. To the west, about two-and-a-half hours by car, is the beautiful monastery of Curtea de Arges and the scenic Vidraru Lake north of Capatineni. Near the lake there is an old fortress of Vlad Tepes, and on a clear day the peaks of the Fagaras Mountains, the highest in Romania, can be seen in the distance. All of these spots provide good picnic areas.

Some interesting museums and a botanical garden are in Bucharest. Also, tours to arts and crafts mills can occasionally be arranged. There are several nice parks for strolling, but they are crowded on weekends.

Numerous spectator sports in Bucharest can be attended by foreigners. The most popular is soccer. Other sports are volleyball, handball, basketball, boxing, tennis, and ice hockey. Tickets are reasonable. A number of international matches are played in Bucharest each year between Romanian and foreign teams. American teams have made a few visits.

Professional tennis lessons can be arranged for visitors at the Club Tineretului or the Bucharest Tennis Club, and admittance to the Club Tineretului for swimming also can be arranged. In winter one can ice skate at the Floreasca rink and ski in the mountains near Sinaia and Predeal.

Local entertainment possibilities for English-speaking visitors are limited. Many inexpensive cinemas exist, but the films shown are generally poor or are in a foreign language. Few American films are shown. Some good operas and ballets are seen each season and many fine concerts and recitals are given. For those skilled in Romanian, the live stage is enjoyable.

Good restaurants are scarce and can be expensive. Selection is limited, and service is fair to poor. Nightclub entertainment is even more limited and monotonous.

Folk festivals with the various

regional dances and colorful costumes can be enjoyed in the countryside. Bucharest holds a growing number of international fairs.

Notes for Travelers

Bucharest is served by numerous foreign airlines which use Otopeni International Airport. Flights are scheduled daily from Frankfurt, and four to six flights a week arrive from Paris, Rome, and London. TAROM, the Romanian state airline, and Pan Am provide service between Bucharest and New York. International shipping arrives at the Black Sea ports of Constanta and Galati. Rail connections are available from Western Europe via Budapest and Belgrade, as well as from Eastern European countries, including the Soviet Union. Travel by car from Western Europe also is possible.

Passports and visas are required. Enforcement regarding immunizations varies, depending on the existence of an epidemic, but valid smallpox and cholera vaccinations are advised.

Certain firearms may be imported for sporting purposes (unmodified shotguns, with a barrel of at least 18 inches, of either 12, 16, 20, or 410 gauge; or rifles within the .30 caliber family). Ammunition not to exceed 1,000 rounds per weapon may be included. All firearms must be registered with local authorities. Hunting trips are usually only possible through the facilities of the National Tourist Office (ONT).

Romanian Orthodox is the dominant religion in Romania, but there are also Lutheran, Catholic, Baptist, Calvinist, and Unitarian churches; several Jewish synagogues; and two mosques in Bucharest. The British community sponsors an Anglican church, with services in English. Christian Science services in English are held in the home of a member of the diplomatic community.

The *leu* is the official unit of currency (the plural is *lei*). There are 100 *bani* in one *leu*. The current exchange rate is U.S.$1 = 12 *lei*.

The metric system of weights and measures is used.

The U.S. Embassy in Romania is located at Strada Tudor Arghezi 9 (formerly Dionisie Lupu), Bucharest.

Spain

SPAIN, after nearly four decades of dictatorship, in now enjoying the beginning of an official parliamentary democracy under the leadership of King Juan Carlos I. Although Juan Carlos has been monarch for six years, the elections and referendum endorsed in December 1978 paved the way for a guarantee of basic civil rights. Prime Minister Adolfo Suárez (González), who played a vital role in the establishment of a democratic government, resigned in January of this year (1981), and was succeeded by Leopoldo Calvo Sotelo.

History

Spain dates back to the Stone Age, and historians believe that the people of the Basque region in the north may be descendants of prehistoric men whose art is preserved in caves at Altamira. The country was colonized by Greeks, Romans, and Carthaginians, was overrun in the fifth century by Vandals and Visigoths, and fell to the Moslem Moors early in the eighth century. It was later recovered by Christians.

The year 1492 marked the fall of Granada, the last Moorish stonghold. Spain became the leader of the western world during Europe's golden era of exploration, and its empire extended into every corner of the earth. It began to crumble, however, in the 19th century—a time of civil war and insurrection. It experienced political and economic crises after the Spanish-American War of 1898, and in 1936 a civil war erupted, lasting for three years. During this time, Generalissimo Francisco Franco began his long dictatorship, which ended with his death in 1975. Spain remained neutral during World War II, although it upheld pro-Axis sympathies.

Area, Geography, Climate

Spanish territory comprises the Iberian mainland, the Balearic Islands, the Canary Islands, the presidios of Ceuta and Melilla, and three smaller presidios. Spain and its possessions total 194,880 square miles, slightly less than the area of Nevada and Utah combined.

Spain's most striking topographical features are its elevation and its internal division by mountain and river barriers. The peninsula rises sharply from the sea with only a narrow coastal plain, except in the Andalusian lowlands. Most of the peninsula is a vast plateau broken up by mountains and broad, shallow depressions. Spain has few bays, virtually no coastal islands, and a scarcity of natural harbors.

266

The climate in Madrid, the capital, is predominantly dry and agreeable, although somewhat variable. Because of its elevation (about 2,000 feet above sea level) and its proximity to mountains, Madrid often experiences wide variations in temperature. These changes in weather make colds and other respiratory ailments common. Winter temperatures rarely stay below freezing for long. The seasonal rain and wind from the mountains, however, make many winter days uncomfortably cold. Summers are warm, with usual midday temperatures of 90° to 95°F. The heat is dry, and usually not particularly uncomfortable. Evenings and nights, except during rare hot spells, are cool. Daily mean temperature ranges from 50° to 68° during eight months of the year. Rainfall is almost nonexistent in July and August. Snow, unusual but not unheard of in Madrid, almost always becomes rain and slush by early afternoon.

Population

Peninsular Spain, the Balearic Islands, and the Canary Islands have a population of about 37.6 million (January 1981). Population density is comparable to New England's and is much lower than in most European countries. Madrid and Barcelona each have well over three million persons. Barcelona, the second largest city, is Spain's principal commercial and industrial city and is a popular port of call for units of the Sixth Fleet.

Peninsular Spain may be divided geographically or ethnically into six major groupings:

Castile. The territory roughly encompassed by the old kingdom of Castile in the center of the peninsula (known today as Castilla la Nueva and Castilla la Vieja) is inhabited by the most populous and ethnically dominant group. Castilian Spanish is the national language. The feudal institutions and grim humor which once characterized this sector of the population form the basis of Spain's esteemed epic literature and legitimate theater. The cities of Burgos, Leon, Valladolid, Toledo, and Madrid are the most populous centers of this region.

Galicia. Galicia, the northwest region of Spain, is inhabited by the Gallegos. The principal city of this region is La Coruna. The cathedral in Santiago de Compostela is world famous.

Basque Country. East of Galicia is the region inhabited by the Basques, known for their unique language and history of regional awareness. Most of Spain's mining and heavy industry are located in this area. Strong regionalist sentiment prevails in the Basque Country, and a small but intense minority wants independence.

Catalonia. Centered around Barcelona, this region is inhabited by the Catalans, famous for their commercial skills and proud of their separate language, Catalan. World-renowned artists of Catalonia include Picasso (who was actually born in Málaga but spent much of his early life in Barcelona), Dali, and Gaudi.

Levante. Levante is located farther south along the Mediterranean coast and is famous for its oranges and *paella*, the Spanish rice and seafood dish. Valencia is the major seaport of this area.

Andalucia. Southern Spain is famous for flamenco music and its distinctive architecture derived from the Moors. Seville is the largest city in southern Spain and is world famous for its Holy Week religious festivities and its April Fair.

Government

Spain is a parliamentary monarchy. King Juan Carlos succeeded Franco as chief of state in November 1975, in accordance with the provisions of the Franco-era Fundamental Laws, but the monarchy was later legitimized by constitutional referendum on December 6, 1978.

Spain's new Constitution, which was drafted and approved by a Parliament elected by free, universal suffrage on June 15, 1977, provides for a freely elected bicameral legislature, governmental responsibility to Parliament, the full range of basic rights and freedoms, an independent judiciary, the creation of autonomous government in Spain's various regions, and the institution of the monarchy.

The head of government is the President of Government, or Prime Minister, who presides over the Council of Ministers, composed of officials who head the government ministries or hold ministerial rank.

Arts, Science, Education

Spain is justly proud of its museums and cultural relics, which abound throughout the country. Madrid boasts the world-renowned Prado and the Royal Palace; Barcelona has its own Picasso and Romanesque museums; and many other provincial cities have artistic, cultural, and historical treasures representative of Spain's long history. The Spanish Museum of Modern Art in Cuenca houses some of the best paintings and sculptures of Spain's "Generation of the 1950s and 1960s." Granada, with its grand heritage of Arab rule, and imperial Toledo are, in fact, cities preserved as museums. Sagunto (near Valencia) and Merida (near Badajoz) offer well-preserved Roman amphitheaters and fortresses dating to the birth of Christ. Some of the oldest and best preserved prehistoric paintings known to mankind are found in the Altamira Caves near northern Santander, but are no longer open to the public.

Also highly representative of Spanish culture are the numerous festivals held throughout the year in the more important cities. Festivals can be religiously oriented, such as Holy Week in Seville (April) or the Fallas in Valencia (March). Other festivals pay homage to local customs as well as to the patron saint, such as the festival of San Fermin in Pamplona—the Running of the Bulls (July). Still others, such as the Sevilla Fair (April) and the Sherry Festival of Jerez de la Frontera (September), popularize the local lifestyle and cultural heritage or the most important agricultural product of the province.

Dance, music, and theater festivals occur frequently. Madrid and Barcelona have excellent local flamenco, folk dance, and Zarzuela (operetta) performances. These cities also attract top foreign artists such as the Alvin Ailey Dancers, Rudolph Nureyev, Aaron Copland, and others. Spanish cities also compete strongly in hosting festivals: Granada hosts an annual international music festival in early summer, Santander an international piano competition in midsummer, and Barcelona an international choir festival in late summer. The Spanish love of the cinema is evidenced by the hundreds of movie houses in the larger cities and by the numerous annual film festivals. The most important of these is the San Sebastian International Film Festival, also known as the "Producers' Festival" since mainly producers and directors attend.

Other annual film festivals include the Festival of Children's Films in Gijon and the Festival of Naval Films in Cartagena. The wide variety of Spanish topography, vegetation, and agriculture has made Spain a popular site for foreign as well as Spanish film-makers. Spain has provided the setting for such films as *Dr. Zhivago*, not to mention the dozens of "spaghetti westerns" filmed in southern Spain.

Spain's educational system has been strained by rapid economic development, over-enrollment, and social pressure. An all-inclusive 1970 educational reform law is the basis for an effort to update and upgrade Spain's educational system to put it in tune with modern needs. New universities have been created, and the Madrid and Barcelona technical schools (university level) have been joined to form poly-technical universities, bringing the number of Spanish state universities to 21 (22 with the summer university of Santander). Spain also has two private universities. New courses of study have been instituted which give the university student a diploma after three years of general study and the traditional licenciatura after two or more years of study in a specialization.

Over 60 U.S. universities operate summer or full-year programs in Spain. American-style junior colleges function in Barcelona and Seville. Two university programs in Madrid offer a complete four-year B.A. degree. Some American students complete language studies or special research through the assistance of the Centro de Cooperacion Iberoamericano or the U.S.-Span-ish Fulbright Commission for Educational Exchange. The Spanish scientific community, led by the Higher Council for Scientific Research, works closely with the American scientific community in a range of mutually rewarding and important research projects.

Commerce and Industry

The Spanish economy has grown rapidly in the past two decades to make it the fifth largest economy in Western Europe. Per capita income was $5,250 in 1979, and the economy is based on a diversity of manufacturing, agricultural, and service industries. The national economy remains distinctly separate from the larger Western European economy formed by the European Communities (EC) and by the European Free Trade Association, but Spain is now negotiating with the EC for full membership.

Spain is the world's 10th largest industrial economy, although Spanish economic development has been uneven within the country, and many rural areas still have not enjoyed the prosperity of urban centers. Nearly half of the nation's national income is generated in the Basque and Catalan regions and the Province of Madrid, although these areas comprise less than 12 percent of the country's land area. To achieve a more equitable distribution of wealth, the 1978 Spanish Constitution provides for a Compensation Fund to transfer funds from the wealthier regions to the poorer.

The national economy is a blend of private and public enterprise; the latter spearheaded the development of heavy industry during General Franco's regime. Many public enterprises are owned wholly or in part by the Ministry of Industry's huge Instituto

Nacional de Industria (INI), which is a holding company for many leading firms such as ENSIDESA steel mills, Iberia Airlines, and a large share of SEAT autos.

The private sector is broad and similar to that of other developed nations, except that during the Franco era it benefited from low-level competition together with subsidies and protectionism. Spanish enterprises now are being pressured to become more competitive, and this is necessary preparation for future competition with EC enterprises. Other special features of the economy include a half-dozen privately owned commercial banks that traditionally have controlled a range of industrial firms and numerous foreign investments. The U.S. is the single largest investor nation, but investments have been made in Spain by many countries.

The Spanish economy was hit hard by the oil price increases of 1973, and the death of General Franco in 1975 delayed the implementation of reforms to deal with long standing structural problems. The basis of Spanish economic growth until 1973 had been heavy inflow of foreign currency from Spain's huge tourist industry, as well as from the remittances of Spanish emigrant workers and from new foreign investments in Spain. Much of the foreign exchange thus earned was invested in industry, through either the government, private entrepreneurs, or commercial banks.

The steeply rising oil prices which began in 1973 caused Spain to spend more of its foreign earnings abroad. The worldwide recession of 1974 and 1975 placed additional pressure on Spanish balance-of-payments because it led to a reduction in tourist and emigrant revenues. Unemployment and inflation began to grow, the latter reaching 26 percent during 1977. In mid-1977 the government began to act energetically to deal with a range of economic ills. The *peseta* was devalued, and a series of measures were announced to fight inflation and to reform old economic structures. A program of tax and financial reforms was initiated almost immediately. That fall, Spain's leading political parties signed the Moncloa Economic Pact, which committed them to fight inflation by means of a restrictive monetary policy and wage limitations. Thanks to these measures, the economic health of the nation has improved, and inflation in particular has been sharply reduced.

Spanish foreign trade is significant but not large, relative to the size of the economy. Basic metals and metal products, mainly ships, automobiles, machinery, and other transport equipment, account for 41.2 percent of Spain's exports, and shoes and citrus fruits supply the bulk of the rest. Crude oil tops the import list at 24.9 percent of the total. Spain is a major customer for American exports; U.S. sales to Spain in 1978 amounted to $2.4 billion, or 14.8 percent of Spain's total imports. Primary U.S. exports to Spain are animal feed, machinery, computers, heavy construction equipment, and aircraft. The U.S. purchased 8.8 percent of Spanish exports for $1.3 billion. Spain's principal exports to the U.S. are shoes, bottled olives, automobile tires, and basic steel products.

Transportation

Air and rail facilities serve most cities and places of interest in Spain. Rail fares other than first class are reasonable and compare favorably with American prices; air fares and first-class rail fares are comparable to or higher than in the U.S. Bus service is also available between most cities in Spain; the quality varies widely and generally is not as desirable as other means of transportation. Rental cars are available, with or without driver.

The Spanish National Railroad System (RENFE) runs several fast trains (known as Talgo or Ter) between all major cities in Spain. These trains have comfortable seats and satisfactory dining facilities. Trains with sleepers, serving selected cities in Spain, connect with rail facilities serving all of Europe.

Travel agencies in Spain's larger cities frequently offer domestic and international economy tours at lower rates than those charged by scheduled airlines. Agencies also will procure rail tickets, charging the same as the carriers. The railway and the airlines sometimes assess a fee when a traveler changes or cancels reservations.

Public transportation in Spain's major cities consists of buses or taxis, with Madrid and Barcelona having good subway systems as well. Buses and subways are inexpensive but crowded, particularly during rush hours. They generally operate on an 18-hour schedule. Taxis are numerous and fares are comparable to those in Washington, D.C. Cabs are difficult to find during rush hours, late at night, or in bad weather. Taxis will travel outside cities to recreation areas not easily accessible by bus or metro, but one should agree on the fare with the driver before making the trip. Most taxis are metered, and the metered fare applies within city limits; the only additions are for baggage, animals, and Sunday or holiday trips.

Highways in Spain are mostly macadam-surfaced. Some city streets and country roads are cobblestone or dirt and gravel, and some macadamized highways frequently need or are under repair. Compact, lightweight cars are most suitable for Spanish roads and traffic conditions, and require less maintenance. All cars should be left-hand drive. Repair facilities are usually adequate but spare parts for imported cars are often unavailable or quite expensive. Automatic transmission, power steering, and other automatic features are not easily repaired. Body work is less expensive than in the U.S. and is of good quality.

The Spanish Government requires that all cars imported into the country have amber rear-turn signals. Complexity of conversion varies depending on where the vehicle was manufactured, but all makes can be converted after arrival in Spain.

Authorities will not issue tourist plates without proof of compulsory insurance from an acceptable Spanish insurance company. Valid international drivers licenses may be used for driving in Spain if obtained in any other country. Spanish drivers licenses are honored in all European countries except the Federal Republic of Germany and Greece.

Communications

Complete telephone and telegraph facilities are maintained in Spain. Long-distance calls may be made to practically any part of the world, and rates within Spain, to other European countries, and to the U.S. are reasonable. The government telegraph office handles all telegrams, regardless of routing.

Postal services also are satisfactory. Airmail letters from the U.S. east coast generally arrive in about two or three days, and surface mail arrives at irregular intervals in about four weeks.

Spanish local radio reception is good, but programs have limited appeal. FM programs broadcast from the military bases may be received on regular FM radio channels; format follows general American-style news and music offerings. Spanish TV is well developed, but the quality of programming varies. American series or movies shown are Spanish-dubbed. Original-language versions of movies or TV specials, some of which are in English, are rarely shown.

European editions of Time and Newsweek are available at newsstands throughout Madrid and also may be found in other major Spanish cities. Many newsstands also carry the International Herald Tribune. American technical journals and household and fashion magazines are not always available on Madrid and Barcelona newsstands, and usually are not found elsewhere in Spain. Publications can be ordered by subscription.

The National Library and many specialized libraries and archives in Spain's major cities make available much material in Spanish. The Biblioteca Nacional houses the national periodical collection. Several Spanish-language daily newspapers and literary, photo-feature periodicals are published in Madrid and Barcelona. Some bookstores in Madrid and Barcelona stock books in English, French, and German.

Health

Many Spanish hospitals and sanatoriums are generally below U.S. standards, but are satisfactory. Two or three of the new large ones, such as La Paz and Concepcion, have modern medical equipment and facilities and serve as general and emergency hospitals. The British-American hospital in Madrid has 35 beds, is equipped to care for medical, maternity, and surgical cases, and provides a wide range of outpatient services at moderate rates. It has English-speaking nurses, and all physicians on duty speak English.

Madrid and Barcelona have general practitioners and specialists in all fields of medicine. Some local doctors understand and speak English. Oculists and opticians are good and their rates are reasonable. A number of U.S.-quality dentists are available. Some speak English, but are in demand and charge prices commensurate with their reputations and ability. The American Embassy and Consulates maintain lists of doctors and dentists in their areas.

Sanitary conditions and facilities are adequate in all of Spain's large cities. Most temporary health problems arise from lack of proper food storage and refrigeration equipment, from deficiencies in the water conduction systems, or from uncooked preparation of vegetables. Streets are cleaned daily, and municipal garbage removal is used in the larger cities. Soft coal burned for winter heating leaves pollutants not normally found in the air of U.S. cities. The pollution can aggravate allergies and may increase susceptibility to respiratory ailments. Air pollution and smog are growing problems and do reach menacing, bothersome levels in all of Spain's large cities.

Local milk and dairy products may not always be as safe as American products. Meats and fresh vegetables and fruits are available all year. The best meat and fish stores have refrigeration equipment, but cuts of meat are different from those in the U.S. Veal, pork, and chicken are particularly popular throughout Spain and are of good quality. Local seafood is excellent. Fresh vegetables and fruit are usually displayed in open bins and care should be taken in their preparation. In some instances, food handlers may not be as sanitary as in the U.S.

Tapwater is normally safe for drinking in Spain's major cities, but occasional breaks in city water systems due to construction or old age require special precautions (i.e., boiling water and treating it with two drops of Clorox per quart, or buying bottled water).

The most prevalent illnesses among the local population are tuberculosis, respiratory and throat ailments, heart trouble, gastroenteritis, sinus trouble, typhoid, typhus, diphtheria, hepatitis, and "liver trouble." Among Americans, gastric disorders are common.

Immunizations should be kept current for tetanus, polio, and typhoid, and a skin test for tuberculosis is recommended. During winter, colds and grippe are common and hard to cure. Family members, especially children, should have current immunizations and receive adequate rest and nutrition.

The dry heat common to most apartment buildings in the winter and the extremely dry summers may cause skin irritations or aggravate existing allergies.

Major Cities

MADRID, the capital of Spain, is in the center of the Iberian Peninsula at an elevation of 2,150 feet. The city is on a large plateau bordered by the mountain peaks of the Sierras of Guadarrama and Gredos and by the mountains of Toledo. Madrid is at the northern limit of the area known as La Mancha—the territory inhabited by Miguel de Cervantes' fictional *Don Quixote*. The plateau region is high and dry, and its soil is rocky and sandy.

A short distance from Madrid the topography changes and the valleys become greener and the soil more fertile. The topography of Madrid and its environs resembles the foothill regions of the Rocky Mountains at about the same altitude as Salt Lake City.

A modern and cosmopolitan city, Madrid also is the seat of Spanish culture and the respository of Spanish traditions. Characterized today by tall, modern buildings and wide boulevards, the city still retains much of its unique charm in the old buildings and narrow streets of the central section.

For a city of its size, Madrid has few large industries. The Spanish Government is the largest single employer. Next are the government-protected automobile and truck manufacturers— SEAT, Pegaso, and Barreiros. A large and booming trucking industry, the local construction industry, and various light manufacturing firms are the major local employers.

As the seat of government and the location of the head offices of most of the country's businesses, Madrid has a large number of administrative and clerical workers. The general level of education in the city is high.

Madrid has a large and growing colony of foreign residents. American citizens number about 13,000; most of them are permanent residents. About

700 nonresident American employees and dependents comprise the U.S. Mission. A large number of American tourists visit Madrid, with the greatest number arriving during the April-through-November tourist season.

BARCELONA was founded by the Carthaginians in about 680 B.C. It is Spain's second largest city (it claims first place in terms of metropolitan area population and is one of the world's most densely populated cities). It also is the country's leading industrial and trade center. The official language is Spanish, but the native language (Catalan) is widely spoken throughout the region of Cataluña.

Barcelona's climate is temperate and usually pleasant, although relatively high humidity makes the warm summer and cold winter days more pronounced. Winter and early spring months often bring heavy rainfall, but it rarely snows or reaches below freezing in the city.

The Barcelona consular district (U.S.) includes the Provinces of Barcelona, Gerona, Lerida, Huesca, Tarragona, Castellon, and Teruel; the Balearic Islands (Mallorca, Menorca, and Ibiza); and the principality of Andorra. Fifty-four nations have consular offices in Barcelona, and many, including the U.K., France, the F.R.G., and some Latin American countries, have large colonies in the area.

The district has 5,000 registered Americans. American tourism is heavy, particularly during summer.

Greater **SEVILLE** (population 700,000) is the largest and most important city in Andalucia, Spain's richest agricultural region. Its history spans many centuries, beginning with colonization by the Phoenicians through

occupation by the Romans (third century B.C.), Vandals (fifth century), Visigoths (sixth century), and Arabs (eighth century). The Moorish occupation ended in 1248 when the city was taken for the emerging modern Spanish nation by King Ferdinard II of Castile.

During the colonial period of the Americas, Seville had a monopoly of New World trade and was the center of the intellectual and economic life of Spain. Today, even centuries after the Christian conquest of Seville, the city reflects a harmonious blend of Western European and Middle Eastern cultural patterns and bloodlines.

The central city is characterized by tiny plazas and narrow, winding streets. Some streets in the Barrio de Santa Cruz, a quarter where the Moorish and Jewish residents were forced to live after the reconquest, can be traversed only by foot or horsecart. In that picturesque area, preserved as a national monument, one finds the more "typical" Sevillian atmosphere, where most homes and shops are fitted with elaborate wrought iron gates and windows that look into a patio filled with potted flowers and ferns. Elsewhere, public parks and gardens enhance the city's array of massive architectural forms.

The city lies on both sides of the Gaudalquivir River, 35 miles from its mouth on the Atlantic Ocean and 26 feet above sea level. It has always been an important commercial port and is the only inland harbor in Spain for oceangoing vessels.

The city is the site of one of the finest educational institutions in Spain, the University of Seville, whose courses in literature, history, and Spanish-American relations are of special interest.

Seville is not a city of foreign colonies. Practically no American business community exists there, although American firms are well represented by local Spanish agents.

The climate is hot and dry in summer, pleasant in spring and fall, damp and chilly in winter. From June to September the temperature often exceeds 100°F, and on winter nights sometimes falls below freezing. Temperatures vary sometimes as much as 20 degrees between day and night.

Seville is the most southerly U.S. consular post in Europe and covers most of the south of Spain, (i.e., the regions of Andalucia, Extremadura, and the two Spanish enclaves in Northern Africa). The post has consular jurisdiction in Almeria, Badajoz, Cáceres, Cádiz, Ceuta, Córdoba, Granada, Huelva, Jaén, Málaga, and Sevilla.

BILBAO, capital of the Province of Vizcaya, has a population of 450,000; inclusion of the adjacent metropolitan area doubles that figure. Bilbao is in the narrow Nervion River valley about 10 miles inland from the Bay of Biscay. In many ways it resembles comparable industrial cities in mountainous areas of the U.S., such as Pittsburgh, with the added charm of "old Bilbao" and its crowded, maze-like *siete calles.*

Bilbao's latitude is roughly that of Boston, but moist winds off the bay bring relatively cool summers and mild winters with mostly above-freezing temperatures. Rainfall averages 55 inches per year. Because of tempera-ture inversion and smoke from the factories, the skies are frequently overcast, and air pollution is recognized as a serious problem.

Bilbao is the largest city in the Vascongadas, or Basque region. Ethnically, culturally, and linguistically, the Basques consider themselves distinct from the rest of Spain. Their origins are unknown and, unlike the rest of Spain, they were barely influenced by the Romans and unconquered by the Moors. They are generally a serious, hard-working, religious people with close family ties. Although only a small portion of the urban population still speaks Basque, most Basques proudly maintain their individuality.

Recreation

Madrid

Madrid and its suburbs offer opportunities for sports comparable to other major cities. Golf, tennis, swimming, shooting, horseback riding, and skiing are the most popular adult sports.

In the Madrid area a number of private clubs provide facilities for outdoor activities, particularly tennis, golf, and swimming. The most exclusive club is the Real Club Puerta de Hierro, which has a 27-hole golf course, tennis courts, swimming pool, riding stables, and polo field. Its clubhouse is attractive and offers bar and dining room service, a large clubroom, and a few living quarters. The club is accessible only by car.

A small shooting club, the Sociedad Tiro de Pichon, is close to Madrid and is popular with skeet- and target-shooting enthusiasts. The Ciudad Deportiva del Real Madrid Club de Futbal y Tenis also is in Madrid and offers excellent tennis and swimming facilities (this club sponsors the well-known Real Madrid football team).

The most popular Spanish spectator sport is soccer, with bullfighting running a close second. Spanish soccer teams are well known in Europe, and an international match at the Estadio de Bernabeu can be an exciting event. The best bullfighters in the world regularly appear at Madrid's main ring, Las Ventas. In fact, a bullfighting custom states that a fighter cannot be called matador de toros until taking an *alternativa* in this ring. In mid-May, the Feria de San Isidro brings a week of daily fights and almost all the current "names" in bullfighting to the Madrid ring.

Other spectator sports worthy of note are cycling, horse racing, and jai alai, a game thought to be Basque in origin.

Commercial sight-seeing tours to nearby places of interest are regularly scheduled. The Royal Automobile Club has the best information and maps for motoring trips in Spain. The club provides service to AAA members without payment of membership charges. Its fees are small.

A number of riding academies on the city's outskirts have facilities for riding in the country. The mountains north of Madrid offer mountain climbing and hiking. Several Spanish clubs organize climbs and maintain mountain huts.

Excellent facilities can be found for fishing (trout and salmon) and hunting (partridge, duck, hare, wild boar, deer, rabbit, and mountain goat). The Spanish fish wet flies much more than dry flies and also use spoons and

spinners. Most shotguns on the local market are double-barreled, either side by side or over and under. Spanish shotguns are of good quality and are inexpensive. Excellent-quality shotguns made by world-famous Spanish gunsmiths are sold, but are not always available at bargain prices.

Madrid has an international ski club which offers inexpensive bus service to the Navacerrada/Los Cotos ski area in the Guadarrama Mountains (about an hour's drive from Madrid) every Saturday during the ski season. The club also sponsors trips to other areas in Spain and to Switzerland. Ski equipment can be rented near the lifts at Navacerrada. Ski boots and clothing can be bought in Madrid, but all good quality equipment and clothing is imported and expensive.

A broad range of entertainment is available in the Madrid area. Many movie houses show American and English films, but almost all have Spanish soundtracks. Some productions of the Madrid legitimate theater are quite good. The Spanish theater is an excellent medium to improve one's Spanish. Madrid also has an amateur English-language theater group which presents several plays each year.

During winter months, weekly concerts are given by the National Symphony Orchestra. In addition, several chamber music groups give concerts during an eight-month season. The opera season is during April and May. Ballet troupes, famous soloists, choral groups, and orchestras occasionally play limited engagements in Madrid.

Restaurants are plentiful and varied in Madrid. Some nightclubs have shows and dance bands. Several restaurant/clubs feature *tablao flamenco,* with flamenco dancing and singing.

Historical sights and museums provide almost endless diversion. The world-famous Prado Museum heads the list. Many authorities consider it one of the finest painting galleries in the world from the standpoint of the quality and variety of its collection. The Prado has works by the best Spanish painters, as well as by painters of the most important schools of foreign painting, particularly Italian and Flemish. Its collection is so large that it would take months of intensive study to see and appreciate the works on display.

Other fine museums are the homes of Cervantes, Lope de Vega, and the painter Sorolla; the Archaeological Museum; the Romantic Museum; the Museum of Decorative Art; the Lazaro Galdiano Museum; Cerralbo; the Instituto de Valencia de Don Juan; and the Museum "Las Descalzas Reales."

Madrid has a number of *verbenas* (carnivals) held in the open in specially designated places. The first of these, the feast of St. Anthony, takes place on June 13; others are the Verbena de la Paloma and the Verbena de la Carmen. Each carnival is devoted to a different saint and district. These festivals are very popular with Spaniards and provide interesting entertainment. Local fairs take place in many towns on special feast days. Most include dances and bullfights.

One of Spain's most popular fiestas is held in Valencia from March 17 through March 19. Large allegorical wood and papier mache sculptures known as *fallas* are built in the streets with prizes awarded to the best. At the end of the fair, on the night of March 19, the sculptures are burned in huge bonfires to the accompaniment of a stupendous fireworks display.

The Fair of San Fermin at Pamplona from July 6 to July 12 is also noteworthy. It is here that young men run through the streets chased by fighting bulls.

Barcelona

Barcelona and its environs offer many opportunities for an active sports life. Golf, tennis, swimming, waterskiing, sailing, hunting, fishing, horseback riding, and winter sports are found in the city or within a few hours' drive.

Besides the travel opportunities presented by Europe, many opportunities are available for weekend tours and sight-seeing activities. The area has two large amusement parks, Montjuich and Tibidabo, and many interesting museums, monuments, and restaurants. The Gothic Quarter is well known for its small, narrow, winding streets and picturesque shops.

Barcelona offers a variety of fine entertainment including opera, ballet, and many excellent concerts. Local theaters present plays, light opera, and musical comedy. Motion pictures are popular, but most films are dubbed in Spanish. The Institute of North American Studies has a movie in English once a week, as well as many other fine artistic and musical presentations. Many interesting local festivals, both religious and secular, are also held.

Seville

Among the outstanding buildings in Seville are the great Gothic cathedral, third largest in the Christian world, with its famed Moorish-Spanish bell tower, La Giralda; the Alcazar, Moorish royal palace; the Royal Tobacco Factory, made world famous through Bizet's opera *Carmen*, and now used to house part of the University of Seville; and the Archives of the Indies, where the most important documents relating to the discovery and colonization of the Americas and the Philippines are preserved.

Southern Spain offers many interesting places to visit on weekends. The beaches along the Atlantic Coast can be reached by car in less than two hours. The internationally popular resorts of the Costa del Sol are about three to four hours away by car. The ski slopes of Granada can he reached by a four-hour car trip. In addition, many small towns and cities of Andalucia are rich with history of the Moorish occupation and the colonization of the New World. Most highways are adequate.

Tennis, swimming, hunting, and horseback riding are the main sports in Seville, but facilities are only available under the auspices of one of the sports clubs.

Seville has many good movie houses offering current U.S and European films dubbed in Spanish. During winter and spring, cultural events include concerts, plays, and dance recitals. The city sponsors several cultural festivals during the year which offer fine entertainment at reasonable prices. Sevillian cultural life, however, centers on the family and church, and the city can be best described as quiet, charming, and somewhat provincial.

Several discotheques and nightclubs in Seville offer modern and fla-menco dancing. Bullfights and soccer (*futbol*) are extremely popular, and the local sporting events are first-quality.

Seville has five radio stations and two TV channels. U.S. television sets must be converted to European standards.

Holy Week processions are held in many Spanish towns, but those in Seville are noted for their color, brightness, and religious enthusiasm. The Spring Fair in Seville in April has festivities which last almost one week. During these periods the city is crowded, lodgings are hard to find, and prices are double or higher.

The Holy Week ceremonies are characterized by processions of robed and hooded members of the city's numerous religious brotherhoods, accompanied by elaborate religious floats carried by teams of stevedores. A couple of weeks later the annual April Fair (Feria de Abril) is celebrated. It consists of six days of festivities including daily horse parades, a trade fair, a carnival, a number of circuses, a series of bullfights, and dancing and socializing in small *casetas* until early morning.

Bilbao

Bilbao has limited sports facilities. Facilities for golf, tennis, and swimming are available, but the climate does not lend itself easily to a great deal of outdoor activity. The city also has a riding stable and boat mooring facilities. Spectator events include soccer, jai alai, and bullfights in summer.

Skiing is good in the French Pyrenees at spots such as Candanchu, north of of Jaca, about a five-to six-hour drive by car. Inland fishing for trout and salmon is popular, especially in Oviedo and Santander. In season, some hunting is possible for birds, small game, and even an occasional wild boar.

The Bay of Biscay provides opportunities for swimming and boating, although possibilities for sailing and waterskiing are limited. Several beaches may be reached within 15 to 25 miles of Bilbao. Since most, however, are near polluted rivers and streams, few are completely safe for swimming. A favorite swimming spot of resident Americans is the extensive beach area of Laredo in the Province of Santander, 75 miles from Bilbao. A number of Bilbao residents have bought new summer condominium apartments on the Laredo shoreline. Sea-fishing enthusiasts can join a yachting club in Legueitio 37 miles from Bilbao.

Bilbao has many movie theatres. All foreign films, including American, are dubbed in Spanish. Spanish plays and musical comedies are presented at fiesta time. Concerts are held during late fall, winter, and early spring. One series is given by the Bilbao Symphony Orchestra and two series, both featuring visiting artists, are sponsored by the Sociedad Filarmonica and Conciertos Arriaga.

After the Semana Grande in late August, Bilbao has a brief season of Zarzuela (Spanish operetta) and opera. The local opera society often features Italian performers. Excellent choral concerts are given by groups such as the Sociedad Coral de Bilbao. (This society welcomes participation by foreigners.) Bilbao has some good nightclubs and cabarets, such as Flash, Bluesville, Garden, Holiday, Tiffany's, House Club, and Cask del Loco.

Notes for Travelers

Many international and local airlines, including Iberia, Pan Am, and TWA, serve the major cities and resort areas of Spain. Rail facilities are good, and several systems connect selected Spanish cities with the rest of Europe.

A valid passport is the only entry requirement, except for those planning a stay of more than six months, when a visa is necessary. Health certificates are not required unless the visitor is traveling from an infected area.

Spanish regulations governing importation of firearms and ammunition are strict. Only diplomatic members of foreign missions are authorized to import hunting weapons and pistols.

Houses of worship in Madrid which conduct services in English include Roman Catholic churches, several Protestant churches, a Jewish synagogue, and a mosque. In Barcelona, the Church of England sponsors a resident English chaplain who offers regular services attended by British, American, and other foreign groups. Roman Catholic masses are conducted once a week at a local church, and a Jewish synagogue holds regular services under the direction of an English-speaking rabbi. Various Protestant sects also exist in the city. Seville has Catholic and Protestant churches, but no synagogue. In Bilbao, besides the numerous Catholic churches, there is the British Cemetery Chapel, which offers weekly services.

The Spanish unit of currency is the *peseta*, with a monetary conversion rate of about 77 *pesetas* to the U.S. dollar (1979). The exchange rate fluctuates.

The metric system of weights and measures is used.

Special note: Street crime has escalated in many parts of Spain during the past few years. American and other foreign-made cars are prime targets, so the installation of an anti-theft alarm system is recommended.

The U.S. Embassy in Spain is located at Calle Serrano 75, Madrid. A Consulate General is at Via Layetana 33 in Barcelona; a Consulate General at Paseo de la Delicias 7, Seville; a Consulate at Avenida del Ejercito 11, Duesto, Bilbao; and consular agencies in Palma de Mallorca, Las Palmas (Canary Islands), Málaga, and Valencia.

Sweden

SWEDEN is a land of remarkable contrasts. At once cosmopolitan and bucolic, it is an industrialized nation with one of the world's highest standards of living, yet in its far northern region, the Lapps still herd their reindeer as they did a thousand years ago. Medieval buildings are preserved amidst the new structures of modern cities, and although Sweden faces the disturbing inflationary problems and increasing crime rates experienced by other countries of comparable development, its beautiful countryside and friendly people continue to beckon travelers from all over the world.

Nonbelligerent since Napoleonic times, Sweden's policy of political neutrality has deep roots and wide support among its citizens. In the past few years, however, Sweden has taken an activist stance on a wide variety of international issues.

Area, Geography, Climate

Sweden is bordered on the west by Norway, on the north by Norway and Finland, and on the east and south by the Baltic Sea. The country is long and narrow and encompasses an area of 173,378 square miles, a little larger than California. Despite its northern latitude, Sweden's climate is not excessively cold, due to the proximity of the Gulf Stream and the Baltic Sea. The mean annual temperature is 48°F. Winter temperature and humidity in Stockholm, the capital, resemble that of the Puget Sound area of Washington State. The winter season is longer, however, and winter daylight hours are considerably shorter than in the northern United States.

During most of December and early January the sun never rises before 9 a.m., and sets as early as 2:30 p.m. Snow usually falls in January, February, and March, but days are often sunny, brisk, and clear. The average temperature for December through February is 27°F. Spring comes late, with snow frequently falling in April. Average temperature for July and August is 62°F. Late June, July, and early August can be warm and very pleasant, and June and July are months of almost continuous daylight. September, although cool even on the brightest days, is frequently characterized by a subarctic clearness; it is said that central and southern Sweden and Stockholm are most attractive in September. But Stockholm is at its best in summer, when sidewalk cafes, numerous sailboats, and cruise ships in the harbors lend a holiday atmosphere.

Average annual rainfall in Stockholm is 22 inches; rainy seasons are in early spring and fall. Heavy snows are infrequent, although 1978 and 1979 had record cold and snowfall. Snow removal is prompt, but snow tires are essential for safe driving outside the cities.

Population

Sweden's population is about 8.3 million, an average density of 49 people per square mile. Stockholm has a population of 680,000, or 1,400,000 including suburbs. The state church is Lutheran, encompassing 93.5 percent of the population, but all denominations have religious freedom.

Government

Sweden is a constitutional monarchy with a parliamentary government. King Carl XVI Gustaf is a member of the Bernadotte dynasty. Sweden has five political parties represented in Parliament (Riksdag): the Social Democratic Party, Center Party, Moderate Coalition Party (formerly Conservative Party), the Liberal Party, and the Communist Party. Parliament is a 349-member, single-chamber legislature elected by direct popular vote every three years. The Swedish electoral system is based on proportional representation.

Arts, Science, Education

Sweden is traditionally a leading nation in the field of education. It has six national universities, including the University of Stockholm, as well as various technological institutes. Specialized professional schools include dentistry, pharmacy, veterinary sciences, agriculture, forestry, economics, social work, art, music, journalism, and library science.

Stockholm University also administers the Institute for English-Speaking Students, divided into three sections: International Graduate School (IGS), Stockholm Junior Year, and Swedish Language courses. The emphasis is on Swedish language and literature, economics, social and political sciences, and international affairs. An American degree is required for admission to IGS.

A number of extension courses are also available and are arranged by Kursverksamheten (KV), TBV, Medborgarskolan, etc. They range from academic subjects to arts and crafts.

Commerce and Industry

Intensive exploitation of three key natural resources—forests, iron ore deposits, and water power—combined with the development of a skilled and disciplined labor force transformed Sweden from a poor, rural society into a highly productive, industrial economy in less than 100 years. Other key factors in this transformation were Sweden's large-scale emigration to the U.S., extensive research and development, and highly developed managerial skills. Today, emphasis has been shifted away from raw materials towards the engineering industries. Machinery, vehicles, ships, metalworking, instruments, and the like now account for over 30 percent of total industrial production and over half of total exports.

During the past 40 years, Sweden has expanded public social services on a scale almost unequaled in the world, but tax rates have risen substantially to pay for those services. Now, with progressive marginal tax rates among the highest in the world, many Swedes fear that productivity and incentive to work are being depressed. A recent long-term Swedish Government prognosis implies that Swedes may have to accept a slower growth rate in private consumption and in public services. As Swedish exports of many goods such as shipbuilding and iron ore face increasing competition from low-cost producers, and as producers of goods such as textiles and shoes struggle to compete against low-cost imports, many changes are in store for the 1980s. The fact that 76 percent of Sweden's energy needs are satisfied by imported oil only adds to the nation's problems. However, the Swedes are well aware of these problems, and there is little doubt that they will find innovative ways to cope with them.

Transportation

Stockholm's Central Train Station is downtown and Arlanda Airport is about 25 miles north of the city. Domestic flights use Bromma Airport on the city's western outskirts.

Stockholm has buses, electric trains, and subways that operate within the city and most suburbs. Mass transit charges are reasonable and transportation commuting tickets economical. Cabs are expensive and plentiful except during foul weather and rush hours. Rush hour transportation facilities are crowded and traffic is heavy.

For personal use, rental cars are available, or privately owned vehicles may be imported into the country with proper documentation. All cars must pass a stringent registration inspection. Recently the Swedish Government tightened these controls as they apply to 1972 and later models, particularly regarding brakes. Models of 1974 and later must be equipped with headlight wipers; new regulations concerning emission controls apply for 1976 and later models. As a result, many new foreign (including American) models are unable to pass inspection without expensive alterations. Foreign cars not manufactured to Swedish specifications need alterations to pass inspection. Cars are still subject to annual inspection. New car registration inspection is good for the first two years.

Most cars, including a few American models, can be purchased in Sweden, but American cars are expensive. Maintenance and repair facilities are adequate for all makes, but parts, repairs, and service are more expensive than in the U.S. All cars should be undercoated. Some people prefer to use radial tires year round; others prefer snow tires for winter use. However, if one uses studded snow tires, all four tires must be studded. Be advised that many other European countries prohibit the use of studded tires.

Third-party liability insurance is compulsory for every vehicle. Only Swedish insurance companies are authorized to provide this coverage, but at initial entry, a "green card" is adequate if the vehicle is driven into Sweden. Policies issued by Swedish companies cover Sweden, Finland, Norway, and Denmark.

A Swedish drivers license will be issued upon presentation of a valid U.S. license. It should be noted that driving after drinking, even in moderate amounts, is considered a serious offense, usually punishable by imprisonment.

Communications

Communications systems are good in Sweden, and cost less than comparable service in the U.S. Excellent direct-dial service is available between Sweden and America, and telegrams can be sent from telegraph offices or by telephone at any time.

International airmail from America generally is delivered from the U.S. east coast within five to seven days, and from the west coast within seven to 10 days. Surface delivery takes four to five weeks, and packages six to eight weeks.

English-language radio programs from Luxembourg, England, and AFN Germany can be received by medium wave in the evenings with a well-placed outside antenna. Medium- and shortwave Voice of America (VOA) broadcasts can be received morning and evening. Reception of local programs is excellent. BBC shortwave can be heard almost 24 hours daily.

Reception of Stockholm's two TV stations is good, but telecast time is limited. Most new black-and-white American TV sets can be converted to operate in Sweden, but this is expensive. English-language TV programs are limited to one or two shows nightly, but radio news, mostly Swedish news, can be heard nine times a day in English.

The Paris edition of the International Herald Tribune is available at newsstands and by subscription directly from Paris. Delivery is generally one day after publication. Some British and continental newspapers are also available. Selected U.S. magazines are available at local newsstands.

Stockholm bookstores have a considerable variety of expensive American and British books and paperbacks, as well as English translations of foreign books and some current American magazines. The American Center Library has about 6,500 American books and 170 magazines and periodicals. Stockholm also has ample public library facilities, with a decent collection of books in English.

Health

Swedish medical and dental standards are high, but appointments are difficult to obtain during summer and at Christmastime, when many doctors and dentists take extended vacations. Swedish socialized medicine is characterized by an impersonal approach and extensive regimentation. Dental fees in Sweden are comparable to those in the U.S. Stockholm has many modern hospitals. Swedish opticians are highly reputable and reliable in filling eyeglass prescriptions.

The Swedish State Institute of Public Health supervises the handling of meats, routine food tests, food handling, water, sewage, garbage disposal, and general sanitation. Public health standards are high and comparable to those in the U.S. The city-owned water supply system is tested regularly. Pasteurized milk is available and dairy products are pure.

Colds and flu are the most common ailments of Americans in Sweden. Rheumatism, bronchial ailments, and sinus trouble may be aggravated during winter. No special health precautions are required, although many Americans regularly take vitamins during winter when sunshine is minimal. Most medicines for colds, sinus conditions, and allergies require a prescription.

Major Cities

STOCKHOLM is Sweden's largest city. Founded in 1250, it has been the principal city since the time of Gustav Vasa in the early 1500s. The walls have long since disappeared and the old houses have been rebuilt. The medieval city plan can be seen in the narrow, winding cobblestone streets and small squares of Gamla Stan (Old

Town). Several restaurants located deep in cellar vaults date from the medieval era. Reminders of Sweden's period as a great power in the 17th and 18th centuries are the Royal Palace and House of Nobility. Other landmarks are the Stock Exchange, Foreign Ministry, Royal Opera House, and the old Riksdag or Parliament building. The burial place of Sweden's nobility, the Riddarholm Church, dates from the city's beginnings.

Modern apartment houses rise tier upon tier on Stockholm's outskirts, and in the suburbs stand many municipal housing projects—large multistoried, utilitarian apartment houses interspersed with grass and play areas.

About 5,000 American citizens reside in Sweden. Other nationalities include Greeks, Turks, Yugoslavs, and Finns. Most Swedes speak English. Outside Stockholm, however, knowledge of the Swedish language is useful and important for shopping, asking information, and finding directions.

GÖTEBORG is Sweden's major seaport to the west, and its maritime traditions are more than 300 years old. When the foundations of the present city were laid in 1619, Dutchmen did the planning and building; Germans, Englishmen, and Scotsmen helped the Swedes to pave the paths and roads of commerce through the city. Viking fleets gathered off the mouth of the Gota River as late as the 10th century to trade at big markets. The canals through the town originally formed the actual harbor area.

Göteborg's harbor is the biggest in Scandinavia and Göteborg ranks 35th among the world's largest seaports. About 85 regular shipping lines include Göteborg in their traffic. A ship arrives or departs, on the average, every 15 minutes. The amount of cargo loaded or unloaded is estimated at 20.5 million metric tons per year. Frequent ferry connections link Göteborg with Jutland in Denmark, the Federal Republic of Germany, the United Kingdom, and the Netherlands.

The city is well laid out and clean. Many parkways and lovely parks with bright summer flowers add much to its charm. Gentle hills surround the city, inviting the hiker to stroll among the woods and lakes.

Göteborg is the home of about 15,000 enterprises and more than 300,000 employees. Some 450,000 people live in the area and about the same number visit the city each year. About 3,000 U.S. citizens live in the Göteborg (U.S.) consular district (the southern third of Sweden).

Other large Swedish cities are Malmö, Norrköping, and Hälsingborg. The city of Uppsala, in the east central part of the country, is the site of the oldest university in Northern Europe, the University of Uppsala, which was founded in 1477.

Recreation

Stockholm

Stockholm offers many opportunities for recreation. Numerous playgrounds are located throughout the city, and some have playground supervisors with whom one may leave children. Each commune offers a program of a wide variety of sports for children and adults.

The temperature of Lake Malaren and the Baltic Sea around Stockholm reaches about 62°F in summer, but

Americans generally find the water too cold for swimming. Outdoor pools are located at various points in Stockholm. Several large indoor swimming pools can be used year round.

Hiking, cycling, and walking are popular. Cycling and strolling paths follow the water in town, and on the outskirts forests and park areas provide pleasant hiking. Cycling paths are found everywhere.

Hunting in Sweden is limited to those invited by proprietors of game land. Duck, pheasant, hare, deer, and moose are plentiful. A good Swedish rifle can be purchased locally, but one must first obtain a license.

Fishing enthusiasts must also obtain licenses. Many game fish are found near Stockholm, and salmon can be caught in rivers about 100 miles from the city. Salmon fishing is tightly controlled and expensive. Trout are found in streams near the mountain range along the Swedish-Norwegian border; fishing rights there are not nearly so restricted. However, trout streams are poorly stocked and catches always small.

Tennis, squash, and bowling facilities are available. Stockholm has good golf courses where visitors can play by paying greens fees, which is generally preferable to joining a particular club due to the short season. Horseback riding may be enjoyed all year; several stables have indoor rings.

Within Stockholm or a short drive outside, are cross-country ski trails and beginners' slopes. Many Americans cross-country ski on various golf courses. The closest ski resort with a ski lift is in Salen, Dalarna, about a seven-hour drive from Stockholm. Two or three rope tows are in the Stockholm area.

In only a few places in the world are yachting and boating so generally enjoyed. The season is short (May 15-September 15) but the Stockholm archipelago is beautiful and easily accessible for either sailing or motorboating. Numerous small secluded harbors among the islands allow boaters to anchor and picnic for a day or weekend. Both sailboats and motorboats can be purchased secondhand. A limited charter market at high prices exists for sail or motorboats, and sailboats can be rented by the day at Saltsjobaden. Several yacht clubs have reasonable fees. Berthing facilities in the city are quite limited.

Sight-seeing tours by bus and boat are available through tourist offices. Places of charm and interest include: Uppsala, a university town and site of a restored medieval cathedral, and nearby, Old Uppsala, where Viking burial mounds are located; Saltsjobaden, a seaside resort on an inlet of the Baltic; Gripsholm Castle, a large fortress containing portraits of European royalty; Skokloster Castle, built at the close of the Thirty Years War and depicting furnishings and armaments from the late 17th century; and Sigtuna, ancient Viking capital, site of several of the earliest churches in Sweden and of original 17th-century buildings. All are near Stockholm.

For longer trips, the walled Hanseatic city of Visby on the island of Gotland, east of the Swedish mainland, can be reached by an overnight boat and train trip, or in one hour by air. Many summer resorts on Sweden's west coast, including Bastad, hold international tennis matches. On holidays many Swedes, particularly in areas north of Stockholm, wear picturesque native costumes. The best time to see them is Midsummer Eve in the Province of Dalarna, when they raise the maypole. A train trip to Rattvik, one of the most popular places in Dalarna, takes about five hours. Lappland, in the far north, is a popular area to visit during the time of the midnight sun. It is also possible to visit the crystal and glass country in southern Sweden, in Smaland: Kosta, Boda, and Orrefors are nearly 200 miles south of Stockholm.

Charter flights are extremely popular and one of the best "bargains" in Sweden. Exotic resort packages include a one- or two-week visit, hotels, and meals at prices less than that of regular airfare. No membership or waiting period is required.

Göteborg

During summer, thousands of Göteborg's inhabitants move to the country. After the dark, sunless winter, everyone wants to fully enjoy the short summer, and coastal beaches and rocks are crowded with sunbathers. The west coast's numerous summer resorts and beaches offer many recreational activities. Göteborg has a few large, modern indoor swimming pools, most of which are open year round. Besides swimming, some pools offer gymnastic rooms, sunrooms, steam baths, and massage. Göteborg also has the largest indoor stadium in Scandinavia, and a centrally located amusement park, Liseberg, open during summer.

Göteborg tennis clubs have numerous indoor and outdoor courts. Squash is a favorite local sport and many courts exist in town. Skating is a popular winter sport and enjoyed on the many area lakes. Skiing is only

occasional due to the lack of snow; the winter sports enthusiast usually goes to northern Sweden or Norway.

The most popular sports on the west coast are boating and sailing. Also popular are fishing, golfing, and horseback riding. The city supports a number of well-equipped children's playgrounds.

Charter travel is popular in this area and air tickets can often be purchased cheaply. A recent advertisement (1980) for a round trip to New York for around $400 is one example. In winter, trips to warmer areas are favored.

Entertainment

There is a wide variety of entertainment in both Stockholm and Göteborg. Stockholm has the Royal Opera and two symphony orchestras with performances from September to June, the Royal Dramatic Theater, and other theaters that feature outstanding modern productions in Swedish. In summer, the Opera performs at Drottningholm Court Theatre.

Swedish, American, British, and other foreign films are shown with their original soundtracks and Swedish subtitles. Half of all films shown are U.S. films. Museums, galleries, palaces, castles, old churches, and gardens provide interesting sight-seeing.

Medium- to high-price restaurants can be found throughout the city, as well as a few nightclubs, bars, and discotheques. Restaurants with music, entertainment, and atmosphere are expensive. Dining out is 50 to 100 percent more expensive than in Washington, DC.

Spectator events in Stockholm include trotting races, horse races, regattas, tennis matches, soccer, ice hockey, speed skating, ski jumping, wrestling, boxing, and international athletic meetings.

Göteborg has three fairly large theaters. The City Theater (Stadsteatern) and the Folk Theater (Folkteatern) usually present plays. The Grand Theater (Stora Teatern) specializes in opera, operetta, and ballet. All productions are in Swedish. Concerts are presented each year from September to June in the Concert Hall (Konserthuset) and during summer, in the Liseberg Concert Hall. American entertainers touring Sweden often include Göteborg on their schedule.

Movie theaters show American, English, Swedish, and other productions with original soundtracks. If the movies are not Swedish, Swedish subtitles are supplied. Numerous restaurants offer a wide range of prices. Göteborg is particularly known for its excellent seafood. Several outdoor restaurants are open during summer, as are numerous sidewalk cafes.

Notes for Travelers

Northwest Orient Airlines has daily flights to and from Stockholm, via New York. No American passenger ships offer service.

No visa is required for an American citizen remaining in Scandinavia for less than three months. No vacci-

nation or health certificates are necessary for entry.

Swedish law prohibits importation of automatic weapons. Importation of ammunition is limited to 200 rounds for each type of permissible firearm, except that 2,000 rounds of skeet-loaded shotgun shells may be imported. Import licenses and registration papers are necessary.

In Stockholm, religious services in English are conducted at the Anglican Church, the First Church of Christ Scientist, and at two Roman Catholic churches. The United Christian Congregation in Stockholm (Old Town) is an ecumenical, English-language church. In addition, Greek Orthodox, Jewish, Mormon, Methodist, Baptist, Mission Covenant, and Pentecostal religions are represented in Stockholm. Services are usually in Swedish, although occasionally it is possible to find services conducted in French, German, Spanish, or English. In Göteberg, the only English services are those of the Church of England.

The official monetary unit is the Swedish *krona*. There are 100 ore to one *krona*. The rate of exchange is about 4.52 *kronor* to the U.S. dollar, but the rate fluctuates daily.

Sweden uses the metric system of weights and measures.

The U.S. Embassy in Sweden is located at Strandvagen 101, Stockholm. The Consulate General is at Södra Hamngatan 53, Göteborg.

Switzerland

Originally inhabited by the Helvetic Celts, the territory which is modern **SWITZERLAND** once was part of the Roman Empire, later was invaded by Teutonic tribes, became part of the empire of Charlemagne, and subsequently passed under the dominion of German emperors until it marked the beginning of its independence in 1291. For centuries it protected itself against the ruling dynasties of Europe. Switzerland's independence and neutrality were officially recognized by the Congress of Vienna in 1815, and since the drafting of its constitution in the middle of the 19th century, its history has been one of continued political, economic, and social improvement for its people. Its determination to adhere to the principle of neutrality kept the Swiss out of both World Wars.

Switzerland is all the travel brochures say it is, and more. The country's natural beauty, the courtesy of its people, and the stability of the Swiss way of life, mirror the charm of a different age. Yet, its modern facilities and cultural opportunities are a stimulating discovery.

The Swiss are proud of their national identity, and of their ability to remain neutral in a swirl of international activity. Geneva, in the southwest corner of the country, and once the home of the League of Nations, now is a major center for worldwide governmental organizations.

Area, Geography, Climate

Switzerland covers an area of 15,944 square miles. About one quarter of the country consists of glaciers, rocks, and lakes; another quarter is covered by forests. Because of the varied topography (from an altitude of 633 feet in the Ticino Canton to 15,203 feet—the Monte Rosa peak—in the Alps), climate and vegetation vary from Mediterranean to arctic. Neither Bern, the capital, nor Zurich have great extremes of hot or cold weather. Rain is common in winter and summer, and snowfalls are frequent in winter. Humidity is high during spring and fall. Winter brings some warm spells, and all-day fog and cloudy weather are common. The *föhn*, a dry south wind that passes over the Alps changing air pressure, has an enervating and otherwise unpleasant effect on some people. Average summer temperature in Bern is 60°F; in winter, 33°F; Zurich temperatures are usually a few degrees lower.

Population

Switzerland's population of about 6.3 million includes one million resident foreigners. More than three-fourths of the people live in the central plain, which stretches between the Alps and the Jura Mountains from Geneva to the Rhine.

Switzerland has four official languages: German, French, Italian, and Romansch. Romansch, based on Latin, is principally spoken by a small minority in the Graubünden Canton. The Swiss version of German is spoken by about 70 percent of the population. Spoken Swiss German differs substantially from German spoken in Germany and Austria. It frequently varies from canton to canton, even from town to town. The written language, however, is High German and is used in most TV and radio shows, on the stage, and in university lectures. French is the first language in the Cantons of Fribourg, Vaud, Valais, Neuchâtel, and Geneva, with English the second language for most educated Swiss. Italian is spoken in Ticino Canton.

The ratio of Protestants to Catholics among the Swiss is about six to five. Three German-speaking cantons are Catholic, and three are predominantly Protestant. Of the four French-speaking cantons, two are Catholic and two predominantly Protestant. Ticino Canton is Catholic.

Switzerland's cantons differ in history, customs, and culture as well as in size and natural setting. Active competition exists among the cantons, perhaps more so than among states in the U.S. Yet, as a national group the Swiss are generally serious-minded, conscientious, hard-working, and determined. Living patterns are similar to those in America, although the Swiss are more paternalistic, formal, and conservative in dress and conduct than Americans.

Their practicality is reflected in their architecture, furnishings, clothing, and food.

Government

Switzerland has a federal government structure with a bicameral legislature. The National Council is the lower house, with members elected by proportional representation. The upper house, the Council of State, is composed of two members from each canton and one member from each half canton (total 46 members) who are elected by methods individually determined by the cantons. Executive power rests in the seven-member Federal Council, a unique Swiss political institution. The Council is elected by the legislature for a four-year term, although in practice councilors are reelected as long as they wish to serve. The President of the Federal Council is also the President of the Swiss Confederation. The office is filled by the council members in rotation for one-year terms. Each councilor heads one of the seven executive departments.

The four major political parties are the Radical Democratic Party, Socialist Party, Christian Conservative Party, and the Swiss People's Party.

Switzerland consists of 20 full cantons and six half cantons. The cantons historically precede the Confederation, which dates from 1291. Within the federal system, each canton has its own constitution and active political life. Cantonal governments have primary responsibility for law and order, health and sanitation, education, and public works.

Under the Swiss judicial system, a single national code exists for civil, commercial, and criminal law. However, the Supreme Federal Tribunal, the only federal court, has final appellate jurisdiction. The application of federal law on civil and commercial matters is entrusted to cantonal courts.

Compulsory military service is mandatory for physically-fit male adults. However, the length of service in the national militia varies. Switzerland can rapidly mobilize more than 650,000 soldiers. The air force has about 300 combat aircraft.

Many organizations in Switzerland represent special economic and occupational interests. The four most powerful are the Swiss Union of Commerce and Industry, the Swiss Association of Arts and Crafts (representing small business groups), the Swiss Farmers Union, and the Swiss Federation of Trade Unions. Geneva is the seat of many international organizations, such as the International Red Cross and various United Nations branches.

Arts, Science, Education

Switzerland is well endowed with cultural institutions. The opera and theater—including the Bern cellar stages—play an important part in the life of the people. Most stage performances are in German, some in Swiss dialect, and some in French. English-language shows, except for movies, are rare.

Music education is important and standards are high. Several composers perform in Switzerland, and the Orchestre de la Suisse Romande is world famous. Many cities, including Bern, have orchestras.

Switzerland has a literacy rate of 98 percent. Institutes of higher education (10 in all) have a total enrollment of 50,000, including over 10,000 foreign students. Two technical universities and many other engineering schools produce excellent engineers and technicians.

Commerce and Industry

The Swiss economy is a highly developed free enterprise system, heavily export-oriented, and characterized by a skilled labor force. The per capita income in 1979 was a very high $15,750. About 30 percent of the national income is earned abroad, of which 70 percent is from the sale of export products. Principal industries include machinery and metalworking, chemical and pharmaceutical products, watches, and textiles. Other important business activities include tourism, international banking, and insurance.

Unemployment is relatively low in Switzerland; nearly one-third of the Swiss labor force is made up of foreign workers, mainly Italian and Spanish. Strikes are rare despite well developed trade union organizations in industry, trade, and government.

Swiss attitudes toward property ownership and investment are similar to those in the U.S. Real estate purchase by a nonresident or a company not incorporated in Switzerland is subject to individual review by cantonal authorities.

The development of regional economic blocs within Europe has been of concern to Switzerland because it feels it cannot join the European Economic Community (EEC), where the political obligations of membership would conflict with traditional Swiss neutrality. Although a member of the European Free Trade Association (EFTA), Switzerland trades mostly with the EEC, with which it negotiated a free trade agreement in industrial products on January 1, 1973.

Transportation

Geneva and Zurich are major European flight centers, and daily flights to the U.S. are available from both cities. Bern has no passenger air service, except for a Bern-London flight that operates daily during the summer and four times a week during winter. A special bus runs between Bern and the Kloten (Zurich) International Airport and the trip takes about one-and-a-half hours. Rail service between Bern and Zurich and Bern and Geneva take the same length of time—just under two hours.

The Swiss Federal Railway system is entirely electric and connects the main cities and towns. Trains are clean and run on schedule; fares are reasonable, with special round-trip and holiday rates. Most points not accessible by train can be reached by postal bus. Over 100 mountain funiculars and aerial tramways with regular steamer services operate on major lakes in spring and summer.

Local transportation systems—trams, buses, trolley buses, taxis, and in Zurich, commuter lake steamers—are efficient. Taxi fares are comparable to those in Washington D.C.; all taxis have meters, and drivers expect a 10 to 15 percent tip.

Fire engines are red; police cars, white or black; ambulances, dark blue; and official postal vehicles, gold and black.

Swiss roads are good although often narrow and winding. A network of freeways is under construction and many sections are already completed.

Many mountain passes are closed by snow in winter, but railway car ferries operate through the St. Gotthard, Simplon, and Loetschberg passes. Road directional signs are excellent and all traffic moves on the right.

A car greatly enhances the convenience and pleasure of a stay in Switzerland. Smaller cars—either U.S., Japanese, or European—are the most convenient, both for city parking and mountain driving. Only a Swiss drivers license is valid (not applicable to tourists) and is issued on the basis of a valid drivers license from any country.

Communications

Telecommunications systems are excellent, with direct dialing possible to all parts of Switzerland, Western Europe, the U.S., and Canada. Telegraph and international mail service also are fast and efficient.

Swiss radio broadcasts in the three principal Swiss languages. Programming is of good quality with more talk programs than in the U.S. Broadcasts from other European countries—such as AFN Frankfurt, VOA Munich, Luxembourg, and BBC—are fairly good, but reception varies.

Radios with a longwave band may be connected to a continuous broadcasting system ("Telephonrundspruch") for an installation charge, plus a monthly fee.

As in most of Europe, radio and TV are run by a public corporation. Swiss television is on the air only in the late afternoon and evening, and program variety is limited. Broadcasting is in German, French, and Italian. Children's programs are broadcast once or twice a week; special programs are sometimes relayed from the U.S.

by satellite. News and sports coverage on both radio and TV is good. The radio cable carries a BBC English newscast at 7 p.m.

Many good Swiss newspapers are printed, representing various political viewpoints, and they originate in all areas of Switzerland. Several weekly and monthly Swiss illustrateds such as news, women's fashion, etc., are also published. French, German, and Italian periodicals are available at local newsstands.

The International Herald Tribune and international editions of Time, Life, and Newsweek can be purchased either at local newsstands or by subscription. Other U.S. and British magazines are also sold locally.

Health

Medical facilities and care are good throughout Switzerland. Dental work is expensive. Public health and sanitation services are available and are similar to those in other highly developed countries. Garbage is collected twice a week, trash is collected weekly, and glass bottles are collected once a month.

Manufacture and sale of adulterated food and beverages are prohibited. Official cantonal inspectors enforce control measures regularly. They inspect the water, milk, and meat, and on a random basis the other foods and containers. Sterilization of food containers is good.

Switzerland has no endemic contagious diseases. No immunizations are required except for smallpox, which is necessary for those traveling from an area of contagion. Special health measures are not necessary.

Major Cities

BERN , the capital of Switzerland since 1848, is a charming city built around the bend in the Aare River. Its "Old Europe" atmosphere is evident in arcaded walks along cobblestone streets, towering cathedrals, fountains, clock towers, and bustling open markets. An elaborate medieval clock tower and a pit in which bears (Bern's heraldic animal for seven centuries) are kept are well known to tourists. Yet at the same time Bern offers modern shopping facilities, and ever-expanding suburbs with new apartment buildings.

The city lies in west-central Switzerland, with Alps on the south and the Jura Mountains on the northwest. Bern has a population of about 175,000 (4,000 Americans), and is the seat of the executive and legislative branches of the Swiss Government. As an industrial center, Bern manufactures precision instruments, machinery, textiles, chemicals, pharmaceuticals, and chocolate.

ZURICH is located at the north end of the Lake of Zurich, and is surrounded by verdant hills with residential areas extending along the lake on either side. To the south, the snow-capped Glarus Alps can be seen on clear days. The city is situated in the Swiss central plateau which extends from the Alps to the German border.

Zurich, Switzerland's largest city, is the center of finance, commerce, and industry in the German-speaking section of Switzerland. It is also the hub of the country's printing and publishing industry. The old part of town reflects a long historical past. Occupied as early as the Neolithic period, Zurich joined the Swiss Federation in 1351. It has a famous polytechnic school, the largest university in Switzerland, and several excellent museums. Shopping facilities are varied and of the highest quality.

About 7,500 Americans reside in Zurich's U.S. consular district, which covers an area with a total population of 3.3 million.

GENEVA is a part, though sometimes an atypical one, of Switzerland. With its nearly half a million residents and its teeming international organizations, it is the center of more intergovernmental activity per capita than any other city in the world. The diplomatic community—members of national missions and intergovernmental organizations and their families—exceeds 22,000; international governmental and nongovernmental agencies with headquarters of major offices in Geneva total 100; and approximately the same number of nations maintain permanent missions in the city.

The hub of all this activity is the Palais des Nations—once the home of the League of Nations and now a major center for U.N. meetings and organizations. Close to 5,000 meetings take place annually in the Palais; other international organizations also house meetings throughout the year.

From time to time Geneva is a front-page dateline, with a summit conference among the "big four" or a meeting of foreign ministers summoned to try to bring peace to some trouble spot like Africa or the Middle East. But even when Geneva diplomacy is not making headlines, it is still working steadily to improve international relations and to make the world a better place.

Major activities in Geneva include

the development of programs for combating disease; for expanding trade; for helping refugees and migrants seeking lives free of tyranny, strife, and hunger; for training people in industry and agriculture; and for utilizing to the fullest weather and communications satellites. Representatives of the U.S. and the Soviet Union meet in Geneva for the Strategic Arms Limitation Talks (SALT). Arms control and disarmament is another major part of continuing Geneva diplomacy; the Conference of the Committee on Disarmament (CCD)—already the author of several arms control treaties—meets here. These major intergovernmental organizations also meet in Geneva:

International Labor Organization (ILO);
World Health Organization (WHO);
International Telecommunication Union (ITU);
World Meteorological Organization (WMO);
World Intellectual Property Organization (WIPO);
U.N. Conference on Trade and Development (UNCTAD);
U.N. Economic Commission for Europe (ECE);
General Agreement on Tariffs and Trade (GATT);
International Bureau of Education (IBE);
U.N. High Commissioner for Refugees (UNHCR);
Intergovernmental Committee on European Migration (ICEM);
World Tourism Organization (WTO);
International Narcotics Control Board (INCB);
Division of Narcotic Drugs (DND);
U.N. Fund for Drug Abuse Control (UNFDAC);
European Free Trade Association (EFTA);

European Organization for Nuclear Research (CERN).

The U.S. participates in the activities of all of the above, except CERN, ILO, and EFTA.

Among major nongovernmental organizations in Geneva are the International Committee of the Red Cross and the League of Red Cross Societies, the World Council of Churches, the World Jewish Congress, the International Commission of Jurists, the Boy Scouts World Bureau, and the European Broadcasting Union.

Geneva is located on the Rhone River where it emerges from Lake Geneva in the extreme southwest corner of Switzerland. The Canton of Geneva is surrounded on three sides by France and is connected to the rest of Switzerland by a narrow strip of land that runs along the west side of Lake Geneva. Lying on gently rolling hills along both banks of the Rhone at an altitude of 1,200 feet, Geneva is dominated on the northwest by the Jura Mountains and on the south by the Saleve, a long, low mountain that forms a distinctive landmark. Mont Blanc, the highest mountain in Europe, is visible on clear days. The other ranges of the Alps of the Haute Savoie in France and the Swiss Alps on the Valais rise steeply at the other end of Lake Geneva, 50 miles away.

Geneva's temperate climate is variable due to the city's location. It is generally pleasant from April to December. Winters are often damp with overcast skies, but are never severe. Although nearby mountains are snow-covered throughout the winter, Geneva itself gets little snow. Temperatures rarely drop below freezing during the day. Summers are generally mild and pleasant with a few hot spells. Frequent rains occur in spring and early summer; temperatures are cool and crisp in both spring and autumn. The normal seasonal weather is affected from time to time by two winds characteristic of many parts of Switzerland: the *bise,* a north wind that blows from Lake Geneva and brings a chilling cold in the winter and clear skies and pleasant temperatures in the summer; and the *föhn,* a south wind that is often oppressively warm and humid.

The bridge to understanding the real spirit of Geneva is the realization that it is an international city. It is not only a geographical crossroads of Europe, but also a crossroads of international minds. Much of its population consists of diplomats and international civil servants who go to Geneva for a few years' assignment and frequently end up staying forever. It is a peaceful city and its name is symbolic of peace.

Geneva, more than any other city of its size, is polyglot. French is the language of everyday dealings, but German, Italian, Spanish, English, Russian, Chinese, Japanese, and Arabic are also heard commonly in its streets. Probably every language can be heard sooner or later in the corridors of the Palais.

Geneva's History

Historically, Geneva is of great interest. Founded in the first century B.C. by a Celtic tribe, it became an outpost of the Roman Empire and an important episcopal see. After the Empire collapsed, Geneva served as a pawn in dynastic and church politics of the feudal period until the 14th century, when it achieved independence. Its first official links with the Swiss

Confederation were in the form of alliances in the 16th century with Fribourg and Bern, undertaken to protect the city's independence. Shortly thereafter, the Protestant Reformation spread to Geneva and, after the arrival of John Calvin in 1536, the city was governed by a Calvinist theocracy. It became the chief center of Reformation doctrine on the continent, and a haven for Protestant refugees from all over Europe. The Reformation and the period of Calvinist rule have had deep and lasting effects on the city's political, cultural, and economic life. French Protestant refugees, incidentally, introduced watchmaking into Geneva, thus establishing Switzerland's highly important export industry.

Another important phase in Geneva's history was its association with the French liberal movement in the 18th century. Before the French Revolution, Rousseau and Voltaire lived in and near Geneva for long periods. Through their contacts and writings, they propagated liberal ideas that had profound repercussions throughout the Western World and on Geneva's own political development. In 1814, the city joined the Swiss Confederation, thus completing the territorial area of present day Switzerland. For the past century, Geneva has progressed into a prosperous and flourishing center of commerce, tourism, and international politics.

Geneva's general appearance belies its long and distinguished history. While the Old City, a section on the left bank of the Rhone, is composed largely of buildings dating from the 16th to the 18th centuries, Geneva is mostly a modern city, reflecting growth in population and expansion in commerce and other affairs of the past century. It seems smaller than it is.

From the center of town one can walk to most of its important landmarks within 10 minutes. From the Old City and its maze of picturesque, narrow streets crowded with antique shops, visitors can stroll along a lakeside promenade for a view of Mont Blanc or the Jet d'Eau. The Jet d'Eau, an incredible "fountain" was created in 1886 by an engineer in charge of Geneva's water supply. The water rushes from the base of the fountain at a speed of 125 miles per hour, with an output of 110 gallons per second.

More than 100,000 American tourists and other temporary visitors pass through the city each year. In 1977, at least 1,000 American delegates participated in conferences held in Geneva. About 200 American business firms are represented in Geneva; many use the city as a center for their European and worldwide operations.

A city of beautiful parks, gardens, and promenades, Geneva can be enjoyed at any time of the year.

Recreation

Bern and Zurich

Skiing is Switzerland's major sport, and there are many ski areas within easy reach of the large cities. Most of the slopes have English-speaking instructors. In Bern, there are ample opportunities for other individual sports, such as golf, hunting, fishing, wind surfing, sailing, swimming, and hiking. Sailing lessons are given on the Lake of Thun, and mountaineering is taught by the Swiss Alpine Club. There are no public tennis courts, but some visitors make arrangements at private clubs. In Zurich, boating and sailing are available on Lake Zurich, and golf and other sports can be played in various spots throughout the city.

Both cities are centrally located for travel, and are within weekend driving distance of France, Italy, Germany, and Austria. Magnificent scenery and charming hotels add to the color.

Countless opportunities exist for camping and hiking near Bern and all over Switzerland. Bern itself boasts a botanical garden, a rose garden overlooking the old town, a small outdoor zoo with play areas for children, the famous bear pits, and a local mountain park with night skiing in the winter. Bern has several museums and a number of small art galleries, plus occasional exhibitions and fairs. Outstanding museums are also found in other Swiss cities.

No restrictions are placed on photography except where posted, such as in military areas.

The variety of entertainment in Bern is impressive, although little cosmopolitan "nightlife" exists. About 20 film theaters show American, French, German, and Italian movies with subtitles in German and French. Most American movies are shown in Bern. The City Theater offers operas, plays, ballets, and operettas, while smaller theaters offer plays and cabarets. Guest performances by Swiss and other international classical and jazz musicians are common, and lectures, travelogues, etc., are given frequently. Most of the performances are presented in German, although some nightclub acts are in French. Bern has four nightclubs, several bars, and many restaurants featuring Swiss specialties. In general, Swiss law prohibits children from attending film theaters at night.

The principal local festivities are: Swiss National Day (August 1); Labor Day (May 1), when small parades are held; and the Onion Market, held on the fourth Monday in November. The Onion Market features hundreds of market stalls selling only onions. Also, on this day restaurants serve only onion dishes.

Zurich has an opera, symphony orchestra, a number of Chamber Groups, and a German theater. Local groups occasionally produce plays in English, and first-run movies, often in English, are shown.

Geneva

Geneva is a skier's paradise, with good slopes just 40 minutes away. Cross-country skiing also is very popular and can be enjoyed in Geneva's immediate environs. Other recreational opportunities include boating, hiking, swimming, mountain climbing, fishing, cycling, horseback riding, bowling, ice skating, basketball, and Little League baseball. Public golf courses are located in Divonne and Evian in France, and Geneva has a private club. All are expensive. Several private tennis clubs are available. Two excellent year-round pools are among the several available. Lac Leman is polluted in some places, and is cold for swimming even in summer.

Geneva boasts beautiful parks with sandboxes, swings, merry-go-rounds, and other play equipment. Among the many amusements for children are excellent circuses, a delightful puppet theater, and frequent small fairs with rides of various kinds. Spectator sports include ice hockey, soccer, boxing, handball, basketball, bicycle racing, horse racing, ski competition, rugby, and sailing.

Most entertainment common to the U.S. is available in Geneva. The city has many movie theaters, and American and British films are shown. Local stage productions are in French, except for plays presented by the Geneva English Drama Society and the Players Theatre, an international group. Occasionally, small professional productions are brought to Geneva from England. Good entertainment is offered at the Grand Theatre, but it is sometimes difficult to obtain tickets as they are sold on subscription.

Excellent programs are offered including concerts, symphonies, soloists in recital, opera, ballet, and jazz. For the art lover, consistently fine exhibitions are shown at the many small galleries throughout the city. Geneva has excellent museums, including the Museum of Art and History, a museum of natural history, and an ethnographic museum.

Fine restaurants abound, most serving French or international cuisine. Others feature native Swiss cooking or foreign specialties. Restaurant prices vary widely but are high, and generally above those in Washington, D.C. The city has a number of night-clubs—all expensive. They are mainly for after-dinner entertainment.

Notes for Travelers

No problems arise in traveling from the U.S. to Switzerland. Direct daily flights are scheduled to both Zurich and Geneva, and many connecting flights are available from major European cities.

Visas are not required for American citizens. Only a valid passport is necessary for entry.

Rifles and shotguns can be taken into Switzerland in any combination up to three (maximum 6.2 caliber). Ammunition is widely available, and need not be imported. In the Canton of Bern, a license or permit is not required to own or carry nonautomatic firearms; in the Canton of Zurich, a license is required to carry or transport all firearms; and in the Canton of Geneva, all arms should be registered, but a special license is not required to carry such weapons.

Religious services in English are conducted in Bern, Zurich, and Geneva. Bern has one Catholic church with a Sunday mass, and an Anglican church which serves as the parish church for the U.S., Canadian, and British Protestant community. Several Catholic and Protestant churches in Zurich schedule English services, and a Conservative synagogue also is available. English-language services are widely available in Geneva churches, including Episcopal, Catholic, Baptist, Lutheran, Quaker, Presbyterian, and Christian Science.

The Swiss franc, divided into 100 *rappen* or *centimes,* is the basic unit of currency. The exchange rate is Sfrs. 1.788 (1979, floating) = U.S.$1. Geneva, an international banking center, has excellent facilities.

The metric system of weights and measures is used throughout Switzerland.

The U.S. Embassy in Switzerland is located at Jubilaumsstrasse 93, Bern. The Consulate General is at 141 Zollikerstrasse, 8008 Zurich; the U.S. Mission, at 80 rue de Lausanne, Geneva.

Turkey

TURKEY's past is as fascinating as its present and future are promising. The country is rich in the relics of a long and varied history. Ankara, the capital, contains Byzantine and Roman ruins, and is said to have been the site of the church of Galatia, which was addressed by St. Paul in his New Testament epistle. Within a day's drive of Ankara are Hittite and Phrygian ruins; ancient Greek cities; several of the biblical Seven Churches in Asia; Seljuk and Ottoman monuments; and Istanbul, the fabled capital of the Byzantine and Ottoman empires.

Area, Geography, Climate

With an area of 296,185 square miles, Turkey is larger than any European country except the Soviet Union. Lying between the Black and Mediterranean Seas, it extends approximately 950 miles east to west and 400 miles north to south. If superimposed on a map of the U.S., Turkey would reach from Washington, D.C. to Kansas City, Missouri.

Turkey is divided into two main geographical areas, Anatolia and Thrace. Anatolia is a high plateau bounded on the north by the Pontic Mountains and on the south by the Taurus Mountains. The average elevation ranges from 2,000 feet in the west to over 6,000 feet in the eastern area.

The central portion has a topography of broad, treeless valleys and plains interrupted by rounded hills. In the east, the valleys and plains give way to more mountainous terrain with peaks rising to over 10,000 feet, including Mt. Ararat where Noah's Ark supposedly landed. The plateau is skirted by narrow coastal plains on the northeast and south. The climate of the plateau region is semiarid, with hot, dry summers and cold winters. Annual precipitation averages about 20 inches on the edge of the region, decreasing to about 14 inches toward the center.

Ankara, in the north central portion of Anatolia, has an annual precipitation of 14 inches, accumulating chiefly from November to May. Clear, cloudless days are the rule from June through October. The mean temperature for January is 30°F, and for July, 74.5°F. Winds are moderate; however, temperatures sometimes reach the low 90s. Nights are normally cool. During winter, the snow is usually sufficient for skiing on Elmadag, near Ankara, and on Uludag, near Istanbul.

The region of Trakya and the coastal areas of (southern and western) Turkey have Mediterranean climates with hot, humid summers and mild to cold winters. South of the Taurus Mountains around Adana or Antalya,

299

annual precipitation exceeds 28 inches, and average temperatures range from 94°F in August down to 58°F in January. Around the Marmara Sea and Istanbul, the average temperature in July is 83°F, and in January, about 35°F.

The Black Sea region has cooler summers and warmer winters than the other coastal areas. Rainfall is also heavier, ranging from 25 inches in the Istanbul area to 98 inches at Rize in the east.

Because of the great differences in climate in the regions of Turkey, the Turks are able to produce a wide variety of crops; bananas, figs, tea, tobacco, cotton, and citrus fruits in the subtropical areas, and cereal grains in the Anatolian region.

Population

Turkey's population is estimated at about 46.1 million, and is increasing at an annual rate of 25 per thousand. Istanbul, Ankara, Izmir, and Adana are the largest cities. Generally, population decreases from northwest to southeast, with parts of southeast Turkey quite sparsely populated. Most citizens of Turkey are ethnic Turks, although a large Kurdish minority is in the southeast, and smaller minorities of Arabs, Azerbaijanis, Turkiz (people born in Turkestan), Lazzes, and Georgians exist. In addition, there are minorities of Greeks, Armenians, and Jews, especially in Istanbul.

The most widely spoken language is Turkish. Although the minorities often keep alive their own languages, they usually speak Turkish as well. The Kurds are the major exceptions to this rule, as many of them speak only Kurdish.

Nearly all ethnic Turks are Sunni Moslems, but some of the Moslem minorities are Shiite. The distinctive flavor of the dervish orders of Islam has almost disappeared from Turkey, as these orders were dissolved by the founder of the Turkish Republic, Ataturk. Despite the overwhelming predominance of Moslems, no state religion has been established, as Ataturk wanted to establish a secular state in place of the religiously dominated Ottoman Empire.

The Koran provides a complete social code, including certain dietary laws, for Moslems. While these Koranic structures are quite rigidly observed in the rural areas, the Ataturk reforms have significantly affected life in the large cities. Although even educated Turks do not usually eat pork, many do drink alcohol and are less than wholly observant of the rules of prayer. For other Turkish citizens, life continues much as it did in the past. Thus, although the veil has been abolished and women in the cities walk about in Western clothes, the baggy pants characteristic of rural Anatolia are still widely worn, and in the country it is by no means unusual for women to cover their faces as a man walks by.

Government

Turkey has been a republic since 1923. Its present constitution came into effect in 1961 following the overthrow of Adnan Menderes by the armed forces. The constitution provides for a President, a two-house legislature, and a Prime Minister. The President is elected by Parliament. The Prime Minister is appointed by the President from members of Parliament and is the effective executive and political leader of the country. The cabinet selected by the Prime Minister and approved by the President must command majority support in the lower house.

The lower branch of Parliament, the National Assembly, has 450 members who serve until elections are called, at least once in four years. The Senate has 150 elected members, one-third elected every two years, 15 appointed by the President to six-year terms, and 18 life members.

Administratively, Turkey is highly centralized. It is divided into 67 provinces (*vilayets*), each governed by a *vali* (governor) who is appointed from Ankara and comes under the Ministry of Interior. While major cities supply their own utilities, police, and public works, the central government provides such services in rural areas. Central government involvement is much greater than in the U.S. In the country, the Jandarma, a military organization under the Ministry of Interior, provides police protection. Local councils are charged with administering those matters not reserved to the central government. In practice, however, Ankara makes decisions on nearly all matters, and these decisions are then put into effect by the *vali*.

The judicial system is based on several continental law codes that have been adapted to the Turkish situation. The system of courts comes under the Ministry of Justice and, like the administrative mechanism, contains a high degree of centralization. Turkish law is framed in general terms in order to leave the power of interpretation with the judiciary. The intent is for the law to be worded in such a way that the judge can fit it to the needs of a particular case.

The Justice Party (JP) government of Suleyman Demirel, which emphasized economic development, an activist foreign policy, and close ties with the United States and NATO, won reelection in 1969. But internal divisions in the Justice Party and widespread student unrest weakened the position of the government. On March 12, 1971, the four senior leaders of the armed forces issued a memorandum indicating they had lost confidence in Parliament and the Demirel government. They called for reforms and the restoration of law and order, implying direct military intervention otherwise.

Demirel resigned and for the next two-and-a-half years the country was ruled by 'above-party' governments headed by Nihat Erim and Ferit Melen, and a coalition government headed by Naim Talu. In 1973, the Republican People's Party (RPP) under its new leader, Bulent Ecevit, won the largest share of the vote in the national elections and 185 seats in the National Assembly. Ecevit finally formed a coalition government with the national Salvation Party in February 1974, but the coalition collapsed the following September.

Turkey then was governed by caretaker cabinets until April 1975, when a Demirel-led "Nationalist Front" coalition of four center-right parties received a vote of confidence.

General elections in June 1977 resulted in large gains for both Demirel's JP and Ecevit's RPP, mostly at the expense of two small centrist parties, the Democratic Party (DP) and the Republican Reliance Party (RR); however, although the RPP won 41 percent of the vote and the JP won 37 percent, neither party succeeded in winning a majority of the seats in the

National Assembly. A minority cabinet headed by Ecevit failed to win a vote of confidence and was replaced, after only a month in office, by a new center-right coalition, headed by Demirel and composed of the JP, NSP, and ultra-nationalist Nationalist Action Party (NAP). The latest Demirel government fell on December 31, 1977, after only five months in office, following the defection of 11 JP deputies.

The present Cabinet, formed by Ecevit on January 5, 1978, consists of 35 ministers, 22 from the RPP, two from the RR, one from the DP, and 10 independents, all of whom had resigned from the JP. The moderate program of Ecevit's government, which does not consider itself to be a coalition, has given main emphasis to ending domestic violence, improving the country's economic situation, and resolving foreign policy problems.

Arts, Science, Education

The religious school system of the Ottoman Empire was abolished during the early years of the Republic. Since then, Turkey has made great strides in establishing a modern educational system. In theory, education is free, compulsory between ages seven and 12, and coeducational. In the large cities the education system offers primary, secondary, *lycée*, and university education, but villages may not even have a primary school. The literacy rate in Turkey is about 62 percent.

Turkey has nine universities and a number of technical institutions, all of which are state-sponsored. Admission to the universities is based on competitive examination. As in many countries, children of upper- and middle-class families more frequently receive the *lycée* education necessary to pass the entrance examination, and their families can best afford to forego the earnings of their children who are in a university.

Ankara University, Hacettepe University, and the Middle East Technical University (METU) are located in Ankara. Ankara and Hacettepe offer degrees in a broad range of fields, while METU provides a science and engineering curriculum.

Istanbul University also offers a broad range of subjects, and Istanbul Technical University gives degrees in engineering and related subjects. Bosphorus University is the newest Turkish institution of higher education. It was established in 1972, when the former college level of Robert College was turned over to the Turkish Government. It offers degrees in engineering, business administration, and the humanities, and, as in the case of METU in Ankara, all its classes are conducted in English. The *lycée* (high school) level of Robert College still continues as a separate institution supported by the U.S. Government and private sources.

Ankara and Istanbul offer extensive and interesting cultural opportunities. Ankara has five state-operated theaters, including one that features opera, ballet, and classical plays. The other theaters offer local productions, light foreign operettas, or current foreign plays. The Presidential Symphony Orchestra in Ankara and the Istanbul State Symphony Orchestra give regular concerts, often featuring soloists of international caliber. The State Conservatory, National Library, and private theaters add to the daily musical and dramatic bill of fare. The theater season in Ankara runs from October through May.

Dancing and folk song programs may be seen in all parts of Turkey throughout the year. In December, the Mevlana Order of Whirling Dervishes has a week-long festival in Konya, during which it is allowed to perform ritual dances.

The Turkish-American Association (the American binational center) in Ankara schedules cultural presentations by American artists, as well as lectures, tours, hobby clubs, discussion groups, film showings, and a theater group.

Of special interest among the activities carried on by other binational cultural centers in Ankara is the French Cine Club, which regularly screens recent French films. Both the British and German cultural centers sponsor concerts, lectures, and solo performances by national artists. Art exhibits are held in major cities, both in binational centers and in local galleries. The Ankara Art Lovers' Club provides a center for those interested in local art.

Of major interest are the archaeological excavations currently under way in various parts of Turkey. Gordium (within 100 kilometers of Ankara), Sardis, and Aphrodisias are among current centers of archaeological work. A foreigner interested in archaeology can visit scores of ruins dating from Hittite through Ottoman times. Among these are Efes, Bergama, and Troy in Western Turkey. A round trip from Izmir to the spectacular Hellenic Ruins of Efes can be completed in a day, with time for sight-seeing.

Commerce and Industry

In spite of a steady rise in the number of new industries, Turkey remains a predominantly agricultural country. Agricultural and animal products, fisheries, and forestry account for about 25 percent of the nation's income. Chief agricultural products are cereals (wheat, barley, corn, and rice), cotton, sugar beets, vegetables, nuts, tobacco, and fruits (including grapes, figs, and olives).

Manufacturing, mining, and utilities also account for about 25 percent of the national income. The major industries are textiles and yarn, food and beverages, iron and steel, cement, petroleum refining, and the mining of coal, lignite, copper, chrome, iron ore, and manganese.

Turkey's chief exports are cotton, tobacco, fruits, nuts, cotton yarn, textiles, food products, and minerals. The country's chief imports are oil, machinery and electrical equipment, motor vehicles and parts, other transportation equipment, chemicals, and iron and steel mill products.

Turkey is moving gradually toward a full customs union with the European Economic Community (EEC) by 1995. The EEC countries as a group account for about 55 percent of Turkey's imports and exports.

In the late 1970s, the U.S. supplied about eight percent of Turkey's imports, and bought 10 percent of its exports. The Federal Republic of Germany is Turkey's major trading partner, supplying about 22 percent of its imports, and buying the same percentage of its exports. Approximately 10 percent of Turkey's imports and five percent of its exports are in trade with countries of Eastern Europe and the U.S.S.R.

The Government of Turkey works under a development plan

which aims at economic growth in all sectors, and particularly at broadening and expanding industrial production. Large expenditures are allocated each year to meet objectives.

Since 1974, Turkey no longer receives major concessional economic assistance from the U.S., although it still receives around $100 million per year from the individual countries of the European Economic Community or from the EEC itself. Project financing to pay for large government investment expenditures now comes primarily from the World Bank and from the Export-Import Banks of the U.S., Germany, the U.K., France, Italy, and Japan. Need for concessional financing to provide investment credits for major projects has also given increased trade opportunities to the U.S.S.R. and the countries of Eastern Europe.

The post-1973 OPEC price increases and the subsequent world recession hit Turkey hard. Imports have increased rapidly, while exports have stagnated and worker remittances have declined. In order to maintain a real annual seven percent growth in GNP over the past several years, Turkey has been forced to borrow heavily abroad, both from public and private sources. Consequently, both the long-term and short-term foreign debt, payable in foreign exchange, have risen rapidly.

A number of Turkish industrial establishments are owned by the state. These include companies manufacturing fertilizers, cigarettes, iron and steel products, sugar refineries, cement plants, petroleum refineries, and breweries. The Government of Turkey is also part owner of various other establishments, including textile mills, banks, cold storage depots, and mineral processing facilities.

Turkey also has a growing and well-established private sector. Its government generally welcomes private foreign investment that benefits the national economy according to certain criteria. New industries receive tariff and quota protection.

Private foreign investment in Turkey, however, is not substantial in comparison to the size of the Turkish economy. Total foreign investment is generally estimated to be about $300 million, of which approximately one-third is American. American companies involved in manufacturing, either through equity or licensing in Turkey, include the Squibb and Pfizer pharmaceutical firms, International Harvester, Ford, Chrysler, Uniroyal, Goodyear, Singer Sewing Machine, CPC, and Mobil Oil.

Turkey has a set of modern labor laws providing for freedom of association, collective bargaining, and the right to strike. The legislation is developing partly by legislative refinement and partly by usage. Two confederations of trade unions are available— the major one devoted to economic, nonpolitical unionism, and the second, a Marxist-oriented small confederation espousing political unionism. On an average, about 1,200 collective contracts are signed each year. About one-and-a-half million workers are organized in the public and private sectors, or about 50 to 60 percent of the nonagricultural labor force.

Transportation

The Turkish state railways provide service to many points within Turkey and have key routes connecting Europe, the Middle East, and Asia. Direct rail service is offered from major European cities to Istanbul by the

Direct Orient/Marmara Express. All European services terminate at Sirkeci Railway Station, Istanbul's European station. The trip from London and Paris takes nearly three days. Passengers continuing on to Ankara and Adana transfer to Haydarpasa Railway Station, Istanbul's Asian station, by ferry service from Karakoy pier near Galata Bridge. Direct passenger service, Istanbul to Izmir, is offered by ferry from Istanbul to the post of Bandirma, and by connecting train from Bandirma to Basmane Station in Izmir. From Haydarpasa Station and Ankara, passengers may continue south to Adana, Beirut, or Baghdad, or east to Lake Van, Tabriz, and Tehran.

Railway service is generally slower than bus service, but dining and sleeping cars on both international and domestic lines help make the trip more comfortable. Meals served in dining cars are considered satisfactory.

Turkish Airlines provides service to many points within Turkey, Europe, and the Middle East with daily flights connecting Istanbul, Ankara, Izmir, and Adana. Pan Am, in curtailing its international service, eliminated all Turkish flights in July 1981. It had previously served both Istanbul and Ankara.

Istanbul is the primary international airport and offers service to Europe, the Middle East, and around the world. Ankara offers service to Europe and the Middle East, Izmir offers service to Europe, and Adana offers connections to Cyprus. More than 20 scheduled airlines connect Turkey with all parts of the world. Bus and taxi service connect airports with city terminals. The airport terminal buildings at Istanbul (Yesilkoy) and Ankara (Esenboga) are inconvenient

and outdated, but a new terminal is under construction at Istanbul.

Ships of American Export Lines and Prudential Grace Lines call at Turkish ports, including Istanbul and Izmir on the Mediterranean Sea, when cargo requires. Schedules may be obtained from the line's agents in major port cities. Turkish Maritime Lines provides ferry service for passengers and automobiles between Europe and Asia at Istanbul (across the Bosphorus) and at Canakkale (across the Dardenelles). Turkish Maritime Lines also provides service to Adriatic, Aegean, and Mediterranean Sea ports, including Barcelona, Marseille, Genoa, Naples, Piraeus, Athens, Alexandria, Beirut, Limmassol, and Hanifa, as well as to Black Sea ports.

Domestic intercity bus service in Turkey features comfortable reclining seats and picture windows. Travel time is somewhat slower than by automobile.

The main intercity highways are generally well-paved and properly maintained. However, many traffic hazards make them dangerous—for instance, slow moving farm equipment, animals, trucks, buses, cars passing on hills, and vehicle repairs made in the middle of the road. In general, the unexpected can, and frequently does, happen. Winter snows and ice require extra caution in city and highway driving.

Traffic moves on the right. Road signs are identical to those used in Europe. In October 1973, the Bosphorus Bridge was opened in Istanbul as part of Turkey's 50th-anniversary celebrations. The bridge enables motorists to drive between Europe and Asia for a small toll, eliminating the wait for ferry boats.

City roads are generally good, but are crowded with all kinds of vehicles, including horse carts. Although traffic moves on the right, the *dolmus* (shared taxi traveling regular routes) and other taxis do not always observe this rule. This eccentricity can be confusing and dangerous, even to the experienced driver. Cities have municipal bus systems. In smaller cities, horse-drawn carts may supplement *dolmus* service.

All taxi fares are fixed. Nevertheless, drivers may attempt to overcharge so it is advisable to settle the fare in advance. Tipping *dolmus* or taxi drivers is not customary.

Official Turkish Government vehicles, including police cars, are painted black; fire engines are red; ambulances are painted white with a red crescent, the symbol of Turkey's equivalent of the Red Cross, on the side.

To import a car into Turkey and obtain license plates, Turkish law requires that the car be covered by Turkish traffic insurance underwritten by a Turkish insurance company (or a foreign firm licensed to do business in Turkey), and that the car be in safe operating condition as certified by Turkish Traffic Police. Required safety equipment which must be in the car at the time of inspection includes a first aid kit, safety reflectors, and snow chains.

Automobile repair shops located all over Turkey are capable of most types of repairs. Labor charges are relatively low, but the quality of work may only be fair. Replacement parts for older American and European cars are generally available locally, but are difficult to find for newer models.

A valid U.S. drivers license may be exchanged for a Turkish license, or an international permit is acceptable for those intending to reside in Turkey. For travelers, the international license is ordinarily recommended.

Communications

Telephone and telegraph services are satisfactory, although rates are high for both domestic and international phone calls. Airmail service to and from the U.S. is fast and reliable, with letters taking from four to seven days between Ankara and Washington, D.C.

The government-owned Turkish Radio and Television operates all transmitting facilities. Private radio broadcasting is not permitted. AM (medium-wave) radio stations broadcast in all parts of Turkey. Programming includes popular music from America and Europe. Turkey also has long-wave radio stations, which broadcast news (in Turkish), as well as music. Ankara has an FM-multiplex stereo radio station broadcasting classical and popular music, plus two regular FM stations. VOA and the BBC broadcast to Turkey via short- and medium-wave bands.

Ankara, Izmir, and Istanbul have television stations broadcasting (in Turkish) news, music, movies, and some children's programs. With well-placed antennas, Izmir residents can receive TV programs from Greek stations, Istanbul receives programs from Bulgaria and Romania, while Adana receives programs from nearby Arab countries, Cyprus, and Israel. Turkish television operates on the European standard of 625 lines, but can be received on a normal American TV set without an adapter. Sound converters are available.

Ankara, Istanbul, and Izmir have many shops selling foreign news publications, including the International Herald Tribune, Time, and Newsweek. In addition, British, French, German, and Italian publications are widely sold. Periodicals usually arrive earlier at the Turkish newsdealers than through the mail. In addition to many Turkish-language publications, several foreign-language publications are printed in Istanbul and Ankara. The Daily News, an English-language daily newspaper, and Outlook and The Week, both weekly magazines, are all published in Ankara and available in other major Turkish cities.

Ankara has libraries of the Turkish Government and of American, British, French, and German governmental cultural services which are open to the public. The American Air Station in Ankara also has a library. American libraries are also in Adana, Istanbul, and Izmir.

Health

Health services and standards in Turkey's larger cities are generally acceptable, but care should be taken in rural areas. Medical facilities for U.S. Government employees are provided by the USAF Clinic in Ankara, and by the U.S.-assisted Bristol Hospital in Istanbul. There are other clinics and small hospitals available to military personnel or, for a fee, to contract personnel.

Local health standards necessitate certain precautions. Water impurities are prevalent due to the absence of filters in the system and irregular water pressure and service. Americans are advised to drink boiled or chlorinated water. Bottled spring water, relatively clear in appearance, is available in

restaurants and from street vendors and grocery shops. It is generally drunk as is, but as a precaution should be treated with chlorine or boiled before drinking. City water is not potable and should be boiled a minimum of 20 minutes, or properly treated with chlorine and then filtered.

Local wine, bottled soda, fruit juice, and beer are considered safe to drink. The USAF Clinic advises that milk and yogurt purchased in bottles from local shops are considered unsafe. Nevertheless, many Americans use local milk products—including milk, yogurt, and cheese—with no apparent ill effects. Many local shops do not, however, have adequate refrigeration. When purchasing local milk and yogurt, one should check the day and date stamp on the lid to determine freshness.

Locally produced beef, lamb, pork, and poultry can be of good quality when care is exercised in patronizing refrigerator-equipped and sanitary shops. In the smaller towns, only lamb may be available. Fresh fish and seafood are available in the major cities in winter; in summer, except near the sea, fish and seafood are out of season and difficult to obtain. Fresh vegetables are generally of good quality, but should be thoroughly washed and soaked in a mixture of water and bleach prior to serving, particularly if they are to be served raw.

Some serious health hazards are peculiar to Turkey. Although the Ankara area has not had an epidemic for a number of years, the incidence of tuberculosis and intestinal diseases among the local population is high. Servants should have medical examinations, particularly if one has young children. Chest x-rays are performed by the Turkish Government at no charge and a complete examination costs about 52 (U.S.) dollars.

Rabies is quite prevalent in Turkey, and children should be cautioned against handling strange or stray animals. Facilities for quarantining rabies-suspect animals are available.

Major Cities

The contrast between old and new, East and West, is apparent in **ANKARA** , the nation's capital. The city is located in the western portion of the Anatolian plateau at an altitude of 3,000 feet, and is dramatically situated at the center of a bowl formed by rugged hills. The climate is generally pleasant; its rare extremes of hot and cold are moderated by the dryness of the air, and in summer by a mild breeze. Particulate smog, caused by widespread use of lignite coal for heating, gives the city a drab appearance for much of the winter.

Although the area around Ankara has been inhabited for many thousands of years, the general aspect of the present city is modern, with wide boulevards and a steadily increasing number of large office buildings and apartment houses. Ankara was a relatively small town when Kemal Ataturk moved the Turkish capital there from Istanbul in 1923. It now has a population of about two million. The Turkish people have worked energetically to create this new city and are proud of their creation. Construction continues at a great rate, and Ankara bustles in an atmosphere of activity, achievement, and progress.

The many government offices, somewhat severe in style, indicate the administrative character of the city. In certain areas, single-family homes may still be found, but these sections, with their pleasant tree-shaded streets and attractive gardens, are decreasing steadily. Ulus (the old city), situated on two steep hills, is dominated by an ancient citadel. Its narrow, winding streets, mosques, and small houses give it a color and interest that is lacking in the newer parts of the city. Possibly the most attractive feature in Ankara is the spectacular view afforded by its location in the hilly Anatolian countryside.

The foreign community in Ankara is predominantly American. The roughly 2,500 Americans include military and civilian employees of the U.S. Government, exchange students and professors, businessmen, and their dependents. The rest of the foreign colony is diplomatic (including 50 diplomatic missions), except for a few businessmen from Western Europe. Generally speaking, American visitors to Ankara go on business rather than as tourists.

ADANA is situated in southeastern Turkey, 30 miles from the Mediterranean Sea, a seven- to eight-hour drive from Ankara or Damascus. The fourth largest city in Turkey, with a population estimated at over 400,000, it is a provincial capital oriented to the rich agricultural land that surrounds it.

Adana is a rapidly expanding agricultural center. It is comprised of an ancient town center located on the banks of the Seyhan River, with growing residential and slum areas surrounding it.

Adana's population is composed of ethnic Turks, Arabs, and Kurds. The vast majority of the American community is made up of U.S. Air

Force and attached civilian personnel stationed at Incirlik, a Turkish air base nine miles east of the city. About 400 American families reside in Adana proper. While Turkish is the principal language throughout the consular district, Kurdish is widely spoken in the eastern provinces, and occasionally some Arabic is spoken in Adana and other southern areas. English and French, however, are second languages for many public leaders and officials.

It is difficult to adequately describe the climate. Essentially, the summers are very hot and humid, with rainfall rare. In winter, the temperature rarely falls below freezing, yet rains that last for days make it seem colder. Fall and spring are magnificent with clear sunny days and pleasantly cool evenings. When compared to the U.S., the climate in Adana resembles the cotton growing areas of Mississippi and Texas, and is not unlike Washington, D.C.

The Adana area is often described as the "Texas of Turkey," and in some ways it is an apt description. Located on the flat Cilician plain where cotton and citrus fruits are the principal crops, and where many wealthy farmers and textile manufacturers live, the province does have some superficial resemblances to that state.

History does not record a period when Adana was not inhabited. Excavations made at Tarsus and Mersin (within an hour's drive of Adana) have shown levels of occupation going back to Neolithic times, possibly as early as 6000 B.C.

Various groups have conquered Adana and have settled there. Alexander the Great passed through the area during his conquest of the Middle East from the Persian Empire. After Alexander's death, Adana became part of the Seleucid State. After centuries of rule by the Greeks, the area was conquered by the Romans. The city received many gifts from the Roman sovereigns, and among them was a bridge across the Seyhan River that is still in use today. During Roman times, the area became very important in the history of the Christian Church; St. Paul's home was in Tarsus, and much of his preaching was done there.

In A.D. 1132, Armenians took Adana, and it became a center of Armenian culture. In 1515, it was captured by the Turks and was a part of the Ottoman Empire until the end of World War I.

With fine, but undeveloped, beaches on the Mediterranean within two hours' drive, the Adana area holds some promise of eventually becoming a center of tourism. Adana is at at the crossroads between Turkey and the Arab areas.

ISTANBUL has a mild climate, considerable natural beauty, and a wealth of historical monuments. It also, unfortunately, is one of the most congested cities in the world. It is the social, intellectual, and economic capital of Turkey. Only the ancient cities of Athens, Rome, and Jerusalem can be said to rival Istanbul as so greatly influencing the course of Western history.

Straddling the Bosphorus Straits, Istanbul is situated in Europe and Asia. On the European side, the city is bisected by an inlet, the Golden Horn. To the south, Istanbul is washed by the waters of the Marmara Sea, while beyond the west walls of the city lie the rolling, treeless farmland of

Thrace. On the Asiatic side, east of the city's suburbs, the terrain for 60 miles consists of low hills, covered with scrub oak.

Istanbul's U.S. consular district includes all of Thrace (European Turkey), the land on both sides of the Bosphorus and Dardanelle Straits, the provinces bordering the Marmara Sea, and an area extending about 175 miles into Anatolia (Asiatic Turkey) and bordering the southern shore of the Black Sea.

Having a continuous history of over 2,500 years of existence, Istanbul is a mixture of ancient and modern, with its three-million population increasing annually by several hundred thousand. The city is a fascinating cross between East and West. Although it is filled with narrow, cobblestone streets, and suffers from traffic congestion and poor public services, the setting of the city is a beautiful one, with its charming old neighborhoods. Newer and more expensive neighborhoods along the Maramara Sea and the Bosphorus are very definitely modern and European in atmosphere.

IZMIR, with a metropolitan population of 900,000, is Turkey's third largest city and the unofficial capital of Aegean Turkey, the country's scenic and fruitful southwestern region. With a fine harbor midway down Turkey's western coast, it is the country's second busiest port. Its hinterland, rich in tobacco, cotton, fruits, and vegetables, makes it even more important than Istanbul as an export center. In recent years, as the Istanbul-Izmir region has become saturated, Izmir has started to develop as the country's second industrial area. The city boasts of being "the pearl of the Aegean." Increasing numbers of foreign tourists are finding that it is surrounded by some of the world's loveliest scenery.

Historically, Izmir was better known under the Greek form if its name, Symrna. It has been an important center for over 3,000 years, and has seen the passage of Hittites, Lydians, Ionian Greeks, Persians, Romans, Byzantines, Saracens, Seljuks, Tartars, Crusaders, Venetians, and Ottomans. A modern Greek invading force was driven into the sea in 1922, and the city was subsequently incorporated into the Republic of Turkey. The surrounding area abounds in relics of earlier times—especially of classical antiquity—but in Izmir itself, the only relics of earlier eras are the foundations of the earliest Greek city, a part of the Roman agora, a hilltop castle of indeterminate age, some handsome Ottoman mosques, and a few streets of rapidly disappearing 19th century buildings.

Not only the monuments, but also the people of old Symrna have given way to the new. Until World War II, the population was largely non-Turkish Greeks, Armenians, Jews, and "Leventines" (Italian, French, British, Dutch, and German nationals whose families had lived in Smyrna for generations). Today, the population is almost entirely Turkish, a large part of it first or second generation Izmirlis whose families were Turkish refugees from Greece or Bulgaria, or migrants from Anatolia. If Izmir is still the most "Western" of Turkish cities, it is so because of its location, its wealth, and its general vitality, as well as a result of its history.

Izmir is spread out along the U-shaped head of a bay which runs east-west and is surrounded mostly by high hills. The major part of the city is on the southern shore. Closest to the city center is the Konak quarter, which is both the traffic hub and the main shopping center. In appearance and atmosphere, this is the most picturesque part of Izmir; it has much of the character of an old Near Eastern marketing center. North of this area is the quarter of Alsancak, most of which is quite modern. It is a level area with well-designed streets, modern apartment blocks, and stores and warehouses.

Like most rapidly developing cities in older countries, Izmir is a city of contrasts. Beneath the attractive and almost serene skyline, seen from a distance, are all the problems of contemporary urban blight, much aggravated by a population that has not yet made the adaptation from rural to metropolitan living. A breathtaking panorama dissolves into a mass of colorless and even squalid details. For all its antiquity, however, Izmir remains a thriving, vital city. Minor frustrations in daily living abound, but the climate, scenery, history, and a friendly population more than compensate for them.

American associations with Izmir go back to the early 19th century, when American traders, shippers, missionaries, and teachers first settled in the then predominantly foreign city. Apart from the U.S. Consulate General, the only remainder of this earlier association is the American Girls' School, a fine secondary school for Turkish girls which is largely managed and staffed by Americans. At a later date, oriental tobacco was exported from Izmir to the U.S. in large quantities. This remains an important trade today, and every important American

tobacco company has its permanent American representative in Izmir.

By far the largest number of Americans to visit Izmir in recent years have been military. The U.S. Air Force maintained a base at Cigli (now the site of the city's civil airport) for many years. This base was relinquished in 1970, and almost half of the American military and their dependents then left the city. A smaller military presence remains, however.

In the future, its seems likely that new Turkish-American ties in Izmir will develop through tourism and industrial investment and development. The latter is already bringing new Americans to reside in the city. The total American population of Izmir is almost 2,500.

Recreation

Ankara

Ankara and the surrounding area have much to offer tourists and history enthusiasts. The citadel and the old city date from Byzantine times. Although the outer citadel walls have been destroyed or have fallen in ruins, the inner fortress still stands. The old city lies within the fortress walls and on several nearby hills. Julian's Column, near Ulus Square (Ulus Meydani), dates from the fourth century; it was set up to commemorate a visit by Emperor Julian the Apostate to Ankara.

The Roman baths, only recently discovered, date from the third century. The ruins give an excellent idea of the original structure of the baths.

The Temple of Augustus and Rome was probably built during the second century B.C.; it was later dedicated to the Roman Emperor Caesar Augustus. In the early sixth century A.D., it was made into a Christian church; in the 15th century, one of its walls was used as a support for the roof of the Haci Bayram Mosque. The side walls and entrance columns of this marble temple are still standing. One can read on the temple wall the bilingual (Latin and Greek) inscription, "Monumentum Ancrynum" or "Testament of Augustus," a discovery that helped ascertain the exact year of the birth of Christ.

The Aladdin Mosque is situated within the walls of the citadel. Inscriptions on its carved walnut pulpit indicate it was built by the Seljuk Turks, the dynasty which ruled Turkey before the establishment of the Ottoman Empire.

The Arslanhane Mosque (the Mosque of the House of Lions) has inscriptions which indicate it was built at the beginning of the 13th century; it is the oldest and largest mosque in Ankara. An unusual feature is a minaret with two balconies. A stone lion dating from Roman times is in the courtyard, and gives the mosque its name.

The Ethnographic Museum contains an extensive collection of old Turkish dress, caligraphy, wood carvings, copper and brass, ceramics, and pottery.

The Archaeological (or Hittite) Museum contains the world's finest collection of Hittite artifacts, as well as specimens of Phrygian and Lydian origin. It is housed in a 15th-century caravanserai, adjacent to the Ankara citadel. Many of the artifacts come from sites within 200 miles of Ankara.

Konya, the ancient Iconium, is a four-hour drive from Ankara. It was the capital of the Seljuk Sultanate and contains many monuments dating from that period. Here also are the tomb and chapter house of the Turkish Islamic mystic, Mevlana Cellaleddin, founder in the 13th century of the Order of the Whirling Dervishes. Every December, many travel to Konya to see the Festival of the Dervishes.

Kayseri, a large marketplace for Turkish carpets, is six hours from Ankara. Built on the site of the ancient Caesarea of Cappadocia, it is one of the largest and most important historic cities of Anatolia. It is also one of the richest in Seljuk architecture and decorative art. Near Kayseri, and about four miles from the village of Urgup, is the Valley of Goreme, containing early Christian dwellings and cave churches carved out of limestone cones or pillars produced by wind erosion, and rising as high as 200 or 300 feet.

Amasya, on the banks of a river, is about seven hours northeast of Ankara. The city is dominated by a fortified crag into which the graves of the kings of Pontus were dug, and contains important Seljuk architectural remains.

Gordium, where Alexander the Great is reputed to have cut the Gordian knot in 333 B.C., is a two-hour drive west of Ankara. It is the site of Phrygian and Hittite ruins and the tumulus of King Midas.

Ataturk's Mausoleum (Anit Kabir) in Ankara is a huge structure of golden limestone enclosing the marble sarcophagus of the founder of modern Turkey. One of the largest memorials in the world, the mausoleum can be seen from almost every part of the city.

The Palace of the President of the Republic is located in the Cankaya district at the southern end of the city, and commands a panoramic view of Ankara. The beautifully landscaped gardens and a museum containing Ataturk memorabilia are open to the public.

The Grand National Assembly Museum in Ulus and a museum adjacent to the railway station provide background for the early days of the Turkish Republic.

Ataturk's Farm (Gazi Orman Ciftligi) was founded by Ataturk as an experimental farm. The area now contains a park and picnic grounds, a zoo, a restaurant with music and dancing in the evenings, and a nursery where shrubs, plants, and cut flowers are for sale. The farm produces dairy products which are sold in Ankara shops and are widely used in restaurants and hotels.

Various locations near Ankara offer freshwater fishing. The rivers and streams of eastern Turkey, although difficult to reach, provide excellent trout fishing, as does the Manavgat River in southwest Turkey. Other denizens of rivers and lakes include giant catfish, carp, pike, and bass. Saltwater fishing is available near Istanbul and Izmir. A fishing license is not required and no limit is established.

Duck, geese, partridge, bear, wild boar, wolf, fowl, and numerous smaller game are prevalent in many areas. Turkey also has its own species of quail and wild turkey. A hunting license permits the hunting of most animals and birds, with no bag limit. The license may be obtained only through a recognized hunting club.

Skiing is growing in popularity in Turkey, although less snow is available than experts would like. The main slope in the Ankara area is at Elmadag, a 55-minute drive from the city, where a fully equipped lodge, a warming hut, and T-bar lifts are available. Bursa is also a favorite spot for skiing for foreigners and Turks alike. Good hotels and lifts are available at Bursa.

The Black Sea towns of Amasya, Akcakoca, and Trabzon are four to eight hours from Ankara. They offer simple hotels and camping places near pleasant beaches. Bolu is about a three-hour drive northwest of Ankara. Nearby is Lake Abant where one may fish, boat, or swim. A hotel overlooking the lake provides good accommodations.

Several other areas of Turkey offer excellent beaches, notably on the Sea of Marmara, near Istanbul, along the Aegean coast north and south of Izmir, all along the Mediterranean coast, and at other resort areas on the shores of the Black Sea.

In Ankara, the sports fan can watch tennis and soccer matches, horse racing, and some wrestling and boxing. Participant sports in the area include tennis, riding, softball, bowling, football, basketball, jogging, paddleball, hunting, handball, fishing, boating, and skiing. Membership in private clubs and organizations is prerequisite to taking part in most of these sports. Opportunities for swimming in the immediate Ankara area are limited.

Entertainment

The Turkish State Opera, Ballet, and the Turkish State Conservatory are located in Ankara. The Presidential Symphony Orchestra performs two concerts a week during its regular season. The State Theater has presented in Turkish such musicals as *My Fair Lady*, *Fiddler on the Roof*, and *Man of La Mancha*.

Several legitimate theaters in the city present plays in Turkish. Touring companies of foreign artists often appear, and each season, various well-known musicians appear with local orchestras. The cultural branches of foreign embassies occasionally sponsor famous orchestras, ballets, musical ensembles, and stage performances. Tickets for all of these are modestly priced. The Turkish-American Association sponsors concerts, lectures, movies, and art and other cultural exhibits.

In addition to Turkish films, Ankara motion picture theaters present American and European movies with Turkish subtitles. However, foreign films are often edited so that the stories are hard to follow.

Adana

Adana is literally surrounded by undeveloped archaeological sites which would be featured national parks or tourist sites if located in Europe. Ruins of medieval castles and cities, dating from the Greek to Armenian eras, are within easy driving distance over good, but heavily traveled roads.

The entire Adana District is rich in historical sites. Crusader castles along the coast are favorite sites for day trips by Americans. Many of them are relatively untouched. The town of Tarsus, located about 25 miles west of Adana on the Mersin Road, is reputed to be the birthplace of St. Paul. Undeveloped resort areas are located in the Taurus Mountains north of the city, as well as at the various beaches that stretch along the Mediterranean coast. These offer pleasant changes from the summer dust and heat of the city.

Adult participation in organized sports is virtually unknown in the local Turkish community, and is limited largely to younger men who play for amateur soccer clubs. Recreation for most Americans revolves around picnicking and swimming. The nearby beaches and mountains provide relief from the heat on weekends. Adana Lake offers swimming, boating, and skiing. Beaches along the Mediterranean are underdeveloped, but beautiful. A few campsites have been established as part of the national program to attract tourists to Turkey. Some beach cottages are offered for rent at Karates, the beach closest to Adana, 30 miles from the city. However, the beach is crowded and not pleasant for family use. Unaccompanied women find beaches unpleasant in some respects, and those wishing to avoid undue attention go in larger mixed groups.

Ample opportunity for hunting and fishing exists within a day's drive of Adana. Wild boar are found near Tarsus, and migratory water fowl gather in the salt marshes south of Adana. Trout fishing is available in the mountains near Maras. Guns must be registered with Turkish authorities on arrival, or when purchased.

Little cultural activity is available in Adana. Evening entertainment is at a minimum. Occasional local theater productions of plays are in Turkish. Numerous indoor and outdoor movie theaters feature Turkish, European, and some American films, all with Turkish soundtracks.

Two hotels offer evening dining, with orchestras on weekends for dancing, but are not widely patronized by married couples. The best food served is Turkish, although some European dishes are offered. Several nightclubs offer dancing, food, and a variety of musical entertainment. Imported drinks are expensive, but Turkish wines and beer are available. Several clubs, hotels, and restaurants patronized by Adana officials and business representatives have been found suitable by Americans for pleasant evening entertainment. Private social clubs have limited appeal because they are expensive and are patronized by businessmen and farmers for stag card parties, rather than for family dining or entertainment.

Istanbul

It is impossible to exaggerate the magnificance of the museums and collections in Istanbul. Interesting collections of artifacts and art of the Greco-Roman, Byzantine, and Ottoman periods are worthwhile, as well as exhibits of Sumerian, Hittite, and earlier findings. Most of the palaces are open as museums, as is the great Byzantine Church, Aya Sofia. The Kariye Museum and Fethiye Mosque, restored by Dumbarton Oaks, have some of the finest Byzantine mosaics and frescoes in existence. The Museum of Antiquities has an extensive collection of Greek, Roman, Byzantine, and Phoenician art, while the Museum of Ancient Oriental Art houses rare artifact collections from Babylonian, Assyrian, Egyptian, and Hittite civilizations. Topkapi and Dolmabache palaces give unrivaled insights into the Ottoman period.

Excellent sight-seeing tours are organized by the YMCA, Bosphorus College, and the Turkish-American University Association. Boat rides on the Bosphorus and excursions to the Princes' Islands in the Sea of Marmara are chartered. Outside of Istanbul, possibilities for visiting interesting Turkish cities are limitless. Of particular interest are the summer cruises along the Aegean coastline, southern Turkey, and the Black Sea coast.

Hiking and camping are not yet well-developed activities in Turkey, but ample opportunities exist for the avid outdoorsman. Camping facilities are improving with the establishment of a series of sites along well-traveled routes. The organization of hiking expeditions requires individual initiative, as few organized groups or facilities exist. The possibilities, however, are practically limitless.

Istanbul offers a variety of sports facilities and activities. A tennis club, located in the center of the city behind the Divan Hotel, is equipped with seven courts and a small clubhouse. The clubhouse is attractive and memberships are available. Bosphorus College has a tennis club, and a court at the British Consulate General accepts foreign members. There are also tennis courts at the Hilton Hotel.

The geographic situation of the city affords numerous swimming facilities located along the Bosphorus, the Sea of Marmara, and the Black Sea. Swimming clubs with private beaches include the Galatasary Club and clubs at the Tarabya, Carlton, and Cinar Hotels. The Lido, a private swimming club on the Bosphorus, has a swimming pool. Memberships are available.

Sailing has many devotees in Istanbul. There are several yacht clubs, the best known of which is the Moda Club, located on the Sea of Marmara. Privileges at this club, including the rental of boats, are for members only, but foreigners may obtain membership. Sailing is a challenge on the Bosphorus, but is not recommended for the novice because of unfavorable winds and strong currents, except when the north wind prevails. Rowboats and runabouts are very popular along the Bosphorus for sports, fishing, and waterskiing.

Hunting is currently forbidden to foreigners; however, some exceptions are made for diplomats who are able to join hunting clubs. Hunting in the vicinity of Istanbul is fair, although available game resources are depleted early in the season by the great multitude of hunters who go afield on opening day. The various seasons are open from September until April. Small game within easy reach of the city are European quail, dove, wild pigeon, woodcock, and duck. Wild boar is fairly prevalent in Turkey. Dogs may be used for retrieving. Only shotguns may be imported into Turkey. Any gun with rifling is strictly forbidden.

Saltwater fishing is good. With a sufficiently large craft, the sportsman can find small to medium tuna and swordfish in the Marmara. The bottom bouncer with small craft can find a wide variety of rockfish seasonally. On the Bosphorus, the small boat enthusiast can fish practically year round for a wide variety of migratory fish, ranging from small tuna to mackerel and bait fish. Freshwater fishing can also be good, but the best locations for it are some distance from Istanbul.

Istanbul has a nine-hole golf course, but it is rarely played because of the lack of maintenance and condition of its greens.

Soccer is Turkey's national game. Everyone has a favorite team and player. Lottery tickets are avidly sought. "Football pools" receive a great deal of attention, and stadiums are filled to overflowing. Football fans have been known to riot when a call is made against their player or team. Turkey's national teams play a confederation of middle European teams, at home and away.

Istanbul has practically no children's public sport facilities and very few playgrounds or parks in which children can play.

A wide variety of entertainment is available in Istanbul. The Istanbul Cultural Center at Taksim Square performs seven or eight operas during the season (October to April) at the Main Opera Theater. The opera orchestra is comprised in part of the Istanbul City Orchestra, which also maintains a concert program during the season. Turkish and Western classical music is presented on alternate weeks. From time to time, guest American and European orchestras on tour play in Istanbul.

The Istanbul International Festival, a month-long event held in the summer, is the highlight of the entertainment year. Top-rated foreign and Turkish groups perform a variety of the arts (music, dance, theater, opera), using the historical sites of Istanbul as their stage. Prices are usually quite reasonable.

In addition to Turkish films, Istanbul motion picture theaters show a limited selection of foreign films, including American, some with subtitles. However, foreign films do not include top-rated or recent releases; those that are shown are often edited so that the stories are hard to follow.

Drama is becoming increasingly popular in Istanbul and many American, European, and Turkish plays, as well as Shakespeare, are staged in Turkish by the Istanbul Municipal Theater and a number of independent companies. Performances in English are rare.

Istanbul abounds in fine restaurants. Turkish food is varied and excellent, and the whole spectrum of atmosphere and cuisine is available at reasonable cost.

Izmir

Touring is the foremost attraction of a visit to Izmir for there is so much to see. An enjoyable outing is a drive (over fairly good roads and through magnificent scenery) to one of the picturesquely located ancient city temple sites for a picnic and a few hours of walking and climbing among the ancient ruins. Sometimes rocky climbs and overgrowth make walking difficult, but it is an activity enjoyed by young and old. In summer, it is often possible to include some swimming in such an excursion.

The ancient ruins alone surpass anything to be found in modern Greece. The mere roster of place names is enough to excite any amateur historian's imagination. Within an hour or so are Ephesus, Sardis, Teos, and Claros; within two to three hours are Priene, Miletus, Didymae, and Aphrodisias. Requiring overnight stays, but within easy reach, are Hieropolis (Pamukkale), Termessos, Halicarnassus (Bodrum), Antalya, Perge, Side, and Aspendos (all in the district), and Troy and Assos.

Although tourism in the area is still in its infancy, acceptable tourist hotels and restaurants are found at or near most of the tourist sites. Camping is also possible at many sites.

European football (soccer) is the great spectator and participant sport in Izmir, but Americans have usually shown little interest in it.

In summer, sea bathing is the most popular outdoor activity for Americans. The local season runs only from the beginning of July to the end of August, but those used to cooler waters find the Aegean pleasant from the end of May through October. Pollution makes the inner Bay of Izmir unfit for bathing, but good swimming is found between 45 and 90 minutes' drive to the south, west, or north. The favored sand beaches suitable for children are at Cesme (75 minutes west), Gumuldur (60 minutes south), and Kusadasi (90 minutes south). Swimming is also possible along some of the rockier parts of the coast, and some areas provide good snorkeling and scuba diving.

Most resort hotels make bathing facilities available for the day at a small cost. Elsewhere, facilities are rustic and informal. A sturdy windproof tent for use in changing is a useful item, as is a large canvas beach umbrella for swimming and sunning in isolated areas. Fitted rubber or plastic bathing shoes are desirable.

The Bay of Izmir—indeed, the whole Aegean coast—is ideal for sailing. The sport is new to the area, with the result that boats are hard to find during the summer either for sale or for rent. For those willing to rough it, small wooden coasters with minimal facilities can be rented, with crew, for cruises along the coast and to the nearby Greek islands. Favorite areas for sailors are the lower Bay of Izmir, Bodrum, and Marmaris.

Sea fishing is good, but seasonal

lake fishing in the interior of the district is only beginning. Good hunting in the Izmir area is in fall and winter. The favorite game are wild bear, partridge, duck, and woodcock. Private hunting parties are usually pleased to take along Americans. Primitive accomodations must be expected.

The Izmir Tennis Club has courts in the Fair Grounds. The Bornova Golf Club maintains an average nine-hole course with sand greens, in Bornova, about five miles from Izmir.

Entertainment in Izmir is largely a do-it-yourself activity. Concerts of Western music are rare, no opera exists, and the occasional plays performed by the State Theater are in Turkish, although a Little Theater Group presents about five plays each season, primarily in English, but occasionally in French. All moving pictures, even imported ones, have Turkish soundtracks. The annual Izmir Fair provides "amusement park" entertainment from August 20 to September 20. Nightclubs with floor shows are numerous, but only two or three are appropriate for foreign tourist clientele.

Notes for Travelers

Air travel to Turkey on American carriers includes stops at major European cities, such as London, Paris, Frankfurt, Lisbon, Barcelona, or Rome. If a stopover is made in Istanbul en route to Ankara, onward travel is by Turkish airlines.

All Americans anticipating a stay of more than three months must have a Turkish visa for initial entry. Arrivals may be requested to present certificates of vaccination against smallpox (valid within three years) and cholera (within six months). Those traveling by train or auto through Europe to Turkey are cautioned to secure transit visas for Yugoslavia and Bulgaria.

Turkish law prohibits the importation of firearms with rifling or grooves. The limit for the allowable shotguns is two, with 1,000 rounds of ammunition.

English-language religious services are provided in Ankara through U.S. military facilities for Protestant, Jewish, Latter-Day Saints, and Jewish groups. Roman Catholic services are also held in the French and Italian embassies, and Anglican services at the British Embassy. A congregation of Turkish Sephardic Jews has a synagogue in the old part of Ankara. At Adana, Catholic and Protestant services are offered at the U.S. Air Force Chapel (Incirlik). Occasionally, other denominational services are held. A small Jewish community and synagogue are in the city. A number of denominations are represented in Istanbul, and some of the larger groups provide English-language services. Jewish synagogues are of the Ashkenazi and Sephardic sects. At Izmir, Air Force chaplains conduct both Protestant and Catholic services at St. John's Cathedral in the Alsancak quarter. In addition, the Anglican Church of St. John has services in English, and a number of Catholic churches offer French and Italian services. A few Jewish synagogues have non-English services.

The Turkish unit of currency is the *lira,* which is divided into 100 *kurus.* The rate of exchange is 31.08 *lire* = U.S.$1 (1979).

Weights and measures follow the metric system.

The U.S. Embassy in Turkey is

located at 110 Ataturk Bulvari, Kavakli-
dere, Ankara. The Consulate in Adana is
at 234/A Sapmaz Apartments on Ataturk Caddesi; the Consulate General in
Istanbul, at 104 Mesruitiyet Caddesi; and
the Consulate General in Izmir, at 386
Ataturk Caddesi. The Izmir post is successor to the Consulate established in Smyrna
in 1803, one of the earliest in the American Foreign Service.

United Kingdom

The **UNITED KINGDOM** is a parliamentary state with a constitutional monarchy. The state's origins and traditions are found in each of its four component parts: England, Scotland, Wales, and Northern Ireland. England was first united under a Saxon king in the ninth century. Wales eventually became part of that kingdom, and Ireland joined it before the end of the 13th century. In 1603, James I of England, who also ruled as James VI of Scotland, united the English and Scottish dynasties. In 1707, the Treaty for the Union of England and Scotland provided that the two countries "should be forever united into one kingdom." One Parliament (the Parliament of Great Britain) served as the supreme authority in both countries.

In 1801, the Act for the Union of Great Britain and Ireland (joining the Irish Parliament with the Parliament of Great Britain) established the present-day U.K. In 1922, however, the 26 counties of Southern Ireland became a self-governing, independent entity (the Republic of Ireland or Eire).

Area, Geography, Climate

The islands which comprise the United Kingdom of Great Britain and Northern Ireland lie off the northwest coast of the European continent. The English Channel, the Straits of Dover, and the North Sea separate the islands from the continent. At the closest point, they are only 17.8 miles from the French coast. The capital city of London is in the southeast with almost the same latitude as Winnipeg, Manitoba, Canada. The U.K. has a total land area of 94,217 square miles, roughly the size of Oregon.

The British Isles have a complex geology with a rich variety of scenery and impressive contrasts in topography. Highland Britain contains the principal mountain ranges, which vary from 4,000 to 5,000 feet and occupy most of the north and west of the country. Lowland Britain, almost entirely composed of low, rolling hills and flatlands, lies to the southeast.

Prevailing southwesterly winds make Britain's climate temperate and equitable year round. Weather patterns frequently change, but few temperate extremes occur. Temperatures range from a mean of 40°F in winter to 60°F in summer. A low of 20°F is sometimes reached during winter, and a high of over 90°F may infrequently occur in summer. Humidity in the summer months ranges from 50 to 80 percent. Average annual rainfall is 30 to 50 inches, until recently distributed evenly throughout the year. (The summers of 1975 and 1976 proved unusually dry and caused drought conditions in rural areas.) Cloud cover is persistent, however, limiting sunshine to an average of about six or seven hours a day in summer and one or two hours per day in winter.

Population

The population of the U.K. in January 1981 was 55,966,000. In addition to ethnic groups indigenous to the British Isles, recent immigration has added large numbers of Indians, Pakistanis, and West Indians to the British population. Britain's urban density, one of the highest in the world, is about 600 persons per square mile. Nearly one-quarter of the inhabitants live in England's fertile southeastern corner, with population declining in the more rugged areas to the north and west. Britain's population is largely urban and suburban.

Today's Briton is descended from varied racial stocks that settled on the island before the end of the 11th century. In its early history, Britain was subject to many invasions and migrations from Scandinavia and the continent. The Romans occupied Britain for several centuries. The Normans, the last of a long succession of invaders, conquered England in 1066. Under the Normans, the pre-Celtic, Celtic, Roman, Anglo-Saxon, and Norse influences were blended into the Briton of today.

The Celtic languages still persist in Northern Ireland and Wales and, to a lesser degree, in Scotland. But the predominant language has long been English, derived from Anglo-Saxon and Norman-French.

Over the past 20 years, the tradi-tional pattern of life in Britain has changed considerably. Not only have distinctions of class and social habits become less rigid, but subjects formerly taboo in public discussions are now openly considered in books, plays, films, and ordinary conversation. A more informed tolerance of behavior that deviates from the usual pattern is emerging. This is reflected, for instance, in the growing popular sympathy for the plight of the unmarried mother. The passing of new laws on matters such as abortion, divorce, and homosexuality, although disliked by some, show public unwillingness to penalize individuals with certain personal problems. Balancing this liberalizing trend is a recognition that, in some areas, restrictions on certain freedoms must be extended in the interests of society as a whole. Hence, legislation is concerned with control of dangerous drugs and firearms.

Relationships between the generations are also undergoing major change. Today, young people are more apt to criticize traditional institutions and to seek more influence in shaping society. This desire for personal involvement is expressed both by those prepared to demonstrate for or against certain courses of action and to bring pressure on the responsible authorities, and by the growing numbers of young people who offer their services to help the old, disabled, illiterate, and others in need.

Religious freedom is guaranteed to all religions. The Church of England (Anglican) has about 29 million baptized members. Established as "church of the land" during the Reformation in the 16th century, it is the major religious denomination in the U.K. A large number of other faiths, including the Roman Catholic (5.5. million),

Jewish (400,000), Methodist (600,000), and Baptist (190,000), are represented. The Unitarian, Quaker, Islamic, Buddhist, and Hindu faiths also have many adherents.

Government

Although one state, the U.K. has adopted flexible methods of government. These are somewhat adapted to the needs of the constituent countries. England, Wales, and Scotland continue, as before the Union, to have different legal, judicial, and educational systems. For most domestic matters, they have different government departments. In Scotland these departments have headquarters in Edinburgh. They are grouped under the Secretary of State for Scotland, who is a member of the Cabinet. To a large degree, the administration of Welsh affairs is delegated to the Welsh Office under the Secretary of State of Wales, another Cabinet minister.

The Government of Ireland Act in 1920 enacted a Constitution for Northern Ireland. This act preserved the supreme authority of the U.K. Parliament and reserved certain matters to that Parliament. But it provided Northern Ireland with its own legislative and executive branches to deal with domestic "transferred" affairs. These arrangements remained in force until 1972 when, following several years of political instability and violence in Northern Ireland, a period of direct rule was introduced. Under direct rule, executive powers were exercised by a Secretary of State and laws made by Order in Council. In 1973, the Northern Ireland Constitution Act established a new type of constitution for Northern Ireland. Among other things, it passed powers to a legislative

assembly and a powersharing executive. These provisions came into force in January 1974. However, they failed to win enough support among all sections of the Northern Ireland community and were brought to an end in May 1974.

In July 1974, the Northern Ireland Act was introduced. This act provides for the election of a constitutional convention to consider what arrangements for the Government of Northern Ireland would be likely to command most widespread acceptance throughout the community. The act provides that, in the interim, the Secretary of State for Northern Ireland is to be responsible to the U.K. Parliament for the delegated services. It also states that laws for Northern Ireland may be made by Order in Council on matters within the competence of the suspended (or prorogued) assembly for one year, subject to extension or termination by the U.K. Parliament. Responsibility for the administration of the Northern Ireland departments rests temporarily with ministers in the Northern Ireland Office.

The Channel Islands and the Isle of Man (which are Crown dependencies and not part of the U.K.) have their own legislative assemblies, systems of local administration and law, and their own courts. At the same time, they have a special relationship with the U.K. because of their proximity to it and the antiquity of their connection with the Crown. The U.K. Government is responsible for the defense, the international relations, and ultimately the good government of these dependencies.

The U.K. Constitution is formed partly by statute, by common law, and by precepts and practices known as conventions. These have never been codified and are not directly enforceable in a court of law. But, nevertheless, they have a binding force as rules of the Constitution. The Constitution is not contained in any document and can be altered by an Act of Parliament or by general agreement to vary, abolish, or create a convention. Therefore, it can readily adapt to changing political conditions and ideas without seriously disturbing existing organs and forms.

The organs of government established by the U.K. Constitution are readily distinguishable, but their functions often intermingle and overlap. They are:

1. The legislature, comprising the Queen and Parliament (the Houses of Lords and Commons). It is the supreme authority in the realm;

2. The executive, comprising: (a) the Cabinet and other ministers of the Crown, who are responsible for initiating and directing national policy; (b) government departments, mainly under the control of ministers and all staffed by civil servants, which are responsible for administration at the national level; (c) local authorities, who administer and manage many services at the local level; and (d) public corporations, which may be responsible for the operation of certain nationalized industries or social or cultural services and which are subject to ministerial control in varying degrees; and

3. The judiciary, which determines common law and interprets statutes. It is independent of both the legislature and the executive.

Arts, Science, Education

London's art scene is dynamic and one of the world's best. Public and private galleries are abundant. They offer a tremendous selection of the works of the old-world masters and contemporary artists. Various festivals, such as the Edinburgh International Festival, attract world attention and participation. Devotion to the arts is rooted in the U.K.'s rich cultural heritage. This devotion has led to maintenance of many museums, concert halls, and theaters offering a wide variety of classical and popular works.

In the last three decades, popular interest in the arts has steadily grown. This development is reflected in the profusion of amateur dramatic and musical societies, the growth in book and record sales, and the large attendance figures at major art exhibitions. These developments largely result from increased leisure time and improved education in the arts. Another factor has been the influence of television and radio, which have made the best in the arts available to people in their own homes.

Artisic activities in Britain receive financial and other support from many sources. Some of the arts, notably drama and classical music, have become more reliant on this support. But others, such as painting and literature, continue to flourish with little outside help. Valuable assistance comes from such private sources as voluntary trusts and commercial concerns. In addition, since 1945 the government and local authorities have played a growing role in encouraging the arts.

Scientific and technological innovation is aggressively pursued by various organizations. These include government departments, universities, many learned societies (six of world renown), professional institutions, public and private councils, industry, and international scientific exchanges through such vehicles as EURATOM, the IAEA, and INTELSAT.

The government is the main source of funds for scientific research and development as a whole, but private industry contibutes a larger proportion of funds for civil research and development. Public corporations, independent trusts and foundations, and learned societies also provide funds. The government reviews facilities for training scientists and insures that adequate research is directed to matters of national interest.

Parents in Britain are required by law to see that their children receive efficient full-time education, at school or elsewhere, between the ages of five and 16. Over 11 million school children attend some 37,000 schools. In England and Wales, about nine million children attend publicly maintained schools. In addition, 131,315 others go to schools receiving direct grants from the Department of Education and Science or the Welsh Office. Also, 432,348 children of all ages attend education-authority or grant-aided schools, and over 17,800 attend independent schools. In Northern Ireland, 369,240 children go to publicly maintained or assisted schools.

In Britain, boys and girls are generally taught together in primary schools. Some 70 percent of pupils in maintained secondary schools in England and Wales and about 48 percent in Northern Ireland attend mixed schools. In Scotland, nearly all secondary schools are mixed. Most independent schools for younger children are coeducational, but secondary schools are usually either for boys or girls.

The higher education system includes universities, colleges of education, and advanced courses at various colleges in the higher education system, particularly the technical schools (or polytechnics). Higher education grew rapidly in the late 1960s and early 1970s. The number of students in full-time higher education in Britain increased from 222,400 in 1962 to 490,000 in 1973–74, and continues to grow. This expansion has been achieved by: (1) increasing the number of universities (currently four): (2) concentrating much of the advanced post-secondary work in the polytechnics, thus giving students a chance to gain a degree outside a university; (3) introducing new courses leading to a bachelor of education (BEd) degree; and (4) establishing the Open University, which provides those with or without formal qualifications the opportunity of studying for a degree.

Commerce and Industry

Although small in area and accounting for only about 1.5 percent of the world's population, Britain is the fifth largest trading nation in the world. It is a member of the European Community, part of the world's biggest trading area, which accounts for about 40 percent of all trade.

For well over a century, international trade has been of vital importance to the country's economy. Britain relies upon imports for about half its total consumption of foodstuffs and most of the raw materials needed for its industries. It is among the world's largest importers of foodstuffs, metals and ores, textile raw materials, and many other products. Its exports of goods represent about one-fifth of the gross national product.

Imports are paid for primarily by exports of manufactured goods and by "invisible" export earnings on overseas investment; travel; civil aviation; British-owned shipping; and financial, banking, insurance, and other services. Britain is one of the world's largest exporters of aircraft, motor vehicles, electrical equipment, chemicals, finished textiles, and most types of machinery.

The important contribution by invisibles to export earnings reflects Britain's position as a major financial center. Its banks, insurance underwriters and brokers, and other financial institutions provide worldwide financial services. The city of London provides perhaps the most comprehensive and advanced capital market in the world.

The U.K. economy is a mixture of public and privately owned firms with a number of joint ventures as well. Several important British industries are under public ownership, including steel, railroads, coal mining, some utilities, and a large part of civil aviation. Proposals for nationalization of other industrial sectors are under consideration.

Within the framework of economic and social policy as a whole, government policy aims to promote the expansion and modernization of industry. At the same time, it seeks to develop an effective solution to the problems of regional imbalances. The government has long sought to influence industrial activity by controlling fiscal and monetary policy and the level of public expenditure; by offering incentives for industrial investment; and by providing services, information, and advice. Legislative arrangements have been developed to control various aspects of employment, monopolies, mergers, restrictive practices, new office and industrial building, and changes in land use.

Britain has long advocated the removal of artificial barriers to trade. To this end, it has taken a leading part in the activities of such organizations as the International Monetary Fund, the General Agreement on Tarriffs and Trade (GATT), the Organization for Economic Cooperation and Development, and the U.N. Conference on Trade and Development (UNCTAD).

Trade between Britain and Western Europe has been increasing in recent years. Thus, the proportion of Britain's exports going to primary producing countries has declined. In 1958, 31 percent of U.K. exports went to Western Europe. But in 1962, these exports began to exceed those to the sterling area, and by 1973 they formed just over half of the total, having risen by 34 percent during the year. Exports to Western Europe rose sharply again in early 1974 to nearly 52 percent of the total. Exports to the enlarged European Economic Community (EEC) rose by 37 percent to account for over 32 percent of Britain's total exports. By 1977, they had risen to over 36 percent of the total.

Trade with Commonwealth countries has tended to decline in recent years and now amounts to about 13 percent (1979) of total exports. The U.S. now accounts for about 9.8 percent of Britain's export and import trade.

Transportation

The U.K. offers comprehensive modern rail, air, and sea transportation facilities. Inland travel is quick and efficient by public and private transportation systems.

In 1981, the railway network operated by British Rail amounted to about 22,000 miles. Passenger services are concentrated on the high-speed, intercity lines and commuter service around the large metropolitan areas, especially London and the Southeast. High-speed train systems carry passengers at speeds up to 125 mph. Motorail services carry both passengers and cars. They have an annual capacity of 135,000 cars on nearly 40 lines.

Subway service in London is fast and frequent, but closes at midnight and is subject to delay in even a little snow. The present network is comprehensive and offers easy transfer to rail and bus. Trips to outlying areas within the greater London limits are fairly inexpensive. Free system maps are available from London Transport.

All major suburban and urban areas have frequent, relatively inexpensive, and fast bus service. Most intracity buses are painted red, and long-distance lines are green. Bus-route maps are furnished free by the various government-operated bus lines. Carrier-owned buses serve major air and sea terminals. Experimental minibus service runs in some suburban areas.

Taxis cruise the streets of all major cities in large numbers (11,000 in London alone). They are easy to find, except in rush hours and in the rain. Taxis are metered and charge a flat rate per mile; subcharges are paid for evening, weekend, and local holiday travel. Many cab companies have telephone pickup services. Taxis may be found at taxi ranks (stands) in front of the larger hotels or may be flagged down on the street, when their rooftop yellow light is visible.

Edinburgh has frequent airline, rail, and bus service to other parts of Scotland and the U.K. Regular airline shuttle service from Edinburgh's Turnhouse Airport to Heathrow and Gatwick Airports in the London area allow the traveler to make connecting flights to practically any part of the world. In addition, daily flights are scheduled from Turnhouse direct to Dublin and the continent. Bus service to major cities in Britain is frequent, reasonably fast, and inexpensive. Trains are more expensive, but they are faster, more comfortable, and include convenient night-sleeper service between Edinburgh and London.

The local transportation system in Edinburgh is clean and efficient but less extensive than that in London. The bus lines seldom run more than every 20 to 30 minutes. Most buses run between outlying areas and the center of town. To ride from one area outside the center of town to another, one must go into town and take another bus to his destination. Trips to nearby towns not served by local buses or trains are more frequent in Edinburgh than in London.

The road network in Scotland is good, but much of it is two-lane—and in some remote areas, one-lane—all-weather roads. Motorways (the British equivalent of the U.S. interstate highways) are scarce in Scotland. Most are near Edinburgh and Glasgow.

Each of the nine major air terminals serves an average of two million passengers annually. Hovercraft and other car and passenger ferries operate regularly to and from the European continent.

Great Britain's extensive network of good roads and motorways (similar to U.S. interstate highways) affords many opportunities for motoring. Most people find a car desirable for recreation and sight-seeing, and foreigners visiting or working in Belfast or Edinburgh will find a car a virtual neccessity for business and shopping. Those in London may find a car optional. Unfortunately, the convenience and pleasure of driving in London is limited by severe parking problems and heavy traffic. Few car owners find it possible to drive to and from work.

Official U.S. personnel may obtain a British drivers permit without a driving test by producing a valid drivers license. British licenses are valid for three years and are renewable if the holder retains official status.

If one is not attached to the Embassy or Consulates General, he may use his U.S. drivers license for one year from date of entry. Thereafter, he must take a driving test and obtain a British license. Driving is on the left throughout the U.K.

Communications

A direct-dial telephone system serves London and most of the U.K. The U.S. and Western Europe can also be reached by direct dialing. Telephones are available on request to private subscribers, but some individuals must accept a party line. Monthly charges for home telephones and charges for domestic and international calls compare to those in the U.S.

Internal and international telegraph service is readily available and highly efficient.

Belfast. Local and long-distance telephone service is good. Telegraph facilities are available through a number of commercial companies and the General Post Office (GPO).

Edinburgh. Telephone and telegraph services, run by the GPO, are excellent. Telephone service is direct-dial. It links Edinburgh to all cities in the U.K., to most of Western Europe, and to the U.S.

Regular British postal channels are safe, quick, reasonable, and widely used for most ordinary mail. Mail is delivered once daily except Sunday. Delivery time for letters to or from the U.S. is about four to five days; surface mail takes about three weeks.

Mail service in Northern Ireland and Scotland also is quick and efficient.

Television, both in color and black-and-white, is broadcast through the facilities of the state-owned British Broadcasting Corporation (BBC) and the commercially financed Independent Television Network (ITV). BBC-1 has a nationwide network reaching 95 percent of the viewing public. Nationwide coverage by BBC-2 is not as extensive but still reaches all major areas. The ITV system of 15 independent stations also provides country-wide programing on a regional basis. All three networks operate in the UHF broadcast range.

Network programing is standard throughout the country in both content and timing. Considerable program flexibility is provided to allow for locally produced shows and news reports between network programs.

Excellent radio programing in AM, FM, and FM-stereo bands is available throughout the country. BBC Radio provides listeners with four alternative national channels. It broadcasts all types of music, news, commentary, adult education programs, and works of artistic and intellectual interest. Two independent commercial radio stations provide general entertainment and news service. Radio broadcasts from Europe can also be reached with a high degree of clarity. Reception of the Armed Forces Network broadcasts is possible.

Newspapers, Magazines, Books

The British press caters to a wide variety of interests and political views. According to the Newspaper Press Director, 130 daily and Sunday newspapers and 1,134 weekly newspapers are published in Britain. Six morning papers—the Guardian, the Daily Mirror, the Daily Express, the Sun, the Times, and the Daily Telegraph—are national. They have a total average daily circulation of 2.1 million. Six national Sunday papers—News of the World, the Observer, the Sunday People, Sunday Express, Sunday Mirror, and the Sunday Telegraph—have a total average weekly circulation of 3.2 million copies. The news media is served by three large British news agencies—Reuters, the Press Association, and the Exchange Telegraph Company. UPI and AP have affiliates in London, as do most major U.S. newspapers (e.g., New York Times, Los Angeles Times, and Washington Post). Many surburban daily papers contain news of a more local interest. The International Herald Tribune is available daily except Sunday.

Britain has over 4,500 periodicals. These publications cater to a broad spectrum of interests. In addition, several prominent journals of opinion are published. The Economist is a politically independent publication covering topics from a wider angle than its title implies. The New Statesman reviews politics, literature, and the arts from an independent Socialist political standpoint. The Tribune represents the view of the left wing of the Labor Party. The New Society covers the sociological aspects of current affairs. The New Scientist reports on the progress of science and technology in lay language. Punch, traditionally the leading humor magazine, also devotes attention to public affairs. Literary and political journals and those specializing in international and Commonwealth affairs are published monthly or quarterly.

The weekly to quarterly publication of trade, technical, business, scientific, and professional journals has become a major aspect of the British publishing industry. These journals cover hundreds of subjects, many in great depth. In addition to circulating in Britain, these journals have wide external distribution. As such, they are an important medium for selling British goods overseas.

Periodicals published in England circulate throughout the U.K. Scotland has three monthly illustrated periodicals (Scottish Field, Scotland's Magazine, and Scot's Magazine), a weekly paper devoted to farming interests (Scottish Farmer), several literary journals (the most famous is probably Blackwood's), and many popular magazines. In Northern Ireland, weekly, monthly, and quarterly publications cover farming, the linen industry, building, motoring, politics, and social work. European editions of Time and Newsweek are readily available at newsstands and bookshops. The large number of bookshops available in London carry such American magazines as Fortune, Forbes, Saturday Review, Harper's Bazaar, and the New Yorker.

Britain is served by a complete network of public libraries administered by local government authorities. These libraries now maintain a total stock of over 110 million books. About half of the libraries lend a variety of phonograph records, and a growing number are adding loan collections of art works, either original or reproduction. Nearly all libraries have children's departments, and most also act as centers for film showings, lectures, adult education classes, exhibitions, drama groups, recitals, and children's story hours.

Books of all types are available in local bookshops and larger department stores. A growing number, including a wide range of nonfiction, are now sold in paperback form. Penguin Books and other large publishing houses sell most bestsellers in paperback.

Health

The U.K. has excellent medical facilities in all major cities. London, Belfast, and Edinburgh have medical training centers offering the full range of medical services. All residents of the U.K. are entitled by law to medical care under the National Health Service (NHS). Medical practitioners may maintain private (fee-for-service) practices in addition to their NHS practices, and many do so. One may establish a private-patient relationship with a local physician, much as in the U.S. Many British physicians accept pay-

ment under U.S. health insurance plans.

Belfast also offers a high standard of medical care. Each individual or family is under the care of a local general practitioner. Complete specialist facilities are available at the Royal Victoria Hospital, which is the major teaching facility of Queen's University Medical School. Edinburgh has long been famous for its medical schools, and the quality of local facilities is uniformly excellent.

Living conditions in Great Britain are excellent; no major health hazards exist. Community sanitation standards are high, and community environmental services are superior. Colds and other upper-respiratory infections are common but no more than in comparable U.S. climates.

Major Cities

"When a man is tired of London, he is tired of life; for there is in London all that life can afford." Dr. Samuel Johnson.

"Hell is a city much like London—A populous and smoky city." Percy Bysshe Shelley.

Opinions of **LONDON** may differ, just as attitudes toward all cities differ. But what is irrefutable is that London is one of the great cities of the world, not only in size and population, but as a seat of government and a center of commerce, education, the arts, and a wide range of enterprise. Like all cities, London attracts people of all backgrounds who come for many reasons, both to visit and to live. As a city which has been preeminent for centuries, it offers a rich and varied history.

The name London has no single

specific meaning. It was originally used to describe the city of London proper (still referred to distinctively as "the City"), which now has an area of only 677 acres and an estimated resident population of 4,200. With the steady growth of the capital since the Middle Ages, the surrounding districts were absorbed into the vast metropolis of today. It had a 1980 population of just over seven million in an area of 610 square miles.

Greater London is actually composed of 32 semi-independent boroughs (plus "the City" and eight new "towns"). Each in turn has dozens of business, residential, and cultural centers of its own. Greater London has followed massive and carefully coordinated postwar reconstruction programs, including intensive efforts to clean the facades of famous surviving buildings. This revitalization effort has been quite successful. Almost anything one would want is available in London's array of shops and stores, large and small, general and specialized. Stores compare favorably with those found in the largest U.S. cities. Household items, personal knick-knacks, cosmetics, and toiletries of most varities are available. Drugstores carry a complete range of medicines, medical preparations, and health aids.

Numerous neighborhood shopping areas are scattered throughout Greater London. One of the first American-type shopping malls opened in early 1976; more have followed. Virtually all shopping areas offer common services: laundry (coin operated and general), dry cleaning, hairdressers, barbers, gas stations, drugstores, hardware stores, appliance repair shops, travel and ticket agencies, restaurants, flower shops, gift stores, banks, libraries, newsstands, bookshops, jewelers, and the ever-present pubs, to mention a few.

BELFAST is the principal industrial city and capital of Northern Ireland. The entire province is small in area, but has a distinct territorial identity within the U.K. It is a fascinating combination of old and new, from Belfast to the most remote rural areas, and its ties to America are traditional and strong. Interestingly enough, 10 of 39 presidents in the history of the U.S. have definite family links with this Province, and several others have close Ulster connections. Northern Ireland is slightly smaller than Connecticut. Its estimated population is 1,540,000 and Belfast's population is 357,000.

The name Belfast is derived from two Gaelic words: *beal*, a river mouth; and *fierste*, hurry or haste. This description pinpoints Belfast's principal feature. It is a port city at the mouth of the river Lagan, a small river which flows into the large and beautiful Belfast Lough (bay). The city is surrounded by bluffs and cliffs to the north. To the south and west the country is open and rolling.

The timing and duration of the seasons are almost identical to those of the American Pacific Northwest, but seasonal changes are less pronounced. The Belfast area has an oceanic climate. Weather is often dull and gray (relieved by bright intervals) with periods of light, misty rain or light fog. Because of Belfast's northern latitude, the amount of daylight varies greatly between summer (about 18 hours in June) and winter (about eight hours in December). May and June are usually sunny months. December through March are the most severe months of the winter, but lasting snow is rare.

British involvement in Ireland dates from Norman times, with the first Anglo-Norman invasion occurring in 1189. The Tudors sought to convert the Catholic Irish to the Church of England and establish "plantations" to inject Protestantism. Scottish and English Protestants settled most of Ulster (traditionally the nine northernmost counties of Ireland). Under English law, these Protestants controlled over 80 percent of the land despite their constituting less than 20 percent of the population. Continued British rule and Protestant ascendancy in Ireland were sealed for over three centuries at the Battle of Boyne in 1690. Here the Protestant William of Orange defeated the Catholic James II.

Penal laws, enacted after 1691, stripped Catholics throughout Ireland of their right to vote, teach, sit in Parliament, hold public office, serve in the army, or marry Protestants. Religion thus became a divisive factor in Ireland and determined political, economic, and social power. The famine of 1845-49 (which caused the large Irish Catholic emigration to the U.S.) intensified Irish bitterness toward Britain and English and Scottish settlers. British rule was never seriously challenged, but uprisings springing from Irish nationalism occurred from time to time.

A nonviolent home-rule movement emerged in the 1870s following relaxation of the penal laws. This movement challenged Protestant ascendancy and enraged Protestants in Ulster. By 1914, home rule appeared assured. The ruling Liberal Party, needing the support of Irish Members of Parliament, passed a home-rule bill, but its effect was postponed because of the First World War. Ulstermen, fearing home rule, set up an unofficial shadow government and militia, resulting in the Catholic nationalists arming themselves.

In 1916, a small group of Irish nationalists revolted in Dublin and proclaimed an Irish Republic. Their rebellion was easily crushed, but the Irish Republican Army gathered increasing popular support among Catholics. By 1920, full-scale guerilla war had engulfed the island. In late 1921, Britain's Liberal government signed a treaty giving southern Ireland independence but permitting the six northern counties to remain in the U.K. Thus Ireland was partitioned into two parts. An Irish Free State was made of the 26 southern counties with a population of three million (94 percent Catholic) The U.K. retained the smaller area of the six northern counties (Ulster) with a population of 1.5 million (about 65 percent Protestant).

Religion, a subject of intense interest and conflict in Northern Ireland, today is still the symbol of political divisions. But it is only one of several areas of life that divide the Province into communities generally identified as Roman Catholic or Protestant. Some progress in intersectarian relations has been made, even during the campaign of violence that began in August 1969 and still continues.

After August 1971, detention without trial caused the almost complete polarization of the community. This greatly intensified the campaign of bombings and shootings, mainly in Londonderry, Belfast, and the border areas. Due to these troubles, the British Government assumed direct control of Northern Ireland in March 1972. This direct rule continues today due to the inability of indigenous political parties to reach a widely-agreed formula for instituting delegated government which is acceptable to the Parliament of Great Britain.

Adding to the strife in Northern Ireland have been the recent hunger-strike deaths in Belfast's Maze Prison, as members of the Irish Republican Army fight for political prisoner status. To date, Prime Minister Margaret Thatcher has refused this request.

Northern Ireland's population tends to be socially and politically conservative. Traditions which are fading in the rest of the U.K. seem to remain strong here. Family and home are the paramount elements in the community. Social life tends to develop along family, professional, club, and school lines. Rarely do they cross class or religious boundaries. Northern Irish people are very hospitable, particularly toward Americans.

Northern Ireland is part of the U.K., but its people are essentially Irish or Scots-Irish. Protestants tend to regard themselves as British and use U.K. passports. Catholics think of themselves as Irish and use Republic of Ireland passports. Feelings of kinship are extended to the Irish of the Republic and to Scotland rather than to their English neighbors acrosss the Irish Sea.

EDINBURGH is the historic capital of Scotland, and one of the most beautiful cities in Europe. The visual focal point of the city is Edinburgh Castle, which sits upon a high, rocky hill in the city center. Much of the city's Georgian and Victorian architecture is carefully preserved in virtually its original appearance.

The city's population of 464,000 (1980) is swollen by tens of thousands of visitors from all parts of the world, particularly during summer and the Edinburgh International Festival of Music, Drama, and the Arts. It begins about August 20 each year and lasts three weeks.

Other Cities

There are several other cities of note throughout Great Britain. They include:

Birmingham, England's second largest city, and the rail and road communications center of the Midlands. Birmingham is renowned for its symphony orchestra and its repertory theater.

Bristol, capital of England's West, and famous for the prominent role it played in American colonization. It was from Bristol that John and Sebastian Cabot sailed to America in 1497. The city also was the birthplace of William Penn.

Liverpool, one of England's great seaports, and a thriving commercial and industrial center. The city is also known as the birthplace of the Beatles, the rock group which emerged in the early 1960s and dramatically influenced the world of modern music.

Manchester, the center of Britain's cotton industry, and the home of the great liberal daily newspaper, The Manchester Guardian, which was founded there in 1821.

Portsmouth, birthplace of Charles Dickens. It is the foremost naval base in Great Britain.

Southampton, chief shipping center for passenger and merchant vessels. In 1620, the Pilgrims embarked from Southampton on their voyage to America.

Dover, the channel port, and once chief of the ancient Cinque Ports, which also included Hastings, Hythe, Romney, and Sandwich.

Glasgow, Scotland's largest city and its leading seaport. It is a great industrial city with a history that dates from the late sixth century. Its university is 530 years old.

Aberdeen, stronghold of royalist sentiment in the religious wars of the 17th century. It is Scotland's third largest city.

St. Andrews, where Scottish kings were crowned, and whose renowned university is the oldest in Scotland (1411). It was the ecclesiastical capital until the Reformation.

Armagh, the religious center of Northern Ireland, and home of diocesan headquarters for both the Church of Ireland and the Roman Catholic Church.

Londonderry, Ulster's well-preserved ancient city which withstood a 150-day siege by the forces of James II in 1689. It was a U.S. Navy base in World War II.

Cardiff, capital city of Wales, and one of the greatest coal-shipping ports in the world.

Recreation

London

London is well known as a sightseer's paradise. Whatever personal interests one may have, London's museums, art galleries, libraries, historic places, pageantry, and numerous parks are bound to fulfill them. Sightseers may explore the city on foot, by bus tours (both public and private), and by boat on the Thames. A full calendar of daily and annual events is available in several weekly publications.

The British also seem to go out of their way to provide entertainment for children. This is especially true during summer and at Christmas. Popular with the youngsters are the special theater productions, pantomime and puppet shows, the zoo, African safari parks, concerts, and film festivals both in- and out-of-doors.

In London, the visitor can participate in virtually every type of popular sport, outdoors and indoors, team and individual. Some facilities are free or very inexpensive.

Many opportunities exist for spectators to view both amateur and professional games. It is always spectator season in and around London. The Oxford-Cambridge Boat Race annually brings thousands to the footpaths along the Thames. Also, the Henley Regatta, held in July, is host to rowing entries from all over the world. Horse lovers find pleasure at the major races of the year—Epsom Downs, Ascot, and Derby.

The most popular sports in Britain are soccer and rugby in winter, cricket and tennis in summer, and golf and horse events year round. TV coverage of these activities is extensive, especially on Saturday and Sunday afternoons.

Tennis at Wimbledon, cricket at Lord's, football (soccer) at Wembley, and dog shows at Olympia are but a few of the highlights of a sporting program that is full, continuous, and always of international championship caliber.

Public sports centers are numerous and close by. Membership in one or more of the many private clubs allows frequent participation in track meets, tennis matches, soccer games, and equestrian exhibitions. Membership in private clubs can be expensive, but some charge only nominal amounts for guests who play without making formal membership application.

Culturally, London is one of the richest cities on earth. It has five symphony orchestras, chamber music ensembles, and pop and rock concerts. The legitimate theater in London is unrivaled. Some 55 plays and musicals are running at any given time. Productions routinely move from Broadway to London and vice versa. Staging ranges from dinner theaters to Broadway-type productions. Practically year round, opera and ballet lovers will find offerings at the Royal Opera House (Covent Garden), the Sadler's Wells Hall, and the Royal Festival Hall. In addition to resident companies, famous continental and American groups often visit.

Central London offers a wide range of first-run films at about 150 theaters including many film clubs and "art theaters." Hollywood productions are the most popular. Cinema-going is easy and informal, as in the U.S.

Restaurants, cafes, and tearooms of every size, grade, and price range abound in London. Food ranges from fast-food fare to exclusive English and international cuisine.

The museums and art galleries in London contain one of the most comprehensive collections of objects of artistic, archaeological, scientific, historical, and general interest ever to exist in one city. The most notable are the British Museum, Victoria and Al-bert Museum, National Gallery, Tate Gallery, National Portrait Gallery, Imperial War Museum, National Army Museum, National Maritime Museum, Museum of London, Wallace Collection, British Museum (Natural History), Geological Museum, and Science Museum.

Belfast

Northern Ireland is beautiful and underpopulated. It offers opportunities for "pony-trekking," waterskiing, camping, hiking, and mountain climbing. All parts of Ireland, including the magnificent west coast, are easily reached by car. Many bus and pony-trekking tours of the country are available in summer, and many of these tours begin in Belfast.

Belfast has a museum and art gallery, a zoo, and a botanical garden. In addition, the Ulster Folk Museum is about 20 minutes by car from Belfast city center. It is a first-rate, open-air museum with representative Irish homes in their natural setting. All parts of Scotland, England, and Wales are only short distances away with good air, rail, and ferry services.

Dublin is an easy three-hour drive from Belfast or about two-and-a-half hours by train. Dublin offers excellent theater and a variety of restaurants. It also has a more cosmopolitan environment than Belfast.

Belfast is an excellent city for the outdoor sports enthusiast. The city environs, for example, have 12 golf courses. Golf carts are common, but caddies are not always available. Many clubs offer squash, tennis, badminton, and yachting. The country offers horseback riding; stag and fox hunts; fishing (salmon and trout); and geese, duck, snipe, and small game shooting.

A few good beaches are within easy access, but the water is cold. Spectator sports include horse racing (flat racing and point-to-point), soccer, rugby, cricket, and motorcycle and auto racing.

Belfast offers a fair amount of enterainment facilities. The city has few movie theaters, but tickets are cheaper than in the U.S. London touring artists and companies occasionally bring opera, ballet, and plays to Belfast, and frequent concerts are given by a good local symphony orchestra. The Lyric Theater is a good company which presents Irish and other plays in a beautiful new theater. A few other small companies also perform. Each November, an arts festival brings two weeks of talent and entertainment to Belfast. Also, occasional fairs and exhibitions are held at local centers.

Because of security uncertainty, Americans seldom frequent the few restaurants remaining in Belfast. Reasonably good restaurants can be found in smaller towns throughout the Province.

Edinburgh

Simple tourist accommodations are available in all cities and towns along the main routes out of Edinburgh. Glasgow is only an hour away by train or car, and a day trip to the Trossachs and to Loch Lomond is possible by car or tour bus. St. Andrews is also of much interest with its university and three famous golf courses. It may be reached from Edinburgh during the summer with ample time for lunch and a round of golf. A trip to Gleneagles offers its world-famous (but expensive) hotel and two fine golf courses.

Another pleasant weekend trip is to the area around Pitlochry, noted for its scenery and fishing. This could be coupled with a trip to Inverness and Loch Ness. A short trip to the north of Edinburgh presents a good view of the famous Firth of Forth Rail and Road Bridges. These are on the way to Dunfermline, with its medieval abbey and home of Andrew Carnegie. Other interesting castles, palaces, and homes are within a one day drive from Edinburgh.

Many fine private and public golf courses exist. Due to the climate, one can play golf year round. The immediate Edinburgh area has approximately 22 courses. Temporary memberships are available in all but the most select clubs.

Edinburgh also has a number of tennis clubs and good squash courts. Several indoor swimming pools are open to the general public at nominal fees. The Meadow Bank Sports Center and the Royal Commonwealth Pool were built to Olympic standards to accommodate the 1970 Commonwealth Games. The cool climate, however, limits outdoor swimming to only a short period in the summer. A number of fine beaches within easy reach of the city are suitable for picnicking, sunbathing, and swimming.

Several riding schools are close to the city and reasonably priced. Skiing is possible around Glencoe and at Aviemore in the Cairngorms. Special ski trains are available when snow conditions are good, and many ski lifts are in operation in that area.

Two active theaters offer first-class dramatic presentations in Edinburgh throughout the year. Two resident stage companies vary in quality. The city has a number of movie houses, and one small theater shows selected films on Sundays to members of a motion picture guild. Another offers a good selection of foreign and art films.

During the Edinburgh International Festival of Music, Drama, and the Arts, the visitor can see three or four excellently produced operas, one or two leading ballet companies, three or four symphony orchestra concerts of international caliber, and three or four plays with outstanding casts. During the main festival, a Fringe Festival presents cabaret, late-night reviews, and student musical and drama productions.

The International Film Festival features a number of first showings with leading performers present on opening night. A "Golden Thistle Award" is made early each September to a movie director of outstanding merit, but no film awards are made on these occasions.

There is much activity in modern art. Edinburgh boasts several excellent art museums. The Scottish National Library, Edinburgh Public Library, and two university libraries offer a wide selection of fiction and nonfiction books, research materials, and children's books, as well as excellent music collections.

Major hotels offer shows and dancing throughout the year. Two leading hotels have dinner dancing on Saturday nights throughout the year and nightly during the tourist season. Other hotels and restaurants have more informal Friday and Saturday night dinner dances. During the tourist season the major hotels also have regular Scottish nights. These are called *ceilidhs* (pronounced "kay-lays"),

and include traditional Scottish dancing, singing, and music.

The city has many public houses or pubs. Some offer musical entertainment, jazz, and even country-western music (which is very popular in Scotland). During the school year, the two universities, Edinburgh and Heriot-Watt, also offer a wide variety of entertainment.

Notes for Travelers

London is one of the hubs of international travel, and its air and sea routes cover all corners of the globe. Britain also is served by modern ferry craft, linking the country to the continent's road and rail systems. Pan Am, TWA, National, Braniff, and Delta offer direct scheduled flights from the U.S. to London, and visitors to Belfast and Edinburgh usually transit London en route.

A valid passport is required. Neither a visa nor evidence of disease immunization are necessary, except (in the latter case) when the traveler is arriving from an area where an epidemic has occurred.

The U.K. has strict gun control laws, and permits are issued sparingly. Local police stations process registration of sporting weapons.

All major religions are represented in London. The Church of England is the established church, but other faiths have houses of worship throughout the London area. Northern Ireland is predominantly Protestant, but the Roman Catholic Church has the largest membership of any single denomination. The Presbyterian Church and the Church of Ireland (Episcopal) have wide membership, and many other faiths are also represented. Most denominations common in America have places of worship in Edinburgh. The Church of Scotland is the established church.

The U.K.'s monetary system is based on the pound sterling. Like the U.S. dollar, the pound is divided into 100 pence (pennies). The floating rate of exchange between the British pound and the U.S. dollar often changes, and in July 1981 fell in the range of £1 = $1.93.

The British use the avoirdupois weight system. Most items are measured in ounces and pounds, but human weight is expressed in stones (one stone = 14 pounds). Road distance and speed are measured in miles.

The U.S. Embassy in the United Kingdom is located at 21-24 Grosvenor Square, London. The Consulate General in Belfast is at 14 Queen Street, and in Edinburgh, at 3 Regent Terrace.

Yugoslavia

YUGOSLAVIA is a land of many contrasts. Its people are comprised of more than seven ethnic groups, each with different customs and traditions. The Orthodox Catholic, Roman Catholic, and Moslem religions all have adherents. In parts of Yugoslavia the Turkish influence remains strong; in other areas the landscape, houses, and people look much like those in Austria, Italy, or Romania.

The land itself has great physical differences. The mountainous interior, the fabled Dalmatian coast along the Adriatic Sea, the lovely lakes of Slovenia, the flat plains of the Vojvodina—all are part of the one land. Although Yugoslavia is still, by European standards, a relatively underdeveloped country, its principal cities, with their well-dressed residents, impressive new buildings, and well-stocked shops, reminds one more of Western Europe than of the Balkans, while in parts of Kosovo and Macedonia, the impression is of the Balkans of an earlier century.

The contrast between the freedom and evident prosperity of Yugoslavia and the condition of its Eastern European neighbors is substantial. The evidences of freedom to travel abroad, to be critical of governmental policies, and to accept Western European standards and tastes are apparent everywhere.

Area, Geography, Climate

The Socialist Federal Republic of Yugoslavia (SFRY) is on the Balkan Peninsula. It shares its borders with Italy, Austria, Hungary, Romania, Bulgaria, Greece, and Albania; its 390-mile coastline along the Adriatic stretches 1,255 miles, including inlets and bays. Yugoslavia's 98,766 square miles make it about the size of Wyoming. Three-quarters of the land consists of mountains and plateaus. The highest point is Mt. Triglav (9,393 feet) in the Julian Alps of Slovenia.

With 220 lakes and 73,500 miles of rivers and streams, Yugoslavia ranks high among the European countries in its waterpower resources. The Danube, its largest river, flows through the northeast portion of the country and forms part of the border with Romania. A giant dam across the Danube at Kladovo, built in cooperation with Romania, has more than doubled Yugoslavia's electric power capacity.

Over 34 percent of the country is covered by forests. Perucica, which lies in a wilderness area between Bosnia and Montenegro, is the last virgin forest in Europe. Animal life is abundant, with many kinds of game, including bear, various types of deer, chamois (antelope), and salt and freshwater fish.

Yugoslavia's climate varies from region to region. The coastal area enjoys a mild Mediterranean climate with a mean temperature around 80°F in summer. By contrast, the interior, which is cut off from the Adriatic by high mountains, has the hot summers and cold winters that characterize a continental climate.

Population

Yugoslavia's population of about 22.4 million is divided among six republics: Serbia, where Belgrade, the capital is located, has a population of 9,200,000; Croatia (principal city, Zagreb) has 4,800,000; Bosnia-Herzegovina (Sarajevo) 4,000,000; Slovenia (Ljubljana) 2,020,000; Montenegro (Titograd) 549,000; and Macedonia (Skopje) 1,840,000. Serbia's two provinces, Vojvodina and Kosovo, have considerable independence in local affairs.

Within these republics are four distinct Slavic nationalities: the Serbs (including the Montenegrins) and Croats, who speak Serbo-Croatian, and the Slovenes and Macedonians, who also have their own national tongues. Other groups include 1.3 million Albanians, 500,000 Hungarians, and more than 100,000 Turks. Both Latin and Cyrillic alphabets are used: the Cyrillic in Serbia, Montenegro, Macedonia, and parts of Bosnia and Herzegovina; Latin in the rest of the country. The most widely used non-Yugoslav language is German. It is the foreign language that shopkeepers, servants, and waiters know best. Along

the Dalmatian coast, Italian is spoken rather widely. The study of English is growing and is beginning to challenge German as a second language, especially among younger people.

The principal religion is the Eastern Orthodox (41 percent), found mainly in Serbia, Montenegro, and Macedonia; Roman Catholicism (32 percent) is practiced largely in Slovenia and Croatia; Islam (12 percent) has most of its adherents in Bosnia-Herzegovina, Macedonia, and the autonomous province of Kosovo.

Government

The political institutions of the SFRY have recently undergone complex modifications. In February 1974, a new constitution was adopted and elections were held to fill positions in the reorganized governments at the federal, regional, and communal levels. In May 1974, the 10th Congress of the League of Communists of Yugoslavia (LCY) approved extensive organizational and personnel changes in the party. With the inauguration of the new political system, four years of political experimentation and change ended.

The Federal government has executive, legislative, and judicial branches. Executive authority is vested in a nine-member presidency, composed of one member from each of the republics and autonomous provinces, and the President of the LCY, succeeding the late Josip Broz Tito as the state executive.

The Federal Executive Council (FEC), which is the Cabinet with responsibility for daily government business, is answerable to the SFRY Assembly. The FEC is headed by the Premier and consists of Secretariats and commissions similar to U.S. departments and agencies.

The bicameral SFRY Assembly has a Federal Chamber and a Chamber of Republics and Provinces. The former has a primary legislative responsibility; the latter, consisting of delegations from the Republican and Provincial assemblies, is the coordinating body between the Federal and regional assemblies.

Each of the six constituent republics and two autonomous provinces has a government patterned after the Federal government: president, presidency, executive council, assembly, and judiciary. At the commune level (*opstina*) the assembly and its president bear primary governmental responsibility. The 1974 Constitution implemented a further development of the unique Yugoslav political institution, self-management. Basic organizations of associated labor, interest communities, and other local bodies are intended to give workers and other groupings direct economic and political control. They participate in decisions on such basic matters as wages, profit distribution, and pricing of products, and express their political will through a series of delegations reaching upwards to the SFRY Assembly.

Arts, Science, Education

Yugoslavia's 11 universities are in Belgrade, Novi Sad, Nis, Pristina, Skopje, Sarajevo, Zagreb, Ljubljana, Titograd, Rijeka, and Split. Several have branches or faculties in smaller communities.

The first Academy of Arts and Science was founded in 1866 by Bishop Josip Strossmayer in Zagreb. Other republican academies have since been established in Serbia, Slovenia, Bosnia, and Macedonia. Several American scholars hold honorary memberships in some of the academies.

Each republic capital and the major cities have theaters and an opera house. Distinguished foreign artists are often invited to perform. Some theaters present American plays, but performances are in the local language.

Yugoslavia has five major philharmonic orchestras and many smaller symphony and chamber groups. The concert season is from October through May. Several professional and amateur folk music and dance troupes have had extensive tours abroad, and have won international reputations.

The country's numerous museums range in subject from ethnography and applied and theater arts, to military history. The Museums of Modern Art in Ljubljana, Belgrade, and Skopje are outstanding and have stimulated interest in contemporary art around the country. The Biennale of Graphic Art in Ljubljana is internationally important, as is Belgrade's Triennale of Yugoslav Art. Many Yugoslav painters and sculptors have exhibited abroad in recent years, including those from the famous schools of naive (primitive) painters.

Yugoslavia hosts several international music, film, and theater festivals each year, the most noted being the annual Dubrovnik Festival, the music Biennale in Zagreb, and the Ljubljana Jazz Festival. Yugoslavia is also the scene of international conferences, congresses, and seminars—many held in summer along the Dalmatian coast.

During the past 30 years, Yugoslavia has made vigorous efforts to modernize and expand its science and technology. Today there are about 600 research institutions and laboratories, over half in the natural sciences and engineering. Institutes are attached to universities, academies of science, and economic enterprises, and are autonomous.

The organization of science and technology in Yugoslavia is different from that in other East European countries. Following its policy of decentralization, the federal government does not dictate to these institutions. Research important to the country is encouraged through grants given by various levels of government. To bring some measure of coordination, a Federal Administration for International Scientific, Educational, Cultural and Technical Cooperation has been set up. Each republic has a similar council to study, stimulate, and coordinate science and technology interests at the local level.

Yugoslavia seeks to become a modern technological state. As a result, it is interested in cooperative programs with other nations. An agreement on scientific-technical cooperation between the U.S. and Yugoslavia was signed in May 1973. Under terms of this agreement, and under previous arrangements, more than 300 joint research projects are being carried out in such fields as energy, transportation, engineering, physics, chemistry, agriculture, public health, biomedicine, rehabilitation, social welfare, and archaeology. These programs create a large interchange of American and Yugoslav scientists.

Commerce and Industry

Yugoslavia's basic economic assets are high quality farmland, 85 percent in private hands; rich mineral resources, including copper, bauxite, nickel, lead, zinc, coal, and uranium; onshore oil adequate to meet about one-third of domestic requirements, with possible additional oil reserves in the Adriatic awaiting full exploration; and timber and landscape suitable for tourism.

Since World War II, an intensive industrialization has taken place. The country now has a developed iron and steel industry and is also a sizable producer of ships, chemicals, automobiles, electronics, appliances, furniture, copper cable, and processed foods. Tourism has become a major and profitable industry. The gross national product has grown by over six percent annually in real terms over the past decade, and now amounts to about $64.4 billion.

The Yugoslav Government exercises influence over the economy largely through fiscal and monetary means familiar in Western countries. Industry and commerce, broadly decentralized, is largely in the hands of individual self-managed enterprises jointly owned by the employees, with management responsible to elected Workers' Councils. Individual industrial enterprises—not the government—decide what and how much to produce, how much to invest, how many workers to engage, and how much to pay them. Market principles are applied to both domestic and external trade.

Yugoslavia has economic problems characteristic of a still-developing country: a steep inflation rate; a shortage of domestic investment capital as compared to development needs; unemployment; and recurrent balance-of-payments deficits.

In order to bring inflation under control, the government is attempting to restrain excess demand and spending, while promoting industrial and agricultural production and productivity. The placement of one million Yugoslav workers in Western Europe has relieved unemployment and brought in large amounts of foreign exchange.

Yugoslavia has succeeded in raising a large amount of capital abroad in terms of both credits and equity investment. A joint venture law passed in 1968 permits foreign firms to own up to a 49 percent share of Yugoslav enterprises.

Of Yugoslavia's trade, 65 percent is with Western Europe and the U.S.; the rest with the U.S.S.R., other Eastern European countries, and less developed countries.

U.S.-Yugoslav economic relations are developing favorably. Principal U.S. exports are complete installations for power plants and for other basic industries, civil aircraft and mining equipment, and agricultural products; principal Yugoslav exports to America are copper and copper products, furniture, and canned meat products. To promote further expansion of commercial and industrial cooperation between the two countries, U.S.-Yugoslav Chambers of Commerce were established July 1974 in Belgrade and New York.

Transportation

Jugoslovenski Aerotransport (JAT), the Yugoslav national airline, has both international and domestic service. Service is frequent and generally good. Several international airlines also serve the country. Rome and Athens are only one-and-a-half hours away from Belgrade by jet; Vienna, one hour; and Paris, two-and-a-half hours.

International trains offering service to points throughout Europe and as far east as Istanbul operate daily all year. Intracountry rail service is also adequate. However, neither the international nor the domestic trains provide dependable dining car service.

In the larger cities, streetcars and trolley and motor buses are available; while these types of public transportation are frequent and inexpensive, they are usually crowded. Taxi service is also available. Taxistands are found at central locations in the cities and they can also be requested by telephone.

Driving in Yugoslavia is on the right. The country has a few four-lane divided highways. The major highway system consists of two-lane paved roads that connect the larger population centers, and paved or unpaved secondary roads which connect the smaller towns. Highways are narrow, not banked for curves, rather poorly marked, and few have shoulders. This makes for dangerous driving conditions, particularly with traffic increasing each year.

Many Yugoslavs drive too fast, both in cities and on the highway. By American standards, their driving judgment is poor and they frequently pass on stretches of road where it is forbidden. Truck and car drivers are often insensitive to driving hazards and frequently fail to observe safety precautions and driving etiquette. Parking on open highways is not uncommon. Night driving is particularly hazardous for all of the previous reasons, and because numerous unlit horse and oxen-drawn vehicles can be found even on main roads. Visitors should try to avoid driving outside the city after dark, and should wear seat belts at all times.

Private cars are a great convenience and are valuable for weekend trips to nearby points of interest. With traffic rapidly increasing and parking becoming more of a problem, particularly in Belgrade, the tendency is to walk or take a cab.

Compact cars equipped with six-cylinder engines and standard brakes, steering, and transmission are most suitable here. Small European cars such as Fiat, Volvo, European Ford, and Volkswagen have servicing facilities in Belgrade. Auto repair and servicing, however, is a chronic problem. Mechanics seem to be inadequately trained, and spare parts—particularly for American cars—are scarce.

A Yugoslav drivers license is required for foreign residents and is issued when a valid U.S. or other foreign license is submitted. The foreign license is returned prior to departure. An international drivers license may also be obtained in Yugoslavia.

Communications

Telephone, telegraph, and wireless communications, both national and international, are good. Airmail to and from the U.S. east coast takes from seven to 10 days.

Yugoslavia has radio broadcasting in all major cities. The latest American and European music is played in addition to national music. Programs include classical and rock music, impor-

tant sports events, interviews, and newscasts.

Belgrade has one UHF and one VHF TV channel. UHF broadcasting is also beginning now in other Yugoslav cities, and a few popular programs are broadcast in color. Eight hours of daily programming (somewhat longer on weekends) include shows for children and educational, sports, news, dramas, musicals, and documentary programs. American movies are shown fairly regularly. Yugoslavia is a member of Eurovision TV, which telecasts live events from other European cities. Live telecasts from the U.S. are occasionally transmitted via communications satellite.

Many European newspapers and periodicals are sold locally. Time and Newsweek also are available on newsstands, and the International Herald Tribune may be obtained by subscription (arrives one to three days after publication).

Health

Hospitals in the large Yugoslavian cities generally are adequate, but U.S. government personnel use military facilities. Belgrade has many qualified medical and dental specialists, some of whom received their training in the U.S.

By American standards, community sanitation in Belgrade is good. The water is potable, garbage is collected regularly, the sewage system is adequate, and streets are washed daily. Community health controls are satisfactory. Belgrade is rapidly following the development of all modern European cities. Dairy and meat plants are in operation and products are controlled and tested.

The general health of Americans living in Belgrade is good. Upper respiratory infections and sinusitis may be somewhat more common during winter, since the soft coal which is the predominant heating fuel produces frequent smog which blankets the downtown areas. Individuals with asthma and emphysema should be cautioned about this potentially severe hazard. Belgrade has no unusual illnesses, but the ordinary immunizations should be kept current.

Major Cities

BELGRADE, capital of Yugoslavia and the Republic of Serbia, is located in the east central part of the country at the confluence of the Sava and the Danube Rivers. Its altitude varies from 224 to 830 feet above sea level.

Belgrade has had a settlement since the time of the Celts in the fourth century B.C. Little evidence of their culture or of the subsequent Roman civilization remains, however. Belgrade today does not appear to have any traces of the ancient city, and few historical monuments of earlier than late 18th century survive. Minimal evidence of the long period of Turkish domination exists, and only a few baroque buildings mark the pre-World War I Hapsburg influence. Belgrade thus lacks the atmosphere and old world charm that marks Eastern European capitals such as Prague and Budapest. Buildings in the center city are gray and somber, and alternate with a few modern concrete and glass highrises. However, the city's parks and tree-lined streets, as well as the numerous sidewalk cafes of the city's center, lend color and charm, particularly in summer.

Contributing to this charm is the contrast between old and new. This is evidenced by the young, well-dressed, even modish Belgraders, and the fur-hatted peasant men in Serbian trousers and upturned sandals with their dirndl-skirted wives in babushkas. They are seen browsing together along the well-stocked shopping streets of the city's center.

The city's economic activity is centered around government, trade, commerce, light industry, and services. The adjacent agricultural area of the Vojvodina is among the richest in Yugoslavia.

Belgrade has an active cultural life, although the activity is somewhat less than it is in major world capitals. Yugoslavs have a deep interest in art and have a long season of opera, ballet, concerts, and drama. Among the young particularly, the taste for popular music, especially American jazz, is evident. Yugosalvs are avid movie-goers, and many Western European and American films can be seen in the original version with Serbo-Croatian subtitles. Many art exhibits of varying quality are presented by contemporary Yugoslav artists; some have well-deserved international reputations, and others show promise of future fame. Several groups of naive (primitive) painters and sculptors work in Yugoslavia today; many have exhibited abroad with considerable success.

ZAGREB, capital of Croatia, is a busy industrial and commercial city, and long has been an important cultural and intellectual center. The oldest part, known as the Kaptol, contains the Bishop's Palace and remains of towers from an 11th-century fortress. Before World War I, Zagreb was the administrative capital of the Austro-Hungarian province of Croatia-Slavonia; the Ban, or Governor, appointed by the Emperor of Austria-Hungary, resided in Zagreb.

The city is on the banks of the Sava River at the foot of an isolated group of mountains. The highest, Sljeme (3,354 ft) is just north of Zagreb. The older parts of the city were built on the rising ground of the Sljeme foothills. In the late 19th century, the city spread out onto the flat area between the hills and the river. Since World War II, extensive high-rise construction has taken place in "New Zagreb" across the Sava to the south. In spring and summer, with trees in bloom, the older parts of the city are quite pleasant; in fall and winter, poorly maintained houses and buildings combine with gray skies and fog to give a rather drab and gloomy look.

With about 625,000 residents in the city proper and another 150,000 in the immediate vicinity, Zagreb is Yugoslavia's second largest city. Since World War II, the population has more than doubled, creating an acute housing shortage. Most inhabitants are Croatians, but there is a significant Serbian minority, as well as scattered representatives of other ethnic groups.

Relatively few foreigners reside in the area. Knowledge of foreign languages—English, French, German—is restricted mainly to the intelligentsia. To shop or converse with servants, some knowledge of Serbo-Croatian is essential.

In summer, the large influx of tourists into Croatia and Slovenia is mostly Italian, German, and Austrian, but the growing number of Americans includes many of Yugoslav descent returning to visit relatives. More than 2,000 Americans are registered in the U.S. consular district, mostly Yugoslav-Americans who have retired to the land of their birth.

Of special importance are Zagreb's series of trade fairs, especially the Spring and Fall International Fairs. A permanent U.S. pavilion is at the Fair where USIA stages a major exhibit each fall. In addition, participation by the Department of Commerce and private American firms in the Zagreb Fair has increased.

Recreation

A number of excursions can be made in the vicinity of Belgrade. About 44 miles north of the city is Novi Sad, which has an interesting fortress overlooking the city. Inside the fortress is a hotel and a good restaurant, and a number of artists have workshops there. En route to Novi Sad is the village of Stara Pazova, where Slovak ladies wear colorful dress on Sundays. The wooded hill country known as Fruska Gora, a pleasant picnic area and site of the Hopovo Monastery, is also en route.

Avala, a 2,000-foot hill 12 miles south of Belgrade, offers a good view on a clear day, and the tomb of the Yugoslav Unknown Soldier, designed by the famous sculptor Ivan Mestrovic, is located there.

The royal crypt of Yugoslavia's former ruling family, containing excellent mosaic reproductions of some of the country's more famous frescos, is at Topola. The ruins of a 15th-century Serbian fort are on the Danube at Smederevo, 25 miles east of Belgrade.

One can also make an excursion by hydrofoil down the Danube to Kladovo, where a dam has been constructed jointly by Romania and Yugoslavia. The boat passes many interesting points, including some remains from Roman times, and Smederevo Fort, and crosses the Iron Gate (Djerdap), which resembles an inland fjord.

Yugoslavia also has some interesting monasteries dating from the 13th to 15th centuries. Visits to the monasteries of Manasiji, Ravanica, Hopovo, and Krusedol make interesting one-day outings from Belgrade; those in southern Serbia such as Sopocani, Studenica, Pee, Gracanica, and Decani can be visited over a long weekend. The frescos in these monasteries are world-famous.

Another interesting day's outing is a visit to the villages of Yugoslavia's primitive artists. Kovacica and Uzdin may be included on the same drive. Oparic is also a village of artists; they are gracious and hospitable and often invite visitors into their homes. En route to Oparic at Svetozarevo is a gallery of Yugoslav primitive art, which has one of the finest collections in the country.

Other interesting places to visit in Yugoslavia include the old cities of Dubrovnik and Split on the famous Dalmatian coast; Lake Ohrid near the Greek and Albanian borders; and numerous lakes in the Julian Alps. Belgrade has beach areas, but health authorities warn against pollution. Boating is good on the Danube and Sava, but mooring facilities are limited. This area also has rivers where one can go kayaking.

In winter there is skiing in many corners of Yugoslavia, primarily in the northwestern part of the country (Alpine region in Slovenia—Vogel, Zele-nica, Kravec, Kranjska Gora, Planica, Pohorje, etc.) where a funicular railway, ski lifts, ski jumps, and ski centers are available. Skiing is becoming increasingly popular in other resorts in the country such as Petekovac and Platak in Croatia; Jahorina in Bosnia; Kopaonik, Brezovica, Zlatibor, Zlatar and Tara in Serbia; and Mavrovo and Popova Sapka in Macedonia, where facilities are quickly improving.

The hunter will find duck, geese, hare, partridge, pheasant, and fox in the immediate vicinity of Belgrade. Bear, wild boar, roebuck (European stag), wolf, and chamois are also in the area, but unless one is invited on an official hunt, game fees are prohibitively high.

There is fishing in the Danube, Sava, and smaller rivers nearby, but catches appear to be "fisherman's luck." Regular spinning tackle will do, but fly is more useful. Seasonal licenses are inexpensive, and each area issues its own; to fish throughout the country requires more than one license.

Soccer (European football) is the great spectator sport in Yugoslavia. The Yugoslavs are avid fans and Belgrade has two large stadiums. A small track just outside the city has horse and harness racing during summer.

Zagreb is central to many of the more interesting parts of Yugoslavia and to Italy, Germany, and Austria. Ljubljana, the capital of Slovenia, is 80 miles west of Zagreb near the mountain and lake resort district.

From Ljubljana, Trieste, the gateway to north Italy, is less than a two-hour drive and is a good shopping center. Graz, Austria is two-and-a-half to three hours by road. Graz also has good shops. Belgrade is 250 miles southeast of Zagreb. Munich, Vienna, Venice, Milan, Lausanne, and Paris can be reached by rail from Zagreb without changing trains. Vienna is 284 miles north of Zagreb.

Entertainment

Movies, opera, ballet, concerts, and drama are offered in Belgrade and Zagreb. The opera and ballet seasons are from October through May or June, and repertoires include both European and Slavic works. The international Review of Festival Winning Films (Fest) in January, the Belgrade Theater Festival of Avantgarde Drama (Bitef) in September, the Belgrade Music Festival (Bemus) in October, and the Newport Jazz Festival in November are outstanding events of the season. Orchestras and chamber music groups are excellent, and frequently present guest conductors and soloists.

American and other foreign films are shown, usually with the original soundtrack and Serbo-Croatian subtitles. Movies are popular in Yugoslavia. Film festivals on various themes are frequent both in major cities and at coast resort cities in summer.

Legitimate theater is offered regularly in many Yugoslav cities, with a repertoire including contemporary plays, classical productions, and musical comedy. These presentations are in Serbo-Croatian, so only those with a knowledge of this language can profitably take advantage of them.

A professional folk song and dance group, the Kolo, performs regularly throughout the year in Belgrade, and other amateur and professional groups give performances frequently in major cities and during the tourist season in resort hotels.

Several museums in Belgrade and Zagreb are worth visiting. Among the best in Belgrade are the National Museum, which has a varied collection of French impressionist works; the Fresco Gallery, which contains copies of frescos found in Serbia's early monasteries; and the Ethnographic Museum, with original examples of peasant costumes, implements, musical instruments, and furnishings from diverse regions of Yugoslavia. The Military Museum in Kalemegdan Park is one of the finest in Europe.

Cultural activities in Zagreb are generally at a high level, although the quality of performance is not uniform. The National Theater, of moderate size but well-equipped, acoustically good, and beautifully restored, is an opera house in the Austrian baroque style of the late 19th century. Here local companies give a 10-month season of classical and modern operas and ballets, frequently with guest artists. Every two years, the Zagreb Festival of Contemporary Music and Dance draws internationally renowned performers.

The Triennial International Exhibition of Naive Art has a worldwide reputation, as does the Biennial Festival of Animated Film.

The Zagreb Symphony Orchestra gives a series of concerts annually, with occasional guest conductors and soloists. It performs in the up-to-date Vatroslav Lisinski Concert Hall, seating 1,850.

An excellent chamber music group has an international reputation. Four smaller theaters are devoted to various forms of drama in the Croatian language. Broadway musicals are popular, and several excellent adaptations have been presented in recent years at the Komedija Theater.

Dining out in Yugoslav restaurants is a popular social activity. Prices are usually reasonable and the food is good, although variety is limited. There are several nightclubs and discotheques to choose from. A number of year-round casinos operate in principal Yugoslav cities, but in resort cities several casinos are open only during the tourist season.

Notes for Travelers

No direct flights to Yugoslavia are provided by U.S. airlines, but transfers can be made at a number of cities in Europe, including London, Paris, Rome, and Frankfurt. The most common overland points of entry are from Austria (Maribor or Jesenice) and Italy (Gorica or Sezana).

Passports and visas are required, but no special immunization certificates are necessary for entry.

Only hunting weapons (rifles or shotguns), and not more than 1,000 rounds of ammunition for each, may be imported, and these firearms must be registered with Yugoslav authorities. In order to hunt, one must join a local hunting club (at considerable expense), or hunt under the auspices of local travel agencies.

Most churches in Belgrade are Eastern Orthodox, but there are also Roman Catholic, Methodist, and Seventh-Day Adventist churches, a synagogue, and a mosque. One Roman Catholic congregation provides services in English, and U.S. military chaplains and British Anglican priests occasionally hold interdenominational services. In Zagreb, services are not held in English (the city is predominantly Roman Catholic), but about four times a year an Anglican priest serves the English-speaking Protestant community.

The monetary unit of Yugoslav currency is the *dinar*, worth about 18.25 to the U.S. dollar (1980).

The metric system of weights and measures is used.

Special note: Yugoslav restrictions on picture-taking are quite liberal in comparison to other Eastern European countries, but there are some banned areas, and these are clearly designated. When in doubt, ask a policeman, or refrain from using a camera.

The U.S. Embassy in Yugoslavia is located at Kneza Milosa 50, Belgrade. The Consulate General in Zagreb is at Zrinjevac 13.

Index

Index

(Boldface numbers indicate Major City section)

A

C

D

E

F

G

H

I

J

K

L

O

P

R

S

T

U

V

W